Revolution & Reaction

Revolution & Reaction
The Paris Commune 1871

Edited by John Hicks & Robert Tucker

The University of Massachusetts Press

Reprinted from *The Massachusetts Review*
Volume XII, Number 3, Summer 1971
Copyright © 1973 by The Massachusetts Review, Inc.

"The Paris Commune and the Artists" by Jeffry Kaplow,
"The Commune and the Revolt of Jules Vallès"
by Gordon Shenton,
Foreword, Chronology, Bibliography and all other
new matter copyright © 1973 by
The Massachusetts Review, Inc.

Library of Congress Catalog Card Number 72-90493
Printed in the United States of America

For J.C., M.H. & S.K.

CONTENTS

FOREWORD

Now, a century after the Paris Commune, it is fitting when commemorating that urban social phenomenon of 1871 to reflect upon it both as unique history and as "news" in Thoreau's sense of that word. These evaluative essays, the result of research into the Commune's causes and its tactics, these perspectives on the violent reaction to it, cannot but reveal the significance of that revolutionary event for current social thought about modes and rates of change in our own troubled time.

The collection argues no special point. Various forces such as the extremes of Jacobin passion and *les pétroleuses* on the one side and the extremes of violence in the name of "order" and the *Versaillais* on the other can be seen with the clarity that comes from a century of retrospect. Many other issues embodied in the rise and fall of the Commune, questions of war and peace and of imperialism, political and industrial bureaucracy, the arrogance and sometimes stupidity of centralized (and decentralized) power, participatory democracy, women's rights, the exploitation of many for the economic and social benefit of few, injustices suffered among the politically deprived, and the frustrations of powerlessness widespread among common people, are still vigorously alive in our time and still demand our intelligent disposition.

The history, the psychology, and the improvisations of the Commune will be compelling in the present period for any American reader disturbed by signs of constitutional crisis in the United States: to persons who see a century's growth in the scope and power of the presidency approach monarchical or fascistic proportion in the police, espionage, and war-making powers of that office; who see effected an unprecedented practical independence of the executive branch of government from the safeguard of traditional checks and balances by separate consulting branches, an immunity from effective review by Congress and no less by the press; who see the role and responsibility of the elected representatives of the people gravely diminished as great decisions of war and purse are veiled from concurrent public discussion; or who ask (against the background of civilian massacre at My Lai, terror bombing in Indochina, and Watergate) how *can* a citizen make his government accountable to the nation's primary values and responsive to critics both internally and publicly.

To such readers revolutionary history has magnified the significance of the Paris Commune of 1871 once more. Nor, as this collection demonstrates, will they be the first similarly concerned to have found in it a particularly absorbing model for their study.

The collection has no particular ax to grind, though we acknowledge the various ideological purposes to which the Commune has often been put. People still must read the evidence as best they can; they will do so, inevitably, in the light of their own pressing needs and convictions. Our intention here is, principally, to view the Paris Commune as a complexly compelling event in the history of human endeavor.

The fascination is severalfold. Not least, certainly, is that unforgettable moment of the victory of women and children over troops on 18 March at Montmartre and Luxembourg and elsewhere in the city; women and children moving among the military files like a wave mixing with, talking sense to, and neutralizing the soldiers and their guns. Or there is the other memorable image: that of humble working people in a major capital city of Europe exercising for a time all the influence normally reserved for establishment elites. Police, military, administrative powers and economic, political, educational functions all passing into the hands of persons who had been powerless and unknown, but who were now freely elected by the majority of the voting population and subject to periodic electoral review. Taking charge of the city as its established elite defaulted, working men and women normally irrelevant to decisions by the government were for once now themselves deciding, improvising vigorously and imaginatively, new patterns for their lives and their community. The wealthy and privileged, the well-connected and normally self-perpetuating establishment cadres, suddenly in confusion and retreat, were bewildered as to where self-interest and safety really lay. An extraordinary turnabout. (Imagine, at a time of intense political division, New York or Washington suddenly abandoned by all its officialdom, and their popular adversaries left to defend and administer a beleaguered city.) New life became everywhere evident where men and women, untutored in politics-as-usual, turned themselves to improving the quality and generosity of their lives. Their intensity in this Paris endeavor only the more betokens the cultural hunger and deprivation of their past. The experience and work of Jules Vallès or of Louise Michel are supreme examples in point. But the Commune numbered others too, by the hundred if not the thousand.

It is fascinating to learn what humble people did exactly with the opportunity afforded them. In the brief period of the Commune's existence what specific energies were released? The savagery of Communard retaliation to the savageries brought against them is not the whole story, as the research in this collection vividly proves. Or, if the relative destructiveness must be quantitatively compared, the butchery of May 1871 should allow no reader conditioned to condemn radical excess to underestimate the blind brutality of a frightened as well as challenged middle class.

There is something very moving about people so precariously placed as the Communards were, surrounded by German' armies and by the hostile forces of the transferred government at Versailles, conducting themselves as if their effort to effect a civil community, generous and responsive to the humane needs of its constituency, would last forever instead of for a few brief weeks. When guns and violent self-defense might understandably have consumed nearly all their energies, the records show us that committees of the Commune met to contemplate, among other urgencies, even the true needs of an effective community theatre and drama program, and, further, took time to reflect upon the social significance of public art. What does one make of such an ample sense of priorities, or of such largesse of imagination?

One perceives frequently in the records of the Commune a desperate effort (not without lapses to be sure) to adopt or to create various implements of social organization that these might keep pace with humane needs. To any reader anywhere, conscious of government unresponsive or insensitive to humane considerations, the events of the Commune, those peaceful and violent alike, present a moving and also sobering record.

Last, perhaps the spectacle, a century past, of France's liberal intellectuals recoiling both from Communard success and excess, their almost unanimous identification with the "order" which the Versailles government finally imposed upon its countrymen, will suggest to many readers questions of social privilege and widespread indoctrination to preserve it; and suggest too the insecurities of conservative governance, and the frantic overkill which threatened class and privilege and power can mobilize. Among the following pages with their illustrations and caricatures, certainly questions of cultural versus political revolutionary action will receive as full interest from our readers as from the editors.

In any evaluation of the Commune and of what it may contribute to our present self-knowledge and sensibility, it is surely time to put aside both attitudes of idolatry and those of hysteria and abuse. The Commune is too valuable a chapter for that, too full of meaning and implication, and our need is too great.

For their assistance the editors would like especially to thank Leonard Baskin, Frederick Busi, Milton Cantor, Jules Chametzky, Wallace Fowlie, Wilbur Frohock, and Sidney Kaplan. We are indebted to Bertha Case and Stefan Brecht for special permission to print in full Leonard Lehrman's translation of Bertolt Brecht's *The Days of the Commune*, less known than other plays in the Brecht canon but having unusual point and merit when placed in the present context. We should like also to thank Eugene Schulkind for his kind cooperation in making available to us once more the essay by Monty Johnstone, "The Paris Commune and Marx's Conception of the Dictatorship of the Proletariat," a paper first delivered at a conference on the Commune sponsored by the University of Sussex, England, in April 1971. We acknowledge, too, various courtesies, scholarly and social, extended by fellows of the Camargo Foundation, Cassis, France, and by Russell Young, the director of the foundation.

JOHN HICKS
ROBERT TUCKER

CHRONOLOGY

Background

Middle Ages

Communes were free, self-determined cities

1776   American Declaration of Independence, American Revolution

1787   Constitution of the United States, Bill of Rights (15 Dec. 1791)

1789   French Revolution

1793   Revolutionary Paris Commune, The Terror

1794   Sans-Culottes

1830   Effects of Industrial Revolution noted in Reform legislation in England

1848   Uprisings throughout Europe
In June, bloody rift between conservatives and leftists in Paris; Thiers (conservative): "[The Clergy who dominate French education] must be strong, stronger than ever, because I am counting on [them] to spread the true philosophy that man is here to suffer"

1850   Marx, *Class Struggles in France; Communist Manifesto* published in *The Red Republican* (England)

1851   Louis Napoleon's coup d'état, creation of the Second Empire

1869   Liebknect and Bebel found German Socialist Democratic Party in Eisenach, gain later electoral successes
Parisian workers strike at the Magasins du Louvre, strike broken by some hundred sisters of Saint Vincent de Paul called from their own charity workshop to replace striking workers

Development and Fall of the Paris Commune of 1871

1870

14 July   Napoleon III's Prime Minister, Ollivier, declares war on Bismarck's Prussia

2 Sept   Surrender of Napoleon III to Prussian Army at Sedan; Marshal Bazaine's army trapped in fortress at Metz

4 Sept   Third French Republic proclaimed, formation of the provisional Gouvernement de la Défense Nationale
German Empire proclaimed
In Paris, conservative Thiers will lead; the center will still hope for a military victory against the Prussians by the National Guard under General Trochu at Paris, who prepares for the Prussian siege of the city, and by General Gambetta in the Provinces; Faure, on the left, will lead insurrectionary demonstration at Hotel de Ville (Paris City Hall) and symbolic destruction of imperial insignia
Provisional government authorizes enlistment of 384,000 men for 254 neighborhood National Guard battalions, in effect the working class of Paris thus becomes armed
The International and the Federation of Trade Unions form Committees of Vigilance in each neighborhood of Paris; delegates from each district form a Republican Central Committee of the Twenty Arrondissements

9 Sept   At this stage, Marx, for the International Workingmen's Association (headquarters in London), warns Parisians not to overthrow the new Republic; but events, as when Thiers seizes his own countrymen's public subscription cannon (see 26 March 1871), will lead Marx to change his position (see 8 April 1871); during the Prussian siege of the city, the Parisian center turns to support the left (or Red) population's aims for Paris and France

18 Sept   Prussian armies complete the encirclement of Paris

21 Sept   Anniversary of the First Republic; Parade in Paris in honor of Liberty

5 Oct   Radical demonstrations at Hotel de Ville

27 Oct   Marshal Bazaine surrenders at Metz
Thiers, through Jules Favre, will agree to Bismarck's harsh peace terms: 5 billion francs indemnity, annexation of Alsace-Lorraine, detention of all war prisoners, occupation of all forts until Bismarck approves final settlement, first payment (to von Bleichröder, Bismarck's personal banker) toward 5 billion indemnity to fall due only after the "pacification" of Paris; Bismarck will later release 200,000 French war prisoners who are used, among other provincial troops, by Thiers for the "pacification" at Paris

31 Oct   Leftist demonstrators and radical National Guard battalions

march on the Hotel de Ville, aiming to establish a Commune de Paris; Government troops fire on the marchers, arrest leaders; insurrectionary force is dispersed

1871

7 Jan   Republican Central Committee of the Twenty Arrondissements of Paris calls for replacement of the provisional Gouvernement de la Défense Nationale by a Commune de Paris to act more vigorously against Prussian siege of the city and increasing physical hardships for the population (production had virtually ceased, with consequent unemployment; prices soared with scarcity of food and supplies; shopkeepers were faced with ruin; working people faced hunger and starvation; government inaction under these conditions increased suspicions of political betrayal of the city)

18 Jan   Proclamation of the German Empire in the Hall of Mirrors at Versailles

19 Jan   Siege of Paris continues, widespread hunger, bread distributed only to people carrying official cards

22 Jan   Insurrectionary demonstrations by some National Guard battalions at Hotel de Ville to oppose Thiers's surrender to Germans
          Breton Mobile Guards fire into demonstrators, severe repressions, clubs banned and seventeen Republican newspapers suspended

25 Jan   Thiers and Favre move to Bordeaux

28 Jan   Armistice signed with newly proclaimed German Empire; settlement terms highly unfavorable to French people and include permit for German troops to deploy in symbolic occupation of Champs Élysées area of Paris; to prevent clashes, public subscription cannons are to be moved far from parade route, many to Montmartre

8 Feb   Nationwide elections create a National Assembly which is two-thirds monarchist; Thiers is designated as Head of the Executive Power

26 Feb   National Guardsmen, civilians, women, children move more cannon from Paris toward Montmartre, Belleville, La Villette, Les Buttes, Chanmont

1 Mar   Prussian troops enter Paris

3 Mar   Prussian troops leave the city (and a power vacuum exists after their departure)

10 Mar   National Assembly transferred to Versailles
          Assembly votes measures that directly provoke beleaguered work-

ing class of Paris: the moratorium on rents and payment of commercial bills (instituted at the beginning of the siege) is discontinued, and debts are to be paid immediately; daily pay for National Guard (for many Parisians the sole source of sustenance) is cancelled forthwith

11 Mar Military governor of Paris suspends six more Republican newspapers; Blanqui and Flourens, popular radical leaders, receive death sentences in absentia

15 Mar Federation of the National Guard (formed after the government armistice of 28 January) now organizes its own elected Central Committee as its ultimate authority (rather than the army chief of staff), 215 out of 270 listed battalions of the guard now adhere to the Federation's statutes, Central Committee endorses defense of the principle of a republican form of government

17 Mar Thiers retreats to Versailles, Conservatives leave Paris
Blanqui arrested and imprisoned for duration of the Commune

18 Mar Thiers sends army division under General Vinoy (at 2:00 A.M.) to Paris to seize public subscription cannons. Vinoy neglects to bring sufficient horses to move artillery. People of Montmartre collect to retain what their subscription money has purchased; women and children advance on the soldiers who fraternize with the population. Regular troops, disobeying the orders of superiors, refuse to fire into their own people. Generals Thomas and Lecomte are taken into custody by army regulars and executed
Thiers orders all government agencies to Versailles

19 Mar Central Committee of the National Guard decrees elections for a Commune de Paris to serve as city government

20 Mar Jules Vallès appointed minister of education

22 Mar A Commune proclaimed in Lyons

23 Mar Communes proclaimed in Marseilles and Toulouse

24 Mar Attempts to establish Communes in Narbonne and Saint-Etienne

26 Mar Fall of the Commune in Lyons
Commune proclaimed in Le Creusot
Commune of Paris proclaimed. 275,000 Parisians participate in elections for members of the Commune. Communards move into Hotel de Ville under a red flag and share rule with Central Committee of the National Guard
The Commune is composed of a neo-Jacobin element led by Delescluze, of old style socialists (like Blanqui), of anarchists, pacifists, humanitarians, and a few Marxists such as Fraenkel of the International Workingmen's Association

Women of the Commune include Elizabeth Dmitrieff, Nathalie Lemel, Aline Jacquier, Blanche Lefebvre, Marie Leloup, Aglaé Jarry. Raoul Rigault becomes chief of police; strongly Jacobin, he will later take hostages and by May approve execution of the Archbishop of Paris and fifty priests in retaliation for mass execution of Communard prisoners by Versailles troops

28 Mar   Inauguration of the Paris Commune
Fall of the Communes in Toulouse and Saint-Etienne

29 Mar   Paris Commune forms nine commissions for administration of the city

30 Mar   Commune decrees renewal of wartime moratorium on payment of rents

31 Mar   Commune of Narbonne falls

2 Apr   Commune of Paris decrees full separation of church and state
Maximum annual salaries for all members of government and civil service set at 6000 francs (the pay of a skilled worker)
Versailles troops attack Courbevoie. During this coming siege by Versailles, incendiary kerosene bombs are often used in the bombardments as well as conventional hardware and explosives. Bulk of world press will minimize this violence of the forces of "order" and exaggerate that of the communard *pétroleuses*

4 Apr   Fall of the Commune at Marseilles. Attempt to establish Commune at Limoges

8 Apr   The International (in London) authorizes an "Address to the People of Paris" declaring loyalty and solidarity; it will later become Marx's *Civil War in France*. The address in final form will come out just after the crushing of the Commune

11 Apr   Union des Femmes organized by Elizabeth Dmitrieff, who was already helping to administer the Comité des Femmes created by Jules Allix to convert workshops to communal uses. The Woman's Vigilance Committee of the 18th Arrondissement had been earlier set up by Louise Michel, Mme. Collet, and Mme. Poirier (Sophie Doctrinal)
Formation of socialist-led Association of Women for the Defense of Paris and Aid to the Wounded

12 Apr   Versailles commences what will become overwhelming attack on Paris
Commune votes extension of moratorium on payment of commercial bills
Commune votes decree, initiated by Felix Pyat, ordering the demolition of the Vendôme Column (see 16 May)

16 Apr   Decree to transfer abandoned factories and workshops to operation and ultimate ownership by worker-owned cooperatives
By-elections to the Commune
Demonstrations of support for Paris Commune take place in Bordeaux and Grenoble

19 Apr   A Declaration to the People of France, a rough sketch of national organization and program issued by the Commune

20 Apr   Courbet elected a member of the Commune

23 Apr   Demonstration of support for Paris Commune by working men in London

25 Apr   Commune votes decree requisitioning vacant lodgings

27 Apr   Employers forbidden to deduct penalties from workers' wages
Commission entrusts Courbet with salvage of art work during Vendôme Column demolition

28 Apr   Commune decrees bakery workers no longer required to work nights

30 Apr   Municipal elections throughout France, substantial gains won by moderate republicans over results of 8 February

1 May   Commune votes 45 to 23 to delegate its powers to a Committee of Public Safety

5 May   Seven pro-Versailles newspapers are suspended

7 May   Decree restituting objects held by national pawnshops

12 May   Decree giving preference to cooperatives in awarding of supply contracts and allowing workers to participate in setting conditions of work

15 May   Delegates of Paris trade unions meet to discuss cooperation with Commune decree (16 April) on abandoned workshops
Efforts to form a federation of neighborhood clubs
Minority Declaration by members of the Commune opposing the transfer of powers to a Committee of Public Safety (see 1 May)

16 May   Vendôme Column toppled

18 May   Committee of Public Safety suspends ten pro-Versailles newspapers
The National Assembly at Versailles ratifies the Treaty of Frankfurt calling for French payment of war costs and cession of Alsace-Lorraine

21 May   Versailles armies under General MacMahon (later president of the Republic) enter Paris at 3:00 P.M. Commune is not in-

formed until 7:00 P.M. Attacking troops, largely provincials mixed with Bismarck's released war prisoners, suspicious of Parisians and what they now stood for

Women convene at Hotel de Ville for final drafting of a Federal Chamber of Working Women

Nathalie Lemel presides over last meeting of the Union des Femmes

25 May   Last meeting of the Commune

21–28   Bloody Week: Fighting is district by district, street by street,
May   house by house, barricade by barricade

Communards burn memorials of the Empire: The Tuileries, the Palais Royal, the Hotel de Ville, Thiers's residence, the Pavillons de Floral and de Marsan; and buildings containing Empire archives: the Court of Accounts, the Council of State, the Ministry of Finance, and any buildings necessary to defense of their street barricades. Between 24 and 26 May sixty-three hostages are executed by Commune soldiers. Archbishop of Paris is also executed

The Versaillais, by the end of the week, had shot 20,000 or more communards and Parisians. Later, more than 30,000 others were arrested and ultimately jailed, deported, or executed. 1,051 women were called before Versailles Councils of War. Louise Michel was deported to the penal colony on New Caledonia near New Zealand

Aftermath

1871–4   Further execution of communards

Liberal intellectuals (Michelet, Sainte-Beuve, Leconte de Lisle, Renan, Taine, Foustel de Coulanges, et al.) turn away from leftist sympathies to conservative concern for order and tradition

1873   Decree for reconstruction of the Vendôme Column at Courbet's sole expense; Courbet imprisoned, fined, later exiled

MacMahon replaces Thiers as president of the Republic and announces a period of "Moral Order"

1875   Vendôme Column reconstructed

1877   Courbet dies 31 December

1879   Partial amnesty for communards (3 March)

1880   Total amnesty for all communards (11 July)

1894   Dreyfus convicted

1917   On the eve of the Soviet Revolution, Lenin cites the achievements of the Paris Commune of 1871

1944   French women demonstrate against the Vichy Government and the Nazi occupation of France

1967   Recommunizing of Chinese bureaucratic structures in Shanghai and elsewhere (May, June, August) on model of Paris Commune of 1871

1968   Manifesto: "Whither China" cites Paris Commune of 1871
        Rebellion of French students and workers in Paris (May)
        In Peking 700,000 Chinese demonstrate in support of French students and workers and display slogan: Long Live the Revolutionary Heritage of the Great Paris Commune.

THE COMMUNE—A CENTURY AFTER

Henri Peyre

*H*istorians of the momentous changes which have completely altered the American psyche in the seventh decade of this century will certainly stress the sudden vanishing of the fear of the word, and of the concept, of Revolution. Courses on the revolutions of the past and on Revolution viewed in its essence, in its myths and in its methods, are now offered in the most respectable American universities. More studies, on the whole sympathetic, on all phases of the French Revolution have been published, in the last twenty-five years, in the English language than in any other; the Terror itself is not looked upon with any repulsion as a monstrous foreign lapse into insanity. The fiftieth anniversary of the Russian revolution was, in November 1967, celebrated in America with almost personal pride; so will some day be Chairman Mao's Long March and perhaps even his bewildering cultural revolution. It is fitting that the centenary of the Paris Commune should be marked by a series of essays of high quality. The event profoundly affected literature, politics, the relation between Paris and the rest of France, and it probably made impossible for long, if not for ever, a leftist revolution in France. The cult of the Commune is fervently celebrated today in Russia, where the 18th of March is a national holiday, and in China, where the London Economist asserted in 1967 that "it was not China alone that was stretched out under Mao's knife, but two centuries of modern history," marked by 1789 and by 1971.

The French have usually proved very adept at covering up with a veil of reverence even the most embarrassing events in their history and at incorporating them into a hallowed tradition. They have written even on the expulsion of the Huguenots after 1685, on the Terror and on the Dreyfus case, even on the St. Bartholomew massacre, with less indignation than one might wish. Still they are embarrassed by the Commune. Thiers may have more boulevards called after him in French provincial cities than any one except Raspail and De Gaulle, but he has not really been forgiven the clumsy flight from Paris which, in March 1871, abandoned power to the Communards, or the bloody and vengeful shooting of some 15 to 20,000 Frenchmen, after the victory of his troops. The rift between the conservatives and the men of the left, deeper even than that which the bloody days of June 1848 had dug, has never been healed in France. Even the far more systematic and horrifying slaughter of millions of Jews by the Germans and the loss of perhaps several millions of human beings during the Bolshevik and the Chinese revolutions have not overshadowed the shame of the panicked conservatives of France, threatened in their

1

attachment to property, or the destruction by fire of several Parisian monuments by the maddened Communards.

The impact on literature and on political thought in France was enormous and far reaching in its consequences. The old men who had fostered the revolutionary mystique and set their faith in the people as being always right in the impulses of its collective heart, like Michelet, or those who had gradually turned liberal, like Sainte-Beuve, were crushed. Flaubert, Leconte de Lisle, Renan, Taine, Fustel de Coulanges and many others, who had been critical of the materialism of the Second Empire and often ill-treated by the régime or by the bourgeoisie, witnessed the shattering of their illusions. They were thrown, temporarily at least, to the right, in their revulsion from the excesses of the mob, infuriated by its suffering and its class hatred. Several decades, marked by accumulated mistakes committed by the army, the Church and the French conservatives, during the crises of Boulanger and of Dreyfus, were subsequently to elapse before French historians, political thinkers, social reformers could again develop a Leftist ideology.

On the opposite side, the Communards, having been the lamentable underdogs in an unequal and desperate fight, have gradually been treated as the idealistic martyrs to a noble cause by those who had no longer anything to fear from the movement which they embodied. The French revolutionary parties too often were content to echo the rhetorical tribute paid to them by Marx, by Lenin and by Trotsky. "We hail in the Paris Commune the dawn, pallid as yet, of the first proletarian Republic," declared Trotsky in a preface to a French Communist, but rather objective, account of the Commune by C. Tales. The Communards themselves, intoxicated with the memories of 1793-94 and imbued with the teaching of the pre-Marx utopian socialists, had indulged high-flown eloquence. Felix Pyat, one of their leaders, a well-meaning and generous but totally ineffectual one, had delivered sonorous speeches to the Paris populace: "You have accomplished a revolution which has no precedent in history. . . . Its peculiar greatness consists in its being completely popular, collective, communal, anonymous and unanimous." For the first time, other Communards declared, recalling the Sans-Culottes of 1794, the proletariat has taken its destiny into its own hands. More than any earlier revolution in France, indeed the Commune counted more men from the working class (artisans, industrial workers, small shopkeepers) than men from the bourgeoisie. If ever a spontaneous élan vital could effect the overthrow of a régime and replace it by another, that miracle should have been achieved by the Paris Commune.

But it failed. And the revolutionary leaders who have woven a myth around the Commune might have been better advised to analyze the reasons for that failure and to draw constructive conclusions. The proletarians, incensed by the sufferings of the Siege of Paris, by the humiliation of France's surrender to the Prussians, deeply patriotic, had no real leaders.

2

The Commune—A Century After

There were too many feuding factions among their inspirers, some devotees of Proudhon (dead since 1865), others of the almost saintly figure of Blanqui, the perpetual prisoner. All revolutionary movements, before the Commune and since, have thus had their factions and devoured their own children and, strangely enough, grown much stronger thereby. But the Commune did not count, or produce, one powerful leader who might have guided it. It had been a spontaneous uprising, but without a revolutionary party behind it which might have given it a strategy, might have conceived an overall blueprint and have imposed its policy through a ruthless discipline. There was little method behind their fury, little clarity of purpose behind their idealism. Auguste Comte had uttered the precept, which proved valid in 1871 as it did in Paris in May 1968, that "one only truly destroys what one knows how to replace."

Not only did the Commune fail to be prepared by an ideological movement such as had preceded 1789, thought out by members of the middle and upper classes bent upon curing all too conspicuous evils; it would not have known what to set up in the way of institutions if it had succeeded in getting rid of the prevailing order. But it did not even know how to destroy. Marx, at first cool to the Commune, decided to espouse its cause. In his Civil War in France (1871), at the same time as he was groping to explain the confused events in Paris into a class struggle, he advanced the thesis which he had upheld in his Eighteenth Brumaire, that a revolution cannot succeed if it merely takes over the previous bureaucratic, financial, military organization. It must shatter it with ruthless determination. Lenin reflected assiduously on the Commune and endorsed the Marxist view: destroying the existing machinery of the state must be immediately accompanied by the construction of a new one. Bureaucracy, army, police must at once be replaced by new ones. The anarchism of Blanqui, the fond hope that all French cities could also have evolved their own Communes and that the whole picturesque disorder somehow might become viable, were pronounced by Lenin in his pamphlet on The Paris Commune a preposterous stupidity. "The road to socialism lies only through the dictatorship of the proletariat."

Some of the forces which defeated the Commune were similarly at work in the Paris riots of 1968. There also, utopianism prevailed. There also a beautifully spontaneous and generous uprising lived its dream for a few days. But it was unprepared by any revolutionary party, unorganized by any strong leaders; it basked for a time in the exhilaration of its own apparent success. But it failed to rally provincial France; it failed to know what to accomplish in order to organize a revolution and even what to put in the place of the much criticized and indeed antiquated and rigid university structure. It, too, became caught up in its own rhetoric and revelled in coining aphorisms. Like the Commune, that movement may have imagined it was the harbinger of a rosy future, that Paris had recaptured its former primacy as the cradle of revolutions. Once again, in the France

3

of 1971, the Left has emerged divided, embittered, weakened in its ability to rally the forces of the future and to direct them firmly to goals clearly conceived and relentlessly pursued. The Russian Marxists have meditated on the failure of the Commune and evolved what some have called a myth around it. The young revolutionaries of France and those of America might well ponder also on an anniversary which may provide them, not with myths doomed to collapse under the impact of events, but with lucid lessons: most revolutions had been preceded and prepared by the disaffectation of the intellectuals; but unless that disaffection also spreads to the working classes, exacerbated by unemployment, injustice, the senselessness of a useless and immoral war, the revolutionary hopes will be frustrated and reaction may well win out.

THE PERMANENCE OF THE COMMUNE

Richard Greeman

*M*arch 1971: Thousands of high school students in Paris greet the centennial of the Commune by organizing a strike, opening their schools, and inviting the population to join with them in a celebration of the 19th century's greatest revolution for freedom. In response to the historically conscious actions of these youth (some of whom were reportedly as young as ten or eleven years old), Official France decrees the occupation of the streets by the force of repression: CRS security police armed with grenade-launchers and submachineguns. One hundred years after the event, the ghosts of Versailles and the Hôtel de Ville eye each other uneasily across the barricades of time.

February 1967: Thousands of workers and youth in Shanghai (People's Republic of China) seize municipal authority, occupy factories and public buildings, and declare the "Shanghai Commune" . . . "on the model of the Paris Commune of 1871."[1] Communist officialdom, after some hesitation, declares this action an "anarchistic" breach of discipline and has it repressed by force of arms. In August 1967, masses of people throughout China respond by applying the Paris Commune principle of "the people armed:" they enter Red Army barracks and seize the weapons in order to defend themselves against the Communist state. Several months later, a mass revolutionary grouping in Hunan declares:

The commune of the 'Ultra-Left faction' will not conceal its viewpoints and intentions. We publicly declare that our object of establishing the 'People's Commune of China' can be attained only by overthrowing the bourgeois dictatorship and revisionist system of the revolutionary committee [the official organ of the Maoist 'Great Proletarian Cultural Revolution' — R. G.] with brute force. Let the new bureaucratic bourgeoisie tremble before the true socialist revolution that shakes the world! What the proletariat can lose in this revolution is only their chains, what they gain will be the whole world! The China of tomorrow will be the world of the 'Commune.'[2]

Again the ghosts of "Versailles" and the "Hôtel de Ville" face each other across the barricades, time and space notwithstanding.

What gives the name of the Commune such astonishing life in a world that has transformed itself so drastically since 1871? How can a century-old event continue to play the role of a "burning issue of the day" when so much has happened since? A sentimental appeal to the heroism of the Communards ("their blood shall never be forgotten") is an insufficient answer to such questions. Rather, it is necessary to see how certain *specific features* of the Commune of 1871, transposed onto the new objective conditions of the 20th Century, have aided revolutionary forces to understand and realize (i.e., make real) their own aspirations. This essay will attempt to elucidate briefly two examples of this phenomenon.

5

Revolution & Reaction

The Paris Commune had been history for nearly a half-century when Lenin, on the eve of the 1917 Soviet Revolution, sat down to review its achievements in his pamphlet, *State and Revolution*. In the interim, the mass socialist organizations of the Second International had arisen to preach the word of proletarian revolution and workers' internationalism in every European country—only to collapse like a house of cards before the guns of August 1914. Socialism was a shambles; its leaders were preaching fratricide in the name of nationalism and the state. For Lenin, the immediate task of the moment was literally to *"resuscitate"* the real teachings of Marx and Engels, and, in this context, the Paris Commune shone like a beacon across the decades to illuminate the present.

It is often said that *State and Revolution* is a mere "rewrite" of Marx's *Civil War in France*. Even if this view were accurate, which it is not, it fails to acknowledge the fact that such a "rewrite," *in the context of an imperialist world war and an incipient Soviet revolution in Russia,* could not fail to be a work of originality and a revolutionary act. What is important to us, however, in Lenin's 1917 return to the Commune of 1871, is how this study revolutionized Lenin's own thinking and prepared him for the revolution to come; for what must be emphasized is that *State and Revolution* represents Lenin's break, not only with the "social-patriot" betrayers of the Second International, but also with his own political and philosophical past.

Where the Marxists of his time, including Kautsky, his teacher, had seen the growth of the state as implicitly "socialistic," as replacing the anarchy of competition with "organization," so that the socialists would need only to "take it over," Lenin, under the impact of the Commune, now emphasized the need to "smash" it and replace it with a Commune-type of non-state. Where all Marxists (and especially Lenin himself, in his 1903 *What Is To Be Done*) had emphasized the need for vanguard leadership, for Organization, Organization, and more Organization, Lenin, studying the Commune, now burst forth with new appreciation for the spontaneous revolutionary creativity of the masses themselves.

This new appreciation, moreover, was not just an abstraction. In Russia, the masses had spontaneously created a new type of autonomous association to express their aspirations: the Soviets, or Councils of Workers' and Soldiers' Deputies. These Soviets had appeared before in Russian history, during the Revolution of 1905; but no revolutionary theorist had recognized in them the actual *form* of workers' power or even bothered to remember them. It was the masses themselves who remembered and recreated them on a grander scale in 1917. Whereas some Marxists had actually seen them as a rival for the Party, Lenin, in the process of writing *State and Revolution,* recognized them as the modern edition of the Paris Commune adapted to Russian conditions, as that "expansive form" of workers' self-government—directly elected by the masses, subject to their immediate recall, capable of arming the people to defend their revolutionary class interests and of smashing the old parisitic, bureaucratic state—which Marx had discovered in the Commune. It was consequently a new and transformed Lenin who was able to call for revolution in Russia under the slogan, "All Power to the Soviets."[3]

There is no more dramatic page in revolutionary history than where Lenin breaks off the manuscript of *State and Revolution* with the phrase, "it is more pleasant and useful to go through 'the experience of the revolution' than to write about it." Unfortunately, however, this circumstance has deprived us of the promised second half of *State and Revolution* where Lenin intended to "sum up the experience of the Russian Revolution" in the light of the past and where we should have found many more explicit comparisons between the Commune and the Soviets than the few hints Lenin has left us in the first part. What we do have is the record of Lenin's attempts to apply the Commune's principles to the almost insuperable problems of an isolated revolution in a war-torn, backward, and predominantly peasant land surrounded by armed enemies, as, for example, in the following declaration, made *after* the seizure of power:

Every citizen *to a man* must act as a judge and participate in the government of the country, and what is most important to us is to enlist all the toilers *to a man* in the government of the state. That is a tremendously difficult task, but socialism cannot be introduced by a minority, by a party.[4] (emphasis added)

The repeated phrase, "to a man," represented for Lenin a new Universal, the criterion which would distinguish between the actual dictatorship of the proletariat modeled after the Paris Commune and a new form of bureaucratic state, which Lenin feared might overcome the fledgling revolution in Russia.

Such a transformation into the opposite did take place in Russia, but it took a bloody Stalinist counter-revolution to establish it. Many modern writers try to lay the blame for this at Lenin's door, both among Western liberals and apologists for the modern Communist state, which, having jettisoned its real founder, Stalin, attempts to justify its existence by mummifying and deifying Lenin's thought. They can only accomplish this end by ignoring the break in Lenin's development exemplified by his return to the Commune and by selectively (and thus falsely) quoting him. There is a genuine ambivalence in Lenin's thought, but the defenders of the modern bureaucratic Communist state which massacres workers in Hungary, Poland, and Czechoslovakia must have a hard time reconciling it with the Lenin who wrote: "While the state exists there is no freedom. When there is freedom, there will be no state."[5]

Just as Lenin needed to return to the Commune of 1871 in order to resuscitate the essential spirit of revolution which lay buried under the reformist rhetoric and actual class betrayals of the "official" Marxists of his time, so today's youthful revolutionaries feel compelled to return to it in a yet different context. For the young Chinese revolutionaries cited above, the image of the Commune with its elected officials paid at workman's wages, its self-armed masses, its multiplicity of newspapers and organizations, and above all its tendency toward what Marx called "the withering away of the state" appears as the direct antithesis of the Communist state and its vast Party, state, and Army bureaucracies of officials chosen from on high. In their hands, the image of the Commune is a unique weapon to use against an oppressor who is officially "revolutionary" and who has usurped the Marxist vocabulary. Small wonder, then, that the Commune is cited no less than forty-five times in their eighteen-page declaration, the conclusion of which we have quoted above.

For the new generation of revolutionaries in France, the connection is much more immediate. The Gaullist state, even by democratic-republican standards, is so obviously a new edition of the authoritarian Bonapartist Second Empire, that the mere attempt to celebrate the long-dead glories of the Communards can easily lead to renewed street-fighting. Moreover, the memory of the near-revolution of May-June 1968 is all too fresh and menacing. For, unlike the Commune, which ended in the massacre or deportation of probably 100,000 workers and revolutionaries, the 1968 May Revolt ended in a draw, with all the contending forces more-or-less intact and ready for the next round.

Our second example of the influence of the Commune on modern revolutionaries comes, appropriately enough, from France. The context, however, is not that of post-1968 *Gauchisme,* but of an earlier period when de Gaulle was still performing his economic miracles, when the official French Communist Party could still pretend to speak for the "Left," and when those who even dared to dream of a second edition of the Paris Commune were confined to a few tiny and isolated radical sects.

On March 18, 1962, three members of one such sect, *L'Internationale Situationniste,* published fourteen numbered paragraphs or "theses" on the Commune as a contribution to the clarification of revolutionary ideas.[6] The authors, Guy Debord, Attila Kotànyi, and Raoul Vareigem, and their obscure *Internationale* were at the time unknown outside the narrowest circles. In 1966, the highly-publicized student rebellion at the University of Strasbourg, which was directly inspired by their ideas, gave them a certain notoriety.[7] The 1968 student-worker uprising put them on the map: the celebrated "Mad Dogs" (*Enragés*) of Nanterre were among their followers, and their ideas were plastered on every wall in the form of popular slogans like "All Power to the Imagination."[8] Their theses on the Commune are thus best understood as part of the process of political and philosophical preparation for the May-June 1968 rebellion, which, it is now universally admitted, was long brewing under the apparently calm surface of triumphant Gaullist society.

The *Situationniste* interpretation of the Commune is highly original and worthy of consideration on its own merits. What interests us here, however, is the striking manner in which the questions and solutions posed in these theses anticipate the ideas and issues raised in the actual practice of the May-June rebellion itself. For, here again, the very fact of rethinking the Commune in the context of the new objective circumstances of the revolutionary movement meant opening new doors to the possibilities of the present. Let us look at some of these theses in relation to the actual revolutionary practice of May-June 1968.[9]

1

It is necessary to rethink the history of the working-class movement stripped of illusions, and first of all of illusions regarding its political and pseudo-theoretical heirs, for they possess only the heritage of its failures. The apparent successes of this movement are its fundamental failures (reformism or the setting up of a state bureaucracy) and its failures (the Commune or the rebellion of the Asturias) have remained open successes, for us and for the future.

Here we have the theoretical basis for the rejection of the so-called "realists" of the Left, the official Socialists and Communists, by the revolutionary masses of 1968. The parties of the "Senile Left" were pushed aside in practice precisely because they insisted on limiting the movement to practical "successes" (e.g. the 10% wage-raises negotiated at Grenelle in order to end the general strike and twice rejected by the workers; the electoral circus imposed by the parties on the masses as a substitute for direct action). These "successes" were in fact defeats for the working class, while the actual process of the open and ongoing revolt was the first real success the European workers had seen since 1936. This lesson in practice has not been lost, for the process of rethinking working-class history has continued in France since 1968 from precisely the viewpoint suggested above, as witness the dozens of new books reviving the traditions of its apparent "failures:" the early Soviets, the Humanism of the young Marx, the Sparticists, the Anarchists, *etc.*

2

The Commune was the greatest *fête* (festival, celebration) of the 19th century. On a fundamental level, the rebels seemed to feel they had become the masters of their own history, not so much on the level of "governmental" political decisions as on the level of daily life in that Spring of 1871 (note how everyone *played* with their weapons; which means: playing with power). This is *also* the sense in which we must understand Marx: "The greatest social measure of the Commune was its own working existence."

The Spring *fête,* the playing with power, the euphoric sense of release and self-mastery, the joy of at last feeling real, responsible, human, the pressing urge to *transform daily life,* the recognition of the *seriousness* of "play"—how better to express the essential spirit of the 1968 May Revolt?

3

Engels' phrase: "Look at the Paris Commune. This was the dictatorship of the proletariat" should be taken seriously as the basis for recognizing what *is not* the dictatorship of the proletariat (i.e. the various forms of dictatorship over the proletariat, in its name).

This fundamental criticism of *all* so-called "socialist" states, drawn from the example of the Commune, lays the basis for the rejection of bureaucratic Communism by the masses of 1968 and draws the dividing line between the "Old" and the genuinely "New" Left. The May-June Revolt broadcast this fundamental idea to the world with its popular slogan: "Humanity will at last be happy when the last capitalist has been hanged with the guts of the last Stalinist bureaucrat." It is also, as we have seen, the basis of the Chinese Ultra-Left's rejection of its regime.

4

Everyone has correctly criticized the disunity of the Commune, the obvious lack of a leadership *apparatus.* But since we today feel that the problem of political apparatus is much more complex than the self-proclaimed heirs of the Bolshevik-type apparatus will admit, it is time to consider the Commune not only as an example of revolutionary primitivism whose errors are to be transcended, but as a positive experience the whole truth of which has not yet been rediscovered or worked out.

To many observers, the May revolt owed its vigor, its expansiveness, its creativity and initiative to the very absence of a traditional revolutionary party-apparatus and to its rejection, partial or total, of the various self-proclaimed vanguards (Communists, Trotskyists, etc.). These apparatuses, with their passion for leading and their pre-formulated slogans and orders appeared positively divisive at times in their efforts to substitute themselves for the self-development of the mass movement.[10] Subsequent to May-June 1968, many on the French Left have concluded, like the critics of the Commune earlier, that the ultimate downfall of the movement was due to the absence of a coherent, recognized leadership. Although many new groupings have been formed, ostensibly to fill that gap, it is significant that this question of the relationship between vanguard leadership and the spontaneous self-development of the masses is being reconsidered within these very groups.

5

The Commune had no leaders. This is an historical period when the idea that leaders were necessary absolutely dominated the workers' movement. The official guides of the Commune were incompetents (if compared with the level of a Marx, a Lenin, or even a Blanqui). On the other hand, the "irresponsible" acts of the time are precisely those which should be claimed as the heritage of the revolutionary movement of our time (even if circumstances limited most of them to the purely destructive stage) . . .

The May-June Revolt, likewise, had no leaders, despite the efforts of the press and government to turn such popular figures as Danny-the-Red into superstars. Moreover, in almost every case its most "irresponsible" (and destructive) acts marked positive turning-points in its development, *e.g.,* the imprisonment of the manager of Sud-Aviation in his office by the workers, the attack on American Express, the student "scandals" of Nanterre, the occupation of public buildings (the Sorbonne, the Odéon), the throwing of paving-stones, *etc.* What "responsible" leader could possibly sanction such actions? Yet how would the movement have deepened without them?

8

The Paris Commune was vanquished less by the force of arms than by the force of habit. The most shocking practical example is the refusal to resort to arms to take over the Bank of France when money was needed so badly. Throughout the Commune's period in power, the Bank remained a Versaillese enclave in Paris, defended by a few rifles and the myths of property and theft. Other ideological reflex-habits were generally ruinous (the resurrection of Jacobinism, the defeatist strategy of barricades—a throwback to 1848, *etc.*).

The May-June 1968 Revolt, with all its *audace,* was marked by the same unconscious timidity and conservatism. Several months afterward, I interviewed participants who expressed outrage at the fact that the banks had been left untouched and that no one had even bothered to "liberate" paper, presses, and printing equipment during the period when the police were powerless to prevent it, and when the material means to continue revolutionary agitation were painfully lacking on the Left. Others felt the official radio-TV should have been seized and used, rather than merely boycotted. Similarly, the conservative weight of the trade unions and official "Left" parties, although ignored during the ascendent stages of the revolt, managed to reassert itself when the movement began to wane. This "dead hand of the past," which today includes not only Jacobinism but every form of reformism and Communism, still weighs heavy on the present, although the French events of 1968 and the rise of a world-wide New Left have done some to counter its effect. It is the counter-revolution *within* the revolution that is the hardest to combat.

9

Theoreticians who reconstitute the history of this movement from the omniscient viewpoint of God, which characterized the classic novelist, have easy work proving that the Commune was objectively doomed, that it had no possible transcendence. It should not be forgotten that for those who lived the event, the transcendence *was there.*

The same could be said for the "events" of May-June. In the Spring of 1968, the attitude of those who stood aloof from the rebellion (*e.g.,* the Communists) was *already* that of omniscient hindsight: "no revolution is possible here." However, the feeling of the mass of actual participants was best expressed in the popular slogan, "Everything is possible." Like the Communards of old, the youth and workers of France experienced their revolt as *actuality;* as possibility, as a future that lay open before them; this in contrast to the Old Left dogmatists for whom history, and hence the future, is *determined.* These contrasting viewpoints reveal two totally opposed conceptions of revolutionary *praxis.*

13

The social war of which the Commune is a moment still continues (although its surface conditions have changed a good deal). As for the task of "making conscious the unconscious tendencies of the Commune" (Engels), the last word has not been said.

11

This last thesis takes the Commune out of "history" and returns it to its place in revolutionary process. The Commune's meaning, therefore, is not just something to be worked out in theory, but also in practice. May-June 1968 certainly reaffirmed the *Situationnistes'* thesis that this struggle still continues (a thesis that was not so obvious in 1962), while its actuality added another "moment" to the revolutionary process, a "moment" whose unconscious tendencies, like those of the Commune itself, are to be elucidated, both theoretically and in the practice of the next stage of revolt. This revolutionary conception of history as process (uniting theory and practice) was clearly alive in the consciousness of the May-June rebels, who united present and future in their favorite slogan, "This is only a beginning; continue the struggle!" This slogan remained popular long *after* the last barricades had been swept away. The process of elucidating and digesting the meaning of 1968 continues to this day.

It is within the dialectic of this movement, rather than in history-books, that the Commune of 1871, with its limitations and its grandeur, its historicity and its open door on the future possibilities for human freedom, continues to live. The very "expansiveness" which Marx noted at the time, contrasting the Commune with the restrictive Second Empire, accounts in part for its permanence. It speaks with a new voice to every revolutionary age and circumstance, from Lenin in 1917 to the masses of Paris or of Peking in 1968. Its brief existence revealed for all time that mankind can be free. All will be compelled to return to it until mankind is free.

REFERENCES

[1] For an analysis and documentation of these and subsequent events in China during the Cultural Revolution, see Klaus Mehnert: *Peking and the New Left, At Home and Abroad,* University of California China Research Monographs, Number 4, June 1969 (Berkeley, 1969). [2] Quoted from "Whither China," a manifesto published in January 1968 by the "Sheng-wu-lien" or "Hunan Provincial Proletarian Revolutionary Great Alliance Committee" made up of more than 20 organizations. The complete document appears as an appendix to Mehnert, cited above. It is more readily available, albeit in a shortened form, under the title "China: Voices of Revolt," through *News & Letters* Committees, 1900 E. Jefferson, Detroit, Mich. 48207. [3] Cf. Raya Dunayevskaya: *Marxism and Freedom from 1776 to Today,* 2nd ed. (Twayne, N.Y., 1964), Chapt. X. "The Collapse of the Second International and the Break in Lenin's Thought." This is by far the best analysis of Lenin's duality I have come across, and the only one to take up his views on the question of the party and of organization in the context of his 1914 rediscovery of the Hegelian dialectic. [4] Lenin, *Selected Works,* Vol. IX, p. 439. Moshe Lewin's *Lenin's Last Struggle* (Pantheon, N.Y., 1968) contains a dramatic presentation of Lenin's struggle to preserve the revolution from incipient Stalinization. The most comprehensive view of the question, however, is still Dunayevskaya's, cited above. Her most recent work on the subject can be found in a recent issue of *Telos* (Dept. of Philosophy, S.U.N.Y. at Buffalo). [5] Lenin, *State and Revolution* (International, N.Y., 1932) p. 75. [6] "Sur la Commune," *Internationale Situationniste* No. 7, pp. 17-18. The same text can be found in a broadside entitled "Aux Poubelles de l'Histoire," published in Paris and dated February 21, 1963. This latter version includes an introduction explaining that the *Situationnistes* had originally elaborated their theses as notes for the use of Henri Lefebvre, the Marxist sociologist, who was then preparing a book on the Com-

mune. This work was eventually published as *La Proclamation de la Commune* (NRF-Gallimard, Paris, 1965). Lefebvre's conclusions are strikingly similar to those of the *Situationnistes,* although his work is a much more elaborate reconstruction of the events of 1871. [7] Cf. Daniel Cohn-Bendit, *Le Gauchisme: remède à la maladie sénile du communisme,* (Seuil, Paris, 1968), pp. 22ff. for an account of the "Strasbourg Scandals." [8] Almost all the chronicles of the May-June Events trace the role of the *Situationnistes* and of the "groupuscules" (mini-groups) in general. René Viént, a friend of the *Situationnistes,* has devoted a 320-page volume to this subject: *Enragés et situationnistes dans le mouvement des occupations* (Gallimard, Paris, 1969). [9] The translations are my own. [10] This thesis is elaborated in one of the best short accounts of the May-June Events available in English. Eugene Walker, *France, Spring 1968: Masses in Motion, Ideas in Free Flow (An eyewitness's critical report),* available through *News & Letters* Committees.

THE FAILURE OF REVOLUTION

Frederick Busi

The dream of reason produces monsters.—*Goya*
There are two tragedies in life. One is not to get your heart's desire.
The other is to get it.—*G. B. Shaw*

The Red flag had its birth in Paris. In 1791 it was unfurled by government troops who were dispersing rioters—ironically former conquerors of the Bastille—on the Champs de Mars. In 1832 it appeared again at the funeral of the anti-monarchist general Lamarque. In 1848 it almost became the national standard, but Lamartine's eloquence persuaded the republican victors to retain the Tricolor. During the Second Empire its increasing popularity among revolutionaries caused it to be the natural symbol for the radicals who would eventually gain control of Paris in the confusion following the Franco-Prussian war. As a symbol the color red was supposed to represent the blood shed by the proletariat at the hands of injustice, but very often it was interpreted by the bourgeoisie as the symbol of revolutionary terror.[1]

These volatile memories served to inflame the passions which led to the Paris Commune of 1871, to its violent suppression and also to obscure a balanced appraisal of its historical significance for France, the middle classes, and the revolutionary movement in general. So distorted has its meaning become that it has required almost one hundred years for the smoke to clear in order to evaluate the Commune's historical importance.[2]

It would be useful therefore to consider, briefly, the social conditions which helped create the Paris Commune of 1871, to follow its rise and fall, and to examine its image and legacy in bourgeois and, more importantly, socialist mythologies. For without its legend there would have been no Bolshevik revolution. Careful attention must be paid to the conditions which spawned it, not merely as an exercise in writing about mid-nineteenth century French society, but to examine the existence or non-existence of revolutionary conditions which permit the overthrow of the state.

To begin with, the effects of industrialization only began to make themselves felt long after the downfall of Napoleon and the restoration of the Bourbons. During the period 1835–1845 industrial complexes started to draw peasants in great numbers searching for work from the land to urban centers. This was the period which witnessed the effective consolidation of bourgeois political and economic power and manifested the precarious position of the workers in a social system that capriciously disregarded their interests. With industrial expansion came the growth of an aggravated urban proletariat. When times were good, workers were faced with increased prices for all commodities and the scarcity of lodgings in

14

overcrowded, unsanitary metropolitan areas: when times were bad, during the periodic economic crises, wide-spread unemployment inevitably followed. Such conditions led, in large measure, to the revolution of 1848. With the end of Louis Philippe's monarchy republican elements tried to institute social as well as political changes. And their most noteworthy success was the creation of the National Workshops as a defense against chronic unemployment.[3] Doubtless due to its limited scope and the obstacles it encountered, this innovative program never fully developed and finally failed. Instead of merely providing work for the urban unemployed, it also served to attract to the city workers from Belgium, thus increasing the jobless and contributing to human congestion and disappointment. Gradually, the revolutionary movement lost its impetus, its leadership, disorganized and divided, its modest programs inefficiently administered, withered away before an aroused reaction and repression. From 1848 to 1851 the only party seemingly capable of restoring order were the Bonapartists, led by Louis Napoleon who, elected president of the republic, broke his oath to the constitution through a coup d'état, then eliminated republican opposition with intensive repression. From 1852, when he proclaimed himself emperor, to 1860 France was an effective police state, the first in modern times.

Despite the initial harshness of the regime, Louis Napoleon desired to demonstrate to his countrymen and the world that he could reestablish France's domestic and international prestige. Thanks to the restoration of order, capital felt safe to invest, and business and industry began to thrive, fitfully, once more. The emperor knew that his reputation was based on his illustrious name, therefore he felt compelled to live up to the Bonaparte legend by engaging France in adventurous expeditions in Italy, the Crimea, and Mexico, for example, which at first seemed to restore former military prestige. This false confidence would later lead to his downfall.

Domestically, the most conspicuous achievement of the Second Empire was the rebuilding of Paris.[4] Under the direction of Baron Haussmann almost three billion francs were spent in the total plan to remake the imperial capital into the most splendid city in Europe. The beneficial results cannot be exaggerated: slums were cleared, water and sewer systems improved, parks established, broad thoroughfares constructed; all these accomplishments made Paris the model city for planning and civic architecture. So vast a redevelopment project naturally provoked criticism; lavish expenditures seemed unjustifiable and did increase inflation, hundreds of thousands of families were disrupted, and conservatives doubted the wisdom of creating the huge labor force required for the project's execution. Considering Paris' revolutionary tradition it was feared this massive concentration of laborers might easily erupt when the building boom ended. Although there was much work for all, the average proletarian scarcely benefited from the renewal projects. In most cases he was forced to move from familiar quarters and seek more expensive shelter in areas far from the place of work, in those districts which even today form the Red belt around Paris. The new social patterns tended to segregate worker and bourgeois to an even greater degree than before. However, while the rebuilding continued, the city's population nearly doubled, and most parties, despite reservations, appeared content with the results.

After 1860 Louis Napoleon felt secure enough to loosen gradually his authoritarian grip on the nation's political life. He began, rather modestly, to liberalize the empire. Elections were permitted in which republicans slowly increased their power, and educational reform, offensive to clerical elements, was furthered. Yet despite these promising signs of change, it could never be overlooked that the whole rotting edifice of Bonapartism was based on a militaristic tradition which must periodically reassert itself. The early successes in Italy and the Crimea were later offset by the Mexican disaster and the growing strength of Prussia. Although reluctant to go to war, the emperor, as champion of Europe's Catholic forces, was quite alarmed by the defeat of Austria. Urged on by the empress, clerical supporters, and conservatives, he clumsily tried to check, diplomatically and militarily, Prussia's ascendancy, and on both scores he was outfoxed by Bismarck.[5] Napoleon's liberal prime minister, Ollivier, allowed himself to be stampeded by the conservative Bonapartists into demonstrating his patriotism by deciding, on the eve of July 14, to declare war.

The war of 1870 exploded the farce of the Second Empire's military prestige, catching France and world opinion completely off guard. The French armies' morale was at first quite high, but in every other category—numbers, equipment, tactics, leadership—they were hopelessly outclassed. Throughout the month of August, French heroism could not stop the tide of German successes, and by the beginning of September, Louis Napoleon was forced to surrender in person at Sedan, and shortly thereafter he abdicated. The only military hope remained with Marshal Bazaine who allowed his army to be penned up inside the fortress at Metz. On September 4th a republic was proclaimed, yet discord and doubt arose over the course the new government was to follow.

Confusion dominated the republican factions. Indeed, there were three major tendencies: led by Thiers, known to the Reds as "the bloodthirsty dwarf," the conservatives, including many of imperialist and monarchist leanings, desired a quick peace with the newly proclaimed German Empire in order to get back to the business of reorganizing France's government. The center group desired to continue the war to regain France's honor, and by far the smallest force, the Reds, sought to constitute a new social order. It must be added that the leading figures of this last group had no coherent plan and were doubtless more unorganized—if this can be imagined—than the other forces. Yet events would in a few months time thrust them into proclaiming the first worker-based state in history.

The center group constituted itself as the Government of National Defense, the aim of which was a military victory. Thanks to the efforts of

The Failure of Revolution

General Trochu in Paris and Gambetta in the provinces, it would soon have at its disposal over half a million men, quickly called into the National Guard. As the Germans moved on Paris, the new government prepared for a siege in the hope that by tying down the invading armies, its sacrifice would bring armed relief from the provinces. It never came.

Weeks turned into months, and as the siege progressed the mood of the city oscillated between vengeance and boredom. Attempts to break through German lines failed; military leaders and soldiers were unjustly accused of cowardice; food stocks rapidly dwindled and many citizens were reduced to eating dogs, cats, zoo animals, even rats. In the face of repeated setbacks, Parisians felt betrayed by the rest of France, and the rest of France felt betrayed by the Parisians who seemed to be obstructing peace negotiations. The upper classes had all but abandoned the city to seek refuge in their country homes, leaving the less fortunate to endure the dangers of war and near starvation; employers were forced to close down their factories, throwing hundreds of thousands out of work. Many of the unemployed found a measure of relief in the National Guard which became in 1870 what the National Workshops had stood for in 1848. As a new source of power its sentiments gradually shifted from center to left. Its early leaders, of bourgeois origins and Catholic sympathies, were replaced by journalists and frequenters of the Red clubs or anyone else who could vociferate his hatred against the class which had led them to this disaster—Flourens, Varlin, Rochefort, new voices to goad the over-cautious government into action. On October 5th, 1870 the radical left marched on the Hôtel de Ville to shake their leaders out of lethargy.

On October 27th the government complied. Its attack on Le Bourget was bloodily repulsed by the Prussians. Shortly thereafter, Marshal Bazaine surrendered his enormous army and was justifiably accused of treason against the new republic which he held in contempt. Finally word reached Paris that Thiers, the leader of the conservatives, agreed to Bismarck's harsh terms in order to gain peace at any cost. On October 31st, the Hôtel de Ville was again marched upon by the Red factions, but this time loyal troops fired on the mob and arrested its leaders. As the siege dragged on, the military government showed itself incapable of defeating the Germans and its reputation, too, went the way of Bazaine's. Incredible though it may seem, after all it had suffered, during the severe winter, the working class still cried for war against the invader. However, because of the government's inability, frustration turned from the foreign to the domestic threat, a sellout at the hands of imperialist sympathizers disguised as republicans.

By the end of January 1871 an unfavorable settlement had been concluded. The new Assembly which approved it was now composed of men unsympathetic to the antics of the Parisian radicals whom they accused of prolonging the war. The radicals of Paris thought as little of the provincials whom they believed betrayed them and the nation's honor. At

17

this point that divisiveness and vengeful spirit, endemic to French politics, continued to increase. The Assembly wished to teach the radicals a lesson by passing a tactless law of maturities which required the immediate payment of all back debts and rents accumulated during the siege. To men and women who had endured war and the humiliating surrender, this was insult added to injury. As part of the armistice agreement, German troops were allowed to parade down the *Champs Elysées*. And in order to prevent clashes between them and the National Guard, artillery of the Paris garrison was moved to areas far away from the parade route. After the conquerors' triumphal march, the government of Thiers decided to retrieve the weapons parked in working class districts.

On the night of March 17-18 Thiers dispatched a division under the command of General Vinoy to seize the cannon, but in an action typical of French military incompetence of the time, he botched the assignment by forgetting to bring enough horses to tow them away. Once the people of Montmartre, where many of the cannon were parked, learned of this treachery, they spontaneously rose to retain the weapons they had paid for through public subscription. Two generals, Thomas and Lecomte, were then captured by the aroused mob and savagely murdered. It should be noted that the killings were not ordered by any political group; they were simply dictated by the blood lust of the mob. But given the mood of France, this distinction was academic and the future leaders of the people would be held responsible by an enraged nation. Also, given the mood of Paris, its leaders could not repudiate so spontaneous and popular an act as the assassinations of despised militarists.

The gulf between Paris and Versailles, Thiers' headquarters, seemed unfathomable. On March 26th the government of the capital officially passed into the hands of the newly proclaimed Commune of Paris, which was to share the rule of the city with the Central Committee of the National Guard, charged with its defense. During the following weeks both bodies faltered between action and inaction, and herein lay, some have maintained, the ultimate reason for the Commune's collapse. It has been argued, since, that the Paris forces could have marched immediately on Versailles in order to dictate its own terms. But this speculation is highly questionable, for although the Commune's army initially was much larger, it was undisciplined, poorly led, underequipped, and surrounded by a superior German force which supported Thiers. The only chance, perhaps, to avoid the ensuing bloodbath was, as John Plamenatz suggests, to come to a compromise with the rest of France during its moment of weakness.[6] However, the Commune's inchoate leadership could scarcely be expected to realize so bold a plan. The power of the Commune was never greater than in the weeks following the abortive attempt to seize their cannon, and Thiers knew it. However, this is all idle speculation, for history, strictly speaking, can only deal with what did happen and not with what should or might have happened; that is reserved for theology and ideology.

The Failure of Revolution

From its inception the Commune was plagued with indecisiveness and a confusing diversity of aims and ideas. An American observer in Paris remarked: "It's a madhouse inhabited by monkeys." From its beginning, lack of discipline and direction hampered its development, and understandably so, for it could never quite decide if it were the vanguard in the struggle against social injustice or for the restoration of national honor through war. The ideological composition of its changing leadership reflected every tint in the spectrum of French radicalism. By far, the largest faction was Jacobin, led by Delescluze, followed by the old-fashioned socialists of Blanqui, and then by the Anarchists. The International of Karl Marx was represented by a Hungarian Jew, Leo Fraenkel, and as a voice this group was, by Marx's admission, the most out of touch with events taking place in Paris. Marx himself had no faith at all in the Commune's chances for success because it did not subscribe to his particular brand of scientific socialism. It is another of history's ironies that Marx would receive credit for an insurrection which he initially discounted.

It is not difficult to understand how this distorted image became accepted by both opposing factions. The very name the uprising gave itself seemed related to the philosophy of communism. Yet the term really referred, nostalgically, to the famous Paris Commune of 1793 and perhaps, to the distant echoes of the independent communes of the Middle Ages, to those free cities which determined their own destinies. By and large, the movement sought to destroy the overcentralized bureaucracy which has characterized French governments since Louis XIV. In the field of social legislation what the Commune proposed seems rather scant. Its only noteworthy achievement was the abolition of night work in the bakeries. The confiscation of factories, seizure of the means of production if you will, was accomplished as a temporary measure taken by municipal authorities to provide work for the unemployed in the owners' absence. These reforms are quite modest compared with the social legislation in most modern welfare states. Aside from this there is little else that could characterize it as ideally socialistic. True, the army and police were at first abolished only to be quickly reinstated to protect the sacred ideals of the revolution. Yet despite all the Commune's shortcomings there was something undeniably unique and captivating about it. Here, for the first time in modern history, was a state, albeit miniscule and weak, which defied imperialism and the bourgeoisie, a state with a proletarian base, a state over which the Red flag flew for two months, a society whose distorted legend was destined to become the model for future revolution.

There would be no revolution this time, however, for the increasingly superior forces of its enemy were gradually whittling away at the defensive position of the Commune. By the time Thiers' armies were poised for the kill, the mood of the Commune had drastically changed. Gone were the idealists who preached freedom and brotherhood. In their place stood a fresh leader, Raoul Rigault, the new chief of police, formerly a bohemian layabout whose only talent was terrorism. He more than all the other figures in the movement would give it a lasting image, and embarrassingly, a model for future dispensers of revolutionary justice. Through the continuing flight, resignation or arrest of the moderates, the character of the Commune turned radically Jacobin. Rigault resigned as chief of police to assume inquisitorial duties of state prosecutor of the revolutionary tribunal. He was a *mangiapreti* who arrested some 3000 Parisians and held them as hostages for bargaining power against the government of Thiers. Among the more notable prisoners were the Archbishop of Paris and some fifty priests, who were executed toward the end of May.[7] And their deaths, along with the memory of the two martyred generals, caused French opinion to demand some sort of revenge.

On May 21, regular troops led by General MacMahon—later to become president of the republic—poured into Paris through an unguarded western gate, encountering little resistance in the traditionally bourgeois quarters. What was to follow, during the next week, was to be one of the most savage repressions of modern times in which the numbers of victims were four times those of the Terror of 1793. In the course of the bitter fighting, the Tuileries palace and the Hôtel de Ville, among several landmarks, were burned by the Commune, and only chance spared the Louvre and the cathedral. All in all the Commune executed 150 hostages in reprisal for which the regular army shot some 20,000 communards, mainly as they surrendered in the streets, were trapped, or identified by priests and respectable people. They were shot down in the Luxembourg gardens, the Parc Monceau, the cemeteries of Montparnasse and Père Lachaise, where Thiers' troops found the unburied body of the Archbishop and proceeded to execute the last fighting group of communards.

Many reasons have been offered to explain the savage butchery of the forces of law and order. Thiers promised no pity and although he warned against acts of unnecessary violence, his troops, mainly provincial recruits, hated everything Parisians stood for, especially their smug superiority and anticlericalism. In retrospect, the Commune appeared just strong enough to arouse its enemy's vindictiveness, but too weak to defend itself, just able enough to start the conflagration which consumed it, thus setting back the working class movement in France by twenty years. Who were the victims? After the barbarous massacres, some 36,000 Parisians were arrested, and it is rather interesting, sociologically, to note that only one fourth were born in that city, the rest coming in from the provinces, doubtless in search of work that did not exist.[8] This large group, the least assimilated, the most unstable, formed the bulk of the movement's following. It is also important to note that despite its vague socialistic rhetoric, this uprising rarely characterized the revolt of slave against master which radical mythology prefers to evoke. The masses seem to have mainly been inspired by patriotic hatred for the foreign invader. Their violence only turned radical when they believed Thiers' policies would betray

France's honor. The greatest irony is that the leaders of the Commune, destined to be models for proletarian revolution, the men who gave it shape and some direction, were petty bourgeois in origin and spirit.

It is doubtless this last observation which caused Marx to be skeptical about the Commune's prospects for victory. As noted earlier, he had little respect for the French section of the International; he felt it incapable of overcoming the burdens of its own glorious revolutionary past, incapable of adjusting to his new vision of the role of the proletariat. Nevertheless, Marx was the chief beneficiary of the Commune. Thanks to reactionary hysteria his own movement would receive most of the credit for fomenting the revolt when in fact he had practically nothing to do with it. The memory of the Commune goes to Marx by default. The notoriety he received propelled him from the status of an obscure German Jewish radical into the role of an evangelist or the antichrist, depending on one's taste.[9] On one score both opposing sides could agree: socialism, after the defeat of the Commune, would never be the same. The failure of 1871 marked the watershed separating reformist and revolutionary elements in the radical cause.

Marx has been accused of being ambiguous about the Commune, and rightly so for he held two conflicting interpretations of its significance.[10] Publicly, he quickly praised the defeated revolt in his *The Civil War in France,* certainly one of the most influential books, by Lenin's standards, ever written. But this pamphlet is least of all a history of the Paris Commune; it is an analysis of its shortcomings, a blueprint for future revolution, and above all it is a call to Armageddon, a hymn of praise to the suffering servants, to the future inheritors of the earth. Privately, Marx could afford to be less enthusiastic about it as he writes to Domela Nieuwenhuis in 1881:

The Commune was merely the rising of a town under exceptional conditions, the majority of the Commune was in no sense socialist, nor could it be. With a small amount of common sense, they could have reached a compromise with Versailles useful to the whole mass of the people.[11]

Upon the first reading there seems to be nothing remarkable about this viewpoint, but where scholarship is free, this letter, compared with his better known opinions expressed in *The Civil War in France,* produces bewilderment. In effect, what Marx is saying is that a peaceful solution "useful to the whole mass of the people" was possible, but he reasons that the bloodbath which followed was somehow more beneficial, almost redemptive, in the long run in forging a new class consciousness. In short, evil bourgeois violence in the future will be purged by massive doses of pure proletarian violence.

The lesson was not lost on Marx's most famous student, Lenin, who writes in *State and Revolution,* "The Russian revolutions of 1905 and 1917 . . . continued the work of the Commune and confirmed the historic analysis made by the genius of Marx." It is of the utmost importance to note here again that Marx's genius also perceived that the Commune's confrontation with the bourgeois republic was not an either/or situation in which one or the other parties was foreordained to seek the other's extermination. Lenin, following Marx, conveniently ignores this insight and chooses to apply the Manichean version to the events in revolutionary Russia where Tsardom had already been overthrown before his return home. His chief contribution consisted in making a coup d'état against the Social Democrats, thus plunging Russia into civil war. Lenin's basic unfinished task was the transformation of a coup d'état into a revolution. This contradiction is still reflected in the third-rate socialisms of the third world, many of which are ruled by "progressive" militarists. Yet Lenin realized and cavalierly dismissed this flaw by claiming that the minor details, the growing pains, would somehow work themselves out. In the meantime there is an example of his philosophy in action:

Ours is a new morality. Our humanism is absolute, for it has as its basis the desire for abolition of all oppression and tyranny. To us everything is permitted, for we are the first in the world to raise the sword not for the purpose of enslavement and oppression but in the name of liberty and emancipation from slavery. We do not wage war against individuals. We seek to destroy the bourgeoisie as a class.[12]

But this new dispensation did not stop with the extermination of the bourgeoisie. After its demise the Tsarists were next, then the Social Democrats, the Kulaks, then the Anarchists, the Reformists, the Zionists, the Revisionists, the rootless cosmopolites, the Trotskyites, then their families and friends and acquaintances until the maelstrom of terror liquidated 20,000,000 enemies of the people; this just to consolidate scientific socialism on the home front, to guarantee the eight-hour day and collectivization. Only the imbecilic logic of Doctor Pangloss makes sense here.

Some will quickly add, with a glimmer of hope in their eyes, that this is not true socialism but Stalinism. By invoking the thoroughly unmarxian notion of ascribing great events to great men they neatly forget that Stalin but inherited and perfected Lenin's terrorist policies: they fervently believe that the real thing will arrive any day now. Like Vladimir and Estragon, by the budding tree, they cannot see that Godot has come and gone twice during their pathetic vigil. It is basically a religious problem.[13]

Radicals have not been totally oblivious to the spectacle of their vision gone awry. For this reason it becomes easier to counterbalance the reality of terror against the ideal of the permanent revolution. Thus in 1968 the disillusioned took heart once again at the outbreak of the benighted Cultural Revolution in China and the Events of May in France. In both countries hordes of obnoxious students disrupted national life in a desperate attempt to unsettle establishment politics, hoping to found a Republic of Virtue. Behind both movements one could perceive the inspiration of the Paris Commune and also the weakness which led to its downfall.[14] The students and their followers were just strong· enough to provoke their enemies into repressing them, thus assuring a firmer power base for the state they hoped to destroy. In China the People's Liberation Army was called out to restore order and now helps the Party to maintain its authority, and in France the Gaullist faction is more solidly in control than ever before. To be sure, these conditions will change, but it is imperative in this context to bear in mind the advice of Marx and Lenin, warning against radicals who attempt revolutions that go off half-cocked.

The conditions which lead to revolutionary situations are mysterious and elusive. A revolutionary situation is not that amorphous backlog of discontent and agitation whose existence is usually recognized by police and radical alike.[15] It is rather that unique opportunity when a disturbance precipitates a governmental crisis in which events may go either way. Even when the proposed revolution goes temporarily amiss, it is still possible for some to entertain the weird logic that repression steels the soul, preparing it for the ineluctable victory. Communists in pre-Hitler Germany were confident, thanks to their interpretation of dialectical historical vicissitudes, that they would succeed the nazi regime. And they did. After a gallant struggle which caused 45,000,000 dead, Walter Ulbricht became the dictator of the German Democratic Republic.

While Lenin was desperately consolidating his grip on Russia, he had nothing but contempt for those inept European revolutionaries who were bungling their historically appointed missions. In his pamphlet, *The Infantile Disease of Leftism,* Lenin warned his western admirers of losing their identity through too close a relationship with the undisciplined discontented. He permitted compromise with them for expediency's sake until communists were in a secure enough position to annihilate their weak-hearted allies. Those who freely indulged in the rhetoric of violence bore a heavy responsibility for mere talk would not produce the revolution. The great danger, Lenin thought, was the uprising that failed and provoked counteraction. Lenin felt that the only equal to socialist wrath was that of an aroused bourgeoisie, preferably petty.[16]

The Paris Commune of 1871 was an appeal back to the vision of an egalitarian and—*pace* Marx—utopian past, an effort to disestablish an overcentralized government, a noble attempt to reduce society to more human needs and dimensions. Marx's genius consisted in giving men practical hope, and the communards' elation, described by Marx, must have been similar to that of Cubans upon the ouster of the Batista regime: "No longer was Paris the rendezvous of British landlords, Irish absentees, American ex-slaveholders and shoddy men, Russian ex-serfowners, and Wallachian boyards."[17] Marx's great contribution to revolutionary thought was the encouragement of opportunism, the necessity to exploit a revolutionary situation and to carry through, ruthlessly, its program for change. In the wake of his ideology's application in Russia, however, there followed the greatest body of dead thought and dogmatism since the dying days of late medieval scholasticism, the boldest perversion of language and ideals required to fill the deafening silence caused by the collapse of a bankrupt liberalism.

What actually occurred during those two remarkable months of 1871 was subsequently interpreted, written large, and applied in vastly different lands and circumstances. It is quite some distance from the ideals of the Commune to the obscenities of Stalinism, however much the latter may claim the former in its search for a respectable genealogy. Ideals, while retaining their original forms, have a habit of spinning away from their authors' spirit. Thus Christ gave the Sermon on the Mount and humanity got the Catholic church; Marx wrote *The Civil War in France* and it got the Communist party. It did not have to turn out quite that way, but perhaps, because of the ethics of achievement, nothing, claims Toynbee, fails like success. The rhetoric of violence tends to condition and confuse the masses to react in a manner alien to their best interests, tends subtly to substitute, institutionalize and glorify the means at the expense of the ends, and thus the state never withers away, violence becomes expiatory, war becomes peace.

The seizure of a city by the disenchanted, the oppressed, by those sick of rotten politics, is in itself no assurance of progress. In 1919, the Italian poet, d'Annunzio (in Lenin's words) "the only real revolutionary in Italy,"[18] at the head of a large group of malcontents, liberated the city of Fiume and held it for fifteen months, defying all the world's corrupt politicians. One year later, Mussolini, impressed by this feat, marched on Rome and established the New Order. One year later, Hitler marched on Munich only to be routed. Chastened by this setback, he adopted a red flag, and ten years later, with the support of the academic community, among others, established national socialism and created the most enthusiastically popular government Germany has ever known.[19] One rarely gets the revolution one expects.

REFERENCES

[1] Concerning the history of the Red flag as a revolutionary symbol see Maurice Dommanget, *La révolution de 1848 et le drapeau rouge* (Paris, 1948) and Gabriel Perreux, *Les origines du drapeau rouge* (Paris, 1930). [2] The critical bibliography on the Paris Commune is immense. For an introduction one may consult Roger Williams' study, *The French Revolution of 1870-1871* (New York, 1969) for its excellent bibliography. Other accounts recommendable for the general reader are: Alistair Horne, *The Fall of Paris* (New York, 1965) and Henri Lefebvre, *La proclamation de la commune* (Paris, 1965). There are specialized studies of various aspects of the Commune, and one, which might be of interest to the university community, is Maurice Choury's *La commune au quartier latin* (Paris, 1961). [3] Donald Cope McKay, *The National Workshops* (Cambridge, Mass., 1965). [4] David H. Pinkney, *Napoleon III and the Rebuilding of Paris* (Princeton, 1958). [5] Lawrence D. Steefel, *Bismarck, the Hohenzollern Candidacy, and the Origins of the Franco-German War of 1870* (Cambridge, Mass., 1962). For a detailed account of the war see Michael Howard, *The Franco-Prussian War* (New

The Failure of Revolution

York, 1962). [6] John Plamenatz, *The Revolutionary Movement in France* (London, 1965) p. 150. [7] Controversy shrouded the circumstances surrounding the death of Archbishop Darboy. Thiers' opponents accused him of not doing enough to secure his release for the simple reason that the prelate's politics were too liberal for his tastes. See Gustave Gautherot, *Thiers et Mgr Darboy* (Paris, 1910) and J. Lucas-Dubreton, *Monsieur Thiers* (Paris, 1848) p. 337. By all standards the nineteenth century was dangerous for Parisian archbishops: another was shot during the revolution of 1848, and his successor was stabbed to death in church by a beserk unfrocked priest. [8] Jacques Rougerie, *Procès des communards* (Paris, 1964) p. 127. [9] The myth of an international Jewish conspiracy received powerful impetus from reaction to the Paris Commune, and this may well signal the beginnings of modern popular political anti-Semitism, at least in France. The talented demagogue and journalist, Edouard Drumont, wrote in his *La France Juive*—which ran through 201 editions—that subversive Jewish forces were responsible for France's defeat. On the left he exaggerated the role of Marx and on the right accused the house of Rothschild of financing a red revolt. In fact, during the hostilities, the Rothschilds and the Bank of France were both coerced by the Commune to grant loans in order to support its activities. Drumont's imagination concocted a Semitic-Aryan confrontation on a global scale, the outcome of which would be determined by what he termed and advocated "national socialism." He even accused Offenbach, the Jew from Cologne, of demoralizing Frenchmen by his comic operettas. More than the army and the church, Drumont was responsible for fanning the flames of anti-Semitism during the Dreyfus affair, and his self-fulfilling prophecy later realized itself in a series of red uprisings partly led by Jews such as Eisner, Luxemburg, and Trotsky. Conservatives saw in Dreyfus' acquittal an insult which would only be later satisfied by the deportation of 100,000 French Jews to Auschwitz. After World War II 20,000 Frenchmen were summarily executed by the left, an act which prompted Charles Maurras, the noted reactionary intellectual, to proclaim at his trial that this new red purge was nothing more than the Jews' revenge since the Dreyfus affair and the debacle of 1870. It is interesting to note, in passing, that *the Protocols of the Elders of Zion* were a direct adaptation—on the part of the Russian secret police—of an anti-Napoleon III pamphlet written by a French lawyer named Maurice Joly. For a detailed history of alleged Jewish subversiveness see Norman Cohen's *Warrant for Genocide* (New York, 1966). [10] Marx's attitudes toward the Commune have been treated in depth by Shlomo Avineri, *The Social and Political Thought of Karl Marx* (Cambridge, England, 1968) pp. 239–249 and by Bertram Wolfe, *Marxism* (New York, 1965) pp. 126–147. [11] Marx-Engels, *Selected Correspondence* (New York and London, 1935) pp. 386-387. [12] Excerpt of an article from the Bolshevik *Red Sword* of 18 August 1919, quoted by David Shub, *Lenin* (Baltimore, 1966) p. 368. [13] For a study of the religious roots of political messianism see Rosemary Ruether, *The Radical Kingdom* (New York, 1970). [14] An example of the unfaltering hope in Utopia—which means "nowhere" in Greek—may be found in Joan Robinson's *The Cultural Revolution in China* (Baltimore, 1969). "There have been three milestones on the road to socialist revolution. The first was the Paris Commune. It failed, but through it the proletariat gained valuable experience. The October Revolution was the first successful proletarian revolution. The Cultural Revolution is the first case of a revolution taking place under an already established dictatorship of the proletariat." p. 45. Paul Lidsky provides a succinct comparison between the Commune and the Events of May 1968 at the end of his *Les écrivains contre la commune* (Paris, 1970) pp. 164–171. See also Daniel Guérin, *La révolution française et nous, '93 dans '68* (Paris, 1969). [15] For an examination of revolutionary situations see Richard Cobb, *A Second Identity* (London, 1969) pp. 267–281. [16] For a detailed analysis and history of middle-class anxiety in the nineteenth century see Romolo Runcini, *Illusione e paura nel mondo borghese* (Bari, 1968). [17] Karl Marx, *The Civil War in France* (New York, 1940) p. 67. [18] Quoted by David Mitchell in his *1919 Red Mirage* (London, 1970) p. 282. [19] Concerning the relationship of socialism and the academic community to Hitler's movement see David Schoenbaum's *Hitler's Social Revolution* (New York, 1966) p. 17 and p. 72.

THE WOMEN OF THE COMMUNE

Edith Thomas

Contemporaries were struck by the importance of women's participation in the 1871 Revolution. . . It is not very important that the critics of the Commune called the women who participated in it "females" and "viragos," and that the supporters of the Commune exalted those "pure heroines." From these contradictory opinions one certain fact can be extrapolated: the massive, extraordinary, momentous participation of women in the Commune. The parliamentary inquiry into the insurrection of March 18th, moreover, confirms this officially: 1,051 women were called before the Councils of War. Others—how many will never be known—were killed at the barricades and in the great slaughter during Bloody Week.

Who were these women? What did they do? What did they want? What did they think? Were the *pétroleuses* a myth or a reality?

One's view of the Commune varies depending upon whether one considers it as the revolt of a people rightfully inflamed by defeat and social injustice, or as an undertaking of criminal subversion against the established order. In the former instance, one will tend to consider the women and men of the Commune as pure, sympathetic heroes; in the latter, as common criminals.

We shall endeavor to escape this naive Manichaeism. Despite its mistakes and shortcomings, the Commune embodies a significant moment in revolutionary history, in the progress of justice. But justice is not upheld by choirboys and Girl Scouts.

What allows me, perhaps, to understand the women of the Commune is that during the Resistance, I took part in the coordinating committee of the Union des Femmes Francais, edited their tracts, and helped them to plan the women's demonstrations against the Vichy government and the Nazi occupation; the barricades of 1944 replied to the barricades of 1871.

Women During the Second Empire

The condition of the workers had scarcely improved at all since 1830. Wages were still beneath the level that would allow a man to live like a human being. Yet within the proletariat itself, women were the more exploited . . . most women could earn a living only doing needle-

After generously consenting to provide an article on the subject of Louise Michel for a special number of *The Massachusetts Review,* Edith Thomas died suddenly in Paris on December 7, 1970.

To honor her and her significant contributions to women's studies, *The Massachusetts Review* in cooperation with George Braziller, Inc., publishers, and The University of Massachusetts Press, herewith offer selections from Edith Thomas' *The Women Incendiaries,* translated from the French by James & Starr Atkinson © 1966, George Braziller, Inc.

work which provided them with little more than a starvation wage. . . . Out of 112,000 working women, 60,000 were employed in needlework, and 6,000 made the artificial flowers that were so much in fashion during the Empire. . .

Le Journal des Demoiselles (February, 1865) called the attention of bourgeois ladies to the lot of their unfortunate sisters: "Among the poor girls who ply the needle, there is a wage scale which goes from 5 francs down to 15 centimes per day. The average comes to 2 francs for a thirteen hour day . . . and still the thread or silk used by the worker must be deducted from this sum." . . . The earnings of a working woman added up, then, to about 500 francs per year, if she was not sick a single day. [Expenses for lodging, heat, light, clothes, etc. often left hardly more than 200 francs a year for food—or about 60 centimes a day.] Many working women ate only bread and milk. If one chanced to become ill, there was no way of paying for a doctor and medicine.

The convents gave the linen-drapers and dressmakers great competition, for the handiwork of the convent sewing-rooms did not cost much . . . the religious orders could supply excellent work at prices 25 percent lower than those of most working women. This competition was not, perhaps, irrelevant to the anticlericalism of the Commune women.

Therefore, it was almost impossible for a working woman to live off her wages alone. She found a mate, legal or not. A shoe-stitcher, Victorine Brochon, describes the life of a working-class family in these terms:

I have seen poor women who work 12 or 14 hours a day for ludicrous wages, forced to leave aged parents and children to shut themselves up for long hours in unhealthy workrooms, beyond the reach of either air or light or sunshine—for they are lit by gas. Droves of women are crammed into factories to earn the modest sum of 2 francs a day, or even less, and nothing on Sundays and holidays. Saturday night, having finished their day's work, they spend half the night mending the family clothing; they also go to the washhouse to soak their clothing, so that they can wash it on Sunday morning.

Prostitution appeared as a normal, and often indispensable, means of supplementing one's wages, or of earning a living when regular employment was unobtainable. Julie Daubié's study *The Poor Woman in the Nineteenth Century* (1867) emphasized the economic character of this prostitution:

The inadequate pay of the urban working-woman sometimes drives her, even during a period of industrial prosperity, into meeting her budget by selling her body; this is called the fifth quarter of the day. During periods of unemployment, this kind of right to work fills the entire day. In various cities . . . women who have decidedly not lost all sentiment of honor are forced into ignominy because they lack means of subsistence. . . Generally the poverty of women is such that among 6,000 registered in Paris, only 2,000 had any resources.

. . . In 1864 the International Working Men's Association was founded in London . . . its French section organized by Tolain, Fribourg, and

Charles Limousin. These men were Proudhonians . . . resolutely hostile to women working. Consequently, the French section of the International drew up a statement against the participation of women in industry. This stand did not keep women from belonging to the International. Victorine Brochon took part in the meetings and brought her husband to them. . . She helped set up a cooperative butcher shop . . . one-third of the profits went to the members of the cooperative, one-third made up the reserve fund, and the final third was lent without interest to establish another cooperative. . . Nathalie Lemel, a bookbinder, started another food cooperative, *La Marmite*, with the worker Varlin. . . . Yet another consumer cooperative, *Société des équitables de Paris,* was set up by Marguerite Tinayre. . .

It was not just working women who had complaints to make of an order that excluded women from society. A century ago, a woman could scarcely exist socially without a protector, either husband or lover. The education she received was mediocre or non-existent. . . . More than 4,000 schoolmistresses earned less than 400 francs annually. Almost 2,000 earned 100 to 200 francs.

The liberal professions were virtually closed to girls of the bourgeoisie. When Julie Daubié sat for her baccalaureate, despite the opposition of the rector of Lyon, and passed that examination, the Minister of Public Education refused in his turn to give her her diploma, for fear of "forever holding up his ministry to ridicule." . . . It was the condition of women itself that had to be transformed, and, at the same time, the whole of society.

The Siege of Paris

When Paris was besieged [by the Prussians] on September 19, there emerged a strange antagonism between a people which believed in the possibility of defense and victory, and a government which did not . . . never had Paris been cut off, as it was then, from all its surrounding land, without which it was nothing but a desert of stone and asphalt, and reduced to asphyxiation and slow death. . . . An egg cost a franc then. Butter rose from 6, to 20, to 28 francs a pound. In the Faubourg Saint-Germain, a rabbit cost 45 francs, a cat 20, a dog's leg 6 francs a pound. No milk for children. Animals from the Jardin des Plantes appeared in the butchershops under the name of "fancy meats." The trees of Paris were cut down, but the green wood smoked and would not heat.

From January 19 [1871] on, the bakers distributed bread only to people carrying cards: 300 grams for adults, 150 for children. Even so it was an unidentifiable mixture, in which straw and paper were to be encountered.

Women suffered more than men: it was they who had to stand in line for hours, in mud, snow, and cold, trying to feed their families. . . . Nathalie Lemel and her *La Marmite* carried out the difficult job of feeding hundreds of starving people. Louise Michel organized a soup kitchen for her students. . . . Mme. Poirier (Sophie Doctrinal) . . . ran a workshop where clothing was made, and employed seventy or eighty women . . . [who] did not earn a salary, but instead shared in the profits. . . . Workshops of this sort were organized in all municipal halls. Work for women was one of the goals of the *Comite des Femmes,* on the Rue d'Arras, founded by Jules Allix [who] advocated the establishment of communal workrooms in which women might find some work and be fed during the length of the Siege. . . One could sign up for work, for nursing, for first aid, or even for the women's brigade being formed on the ramparts. . .

During the Siege, then, women served in the fighting . . . as ambulance nurses or canteen workers; but at the same time they were serving their apprenticeship in political life. Vigilance committees were organized in various quarters; there were two in Montmartre, one for men, the other for women. Louise Michel participated in both at once: "No one was very much bothered by the sex of those who were doing their duty. That silly problem was done with." The Women's Vigilance Committee of the 18th arrondissement had been set up by Louise Michel, Mme. Collet, and Mme. Poirier. . . . "This committee had the job of allocating work, receiving and distributing contributions, visiting the sick and the poor and caring for them in their homes." . . . Women also participated in street demonstrations . . . as on January 22nd, in the square of the l'Hotel de Ville when an enormous crowd [gathered] to oppose surrender [to Prussian forces] [and] Breton Mobile Guards fired into the crowd. . . .

On January 28 [the provisional government made an armistice with the Prussian invaders], four hundred thousand armed men surrendered to two hundred thousand. They thought it easier to reach an understanding with the Prussians—men of order—than with the workers. . . . Paris felt not vanquished, but betrayed. . . One thing, at least, that the Prussians did not have was the cannons. The Parisians considered these their property; they had paid for them by subscriptions—from 10 centimes up—of the common people. On February 26 a singing crowd, an entire population— National Guardsmen, women, children, all together—triumphantly brought the cannons from the good neighborhoods toward Montmartre, Belleville, La Villette, and Les Buttes-Chanmont.

The 18th of March

It would without a doubt be an exaggeration to say that this day of revolution was the work of women. But they contributed a great deal, at least to the first part: the neutralization of the troops.

At the order of Thiers, the government army had entered Paris during the night [to appropriate the cannons]. It had occupied the strategic points, and had effortlessly laid hold of the cannons at Les Batignolles.

On Montmartre, a post of the National Guard's 61st Battalion stood watch in the Rue des Rosiers.

The government army had encountered no resistance, and it seemed that the whole business would quickly be taken care of. But General Vinoy had forgotten that, in order to move cannons, one has to have horses. . . The cannons from La Butte would have to be brought down by manpower.

During this time Montmartre had awakened. The housewives, out to get their bread and milk, began to flock together and spread the news. Inquisitive groups formed about the soldiers.

"The alarm had been sounded. The tocsin rang out in the churches of Paris. I went down, my rifle under my coat, crying 'Treason,' " wrote Louise Michel. "A Column was formed. The whole Vigilance Committee was there . . . Montmartre arose . . . to the attack on the fortified heights; we went up with the speed of a charge, knowing that at the top there was an army in battle formation. . ."

Groups of housewives with their children—merely curious or bantering at first—had swelled and become threatening. Now, among the soldiers of the 88th Battalion and the National Guard, they formed a veritable "human barricade." General Lecomte gave the order to fire. Then the women spoke to the soldiers: "Will you fire upon us? On your brothers? Our husbands? Our children?" The statement of General d'Aurelles de Paladine on this subject is very significant:

The women and children came and mixed with the troops. We were greatly mistaken in permitting these people to approach our soldiers, for they mingled among them, and the women and children told them: "You will not fire upon the people." This is how the soldiers of the 88th, as far as I can see, and of another line regiment found themselves surrounded and did not have the power to resist these ovations that were given them. People were shouting, "Long live the line."

Faced with this unexpected intervention, the soldiers hesitated. Then the 88th Battalion fraternized with the crowd. The soldiers arrested their general.

The women had also assembled in the Rue Houdon. General Susbielle gave the order to charge. But, intimidated by the women's cries, the cavalry "backed up their horses," which made the people laugh. Everywhere—in the Place Blanche, Place Pigalle, in Belleville, at the Bastille, at Le Chateau-d'Eau, and in the Luxembourg Gardens—the crowd, mostly composed of women, surrounded the soldiers, stopped the horses, cut the harnesses, forced the "bewildered" soldiers to fraternize with their "brothers" in the National Guard.

Disconcerted by this strange, this scandalous, victory of the people, General Vinoy ordered his troops to withdraw to the Champs-de-Mars. The field was left to the women. They had nothing to do but to go back home and fix dinner—which, for the most part, they did. . . .

Ten days later, when the Commune, elected on March 26th, moved into the Hotel de Ville, a crowd that included many women joyously welcomed the new power—the power of the people, and of hope. . . .

But the government that had taken refuge in Versailles could not tolerate this other power holding its own in Paris. On April 2, Versailles [troops] attacked Courbevoie.

The Union des Femmes

The *Union des Femmes* was organized . . . by a friend of Karl Marx, Elizabeth Dmitrieff, who was already helping to administer the *Comite des Femmes* created by Jules Allix. . . . Under her stimulus the *Union des Femmes* was formed on April 11, 1871. From then on meetings were held regularly in different neighborhoods of Paris. . . The general staff . . . was composed of . . . Nathalie Lemel, Aline Jacquier, Blanche Lefebvre, Marie Leloup, Aglaé Jarry, Elizabeth Dmitrieff, and a Mme. Collin. . .

The Union's organization is detailed in statutes: "A responsible organization among the *citoyennes* of Paris who are resolved to support and defend the cause of the people, the Revolution, and the Commune, has just been founded to give assistance in the work of the government's commissions, and to serve at ambulance stations, at canteens, and at the barricades."

But if the defense of Paris and first aid for the wounded appeared as the primary objectives of the *Union des Femmes,* the organization of work seemed to be even more important, for this carries within itself the seeds of that social reform which gave the Commune its historical significance. . . Paris was not only to think of defending itself, but also was to enter vigorously upon the path of social reform. The Commune had an imperative duty toward the workers from whom it had sprung: to take decisive measures in their behalf. While the men were fighting, the Commune should concern itself with their wives and children, should give them support and work. . .

This organization of work would be taken in hand by the *Union des Femmes.* Elizabeth Dmitrieff, representing the *Union,* sent a very detailed report to the Commission for Labor and Exchange.

The reorganization of work, which tends to assure the product to the producer, can be effectuated only by means of free productive associations, which make advantageous use of the various industries for their collective profit . . . . the formation of these organizations would eventually allow the workers to run their own business.

It would modify not only the social relations of production, but also the forms of work, which were inhuman. It was absolutely necessary that there be variety, for "the continual repetition of the same manual movement has a deadly influence upon the organism and the brain." The shortening of the working day should also be taken into consideration, for the "exhaustion of physical strength inevitably brings about the extinction of

31

moral strength." Finally, it would be a good idea to abolish "any competition between workers of both sexes," since, in the struggle they were waging . . . their interests were identical. Wages ought to be equal for equal work. . . .

But the state of a society is not altered in a few weeks. Despite the willingness of the Commune and the *Union des Femmes* to make a radical change in working conditions, the situation of working women remained precarious, and worsened from day to day. There were too few cooperative workshops to prevent factory managers from bringing wages even lower, or to force them to set more equitable prices. . . . The women who sewed National Guard uniforms wrote in *Le Vengeur,* May 14: "The intelligent, hard-working woman must cease being the victim, slave, and dupe of the owners, who enrich themselves by her suffering and at her expense. . . ."

The men and women of the Commune, in an isolated city in the heart of a hostile country, entered into a merciless struggle against a government that had both army and money on its side. As if they had the future before them, these men and women were getting ready for a basic transformation of production, and seeking to blaze a path of social justice. . . Moreover, the *Union des Femmes* did not limit itself to these projects. . . . On Sunday May 21, the working women were again brought together at the Hotel de Ville for the final drafting to make up the Federal Chamber of Working Women.

But on that same Sunday Versailles troops entered Paris.

Bloody Week

Never had there been so many flowers as there were that Spring. On Sunday, May 21, the weather was fine and people felt much more like going for a stroll than like fighting. Many Parisians attended the concert at the Tuileries, for the benefit of the widows and orphans of the Commune. During its May 19th session, the Commune concerned itself with theatres, and the Versailles bombardment of Paris had stripped the ramparts bare.

The Versailles troops entered the city that Sunday at three in the afternoon. The Commune was not informed of this until seven o'clock; the Parisians did not learn the news until Monday morning, the 22nd. . . . Paris would fight, then, district by district, street by street, house by house, barricade by barricade, without an over-all plan, but with savage, insane, desperate heroism.

The entire population was summoned to the barricades. "Let even the women join their brothers, their fathers, their husbands! Those who have no weapons can tend the wounded, and can haul paving-stones up into their rooms to crush the invader. Sound the tocsin; set the bells ringing; fire all the cannons."

The Women of the Commune

Everywhere the streets bristled with barricades, despite the admirable plans of Haussmann, who had taken all possible precautionary measures to prevent them. "What could I have been thinking of," wrote Jules Vallès; "I believed the city was going to play dead before being killed. And here are all the women and children getting into the fight. A beautiful girl has just raised a brand new red banner, and above these grey stones it has the effect of a poppy on an old wall. . ." Women in rags and women in silk dresses, young girls and old ladies, were sewing and filling sandbags, were working with pickaxes and mattocks, all day and, by gaslight, all night. The ladies of La Halle erected, in half a day, a sixty-five foot barricade at the intersection of the Place Saint-Jacques, and the Boulevard Sebastopol. In the Place du Panthéon, a barricade was built by women and children. . .

Who were these women who were building the barricades? Some can be identified by means of the proceedings of the Councils of War which have come down to us, and which condemn them "for having made, or helped to make, barricades in order to oppose the action of the civil police." There was the wine merchant Modeste Trochu. . . And Josephine Mimet. . . And the braidworker, Rosalie Gaillard. . . And Virginie Lenordez, who ran a small snack shop. . . And Élodie Duvert, who kept a little restaurant. . . Then there was Eugénie Dupin, widow of Leger. . . And Alphonsine Blanchard. . . And Céline Chartrus. . . And Josephine Courtois, who was no longer young, she had already fought at Lyon in 1848. . . Around her there were other women, among them Marie Cartier. . . And also there was Jeanne-Marie Quérat. . . And Madeleine Billault. . . And Marguerite Fayon. . . And Marie-Augustine Gaboriaud. . . And Eugénie Rousseau. . .

The women fought shoulder to shoulder with their men: mostly unorganized, they had come there either because a husband or lover was in the battle, or a barricade built at the end of their street. But a committee of the *Union des Femmes* had met one final time on May 21, presided over by Nathalie Lemel. On the orders of the Commune, they left, red flag in the lead, to defend Les Batignolles. One hundred twenty women held the barricade at the Place Blanche and halted the troops of General Clinchant for several hours. Not until 11 o'clock, exhausted and without ammunition, did they withdraw; those who had been taken were killed on the spot. Among them fell the dressmaker Blanche Lefebvre of the Organizing Committee of the *Union des Femmes*. . . The survivors doubled back onto the Place Pigalle, where they held out for three hours more; then the last of them retreated to the barricade at the Boulevard Magenta. . . Louise Michel held the Montmartre cemetery with about fifty men from the 61st Battalion. Soon they were no more than twenty; then fifteen; they retreated to the barricade on the Chausée Clignancourt. . . .

At this point we must bring up the question of the fires for which eyewitnesses and bourgeois historians have ascribed full responsibility to the

Communards. These fires had several causes: first, the incendiary shells and kerosene bombs the Army of Versailles had used since the beginning of April. Many houses in Paris and the suburbs were burned . . . by the shells of the friends of order and property. . . Some of the fires during the last week of May were also attributable to Bonapartist agents, trying to eliminate any traces compromising for the personnel of the Empire. It is strange to note that the *Communards* did not attack the houses of the rich; that the *Communards,* those anticlericals, did not burn down churches; but that what disappeared in flames were buildings like the Court of Accounts, the Council of State, or the Ministry of Finance— buildings that contained the archives of the Empire's administration. . . . But having made these reservations, it is certain that the Federals bore a great part of the responsibility for the Paris fires . . . the Federals set fire to buildings near the barricades; thus they flushed the Versailles soldiers out into the open. Marx vindicated the Commune, which "used fire strictly as a means of defense," . . . But . . . no rationale of a military nature justified the burning of, for example, the Tuileries; we must have recourse to another explanation. Benoit Malon is the one who gives it to us: "It was permissible for the people of Paris . . . who for a century had sacrificed the best of each of its generations . . [and] was being slaughtered for its republican faith—to burn the Palace of Kings. . . ."

In spite of bitter local defenses, the Versailles troops advanced little by little. At the corner of the Rue Racine and Rue École de Médecine, the barricade was held by women. On the Rue du Pot-de-Fer, women were fighting. . . In the Place du Panthéon, women prepared rifles, while the men fired . . . on the Place du Chateau-d'Eau . . . at the moment when the National Guards began to retreat, a women's battalion . . . came forward and began to fire. . . .

But repression struck not only the fighting men and women taken with weapon in hand, or those who openly proclaimed themselves responsible for their acts; it struck at random. Every poor woman was suspect. Even more so if she carried a market basket or a bottle; she was a *pétroleuse,* and was executed on the spot. . . Any expression of grief alongside the common graves in which the Federals were heaped up was proof of complicity. Any weeping woman was an "insurgent female."

As for the women who were executed, they were treated somewhat like unfortunate Arabs belonging to insurgent tribes. After they were shot, while they were still in their death throes, they were stripped of some of their clothes, and sometimes the insult went further, as in the Faubourg Montmartre or the Place Vendome, where women were left naked and sullied upon the sidewalks.

It is officially acknowledged that thirty-thousand Federals disappeared during the struggle. Others have said a hundred thousand . . . we shall never know the exact number of the victims, men or women, of the week in May.

THE COMMUNE AND THE
REVOLT OF JULES VALLÈS

Gordon Shenton

Since 1968, Jules Vallès has been enjoying a widespread popularity and a prestige in France which were denied him after the collapse of the Commune when his books were condemned as the work of a danger to society. For not only was he an unrepentant rebel and a proud communard, but, perhaps even worse in the eyes of a nervous middle class, he denounced the sacrosanct institution of the family and exposed the socially repressive basis of bourgeois culture in the schools and universities. But all this, of course, is grist for the mill of '68. Now, his trilogy *Jacques Vingtras* is available in two rival paperback editions,[1] and his works are the subject of discussions and commentaries in the classroom and on radio and television. His best-known work, *L'Insurgé*, which succeeds magnificently in capturing the atmosphere of the heroic, tragic days of the Commune, reveals through the voice of Jacques Vingtras the intransigence, the generosity, and the purity of a revolt which in some ways seems to make Vallès a forerunner of the rebellious students of our time. His defense of the child, his nostalgia for the artisanal community of ordinary people, his anarchistic conception of revolution, his hatred of authority and the state, his suspicion of political parties, his search for a transformation of life in the liberating happening of the Commune are themes which resound as so many prophecies of the spirit of May 1968. It is precisely what sets Vallès apart from the main orthodoxies of the revolutionary movement in the nineteenth century that brings him closer to today's conception of cultural revolution. It is because *L'Insurgé* is resolutely not an objective analysis of the failure of the Commune or a lamentation upon its demise, but rather a reliving of the event as something meaningful in itself, that Vallès is able to speak directly across the years as from one revolutionary generation to another. And, of course, the fact that in the series of Parisian insurrections the Commune was the immediate predecessor of May 1968 has produced an effect of historical foreshortening from which he has benefited. The *contestataires* of the Gaullist years cannot help but feel a certain fraternal solidarity with the *réfractaire* of the Second Empire.

Vallès appears particularly meaningful to those who participated in

---

[1] All references in the discussion which follows are to the Garnier-Flammarion edition: *L'Enfant* (1968), *Le Bachelier* (1970), and *L'Insurgé* (1970).

the Events of May because his vision of revolution and of the Commune underlines many of the values of '68. By adhering closely to the unfolding present in all its lived immediacy and by his elimination of any sustained narrative and explicative account of the event, he is successful in rendering the chaos, the discontinuity, and the improvisation of the Commune. We follow Vingtras as he races back and forth across Paris, sometimes close to the center of the action, sometimes on the sidelines, but always involved and frantically busy. *L'Insurgé* brings out the popular and spontaneous nature of an insurrection which was not without its causes and its premonitory episodes, but which exploded and developed independently of political parties and sectarian leaders. The people of Paris seemed to draw on their own collective memory of earlier revolutions. The Commune, and May 1968 after it, placed themselves in a characteristically Parisian tradition of revolt. The people descended into the streets, took up arms against the forces of oppression, occupied public buildings, built barricades, and for a while lived an anarchistic popular democracy.

We must not forget, however, that whatever the similarities, the circumstances of the Commune and of Vallès's situation were not at all the same as those of 1968. The Commune was a real revolution by violence, and it was spearheaded not by students, but by the working people of Paris. Vallès presents himself to his readers as a disenchanted product of the French school system and as a dropout from the Second Empire, but he was not typical of the students and ex-students of his time. Jacques Vingtras laments in *L'Insurgé* that the only combatants the Latin Quarter ever sent into the social battles were all on the side of the repression. Furthermore, Vallès was poor and far down on the social ladder. His revolt was first and foremost against social injustice. In this respect he was much less complicated than the sons and daughters of the affluent whose insurrection was directed against the values and psychological structures of their own class, however much they may have attempted, by their recourse to the themes of ultraleft radicalism, to place themselves in the context of a traditional class confrontation. However, we know that the student movement is not just a new formulation of socialism, but a demand for a more authentic, more honest, and more real mode of existence; a yearning for a more human community and a fresh start in which men can feel that they control their own destinies and the institutions made to serve them. There was no such feeling prior to 1871, except inasmuch as the myth of the revolution carried an element of liberation and festival with it, but Vallès did find in the event something akin to what the modern generation is searching for. But again,

36

one must underline the differences: Jules Vallès's revolt is the attempt of a solitary individual to break out of his solitude by way of revolution. His drama is very much a drama of the nineteenth century and very different from the malaise of the present generation.

Born in 1832, Vallès was brought up in the schools of the Bourgeois Monarchy in Le Puy, Saint-Etienne, and Nantes, until he was old enough to be sent to Paris to finish his baccalauréat. These moves reflect the stages in his father's painful ascension up the hierarchical ladder of the teaching profession. In the fervor of February 1848, the boy discovered the romanticism of revolution and enthusiastically participated in meetings and demonstrations in Nantes. His hopes were dashed by the betrayal of the Second Republic and the coup d'état of 2 December 1851. On this fateful day, which was to remain engraved in his memory until it was redeemed by 18 March 1871, Vallès desperately attempted to organize a token resistance, whereupon his father brought his son back from Paris and had him confined to an asylum!

This was the beginning of that long crossing of the desert during which he led the double life of a bohemian and an *insoumis* under the Second Empire. In 1853, he was implicated in a plot against the emperor at the Opéra Comique and imprisoned for a few weeks at Mazas. During these years, he refused to follow the only career open to a *bachelier* (holder of the baccalauréat diploma) because of the memory of his father's humiliations in the teaching profession, and because he would have had to swear an oath of allegiance to enter the state schools. He preferred to live a hand-to-mouth existence by doing such odd jobs as he could find with his intellectual baggage of Latin and Greek: private tutor, composer of dictionary items, copyist, employee at city hall, hack journalist. Meanwhile, he pursued his ambition to be a writer by contributing articles whenever he could find a publisher who would accept his subversive ideas. In 1865 he put out a collection of his articles under the title *Les Réfractaires*. By this time he had acquired a certain reputation, and in 1867 he became editor of *La Rue*, a publication which was shortly to be honored by official seizure. In 1868 he was back in prison twice for his attacks on the regime, but these setbacks in no way dampened his ardor. He founded two other short-lived papers, *Le Peuple* and *Le Réfractaire*, predecessors of the famous *Le Cri du peuple* which appeared just before and during the Commune of 1871. He participated in many of the events which led up to the revolt of Paris in March of that year, notably when he took over the city hall of La Villette for one night as his contribution to the abortive insurrection of 31 October 1870. After 18 March 1871 he was directly involved as an elected member of the Commune and as the hard-working editor of a popular newspaper. In May, Vallès managed to slip out of Paris and escape to Belgium to begin the long years of exile, many of them in London, until MacMahon's amnesty allowed him to return to France in 1880. The three volumes of *Jacques Vingtras* were first published as serial novels in various reviews; *L'Enfant* in 1878, *Le Bachelier* in 1879, and *L'Insurgé* in 1882. *L'Enfant* and *Le Bachelier* appeared in book form in 1881 and *L'Insurgé* after his death in 1886.

II

By virtue of his political commitment, Vallès stands out as a solitary figure among the writers of the latter part of the nineteenth century. He was truly *engagé* in the sense that writing was for him an act of solidarity with the oppressed and the poor. Most writers during this period were either apolitical or inclined to hold conservative views (see the articles by W. M. Frohock and Henriette Psichari in this collection). Vallès wrote his trilogy in the same period that saw the rise of symbolism and the emergence of writers like Huysmans, Bourget, and Barrès. Certainly Zola had a social conscience which was reflected in his works, and Victor Hugo was a champion of the poor and himself a victim of the Second Empire; but how different from them was Vallès in his truculent, obstinate poverty! He was spiritually closer to Rimbaud and Léon Bloy than to these men.

In some respects, Vallès can be seen as the lone continuer of a republican and revolutionary tradition in literature which had arisen at the beginning of the century, but which had been largely stifled by the shock of 1848. However, after 1870, this makes him a unique and in some ways very modern figure. Revolt was a common theme throughout the century, but how rarely during the second half is it expressed as social revolt! The artistic revolt of the 1880s was also rooted in a hatred of bourgeois society and in a feeling of alienation; but it was usually expressed in withdrawal and escapism, in a sense of disdainful superiority, in dandyism and decadent estheticism, and in the feeling that one's very malediction was a sign of election—in a word, in Baudelaireanism. It is because he refused to cultivate his suffering and inadaptation as an inescapable evil; because he put the blame where it belonged: on the class structure of society; because he proclaimed that men can be happy and free that Vallès is an original figure in the literary world of the nascent Third Republic.

From the very beginning, Vallès felt that his experience was exemplary, that he was a spokesman for the destitute and a witness to their miseries.

In writing *L'Enfant,* he was writing for all the victims of family and school. Similarly, *Le Bachelier* grew out of his desire to write the history of the defeated generation of 1848. These *Mémoires d'un révolté,* as the book was first entitled, are a testimony to the deprivations suffered by those who refused to submit to the tyranny of Napoleon III. The definite article which precedes each of the three volumes of the trilogy gives them a representative and general value beyond mere personal reminiscence. As he looked back over his past from the distance of exile, he sought not just to capture the significant thread of his own life, but also to schematize the formation and experience of a *déclassé* turned revolutionary in the years leading up to the great event of the Commune.[2]

For the Commune was a decisive moment in Vallès's life, an event for which all his previous existence had been a period of preparation and expectation and which, once it had been lived, made it possible for him to consider his life complete so that even the unhappy years of exile seemed already to have had their recompense. The movement of the trilogy, the unfolding of its meaning, and the articulation of its themes find their necessary culmination in the coming of revolution. The genesis of the work is significant in this regard. In 1869, before the fall of the Second Empire, Vallès had made a first attempt with *Le Testament d'un blagueur* to utilize the autobiographical material which was eventually to constitute *Jacques Vingtras.* And, in that same year, he had been thinking of writing *Une Histoire de vingt ans* to record the years 1848 through 1868. But it was the experience of the Commune which made it possible for him to rise above the episodic nature of his material and unify it into an organic whole. The three books relate to the main divisions of his life, not only chronologically, but dialectically. The humiliated child and the starving *bachelier* are subsumed into the figure of the rebel and redeemed in the social struggle. The Commune is thus the event towards which the entire work looks forward, and which provides the resolution of its themes.

III

Vallès has been criticized for his inability to write a real novel. It is true that the books of the trilogy are not organized as continuous narration: there is no dramatic structure; little sustained character development; no long scenes in which character, action, and description come together into a fictional illusion. The chapters are built around certain key mo-

---

[2] For an interesting discussion of the revolt of the alienated *déclassé,* see "Vallès and the Pathos of Rebellion" in Victor Brombert, *The Intellectual Hero* (Philadelphia: J. B. Lippincott Co., 1961), pp. 43–51.

ments or around groups of impressions in a juxtaposition of short episodes, anecdotes, descriptions, and portraits. There is very little analysis or commentary. As a result, the text is discontinuous, even elliptic, especially in *L'Insurgé* where the pace is particularly fast and the historical situations are unexplained. This form of structure does at times become repetitious, when each succession of incidents seems to be making the same point; this weakness is most noticeable in *Le Bachelier,* where Jacques goes from one mortifying setback to another. However, these objections really pertain only when the reader considers just the surface of the text and takes the books individually. The coherence of the trilogy is to be found at the deeper level of the structure of the thematic material. It is this highly schematic framework which determines the selection and meaning of the episodes.

L'Enfant is the drama of a fundamental rupture, of a tearing apart of the child's being which is a result of the social circumstances in which he grows up. Jacques Vingtras is a *déclassé,* but unlike many such socially uprooted persons who are not consciously unhappy in their situation he suffers because of his separation from the class to which he instinctively feels he belongs, and he hates the class to which his parents try to force him to conform. His mother and father are peasants by birth. His father's father had wanted his son to become a priest (in rural France this used to be a substantial honor), but his father chose to acquire academic "honors" and seek social advancement within the University.[3] So, of course, it is understood that Jacques is to follow in his father's footsteps, and—who knows?—with better protection than his father had, rise to even greater heights in the hierarchy.

But Jacques wants to learn a trade and be a workman. Born in the small provincial city of Le Puy, he is close enough to his peasant origins to have frequent occasions to be with common people. Compared to his own sad existence, their life becomes for him an ideal of liberty and happiness. Whenever he can escape from his mother's tyranny and the prison of school, he wanders happily around the busy streets watching all the bustling activity of the market town with its shopkeepers, artisans, workmen, and peasants. And what a joy it is for him when he goes out to visit his peasant relations on the farm at Farreyrolles! He adores his uncle Joseph, a vigorous young carpenter who takes Jacques along with him sometimes when he and his fellow workers get together to drink and sing and laugh. They play with him and let him touch their rules

---

[3] In France, *L'Université,* used absolutely, means the teaching profession as a whole.

and dividers. One day, Jacques stops to watch a cobbler at work and from then on his childhood dream is to be a cobbler too and tap away happily all day long.

The boy loves these people for their honesty and strength, for their spontaneous joy and anger, for their simple pleasures. He loves the way they are at ease in their own familiar world. Jacques constantly opposes their free and easy vulgarity with the elaborate and stilted manners which prevent him from being natural. He loves the concrete world of things in which they spend their lives. The sights, sounds, and smells of rural France are associated with fullness of life and authentic being. Vallès's metaphors, which give such a rich and fresh quality to his writing, are often inspired by this memory. And it is from the same vision that words like "the people," "the workers," "the street" derive their affective force in his works.

By contrast with these people, Jacques finds himself a paltry figure. At home, he is beaten and upbraided in the name of virtues that seem merely a negation of life. His spontaneity is checked by endless interdictions and admonitions. His parents prevent him from developing his natural energies and appetite for life, so that life comes to be at once the greatest value and the one thing from which he is excluded. He finds himself in a cruel world of strange distortions in which natural values seem to be reversed. His parents have been obliged to go against their own natures in order to adapt to their hard-won social position. The humiliations, the overwork, and the fear of both students and superiors have made his father unrelentingly authoritarian, even toward his son. His mother, too, is warped by the stresses of the family's social situation. Her peasant sense of economy becomes absurd stinginess, her simple tastes become grotesque vulgarity, and her natural energy becomes nagging tyranny. She calls on moral principles to justify all her cruelties. However, Jacques shows that her bad faith is only half conscious, for, if she is guilty of blatantly using these principles to impose her will or cover up her avarice, she nonetheless believes in the austere code which she preaches.

Yet Vallès shows that the flow of high sounding words, the constant sermonizing, are merely the mask of his parents' fear and ambition. In the name of parental authority and the child's absolute duty to obey, his father and mother commit a perpetual aggression, both physical and moral, against the boy. Jacques ruthlessly exposes his father's weakness, his bad faith, and his attempts to make his son feel guilty for the indignities which he suffers in his professional life. *L'Enfant* opens with two early memories which are carefully chosen to set the tone for the whole book. The first is of a thrashing administered by his mother, the second is of an occasion when his father cuts his finger while carving a toy for Jacques. "It's your fault," his mother shouts as she deals the boy a vigorous slap (p. 46).

In their struggle to maintain their position in society, his parents cling desperately to a life-denying petit bourgeois morality. Work, discipline, economy, sacrifice, renunciation, self-control, good manners, cleanliness, moral strictness: these are the guarantees that one will not degenerate and slip down the social ladder to rejoin the common folk below. At all costs one must hold on to what one has; one must not dilapidate or disperse one's vital forces. Life becomes a holding back, a retention, and a concentration, the opposite of the thoughtless, spendthrift unconcern of the people. When Jacques has earned a coin that he was promised if he was top of his class, he asks if he may keep it, meaning, "You're not going to put it into my piggy bank?" His mother assures him that he can indeed keep it, but the luckless Jacques soon learns that she means this literally. He can have it, but he must not spend it (p. 140).

This fear of spending which haunts his mother is carried over into the moral sphere. She instils into her son that it is bad to eat what one likes, that it is immoral to enjoy oneself, that punishment is good for you. Words come to denote the opposite of what they seem to mean or their meaning is pulled out from under them by a sleight of hand like his mother's play on the word "keep." Maternal love has to be expressed in unforgiving rigor; the child's own good is furthered by making him unhappy; a bad mother is one who sends her son candies and consoles him when he is punished at school. An honest woman is one who is too ugly and stupid to attract men.

This repressive morality at home is continued at school. Jacques is a prisoner of a dead world in these drab, ill-smelling, cheerless rooms where arrogant and stupid masters fill his head with classical culture. The education that the children receive is rhetorical, formalistic, moralizing, and completely foreign to their experience of life. At school they are plunged into a strange fiction which, for some unknown reason, adults take seriously: Greek harmony, Roman *virtu,* French clarity and measure, noble sentiments, grandiloquence, uplifting orations addressed to long dead peoples. The result is an absurd combination of trivialization (for his homework, Jacques is asked to write an ode in Latin verse on the death of a parrot) and exaggerated reverence (in class one day, the French teacher cries to the children, "On your knees, on your knees before the divine Racine" [p. 266]).

However, the boy observes the social reality of this absurdity. He sees that behind the disinterested, noble mask of classical letters is an institutional hierarchy in the service of the established order. He sees the scorn of the rich for the poor, the system of protections, and the fear and impotence of those at the bottom of the ladder.

Vallès is very modern in his exposure of the repressive and self-serving mechanism of bourgeois culture. Through concrete anecdotes and caricatural portraits, he shows how it is used to further ambition, pride, and the will to hold power over others. By encouraging competitiveness through a system of grades and prizes, the system creates products that are able to function well within the system. But what is the point of it all? In fact, the system functions mainly to perpetuate itself and to provide a field of success for the successful, while mystifying the general public with its hallowed inanities. One is reminded in our time of Ivan Illych's denunciations of a schooling which is designed not so much to prepare children for life as to program its products for the economic system. During his brief career as a *pion* (the lowest of the low in French schools: the person responsible for discipline when the children are not in class with the professors) in a provincial school, Jacques of the Vallès novel has a glorious moment of revenge when he is asked to replace one of the professors who has been taken ill. He gets up before the astonished class and tells them that they should learn *nothing* that school tries to teach them (*L'Insurgé*, p. 64).

Jacques insists on the irrelevance of this education to the real world. The *bachelier* is unprepared for life, good for nothing except to become in his turn a *pion* and schoolteacher. His misfortunes are due to the fact that outside of the university he is incompetent and useless. Even on the barricades during the final battle of the Commune, Jacques regrets that school has never taught him anything practical. And the tragedy is that not only does school teach him nothing useful, it also gives its products a turn of mind which they can never slough off and which makes it impossible for them to revert to a simpler state.

As a result, Jacques's real nature is frustrated and deformed. Left to himself, he would have been a robust, vigorous, expansive child; but all his vital instincts are denied. Cut off from those he would instinctively choose as his companions, he is condemned to loneliness; but even in his moral isolation he cannot feel that he *belongs* to himself, for he is constantly forced into the role which his parents impose upon him. In this distorted world where words are separated from the things they denote, where men are alienated from their true selves, where values are reversed, where morality is the mask of a repressive society of which his

43

parents are the unconscious instruments, Jacques becomes an absurd creature. He is rendered grotesque by a grotesque system. In episode after episode, Vallès shows us Jacques's clumsiness and incompetence. In *L'Enfant,* the situation is usually the same: his mother has dressed him up and drilled him in preparation for some event, a prize giving or a party, for example, but Jacques ruins everything. He trips up or drops what he is carrying, or he is so bizarrely stilted and unnatural that people are stupefied.

Not only does Jacques act like a clown, he also looks like one. His mother's miserliness is such that she will go to any lengths to avoid buying new clothes for her son. Sometimes his trousers are so tight that he cannot bend over, sometimes the seat bags so much that he seems to waddle along like a duck. To make them last a little longer, his mother patches up his clothes with whatever comes to hand. But she is not without pride in her son: she wants him to be a *Monsieur* and she wants people to notice that she has a sense of style when she dresses him for a special occasion. Her penny-wise imagination is fertile in ways to put together odd pieces of secondhand finery. For one occasion she makes him an overcoat out of a piece of material left over from grandma's days (and which cost the earth even then!), rough as a rasp to the skin, of so loud a yellow that it flashes like a tiger in the sun, and with vivid green buttons shaped like olives to add something special. "Oh, Lord, deliver me from this coat!" (*L'Enfant,* pp. 76–77).

The caricature, the exaggeration, and the repetitious insistence on these themes in the *Vingtras* trilogy are not just structural weaknesses or a deficiency of imagination as some readers feel. They serve the same function as they do in Sartre's *Les Mots,* a book which is similar to *L'Enfant* in several ways. The problem of identity, of true being and its opposite, inauthenticity and the unreality of being, are central to both books. In each case, the child feels that he is an artificial creation of an adult world. Beyond the great differences in the respective situations of the child and in the manner of their presentation, these books have in common a very schematic reduction of that situation.

Jacques's ridiculous appearance is a literalization of a more fundamental deformation of his soul. He is forced into a patched-up, ill-fitting culture against which his heart cries out, but which he is obliged to make his own. The self-deprecating irony which runs through *L'Enfant* and *Le Bachelier* is directed against this disjointed marionette that his upbringing has created. Since Vallès adopts a point of view which is concrete, direct, and extremely close to the unfolding present being lived by Jacques, the irony, whether directed against others or against himself, is an important device, superimposed upon the immediate vision, for conveying the meaning of his books. Jacques suffers because of his alienation from his real nature and from the community of other men and women. His "individualism" is a grotesque and unwanted apparel that he would gladly cast off, but which clings to his very skin.

Jacques's desire, then, is to break out of his solitary inauthenticity, to reintegrate his identity and to reestablish solidarity. At home, he feels that he is never allowed to exist *in his own right* and that he is never accepted as a *person* by his parents. By contrast, some of his happiest moments are when he is in the company of ordinary people who treat him as "someone," who talk to him as if he were a "personage" (*L'Enfant*, p. 151). He is proud to be greeted "as if he were a man" by one of the older boys (p. 162). And on one glorious occasion on the way to Nantes, while his mother was ill down below, father and son sit down as friends and equals to drink and laugh in the boat's restaurant with one of M. Vingtras's old classmates (pp. 201–4). But he is usually thrown back into his unnatural isolation. "Until now," he complains, "I have had nothing which I could call my own, not even my skin" (p. 138). On vacation away from his parents, he rejoices that his room is truly his *own*: "encore un *chez moi* d'un soir" (p. 159). From the time when, at last, he escapes the prison of his family, Jacques's constant concern will be to defend the integrity of his self. In *L'Insurgé*, he looks back on all the years of hunger and humiliation during the Second Empire as an attempt to remain *himself*.

The intransigence of the *réfractaire* stems from this obstinate determination to be his own man. But he is powerless in the face of society and worn out by incessant poverty. A particularly painful episode in *Le Bachelier* dramatizes the bitterness and frustration which have accumulated in his soul. One day a terrible quarrel breaks out between Jacques and Legrand, his roommate and companion in poverty. Jacques demands reparation in the form of a duel, and henceforth nothing will deter either of the young men from their implacable resolution not to back down. Their suicidal rage is such that they decide on the most deadly form of confrontation possible: with pistols until one of them is incapacitated. Jacques explains that this cruel absurdity is a kind of revolt against the wretchedness of their lives. They are impelled to act out the tragedy to its bloody end, because each has the illusion that he is firing at the mirror image of his own poverty and humiliation (p. 291). Jacques experiences an intoxicating feeling of liberation and revenge. For once he is master of his own destiny, imposing his own will upon the event and demonstrating his worth to himself and to others. "I have never yet been *myself* under the vault of heaven," he says. "I have always been squeezed into clothes that were too tight or made for others, or into traditions which disgusted and crushed me" (p. 297). Already in a less serious affair described in *L'Enfant,* when he crossed swords with a *saint-cyrien* who had threatened his father, he had described the duel as a new coat which his mother had not chosen for him.

Jacques finds much the same personal exaltation in the experience of the Commune as he did in his duel with Legrand: revenge, liberation, self-affirmation, recognition by others, and a feeling that he has entered a new dimension of existence. However, revolution is a collective enterprise, and these emotions arise in a warm human feeling of solidarity and love. Although the Commune is an occasion for him to merge his personal revolt in a generalized insurrection, he nevertheless talks about it in much the same terms as when describing the duel, as if revolution had the same value for the people of Paris as his duel had had for him. In his eyes, the poor and disinherited of Paris are living a moment of freedom which, whatever the outcome, is self-justifying. Vallès is inclined to look for the meaning and value of the Commune in the event itself and not in its revolutionary effectiveness.

This solitary affirmation of self is one pole of Vallès's revolt. In a duel two individuals face each other, each isolated in the circle of a ritual which separates him as much from his own seconds as from his adversary. But there is another way, which Jacques discovers in the excitement of 1848. When he is introduced to the idea of revolution, he has the experience of a sudden revelation, as of a new life opening up before him. All the emotions of his childhood seem to have prepared him for an instinctive sympathy with the revolutionary cause. He is deeply moved when he learns that those who had made the revolutions of the past were simple people like the peasants and workmen he has known in Le Puy and Saint-Etienne. His own suffering as a child makes him immediately sympathetic to the cry of the victims against the social injustice of the world. There is a deep affective link in Vallès's works between the child and the poor man. Furthermore, he finds within the revolutionary gatherings a fraternal, virile community in which he enjoys a sense of vital belonging. "I have leaped from a dead world into a living world," he exclaims (*L'Enfant,* p. 287).

It is significant that Jacques has his first contact with the world of journalism at the same time that he discovers revolution. Typically, he is at first drawn to the material side of the production of a newspaper. He loves the rhythm of the press spitting out wet sheets, the smell of resin and ink, the heat and bustle, and most of all the workmen around whom

46

all this activity turns. He even forms the ambition to be a printer himself. But it is through the power of words and not the strength of his arms that he will be able to take his place among the revolutionaries. In Jacques's mind, journalism always benefits from this association with the idea of work, even if he is never entirely successful in escaping from the *bachelier's* bookish calling. For although his constant desire throughout his childhood was to be a worker, it is clear that his education has made him above all a manipulator of words.

Jacques is the victim of culture and the word, but it is nonetheless by the word that he attempts to reestablish that solidarity with the world that he lost as a child. Solidarity with life, which he strives to evoke in all its succulent, concrete reality: this is the mainspring of Vallès's naturalism and impressionism. And solidarity with the people: this is the driving force of his revolutionary journalism. Jacques does not hide his literary ambition, but, beyond the usual satisfactions of reputation, he values primarily the way it brings him closer to others. He speaks of the "family" of his admirers (*L'Insurgé*, p. 92). At the height of the Commune, he experiences a moment of profound joy when he hears his articles in *Le Cri du peuple* acclaimed by the crowd. His ambition is above all to find the words which will speak *for* and *to* the people.

The qualities of Vallès's language are reflections of the values which inspire his revolt. That is to say, they are rooted in an ideal of being. His language is robust, colorful, and savory in its effort to adhere to the material world. It is virile, combative, and, at times, violent in the image of the *réfractaire*. Vallès tries to give to his style something of the original force of the cry of pain and scandal uttered by the victims of this world. It is to a great extent marked by his experience of journalism which, particularly when it is militant in nature, seeks an immediate, visceral reaction from its readers. Even closer to his public than the journalist is the orator, and Jacques has frequent opportunities to address the people directly during the period between 1869 and 1871. He is exhilarated by his ability to communicate his emotion directly and see it reflected in the eyes of his audience: "It was almost like armed combat," he remembers (*L'Insurgé*, p. 91).

Vallès's revolt against his classical education leads him to write in a manner as different as possible from the literary style which he had been taught to revere. He rejects periodic elegance, inflated sentiment, and the whole baggage of classical allusion. In fact, his stylistic reaction is so pronounced that it carries him well beyond the realist and naturalist mode. His sentences and paragraphs are short. The paragraphs usually occupy just four or five lines and often no more than one line, with the result that the pages give an impression of space and movement. The sentences stand out forcibly; their value, ironic, exclamatory, dramatic, pathetic, are heightened by their isolation in a single paragraph. His descriptions are rapid series of notations, adjectives, and appositional phrases cast one after the other on the page. The great use that Vallès makes of the rhythms and vocabulary of spoken French gives his books a racy, slangish directness of tone. Perhaps most significant of all is the way he entirely rejects the narrative system of *passé simple* and *imparfait* which is the foundation of the naturalist novel in the nineteenth century. Instead, he uses a combination of present tense and *passé composé* which allows him to adhere very closely to the event while maintaining a non-literary, conversational tone. Thus, he places himself at the opposite pole from such a characteristically Second Empire man of letters as Flaubert. These traits of style give his writing a modernity of tone and point of view to which the present generation is particularly sensitive.

It is certain that Vingtras as well as Vallès himself never bridges the gap which separates the *bachelier*'s *redingote* from the worker's *blouse,* even in the finest moments of the Commune; and that he never entirely ceases to be a solitary figure. The people of Paris accept him to a point, but he can never be one of them. He is always on the side of the leaders and intellectuals whose job it is to think up what should be done rather than to do it. And even among the other leaders of the Commune, he is not altogether comfortable. He is enthusiastic about the spontaneous, anarchistic federation of sections and districts which springs into being as a "free association of citizens" (p. 186), but he is uneasy as soon as a superstructure of leadership has to be created. In spite of all his enthusiasm for revolution, he becomes increasingly suspicious of organized revolutionary groups with their discipline and their dogmaticism. The ruthless fervor of the fanatics, the Jacobin spirit, are almost as repugnant to him as the base politicking of the bourgeois republican left.

But the Commune is nonetheless a profoundly liberating experience for Vingtras—as for Vallès—in which his entire previous existence finds its justification and its recompense. All the threads of his revolt and his desire come together for a few brief months. He is no longer the bo-hemian outcast, the pariah of a hated society, the useless, clownish *dé-classé,* but a man with a task who is recognized and admired by his com-rades. His past sufferings and humiliations now stand as his revolutionary credentials in the eyes of his peers. His revolt is no longer the solitary negation of the world around him or the clandestine, sterile gesticulation of the equally isolated revolutionary clubs. Revolution has at last brought him close to the people, given him an affirmative voice within the great

48

outcry of a mass insurrection, and restored him to a sense of authentic being. The paradoxes of his own alienation are subsumed into that "grande fédération des douleurs" to which *L'Insurgé* is dedicated.

The trilogy thus embodies the passion with which Vallès lived through the experience of the Commune, and the terms in which he realized its significance, not as social abstraction, but as human moment.

FEMINISM AND ANTI-CLERICALISM
UNDER THE COMMUNE

Persis Hunt

In mid-nineteenth century France the consciousness of working-class women labored under a triple burden, that imposed by the Church, that of secular, bourgeois society in general, and that of the anti-feminism of the workers' movement in particular. All three defined woman and her concerns in religious or quasi-religious terms, "the sanctity of the home," the "self-sacrificing nature of motherhood," and so on, myths which formed a convenient rationale for severe material and psychological repression of women and denied them any productive or dignified role.

When, during the Commune, women rebelled against these burdens, the one which seemed to absorb most of their attention was the Church. Though anti-clericalism may not seem to us now an overwhelming force for social change, it was daring and potentially revolutionary for women to espouse it then, for they were considered by nature religious and submissive to clerical authority.

This is the reason why the anti-clericalism of the women of the Commune seemed such a horrible aberration to contemporaries. If the normal woman was a self-effacing, obedient believer, what a monster the woman must be who would dare to defy the Church and its works. Since the keystone of woman's morality was supposed to be her piety, the female communard, as reactionary writers never failed to remark, must be utterly perverted and lost to all wifely and motherly sentiment.[1]

Even though these ideas are ridiculous, it is still worthwhile looking at the relationship between women's anti-clericalism and their attitude toward marriage, the family and their sex-role in general. Did the Commune really make any fundamental difference in their views? Both friends and foes of the Commune have made exaggerated claims for its effectiveness in breaking down the barriers of convention. For instance, Henri Lefebvre's remark that it destroyed the "habitual barriers between public and private life, between the street and the household, between daily life and political life," is only partly true.[2] To expect the women, much less the men, suddenly in the spring of 1871 to depart from the accustomed structures, to rise above the mystique of the family, would be unrealistic.

In fact, it seems as though the women wanted to protect and strengthen the family bond, and expected the destruction of the Church to accomplish this, for they considered the Church at best a totally inadequate support for family life, and at worst, a real threat to its stability. On the one hand, religious schools, workshops, and orphanages offered a small amount of material aid. On the other hand, the Church demanded of the recipients a kind of acquiescence and acceptance of the economic order, which by its miserable working conditions and low wages, especially for women and children, attacked the health and prosperity of the working-class family in the most obvious ways.

The testimony of the great *communarde*, Louise Michel, is interesting in this matter. In a letter to a newspaper she stated that she could give the names of many workers' families of her acquaintance who had tried to enroll their children in the schools belonging to the religious orders, only to be turned away because of the overcrowding. But, she concluded, so much better if the nuns refuse the children of the people, it is high time their institutions disappear, along with the "daughters of Torquemada" who run them.[3] An opinion as forceful as hers might not have found much echo among French women before the Commune. To see why many of them were ready for such ideas in 1871, we must look at some of the developments which helped to form the mentality of women before then.

The predicament of women after the revolution of 1848 was especially difficult for those who may have wanted to break free of the Church, for in the aftermath of the uprising, the government took a renewed interest in tying the lower classes to the clerical form of education. It was none other than Thiers who said in 1849 that the religious orders must reign supreme in the education of the people, and that "the curé's action must be strong, stronger than ever, because I am counting on him to spread that true philosophy that man is here to suffer. . ."[4] The law on education which was promulgated in 1850 and remained in force until the 1880's, was directed at the education of both sexes, but bore especially hard on that of girls. It provided that nuns could teach without obtaining the certificate of capacity which was obligatory for lay teachers. The congregations' schools were thereby given an enormous competitive advantage over the secular schools and quickly outnumbered them.

More serious perhaps than this was the hegemony of the religious ideal, the image of women as resigned, passive and subservient, in the secular schools as well. The government school inspectors, charged with looking after both the religious and the lay schools, made some revealing statements in this respect. For instance, the report of June, 1870 for the school district of Bordeaux:

In the girls' schools as well as the boys', the education offers all the guarantees of morality which families could desire. The schools are run by teachers, both nuns and laywomen, who bring to their task, from the standpoint of moral education, the most attentive care. Both nuns and laity receive with deference and docility the instructions which are given them by the administration. As I always say, devotion and a sense of duty, generally stronger in persons of this sex, help to compensate for their weakness in other respects. . .[5]

The report for Paris the same year observed that

The women teachers, both lay and religious render perhaps even greater services

51

[than the men]. Their knowledge and teaching ability leave something to be desired, but they are morally superior, more tactful, and more devoted.[6]

To this mentality the role of women was service and nothing more. There was no basic difference in function between nuns and laywomen. Given this attitude, it is no wonder that the congregations' schools outstripped the secular ones, for the religious personnel was from many points of view more desirable. A nun demanded less financially, had no family responsibilities, and was willing to perform extracurricular tasks that others would not, such as caring for the sick and the elderly.[7] No laywoman could hope to compete with this model employee.

Not only to the lay teacher did the religious offer an unbeatable competition, but also to other kinds of working women. The workshops of the convents consistently turned out cheaper goods than the products which women made on the open market, easily underselling them. Furthermore, the orders sometimes co-operated directly with private enterprise. They acted as surveillants in factories where young girls were employed, to guard their morals and keep their work up to standard.[8] At least one case of strike-breaking is known to us, when in 1869 the sisters of Saint Vincent de Paul sent about a hundred women from their charity workshop to replace the striking workers at the department store, the Magasins du Louvre, in Paris.[9]

Against this background, we can understand the value of the Commune for women. It was a chance for them to remove clerical influence from their lives and replace it with a system giving them more control over their own and their children's destinies. The Commune's basic program rested on the idea that women had a right to the same amount of education, work, and salary as men and an equal share of social responsibility. For the first time a woman, Marguerite Tinayre, was appointed an inspector of schools;[10] for the first time the salaries of women teachers were made equal to those of men, because as the decree said, "The necessities of life are as numerous and imperative for women as for men, and, as far as education is concerned, women's work is equal to that of men."[11]

The basis of the Commune's educational program was the decree of April 2, which laicized all church property and turned it over to the community. The schools were from then on to give a purely secular instruction and to be opened to all children. Those inhabitants of each arrondissement who had the credentials were invited to teach.

The congregational workshops were reopened as professional schools. This move was especially significant for the education of girls, for a number of the schools were devoted particularly to their training, an indication of a change of opinion on the part of at least some of the men, who had traditionally been against women working for a living. One such school, for example, was founded by a Mme. Manière, a teacher by profession. Her program, which she submitted to the Commune for approval, was to combine general and professional training in "a milieu favorable

LOUISE MICHEL *Paintings by* Louis Tinayre

NATHALIE LEMEL   *Photograph*

ELIZABETH DMITRIEFF   *Photograph*

JULES VALLES *Painting by* Gustave Courbet

AUGUSTE BLANQUI *Painting by Eugène Carrière*

PIERRE-JOSEPH PROUDHON *Painting by* Gustave Courbet

ARTILLERY AT MONTMARTRE, MARCH 18, 1871

PLACE de L'HOTEL de VILLE. PROCLAMATION OF THE COMMUNE,
MARCH 26, 1871 *Wood Gravure from* London Illustrated News

BARRICADES

LE SPECTRE ROUGE de 1870   *Caricature by* J. Lemot

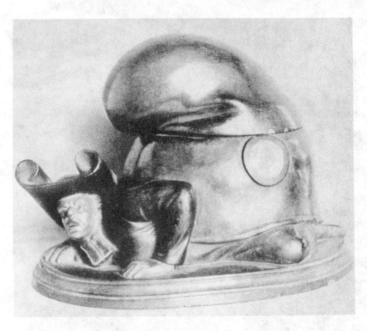

PRIEST CRUSHED BY CAP OF LIBERTY   *Communard Tobacco Jar*

to progressive education," as opposed to the milieu of the conventual workshop, which she aimed specifically to replace.[12]

The type of feminism which demanded careers for women most naturally appeared in those women who had suffered directly from clerical competition and from the anti-feminism of men. The Commune was a chance for them to get some of their own back from these two oppressors. An unnamed woman schoolteacher is described for us by an observer of the Commune who heard her speak one evening at a meeting of one of the women's clubs. This teacher, it was claimed by one of her friends in the audience, had been hounded from her job and imprisoned under the Empire, by "the jealousy of the nuns and priests." Her speech was an impassioned denunciation of men and a demand for the career open to talents for women. "Men are like sovereigns," she announced, "softened by their too constant authority. . . It is time that women replace them in the direction of public affairs. . . Make way for women, for their talent, their valor, their patriotism. . ."[13]

The existence of this strain of feminism in the Commune should not hide the fact that marriage and motherhood were still the most important things for women, in the eyes of many *communards* of both sexes. Jean Allemane is a good example of a *communard's* attitude. He was in charge of laicizing the Church properties in the fifth arrondissement. He describes how he went to expropriate the orphanage and workshop of the sisters of Saint Vincent de Paul. Addressing the nuns, he asked them if they would not prefer to leave their order and "fulfill their simple duty as women." In the face of their refusal, he sadly remarks that they were "enemies of humanity in renouncing the most noble title of all: that of mother." He is less distressed by their political opposition to the Commune than by their rejection of motherhood.[14]

A similar theme is developed in the memoirs of a Celeste Hardouin, a schoolteacher who lived through the Commune and in June of 1871 was arrested on the mistaken charge of having been an active participant. Although she was no *pétroleuse,* her political state of mind can be judged to some extent by the fact that she was a great admirer of Louise Michel, whom she met while they were both imprisoned by the Versailles government. (Mme. Hardouin later organized petitions to have Louise Michel released from her imprisonment in New Caledonia.)

Celeste Hardouin's thoughts are particularly interesting as they relate to the religious orders, a subject about which she became rather knowledgeable, for she served part of her detention as a prisoner in a convent, guarded by the nuns, another disturbing manifestation of the willingness of the congregations to cooperate with the state. Mme. Hardouin had a lively hatred of them, not only for their satisfaction at the repression of the Commune, which they expressed many times, but also because of what she considered to be their "suicidal" attitude toward life, that is, their refusal to bear children. "Poor dried up flowers of mysticism," she addresses them, "understand once and for all the sole reason for being and give children to the earth which gave you father and mother."[15]

Educator that she was, Mme. Hardouin considered mis-education responsible for all ills, as for instance, when she said that religious schooling among the upper classes, especially the women, accounted for their vicious attitude to the Commune. Even though there is certainly a good deal of truth in this, we see that Mme. Hardouin ignored completely the role of class hatred and the fact that even without the influence of the Church the suppression would have been just as ruthless.

This is the essential flaw of the kind of feminist anti-clericalism which was so widespread in the Commune: the idea that the Church was responsible for everything. This narrowness of view is no doubt related to a fact that has been cited time and time again, the lack of a philosophy of economic determinism on the part of the Commune as a whole. The same attitude, one might say, which prevented the Commune from expropriating the Bank of France, prevented the women from seeing through the Church to the real causes of their oppression.

But, by attacking the Church, they made an important beginning which must not be forgotten. Even, or perhaps especially, by their mistakes, they left a valuable lesson. They took anti-clericalism as far as it can go and showed its strengths and weakness as a basis for political action. Most important of all, they challenged society at large and working-class men in particular to take them seriously by showing that women are not necessarily the servants of the clergy.

Did the lessons of feminism in the Commune leave any permanent mark on the world? Certainly their effect on the Church and the *bien pensants* was to make them more obdurate than ever. As to their mark on the workers' movement it is difficult to be sure, but there are some slight traces. The thoroughness with which the Commune was put down and the death or imprisonment of so many of the important militants, such as Louise Michel, left the movement in such disarray that we must be grateful for any continuities, no matter how small, between the Commune and that which came after.

In 1876 in Paris was held the first national congress of workers since the Commune. Among the delegates we encounter Mme. Manière and Mme. Hardouin, both of whom spoke in the session devoted to the problems of women. Mme. Manière, true to her old ideas, defended the right of women to learn skills and to work. Mme. Hardouin, as we might expect, discussed the harm done working women and their children by the congregations' workshops, and demanded a socialist alternative, controlled and staffed by mothers, rather than by celibate women.[16]

Although these speeches were warmly applauded, according to the minutes, it is not really possible to tell whether they were a reflection of the general sentiment. We can certainly say that the question of woman's role was not done with, for at the next two congresses, in 1878 and 1879,

Feminism and Anti-clericalism

the arguments still raged. In 1878, Mme. Hardouin attacked Proudhon's famous dictum that woman is either housewife or courtesan. "We must be more than the one; we must suppress the other." But there were still delegates at that convention who believed that women should not work and that they could not be trusted on the religious question.[17]

There is hardly any mention of the Commune at any of these meetings, probably because any approving references would have brought down the suspicions of the government. Though we cannot conclude from the delegates' silence alone that the Commune had been forgotten, one has the sense that they knew the experience was never to be repeated. They spoke of founding mutual aid societies, of general "cooperation," but never of revolution, never of taking the initiative to create their own society, such as the Commune had been. Such talk would have been too dangerous at the time, and when the time came again in France to talk of revolution, it was in a very different context from that of 1871.

Now, in the aftermath of the Commune, it was only possible to talk, as Mme. Hardouin did in all of her speeches, of self-help while waiting for the state to fulfill the workers' demands. In a way she was right, because in the end, it was the state which created the lay school and gave educational opportunities to women. But the political philosophy and the social context in which they were bestowed were entirely different from that of the Commune, where they had been part of a complete program of equality and justice.

REFERENCES

[1] Paul Lidsky, *Les écrivains contre la Commune*, Paris: François Maspero, 1970, p. 128. [2] Henri Lefebvre, *La proclamation de la Commune*, Paris: Gallimard, 1965, p. 181. [3] Edith Thomas, *Louise Michel, ou la Vellèda de l'anarchie*, Paris: Gallimard, 1970, p. 71. [4] Antoine Prost, *L'Histoire de l'enseignement en France, 1800–1967*, Paris: Armand Colin, 1968, pp. 168-169. [5] Archives Nationales, F^{17}9376. [6] *Ibid.* [7] Prost, *L'Enseignement*, p. 155. [8] Jules Simon, *L'Ouvrière*, Paris: Hachette, 1861, p. 55. [9] *Séances du Congrès ouvrier français, 3e session*, Marseilles, 1879, p. 172. [10] Jean Bruhat, Jean Dautry, Emile Tersen, *La Commune de 1871*, Paris: Editions sociales, 1970, p. 175. [11] Edith Thomas, *The Women Incendiaries*, N.Y.: George Braziller, 1966, p. 118. [12] Maurice Dommanget, *L'Enseignement, l'enfance, et la culture sous la Commune*, Paris: Editions-Librairie de l'Etoile, 1964, p. 61. [13] Marforio, pseud. Mme. Louise Lacroix, *Les écharpes rouges, souvenirs de la Commune*, Paris: Laporte, 1872, p. 20. [14] Jean Allemane, *Memoirs d'un communard, des barricades aux bagne*, Paris: Librairie socialiste, 1910, p. 83. [15] Celeste Hardouin, *La détenue de Versailles en 1871*, Paris: published by the author, 1879, pp. 25-26. [16] *Séances du congrès ouvrier français, 1e session*, Paris, 1876, p. 241. [17] *Séances du congrès ouvrier français, 2e session*, Lyon, 1878, p. 54.

THE COMMUNE IN 1971

C. L. R. James

MARX AND LENIN are in no way responsible for the grave deficiencies in contemporary analyses of the Commune. The deficiencies are these:

1. Commentators do not relate Marx's 1871 analysis of the Commune to his analysis of what happened in France after the 1848 revolution: one of the most significant (and personal) passages in that greatest of all historical treatises, *The Eighteenth Brumaire of Louis Bonaparte*. All agree (following Lenin) that Marx signaled the notable advance that had been made in history (and therefore in theory) by emphasizing that the Commune had struck a mortal blow at bourgeois parliamentary democracy. The apparently inevitable structure of the bourgeois state was the division between the legislature (the elected parliament) and the executive (the governmental machine which carried out, administered, executed the decisions of the legislature). The elected leadership of the Commune was responsible for *both* the legislation and executive duties, which had formerly been distinct and separated functions. So far, so good. Everybody knows that. What is not discussed is Marx's analysis of the bourgeois state, which was so drastically replaced. Most unusually with him, in the tightly constructed *18th Brumaire,* he makes his first analysis:

It is immediately obvious that in a country like France, where the executive power commands an army of officials numbering more than half a million individuals and therefore constantly maintains an immense mass of interests and livelihoods in the most absolute dependence; where the state enmeshes, controls, regulates, superintends and tutors civil society from its most comprehensive manifestations of life down to its most insignificant stirrings, from its most general modes of being to the private existence of individuals; where through the most extraordinary centralisation this parasitic body acquires a ubiquity, an omniscience, a capacity for accelerated mobility and an elasticity which finds a counterpart only in the helpless dependence, in the loose shapelessness of the actual body politic—it is obvious that in such a country the National Assembly forfeits all real influence when it loses command of the ministerial posts, if it does not at the same time simplify the administration of the state, reduce the army of officials as far as possible and, finally, let civil society and public opinion create organs of their own, independent of the governmental power. But it is precisely with the maintenance of that extensive state machine in its numerous ramifications that the *material interests* of the French bourgeoisie are interwoven in the closest fashion. Here it finds posts for its surplus population and makes up in the form of state salaries for what it cannot pocket in the form of profit, interest, rents and honorariums. On the other hand, its *political interests* compelled it to increase daily the repressive measures and therefore the resources and the personnel of the state power, while at the same time it had to wage an uninterrupted war against public opinion and mistrustfully mutilate, cripple, the independent organs of the social movement, where it did not succeed in amputating them entirely. Thus the French bourgeoisie was compelled by its class position to annihilate, on the one hand, the vital conditions of all parliamentary power, and therefore, likewise, of its own, and to render irresistible, on the other hand, the executive power hostile to it.

And not satisfied with that, a few pages later he takes it up again

This executive power with its enormous bureaucratic and military organisation, with its ingenious state machinery, embracing wide strata, with a host of officials numbering half a million, besides an army of another half million, this appalling parasitic body, which enmeshes the body of French society like a net and chokes all its pores, sprang up in the days of the absolute monarchy, with the decay of the feudal system, which it helped to hasten. The seignorial privileges of the landowners and towns became transformed into so many attributes of the state power, the feudal dignitaries into paid officials and the motley pattern of conflicting mediaeval plenary powers into the regulated plan of a state authority whose work is divided and centralised as in a factory. The first French Revolution, with its task of breaking all separate local, territorial, urban and provincial powers in order to create the civil unity of the nation, was bound to develop what the absolute monarchy had begun: centralisation, but at the same time the extent, the attributes and the agents of governmental power. Napoleon perfected this state machinery. The Legitimist monarchy and the July monarchy added nothing but a greater division of labour, growing in the same measure as the division of labour within bourgeois society created new groups of interests, and, therefore, new material for state administration. Every *common* interest was straightway severed from society, counterposed to it as a higher, *general* interest, snatched from the activity of society's members themselves and made an object of government activity, from a bridge, a schoolhouse and the communal property of a village community to the railways, the national wealth and the national university of France. Finally, in its struggle against the revolution, the parliamentary republic found itself compelled to strengthen, along with the repressive measures, the resources and centralisation of governmental power. All revolutions perfected this machine instead of smashing it. The parties that contended in turn for domination regarded the possession of this huge state edifice as the principal spoils of the victor.

Marx had written these pages in 1851. One can imagine how much this monster had grown by 1871. Therefore one can only understand (and expound and teach) Marx's idea of what the Commune had achieved by understanding Marx's view of what the bourgeois state had become in 1871. I respectfully but immodestly submit that I never see anywhere any understanding of what the Commune had set out to smash. It is enough I hope to state here that both Marx and Engels realized that there had been a mistake in the second passage. The French Revolution did not centralize. It broke up the centralization of the monarchy. It was Napoleon who restored it.

II.   The second deficiency in contemporary analyses of the Commune can be briefly stated. Lenin used to say that in preparing for the future you always *began* at the highest pitch previously reached. Thus in preparing for the Russian Revolution he always had as his starting point, not the backwardness of the Russian masses, but the highest point so far in the

European proletarian revolution: the Commune. Not many today recognize the Hungarian Revolution of 1956 as the starting point of any future proletarian perspectives. I can barely state the reason here. The reason is something I am quite certain that both Marx and Lenin understood: Such dramatic explosions as the Commune and the Hungarian Revolution of 1956 are not perceived as significant or illuminating historical episodes. They are strictly logical stages in a Hegelian dialectical conception of historical development. That however, is another story.

THE IMPACT OF THE PARIS COMMUNE
IN THE UNITED STATES

Samuel Bernstein

T he Paris correspondent of the New York *World* reported in April
1871 that the Commune had been plotted by the International Workingmen's Association.[1] His source was *Le Gaulois*, a monarchist tinged
sheet, which charged that the rise of the Paris Commune on March 18th
had been the denouement of a well-laid conspiracy of which the principal
ringleaders were Karl Marx and the General Council of the International.
The charge was correct insofar as the Commune was the intellectual off-
spring of the International. But this sprawling body, centered in London,
had done absolutely nothing to bring it about, as Frederick Engels later
wrote to F. A. Sorge in America.[2] Everything about the Association refuted
the charge of the French paper—its loose make-up, the weakness of its
branches, and its incurable impecuniousness. It had never been a secret
body, organized for conspiratorial purposes; its French branch was completely disordered on the eve of the Commune, as the General Council's
emissary in Paris reported on February 28, 1871;[3] and its treasury was so
empty that the Council in London was often embarrassed by rent-arrears
for its modest meeting place. Actually the International had already been
the object of calumny. A short time before the outbreak of the Franco-
Prussian War, Marx told his colleagues of the Council, "the International
was made the general scapegoat of all untoward events."[4] But the charge
against it respecting the Commune was of another character, for it had
rallied to the defense of the revolution in Paris after its outbreak. To be
sure, The Second Address of the General Council on the Franco-Prussian
War, dated September 9, 1870, had forewarned the Parisians against any
attempt to upset the French Republic.[5] However, the Council was powerless before the events. As its minutes show it accepted the inevitable and
stood loyally by the Commune. Ten days after it became the revolutionary
government of the French capital the Council unanimously accepted
Marx's proposal "that an address be issued to the people of Paris."[6]

I

The Paris Commune had international significance, and therein lay its
historical importance. In all countries of the western world it had numerous vilifiers as well as defenders. In the United States the chorus of abuse
grew crescendo-like. Calumny of the Parisians became a pattern of thought.
Press and pulpit, platform and pamphlet alike drew heavily on the dictionary of defamation to paint the Communards as the vilest specimens
of the race of bipeds. American newspapers and periodicals in general,
like the British, aligned themselves with Versailles and systematically

59

presented Paris as the hotbed of savages and bandits. They were at once foes of family and religion, antagonists of private property and government. Consequently no quarter was to be given them.

No one, as far as we know, has yet found a way of measuring the extent to which the American press and pulpit shaped public opinion on the Paris Commune. But it is safe to assume that the volume of abuse caused Americans, irrespective of social status, to look upon it with repugnance. Its defenders formed but a small fraction of the population. Their brief in its behalf will find space later in the article. For the present we shall concentrate on the case presented by its revilers.

No political or economic issue in the United States, save governmental corruption, received more headlines in the American press of the 1870's than did the Paris Commune and the International Workingmen's Association. Every big newspaper gave readers the impression that the foundations of organized society had crumbled. Anarchy, assassination, slaughter, incendiarism, streets covered with human gore—such blood curdling scenes were monotonously reported in the news. There were predictions that other Marats and Robespierres would arise and the screaming mobs, too, to demand the heads of the rich. An example of the irresponsible reporting was the case of Auguste Blanqui, the dreaded revolutionary of the nineteenth century. Though he had been arrested the day before the rise of the Commune and was a well-guarded prisoner,[7] the American press advertised him as the mastermind of its Central Committee.[8] One correspondent wrote, as if under Thiers' direction, that he had inherited Marat's mantle. "His presence signifies constant turmoil and insurrection." If he ever achieved power, the Guillotine would be set up again.[9]

Newspapers, outside of New York City, by and large followed its press. Thus, according to the Cincinnati *Daily Gazette,* Paris was still the "den of wild beasts" it had been during the first French Revolution,[10] a view shared by the Chicago *Tribune.*[11] Less original was the Wisconsin *State Journal* with such commonplace epithets as "mob rule" and "reign of terror."[12] Both the *Morning Bulletin* and *Evening Bulletin* of San Francisco were persuaded that the "violent reds" were "destroying genuine republicanism and individual liberty, and reviving the worst events of the First Revolution."[13] The warning by Versailles that the Commune was but the initial stage of a worldwide conflagration, directed by the First International, was echoed by the Washington *Star.*[14] Frederick Douglass' weekly charged the Communards with mobocracy, vandalism and terrorism like that of 1792.[15] The Philadelphia *Ledger* and the Pittsburgh *Daily Gazette* reiterated the fabrications of the better known newspapers.[16]

Since the press in American cities leaned by and large on the major newspapers of New York our purpose would be better served if we centered attention on them. From their lead articles and editorials on the Commune several theses emerge which can be stated as follows: The people in France, and by implication the people in the United States, were

60

unfit to have a hand in government; given the socialist character of the Commune, violence was inevitable; the Communards were communists, commanded by the International, awaiting the order to overrun other countries; finally, the Commune might also come to America. Let us consider the theses in their order.

The common people exhibited their political incapacity by their reliance on terror and theft, contended the Commune's denigrators. From the viewpoint of the New York *Tribune*, Paris was a "burlesque Republic," backed by recruits from the gutters and drinking shops, and supported by the seizures of property.[17] The New York *Times* confessed a nostalgia for the dictatorial system of Louis Napoleon. Bad as his Empire was, "it at least kept off a worse thing—The Universal Republic."[18] The New York *Herald* was more blunt. The Bonapartes, it said on April 1, 1871, "were the proper doctors for those virulent revolutionary disorders of Paris." Americans should revise their opinion of Bonapartism, urged the New York *Journal of Commerce*. Louis Napoleon's coup d'état of 1851 had been "a good investment in human life." The shortest way to end the Parisian madness was to free the Emperor and allow him to march on the capital at the head of an army. Failing that, the Germans should intervene.[19]

It may be noted parenthetically that there were dailies and weeklies that rejected the Napoleonic straitjacket. For the Commune, they claimed, had at least demonstrated the failure of arbitrary rule and centralization. It had shattered the machinery of both and raised the banner of federalism.[20]

The Commune was socialistic, declared its foes, and they were correct in estimating it so. Not that its program spelled out socialism. Such as it was, it reflected Proudhonist aspirations and revealed an abiding respect for private property. But the Commune showed its ultimate, socialist, intentions both in its social legislation and in its policies. Its socialistic character, however, did not have violence as its sequence, save in the imaginations of reporters. They equated the Commune's socialism with anarchy, which they in turn gave a forbidding definition;[21] they described it as Fourierist or Saint-Simonist, or even as Marxist. Whatever label they pinned on socialism, they saw it attended by violence. Yet, correspondents visiting Paris, we shall show, were surprised by the courtesy and orderliness of the people, and by their respect for property and churches.

People were led to believe that Commune was synonymous with communism. The Parisians were therefore ipso facto partitioners or destroyers of property. The equation was widely accepted in America and was used to overawe striking workers. A coal miners' strike in Pennsylvania was called "The Commune of Pennsylvania,"[22] and the strikers were likened to Communards.[23] The Internationalists in the Commune, the indictment continued, were communistically inclined and were in league with other Internationalists to bring about a worldwide communist revolution. The accusations were inventions. In the first place, the Internationalists in the

Commune were a small minority, opposed and outvoted by the Blanquists and neo-Jacobins; in the second place, they were Proudhonists, far removed from communism in its social and economic outlook;[24] in the third place, as we have said, the International was badly equipped to organize a general revolution. Whatever plots were laid to it with that end in view were but police tales that became the themes of a large, spurious literature both in Europe and in the United States. The organization was credited with countless forces and limitless resources. No country was safe from it. It was "a constant source of anxiety and trouble."[25] Rumor had it that its affiliates in Italy were plotting the assassination of the Pope.[26] Strikes, it was maintained, were skirmishes to test the resistance of established systems; and demonstrations were but reviews of its forces before entering upon the final struggle. The French police metamorphosed Marx into Bismarck's secret agent, for how else, asked they, could one explain his comfortable style of living?[27] The North American Federation of the International, that had about 5,000 members at its height, early in 1872, was believed by French police observers in the United States to have around 1,400,000 in April 1876, just as its end was nearing.[28]

The press sounded the alarm that the Commune might rise up in America. The "roughs of New York," wrote the *Evening Telegram,* were the sort of element that could become communist.[29] To be sure, the threat was not imminent, the *Times* assured the public, but the horizons looked somber. Labor was organizing in the United States; the workers of all lands were steadily uniting and asserting that capital had all the advantage in the production of wealth, while those who worked were left empty-handed. Through their trade unions they were counting on "a wider and more nearly universal Republic" that could claim the obedience of every laborer . . . from Archangel to San Francisco.[30] Thanks to the absence of feudal traditions in America, thanks to her boundless resources and her republican system, the *Times* felt confident about the future. Still the materials which caused the Commune in Paris were in every large metropolis. New York had beneath its busy surface "a volcano of deep passions and explosive social forces." Fortunately the pressure on American workers was not as heavy; and they had dreams of becoming capitalists.[31]

The dangerous elements were present nonetheless, the warning re-echoed. The more informed among them had heard of the division of property and socialism. Others belonged to trades unions that had sworn bitter war against capital. In other words America was not immune to Communes, wrote the *Times.* "Let some such opportunity occur as was presented in Paris . . . ; let this mighty throng hear that there was a chance to grasp the luxuries of wealth, or to divide the property of the rich, or to escape labor and suffering for a time, and live on the super-fluities of others, and we should see a sudden storm of communistic revolution even in New York such as would astonish all who do not know these classes." A mine was "beneath every large city—not so easily exploded in America as in Europe—but existing with all its terrible elements even here."[32] The spectre that rose above the flames of Paris haunted the United States. It was the spectre "of a toiling, ignorant and impoverished multitude, demanding an equal share in the wealth of the rich."

What was the remedy? The *Times* proposed free schooling and better facilities for acquiring land. It also saw merit in the Rochedale cooperative plan and in some form of profit sharing.[33] The New York *Herald* put its trust in the teaching of religion.[34] The *Tribune* relied on the untrammeled laws of economics to remove social friction.[35] The New York *Standard* was partial to the correctives of the *Times*[36] and the *World* to those of the *Tribune*, provided the government held on to the national domain.[37] At bottom the remedies were all alike in that they in no way impinged on the foundations of the status quo.

Something needs to be said, however briefly, on the role of clergymen in shaping public opinion on the Commune and the International. Among the more prominent and influential were Archbishop Manning of New York, and the Reverends Frothingham and Henry Ward Beecher, both of the same city. The first charged that the principal threat of the Commune was its atheism and materialism. The answer to them, he said, lay in authority and obedience.[38] According to the Reverend Frothingham the danger to America stemmed from the alliance of the trade unions with the Communist International,[39] even though it was common knowledge that American unions, in the great majority, were either indifferent or hostile to it. The third clergyman, the eloquent Henry Ward Beecher, told a large attendance in his church that the scenes of the Paris Commune were but enactments of those of the French Revolution. And since there was a certain likeness in human nature, Americans could not ignore the awful possibilities of the future. It could also happen here, unless the dangerous elements were inoculated with faith in God. He proposed, in addition to the free distribution of land, free schools and indoctrination in the belief in the next life.[40]

II

Any consideration of American opinion on the Paris Commune must take into account publications and public figures who endeavored to contain the tide of denunciation. They were of course a minority, but a sturdy one, including liberals and American Internationalists. The *Weekly New York Democrat* not only blamed the Thiers government for having provoked the Parisians into revolt; it also considered the political program of the Commune worthy of incorporation into the American Constitution.[41] Another weekly, the *Golden Age*, attributed the Revolution in Paris to the misrule of the Second Empire. It then proceeded to clear the Commune of the stigma of communism. The Commune, said the *Golden Age*, was nothing but republicanism. "If the Republic of America is right, the Commune of Paris was right." Had the Commune been victorious as had been the Republic in America, it would have been acclaimed rather than execrated by the same people who lashed it.[42]

Such dissent from the run of opinion must have been welcome to American friends of the Commune, even though the dissenters did not understand its real essence. In this respect *The Nation,* edited by E. L. Godkin, came closest, even before the publication in the United States of the General Council's *Address on the Civil War in France.* However much the periodical marked the Commune as "one of the greatest pieces of folly and wickedness . . . ever witnessed," it nevertheless saw its true meaning: "Veritable workingmen sit in council in the gilded saloons of the Hotel de Ville," doing everything "that can be done to put out of sight or abolish all the machinery, whether moral or material, which the rich and educated classes have invented and declared to be necessary for the proper conduct of human affairs." *The Nation* thus agreed with Marx that, by destroying the old machinery of government, the Commune had taken the requisite steps to what he termed a proletarian dictatorship. The journal went on to say that the workers' government "has shown itself capable of maintaining an army, and carrying on war for two months," so that it not only gave "an air of practicalness to what all the rest of the world sneered at as impractical"; it also showed "that it is not impossible for a great crowd of persons, whom society denounces as lunatics and loafers to seize on the government of a great capital, and administer it for a time, at all events."[43]

No contemporaneous American publication, as far as we know, assessed the Commune as well as did *The Nation.* It saw the Revolution in historical perspective and foretold its future impact. Those who hoped that its fall would spell the end of its ideas were mistaken, it declared. "These ideas . . . will live and grow." They will "not cease to spread until they have made one great attempt for the conquest of modern society, and have in that attempt shaken our present civilization to its foundation."[44]

Amidst the general hysteria new ideas on the Commune were invading the public mind. Even the New York *World,* that had printed so many fantastic tales and excerpted Mazzini's indictment of the Commune,[45] gave ample space to interviews with high ranking Communards and Internationalists.[46] It did still more. On June 29 it published almost the entire text of the *Address on the Civil War in France.* Thereafter it was printed in full by *The Workingman's Advocate* in Chicago and *Woodhull & Claflin's Weekly* in New York. Special editions of the *Address* were issued to meet increasing demands, so that the above-named *Weekly* could say candidly: "No public document has ever been more sought after."[47]

The press could not avoid noticing the International's statement on the Commune. The *Golden Age* and *The Nation* each found in it confirmation of its own forecast; the one regarded the *Address* as "a pungent, angry and manly defence of the Paris Commune"; it attested to the fact that the Commune was a praiseworthy example of self-government; the other weekly, in keeping with its prediction, believed that the *Address* would make the International more audacious.[48] Metropolitan dailies, too, looked upon the piece as a validation of their earlier views. For the *Star* it dispelled all doubts about the Commune's aim of controlling all economic life.[49] The *Times* discovered in it evidence to justify its premonition that the Commune was but the first of further conflicts for the achievement of a new social order.[50] The *World*, though full of praise for the vigor and literary merit of the *Address*, saw in it a warning to statesmen and men of property. No people was exempt from the plague of popular movements.[51]

The controversy over the Commune was becoming less one-sided as its defenders were entering the debate. The weeklies cited above were aided by the press of the American sections of the International that were increasing in number and uniting under a central committee. True, this press was limited in circulation. *Le Socialiste,* founded in New York on October 7, 1871, which soon became an official organ of the International, reached only French-speaking people. It was in this small sheet that appeared serially, from January to March 1872, the first French translation of *The Communist Manifesto. Woodhull & Claflin's Weekly,* another official organ, represented the English-speaking Section 12, which in time developed into a dissident group. Despite the *Weekly's* lapse in discipline and its criticism of the Commune's policies, it stood by the Parisian government and, as we said above, published the full *Address.* On December 30, 1871, it reprinted the first English translation of *The Communist Manifesto* that had appeared in England in 1850 in the *Red Republican.* The most important labor paper of the time, *The Workingman's Advocate,* did not endorse all the principles of the Commune. Still it reprinted the *Address* and rejected the villainous charges of the newspapers. It furthermore declared that the Commune had arisen out of conditions that were also present in the United States.[52] The coal miners' strike in Pennsylvania, it owned, was not unrelated to the Revolution in Paris. Both aimed "to establish and define strictly the rights of producers."[53]

The limited press, it is safe to say, had less effect in dispelling the misrepresentations of the Commune than had a small number of American journalists in Paris. Notable were Frank M. Pixley, writing in the San Francisco *Chronicle,* William Huntington in the Cincinnati *Commercial,* George Wilkes in the New York *Herald* and finally Alfred Russell Young in the New York *Standard.* The accounts of the last two were the best considered and the most convincing. Wilkes' reports to the *Herald* disputed everything printed on the Commune. Moderation, decency and justice were virtues discovered in the government of Paris. It had guarded public morals, religion and property, he wrote; the stories of plunder and incendiarism merely testified to their authors' wild imaginations.[54]

The most authoritative report by an American and the one which provoked chroniclers of the Commune was that of Alfred Russell Young. His paper, the New York *Standard,* had vied with others in heaping abuse on the Communards. It happened that in May 1871, the State Department sent him on a secret mission to Europe. Curiosity led him to every part of Paris. He examined barricades, attended club meetings, entered churches and roamed the streets of Montmartre, reputed to be the center of "ruffians." He soon learned that the Communards had been libeled. A study of the facts showed him that not they but the Versaillese had begun the shooting of prisoners "and unarmed men in cold blood." What about the pillaging? In making the rounds of the clubs, he wrote, he had not heard a single proposal for partitioning, not an appeal for plunder. Never had he seen "a more orderly city." Montmartre was quiet, although it had no police. In his walks through its narrow streets he had never been troubled or questioned. "I saw no drunkenness, no ruffianism, no pillage. I saw one crowd of at least thirty thousand men and women, and it was orderly and good-humored as though it were a gathering at a New York county fair." Were the Communards infidels, ransackers of churches? Young had expected to find the Church of the Madeleine converted into "a stable or wine cellar." Instead it was a quiet place of worship, guarded by a sentry. "The Madeleine," he said, "received more harm from the shots of the Versailles soldiers in combat than from the Commune during the siege."[55]

To newspaper editors who reproved him for his exposé of their mendacious stories, he replied:

It would have been so much easier, so much more popular, so much more acceptable, to home people, to have united in the chorus of anger that seemed to come from the English written press; to have shared the agitations of correspondents, who looked at Paris from the terrace of St. Germain and telegraphed their emotions to New York; to have written a wild article or two, freshened up with the rhetoric of the Reign of Terror. But what we saw and what we heard and what impressions they made upon us—a stranger in a strange and deeply interesting land, among people whose history we had read with affection and deep emotion—we felt called upon to write and print. In that shape truth came to us, and we spoke it.[56]

Young's report was one of the most valuable aids to the sobering of American opinion on the Commune. Wendell Phillips, the former Abolitionist, appraised it as "the ablest, most brilliant and searching of all essays on the Commune."[57]

The same paper that carried Phillips' estimate of Young's story also carried articles by W. J. Linton, the renowned engraver and former British Chartist. Their purpose was to clear the Commune of the slander that had been flung at it. Linton did not share all its principles, but he was at one with it "as far as wanting *some better social ordering than that of the Bonapartes and the Fisks.*"[58] Perhaps his association with Chartists and European socialists had equipped him to get at the underlying objective of the Commune. He could see from his vantage point that it had brought to the surface "the question of the abolition of misery."[59]

66

The bulk of American intellectuals and men of letters, like the European, either gave little thought to the Commune or were downright hostile. Only a small minority sided with the Commune and even with the International. Of that number were Wilkes and Young, Linton and Phillips. One could also find among them American Positivists, champions of moral persuasion, who, though critical of the Communards' political and repressive acts, praised them for having abolished the standing army and repealed the capital penalty. Like their British confrere, Frederick Harrison,[60] they rebuked the Commune's defamers and the falsifiers of its record.

Prominent in the tiny category of intellectuals who stood by the Commune was Wendell Phillips, of one of the first families of Massachusetts. His name had been a symbol of Abolitionism. Once its cause had triumphed, he declared: "We sheathe no sword. We turn only the front of the army upon a new foe."[61] The foe was corporate wealth and the wage system. Unlike other Abolitionists, he had the faculty of seeing the cadenced flow of change and continuity. Slavery once gone, the problem of wage labor absorbed him thereafter.[62] It came upon him slowly that the slave question was but part of the labor question.

His objective was workers' welfare, and his understanding of it was akin to what Jacksonian democrats had advanced. Capital, by his definition, was "but frozen, crystallized labor"; and labor, "but capital, dissolved and become active." Their antagonism was injurious to both, for neither one could exist without the other.[63] "Laws to protect labor from capital, and employer from his workmen," he said in January 1871, "will be needless when each man is both capitalist and workman, equally interested as employer and employed."[64] His ideal society was one of small, independent producers, bound together in a community. It was the sort of ideal once exemplified by a New England town, where, to cite him, were neither rich nor poor, "all mingling in the same society, every child at the same school, no poorhouse, no beggar, opportunities equal, nobody too proud to stand aloof, nobody too humble to be shut out."[65]

Phillips never squared his economic theory with advancing capitalism. He never penetrated its inside to study its workings. The best he could do was to place his trust in labor and in its international solidarity.

Consistent with this trust, he stood firmly by the Paris Commune. It was fallacious to present it as communist, he declared, for it had no such program. Nor had it been concocted by a cabal of cutthroats, as slander had it. The evidence showed that "the movement was the unanimous wish of all Paris." The city was so peaceful that the Stock Exchange refused to close. To the charge of pillage he replied: "The leaders arrested are poor. Those who fled are poorer still." But the indictment accused them of wilful bloodshed. Thiers "set the example," he answered. He refused all exchange of prisoners and shot every Communard, "men, women and children, especially every leader." The Communards, he continued, were genuine patriots who had refused to make peace with Napoleon and who made a desperate effort to lift France from her degradation. Phillips chided American journalists for having catered to prejudice. Had they appreciated the merits of the Communards they might have likened them to the American revolutionaries of 1776.[66]

Phillips held his convictions to the end. He told a reporter in 1878, when the issue of socialism was warmly debated, that America had nothing to fear from it. The press had misrepresented it as it had the Paris Commune. The Commune "was not socialistic primarily," he said, "but grew more and more that way." Was America suited to the spread of socialism? asked the reporter. Phillips did not think so, but he saw no harm in publicizing its principles. If America ever became socialist, it would be through the ballot-box, provided, he added, "force is not used by the other side."[67]

Did Phillips join the First International? We cannot say with certainty. Our only evidence is the news from New York to the General Council in London that he entered the ranks of the International.[68] But news from that source sometimes conveyed anticipation rather than fact.

III

During the hard times of the seventies, the hysteria over the Paris Commune and International took on new life. Meetings of unemployed and peaceful demonstrations to present demands to municipal officials were, in the opinion of the *World,* for example, "The Commune in City Hall" and "The Red Flag in New York."[69] The hand of the International was seen in every strike and every petition. They were the doings of foreign subversives, the *Times* charged, of a "dangerous class" that looked for an opportunity "to spread abroad the anarchy and ruin of the French Commune."[70] The explosive rhetoric might have caused city dwellers to lock their doors, but they were not an answer to the bread and butter question raised by the Long Depression begun in 1873. Perhaps on account of that the terrifying headlines were persistently spread throughout the nation.

It is not the intention here to enter into the many solutions of the social problems that cropped up during the seventies. Suffice it to say that many *isms* were laid before the public, from Social Darwinism and Positivism to Christian Socialism and Socialism. Of all these solutions the last one alone caused deep apprehension, for in July 1876, four parties and societies, totalling nearly 3,000 organized socialists, united to form The Workingmen's Party of the United States. Press and pulpit again sounded the dreadful warning that it could happen here. Socialism, they said, had been the aim in Paris; its emergence as a nation-wide movement in the United States was the best evidence that the hydra-headed monster had crossed the Atlantic. At the time of the railroad strike of 1877, captions like these were carried by newspapers and placards: "Commune in Pittsburgh," "Commune in Reading," "Commune in St. Louis," "Commune in Chicago," "Commune in Philadelphia," "Commune in New York," and the "Reign of the Commune."[71]

A drift to reaction set in during the decade, manifested in part by a sizable anti-socialist and anti-communist literature. It professed to show that socialism and communism were but reversions that had had their vogue in primitive societies, but they were inadaptable to America. Furthermore, the ruins of the Utopian experiments in America were proof of the utter hopelessness of ever replacing the existing order based on private property. Writers went on predicting a Commune in 1880. It would be launched by a secret workers' organization and popular uprisings that would be followed by foreign intervention and the dismemberment of the nation. It was all so fearsome.[72]

Carried by the reactionary drift was the argument that property was insecure under universal suffrage. What America needed was a strong man, a Thiers or a MacMahon, who would make short shrift of the red menace. For if the Commune was the consequence of the popular approach, the ballot in the hands of the people was a bombshell, declared its faultfinders. Nearly all of them agreed that some form of élitism was best calculated both to cleanse the prevailing political system of corruption and to prevent classes from mauling one another.[73]

Reaction failed to swell into a movement for want of mass support. Its principal promoters were cultivated men, wealthy and well-born, without the know-how of reaching the people. Besides, a rising economy after the Long Depression temporarily alleviated the distressing and disquieting problem of unemployment. The bogies, Commune and International, lost their hobgoblin aspects. Actually they were going out of fashion. They were replaced by the spectre of socialism.

REFERENCES

[1] New York *World,* April 14, 1871. [2] Fr. Engels–K. Marx et divers, *Correspondance* publiée par F. A. Sorge (Paris, 1950), I, 204; also Marx–Engels, *Selected Correspondence* (New York, 1935), 330. [3] The General Council of the First International, 1870-1871, Minutes (Moscow, n.d.), 139–144, hereinafter referred to as *Minutes.* [4] *Ibid.,* 158. [5] Karl Marx, *The Civil War in France* (New York, 1940), 34. [6] *Minutes,* 166. [7] See my *Auguste Blanqui* (Paris, 1970), 323. [8] *E.g.,* New York *World,* April 14, 18 and 19, 1871. [9] *Appleton's Journal,* June 10, 1871, V, 679. [10] April 11, 1871. [11] March 22, 1871. [12] *E.g.,* March 28, 1871. [13] *Morning Bulletin,* March 21 and 30, 1871; *Evening Bulletin,* April 18 and 22, May 20, 1871. [14] April 15, 1871. [15] *New National Era,* May 4 and 18, June 1 and 22, 1871. [16] Philadelphia *Ledger,* April 7, 1871; Pittsburgh *Daily Gazette,* April 14, 1871. [17] April 17 and May 3, 1871. [18] April 4, 1871. [19] April 4, 1871. [20] *The Evening Post,* April 14, 1871; *The Sun,* April 15, 1871; *Weekly New York Democrat,* March 31, 1871; *The Golden Age,* June 3, 1871. [21] See *e.g.,* The New York *Herald,* April 13, 1871. [22] *The Evening Post,* April 24, 1871. [23] The New York *Times,* April 8, 1871; The Washington *Evening Star,* June 6, 1871. [24] On this point see Samuel Bernstein *The Beginnings of Marxian Socialism in France* (New York, 1965), 37–47, reprint with new preface; and by the same author *The First*

Revolution & Reaction

International in America (New York, 1962), 74. [25] The New York *World*, July 28, 1871. [26] *Ibid.*, July 1, 1871; New York *Times*, June 20, 1871. [27] This was the tenor of reports by French detectives in London. Their reports belong to the dossier on Karl Marx in Archives de la préfecture de police, Paris, Dossier 1 B.ª/1,175. [28] Archives de la préfecture de police, dossier "L'Internationale en Amérique, 1867–1877," and *The First International in America*, 255. [29] April 28, 1871. [30] March 24, 1871. [31] June 2, 1871. [32] June 18, 1871. [33] April 13, July 6, 1871. [34] February 20, 1871. [35] May 11 and August 26, 1871. The same faith in laissez-faire economics was shared by the weekly, *Every Saturday*, May 13, 1871, II, 450. [36] September 20 and 25, 1871. [37] July 1, 1871. [38] New York *Times*, June 20, 1871. [39] New York *World*, June 17, 1872. [40] New York *Standard*, May 29, 1871; Henry Ward Beecher, *The Sermons in Plymouth Church, Brooklyn* (New York, 1871), 6th series, 233–248. [41] March 24 and 26, April 7 and 21, 1871. [42] April 8 and 22, May 13 and 27, June 3, 1871. [43] May 18, 1871, XII, 334 ff. [44] *Ibid.*, June 1, 1871, 375. [45] June 15 and August 4, 1871. [46] July 18, September 21 and 24, 1871. [47] *Woodhull & Claflin's Weekly*, August 19, 1871. [48] *Golden Age*, cited in the *Workingman's Advocate*, September 23, 1871; *The Nation*, July 6, 1871, XIII, 2. [49] July 5, 1871. [50] June 29, 1871. [51] July 1, 1871. [52] *The Workingman's Advocate*, July 8, 1871. [53] *Ibid.*, May 13, 1871. [54] The New York *Herald*, September 16 and 20, October 3 and 13, 1871; Wilkes' account was published separately in pamphlet form, *The International, its Principles and Purposes* (New York, 1871). Excerpts were printed in *The National Standard*, December 9, 1872. [55] New York *Standard*, June 15, 1871. Young's account was republished in his *Men and Memories: Personal Reminiscences* (New York, 1901), 166–207. [56] New York *Standard*, November 8, 1871. [57] *The National Standard*, August 26, 1871. [58] *Ibid.*, April 15, 1871. The italics are Linton's. [59] Linton's articles in *The National Standard* were assembled in a pamphlet, *The Paris Commune* (Boston, 1871). [60] See his articles in the *Fortnightly Review*, May 1 and August 1, 1871. [61] Cited in Franklin H. Wentworth, *Wendell Phillips* (New York [1906]), 18. [62] On Phillips and American labor, see Charles Madison, *Critics and Crusaders* (New York, 1947), 60–79; Carlos Martyn, *Wendell Phillips, the Agitator* (New York, 1890), *passim*; and Samuel Bernstein, "Wendell Phillips: Labor Advocate," *Science & Society*, 1956, XX, 344–357. [63] A speech by Phillips, printed in *The Workingman's Advocate*, March 25, 1865. [64] *Ibid.*, January 21, 1871. [65] Wendell Phillips, *Speeches, Lectures and Letters* (Boston, 1892), 2nd series, 163. [66] *The National Standard*, July 8, August 19 and 26, 1871. [67] *The National Socialist*, June 29, 1878. [68] *Minutes*, 258. [69] *E.g.*, the issues of February 25 and March 5, 1872. [70] December 28, 1873, January 20, 1874. [71] J. A. Dacus, *Annals of the Great Strikes* (Chicago, 1877). [72] It may be instructive to list a number of the anti-socialist and anti-communist titles: [Anon], *The Commune in 1880: The Downfall of the Republic* (New York, 1877); Joseph Nash, *The Relations between Capital and Labor in the United States* (Boston, 1878), awarded a prize by the Boston Young Men's Christian Union; Henry Ammon James, *Communism in America* (New York, 1879), awarded the John A. Porter prize at Yale; Abram S. Hewitt, *The Mutual Relations of Capital and Labor* (New York, 1878); Jos. R. Thompson, D.D., *The Workman: His False Friends and His True Friends* (New York, 1879); T. T. Bryce, *Economic Crumbs, or Plain Talks for the People about Labor, Capital, Money, Tariff*, etc. (Hampton, Va., 1879); Roswell D. Hitchcock, D.D., *Socialism* (New York, 1879); J. H. Rylance, D.D., *Lectures on Social Questions* (New York, 1880); Joseph Cook, *Socialism, with Preludes on Current Events* (Boston, 1880), a series of lectures, estimated to have reached a million readers weekly. The list does not include numerous articles in periodicals. [73] The following publications exemplify the anti-democratic trend: Brooks Adams, "The Platform of the New Party," *North American Review*, 1874, CXIX; Thomas A. Scott, "The Recent Strikes," *ibid.*, 1877, CXXV; Francis Parkman, "The Failure of Universal Suffrage," *ibid.*, 1878, CXXVII; W. M. Grosvenor, "The Communist and the Railway," *The International Review*, 1877, IV; J. S. W., "The Next American Revolution," *The Penn Monthly*, 1876, VII; [Jonathan Baxter Harrison], "Certain Dangerous Tendencies in American Life," *Atlantic Monthly*, 1878, XLII; Henry Adams, *Democracy, An American Novel* (1880).

INTERVIEW WITH KARL MARX

Philip S. Foner, Editor

A s Dr. Samuel Bernstein has made abundantly clear elsewhere in this book, the Paris Commune was the object of slander and calumny in the American press. Along with this, of course, went a campaign of vilification of the International and its foremost spokesman, Karl Marx. Although Marx was residing in London, he was pictured as directing the Commune from Berlin where he was also said to be functioning as the private secretary of Bismarck. All of this, however, had the effect of arousing curiosity as to what Marx really thought about the Commune— the newspapers conveniently overlooking the fact that the International had warned against an uprising—and led American newspapers to assign correspondents to seek interviews with the leader of the International. The New York *Herald's* correspondent proceeded to distort Marx's statements on the Commune and the International, and the *Herald* refused to publish his reply to "the trash and positive falsehoods" which he charged its correspondent with having attributed to him. However, an interview with Marx published in the New York *World* of July 18, 1871 (and reprinted in *Woodhull's & Claflin's Weekly* on August 12) appeared without mutilations, and gave American readers a clear picture of his views on the Commune and the role of the International as well as a number of other current issues. Marx explained that it was absurd to attribute the Paris Commune to the International which he described as "not properly a government for the working class at all" but "a band of union rather than a controlling force." The International was not a conspiracy, for its aim, openly proclaimed, was "the economical emancipation of the working class by the conquest of political power."

The interview with Karl Marx, published in the New York *World* (Vol. XI, No. 3622), is here reprinted for the fourth time since it appeared over one hundred years ago.

THE CURTAIN RAISED

Interview with Karl Marx, the Head of L'Internationale

REVOLT OF LABOR AGAINST CAPITAL

The Two Faces of L'Internationale—
Transformation of Society—
Its Progress in the United States

What the Association Had to Do with the Commune, &c.

LONDON, July 3.—You have asked me to find out something about the International Association, and I have tried to do so. The enterprise is a difficult one just now. London is indisputably the headquarters of the association, but the English people have got a scare, and smell international in everything as King James smelt gunpowder after the famous plot. The consciousness of the society has naturally increased with the suspiciousness of the public; and if those who guide it have a secret to keep, they are of the stamp of men who keep a secret well. I have called on two of their leading members, have talked with one freely, and I here give you the substance of my conversation. I have satisfied myself of one thing, that it is a society of genuine working-men, but that these workmen are directed by social and political theorists of another class. One man whom I saw, a leading member of the council, was sitting at his workman's bench during our interview, and left off talking to me from time to time to receive a complaint, delivered in no courteous tone, from one of the many little masters in the neighborhood who enjoyed him. I have heard this same man make eloquent speeches in public inspired in every passage with the energy of hate towards the classes that call themselves his rulers. I understood the speeches after this glimpse at the domestic life of the orator. He must have felt that he had brains enough to have organized a working-government, and yet here he was obliged to devote his life to the most revolting task work of a mechanical profession. He was proud and sensitive, and yet at every turn he had to return a bow or a grunt and a smile for a command that stood on about the same level in the scale of civility with a huntsman's call to his dog. This man helped me to a glimpse of one side of the nature of the International, the result of labor against capital, of the workman who produces against the middleman who enjoys. Here was the hand that would smile

72

hard when the time came, and as to the head that plans, I think I saw that, too, in my interview with Dr. Karl Marx.

Dr. Karl Marx is a German doctor of philosophy with a German breadth of knowledge derived from observation of the living world and from books. I should conclude that he has never been a worker in the ordinary sense of the term. His surroundings and appearance are those of a well-to-do man of the middle class. The drawing-room into which I was ushered on the sight of my interview would have formed very comfortable quarters for a thriving stockbroker who had made his competence and was now beginning to make his fortune. It was comfort personified, the apartment of a man of taste and of easy means, but with nothing in it peculiarly characteristic of its owner. A fine album of Rhine views on the table, however, gave a clue to his nationality. I peered cautiously into the vase on the side-table for a bomb. I sniffed for petroleum, but the smell was the smell of roses. I crept back stealthily to my seat, and moodily awaited the worst.

He has entered and greeted me cordially, and we are sitting face to face. Yes, I am tete-a-tete with the revolution incarnate, with the real founder and guiding spirit of the International Society, with the author of the address in which capital was told that if it warred on labor it must expect to have its house burned down about its ears—in a word, with the apologist for the Commune of Paris. Do you remember the bust of Socrates, the man who dies rather than profess his belief in the gods of the time—the man with the fine sweep of profile for the forehead running meanly at the end into a little snub, curled-up feature like a bisected pothook that formed the nose. Take this bust in your mind's eye, color the beard black, dashing it here and there with puffs of grey; clap the head thus made on a portly body of the middle height, and the Doctor is before you. Throw a veil over the upper part of the face and you might be in the company of a born vestryman. Reveal the essential feature, the immense brow, and you know at once that you have to deal with that most formidable of all composite forces—a dreamer who thinks, a thinker who dreams.

Another gentleman accompanied Dr. Marx, a German, too, I believe, though from his great familiarity with our language I cannot be sure of it. Was he a witness on the doctor's side? I think so. The "Council," hearing of the interview, might hereafter call on the Doctor for his account of it, for the *Revolution* is above all things suspicious of its agents. Here, then, was his evidence in corroboration.

I went straight to my business. The world, I said, seemed to be in the dark about the International, hating it very much, but not able to say clearly what thing it hated. Some, who professed to have peered further into the gloom than their neighbors, declared that they had made out a sort of Jesus figure with a fair, honest workman's smile on one of its faces, and on the other a murderous, conspirator's scowl. Would he light up the case of mystery in which the theory dwelt?

The professor laughed, chuckled a little I fancied, at the thought that we were so frightened of him. "There is no mystery to clear up dear sir," he began, in a very polished form of the Hans Breitmann dialect, "except perhaps the mystery of human stupidity in those who perpetually ignore the fact that our association is a public one and that the fullest reports of its proceedings are published for all who care to read them. You may buy our rules for a penny, and a shilling laid out in pamphlets will teach you almost as much about us as we know ourselves."

R.—Almost—yes, perhaps so; but will not the something I shall not know constitute the all-important reservation. To be quite frank with you, and to put the case as it strikes an outside observer, this general claim of depreciation of you must mean something more than the ignorant ill-will of the multitude. And it is still pertinent to ask even after what you have told me, what is the International Society?

Dr. M.—You have only to look at the individuals of which it is composed—workmen.

R.—Yes, but the soldier need be no exponent of the statecraft that sets him in motion. I know some of your members, and I can believe that they are not of the stuff of which conspirators are made. Besides, a secret shared by a million men would be no secret at all. But what if these were only the instruments in the hands of a bold, and I hope you will forgive me for adding, not over scrupulous conclave.

Dr. M.—There is nothing to prove it.

R.—The last Paris insurrection?

Dr. M.—I demand firstly the proof that there was any plot at all— that anything happened that was not the legitimate effect of the circumstances of the moment; or the plot granted, I demand the proofs of the participation in it of the International Association.

R.—The presence in the communal body of so many members of the association.

Dr. M.—Then it was a plot of the Freemasons, too, for their share in the work as individuals was by no means a slight one. I should not be surprised, indeed, to find the Pope setting down the whole insurrection to their account. But try another explanation. The insurrection in Paris was made by the workmen of Paris. The ablest of the workmen must necessarily have been its leaders and administrators; but the ablest of the workmen happen also to be members of the International Association. Yet the association as such may in no way be responsible for their action.

R.—It will still seem otherwise to the world. People talk of secret instructions from London, and even grants of money. Can it be affirmed that the alleged openness of the association's proceedings precludes all secrecy of communication?

Dr. M.—What association ever formed carried on its work without private as well as public agencies? But to talk of secret instruction from London, as of decrees in the matter of faith and morals from some centre of Papal domination and intrigue is wholly to misconceive the nature of the International. This would imply a centralized form of government of the International, whereas the real form is designedly that which gives the greatest play to local energy and independence. In fact the International is not properly a government for the working class at all. It is a bond of union rather than a controlling force.

R.—And of union to what end?

Dr. M.—The economical emancipation of the working class by the conquest of political power. The use of that political power to the attainment of social ends. It is necessary that our aims should be thus comprehensive to include every form of working class activity. To have made them of a special character would have been to adapt them to the needs of one section—one nation of workmen alone. But how could all men be asked to unite to further the objects of a few. To have done that the association must have forfeited its title of International. The association does not dictate the form of political movements; it only requires a pledge as to their end. It is a network of affiliated societies spreading all over the world of labor. In each part of the world some special aspect of the problem presents itself, and the workmen there address themselves to its consideration in their own way. Combinations among workmen cannot be absolutely identical in detail in Newcastle and in Barcelona, in London and in Berlin. In England, for instance, the way to show political power lies open to the working class. Insurrection would be madness where peaceful agitation would more swiftly and surely do the work. In France a hundred laws of repression and a moral antagonism between classes seem to necessitate the violent solution of social war. The choice of that solution is the affair of the working classes of that country. The International does not presume to dictate in the matter and hardly to advise. But to every movement it accords its sympathy and its aid within the limits assigned by its own laws.

R.—And what is the nature of that aid?

Dr. M.—To give an example, one of the commonest forms of the movement for emancipation is that of strikes. Formerly, when a strike took place in one country it was defeated by the importation of workmen from another. The International has nearly stopped all that. It receives information of the intended strike, it spreads that information among its members, who at once see that for them the seat of the struggle must be forbidden ground. The masters are thus left alone to reckon with their men. In most cases the men require no other aid than that. Their own subscriptions or those of the societies to which they are more immediately affiliated supply them with funds, but should the pressure upon them become too heavy and the strike be one of which the association approves, their necessities are supplied out of the common purse. By these means a strike of the cigar-makers of Barcelona was brought to a victorious issue the other day. But the society has no interest in strikes, though it supports them under certain conditions. It cannot possibly gain by them in a pecuniary point of view, but it may easily lose. Let us sum it all up in a word. The working classes remain poor amid the increase of wealth, wretched among the increase of luxury. Their material privation dwarfs their moral as well as their physical stature. They cannot rely on others for a remedy. It has become then with them an imperative necessity to take their own case in hand. They must revise the relations between themselves and the capitalists and landlords, and that means they must transform society. This is the general end of every known workmen's organization; land and labor leagues, trade and friendly societies, co-operative stores and co-operative production are but means towards it. To establish a perfect solidarity between these organizations is the business of the International Association. Its influence is beginning to be felt everywhere. Two papers spread its views in Spain, three in Germany, the same number in Austria and in Holland, six in Belgium, and six in Switzerland. And now that I have told you what the International is you may, perhaps, be in a position to form your own opinion as to its pretended plots.

R.—I do not quite understand you.

Dr. M.—Do you not see that the old society, wanting strength to meet it with its own weapons of discussion and combination, is obliged to resort to the fraud of fixing upon it the imputation of conspiracy?

R.—But the French police declare that they are in a position to prove its complicity in the late affair, to say nothing of preceding attempts.

Dr. M.—But we will say something of those attempts, if you please, because they best serve to test the gravity of all the charges of conspiracy brought against the International. You remember the last "plot" but one. A plebiscite had been announced. Many of the electors were known to be wavering. They had no longer a keen sense of the value of the im-

76

perial rule, having come to disbelieve in those threatened dangers of society from which it was supposed to have saved them. A new bugbear was wanted. The police undertook to find one. All combinations of workmen being hateful to them, they naturally owed the International an ill-turn. A happy thought inspired them. What if they should select the International for their bugbear, and thus at once discredit that society and curry favor for the imperial cause. Out of that happy thought came the ridiculous "plot" against the Emperor's life—as if we wanted to kill the wretched old fellow. They seized the leading members of the International. They manufactured evidence. They prepared their case for trial, and in the meantime they had their plebiscite. But the intended comedy was too obviously but a broad, coarse farce. Intelligent Europe, which witnessed the spectacle, was not deceived for a moment as to its character, and only the French peasant elector was befooled. Your English papers reported the beginning of the miserable affair; they forgot to notice the end. The French judges admitting the existence of the plot by official courtesy were obliged to declare that there was nothing to show the complicity of the International. Believe me the second plot is like the first. The French functionary is again in business. He is called in to account for the biggest civil movement the world has ever seen. A hundred signs of the times ought to suggest the right explanation—the growth of intelligence among the workmen, of luxury and incompetence among their rulers, the historical process now going on of that final transfer of power from a class to the people, the apparent fitness of time, place, and circumstance for the great movement of emancipation. But to have seen these the functionary must have been a philosopher, and he is only a *mouchard*. By the law of his being, therefore, he has fallen back upon the *mouchard's* explanation—a "conspiracy." His old portfolio of forged documents will supply him with the proofs, and this time Europe in its scare will believe the tale.

R.—Europe can scarcely help itself, seeing that every French newspaper spreads the report.

Dr. M.—Every French newspaper! See, here is one of them (taking up *La Situation*), and judge for yourself of the value of its evidence as to a matter of fact. [*Reads:*] "Dr. Karl Marx, of the International, has been arrested in Belgium, trying to make his way to France. The police of London have long had their eye on the society with which he is connected, and are now taking active measures for its suppression." Two sentences and two lies. You can test the evidence of your own senses. You see that instead of being in prison in Belgium I am at home in England. You must also know that the police in England are as powerless to interfere with the International Society as the society with them. Yet what is most regular in all this is that the report will go the round of the continental press without a contradiction, and could continue to do so if I were to circularize every journal in Europe from this place.

R.—Have you attempted to contradict many of these false reports?

Dr. M.—I have done so till I have grown weary of the labor. To show the gross carelessness with which they are concocted I may mention that in one of them I saw Felix Pyat set down as a member of the International.

R.—And he is not so?

Dr. M.—The association could hardly have found room for such a wild man. He was once presumptuous enough to issue a rash proclamation in our name, but it was instantly disavowed, though, to do them justice, the press of course ignored the disavowal.

R.—And Mazzini, is he a member of your body?

Dr. M.—(laughing)—Ah, no. We should have made but little progress if we had not got beyond the range of his ideas.

R.—You surprise me. I should certainly have thought that he represented the most advanced views.

Dr. M.—He represents nothing better than the old idea of a middle-class republic. We seek no part with the middle class. He has fallen far to the rear of the modern movement as the German professors, who, nevertheless, are still considered in Europe as the apostles of the cultured democratism of the future. They were so at one time—before '48, perhaps, when the German middle class, in the English sense, had scarcely attained its proper development. But now they have gone over bodily to the reaction, and the proletariat knows them no more.

R.—Some people have thought they saw signs of a positivist element in your organization.

Dr. M.—No such thing. We have positivists among us, and others not of our body who work as well. But this is not by virtue of their philosophy, which will have nothing to do with popular government, as we understand it, and which seeks only to put a new hierarchy in place of the old one.

R.—It seems to me, then, that the leaders of the new international movement have had to form a philosophy as well as an association for themselves.

Dr. M.—Precisely. It is hardly likely, for instance, that we could hope to prosper in our war against capital if we derive our tactics, say from the political economy of Mill. He has traced one kind of relationship between labor and capital. We hope to show that it is possible to establish another.

R.—And as to religion?

Dr. M.—On that point I cannot speak in the name of the society. I myself am an atheist. It is startling, no doubt, to hear such an avowal in England, but there is some comfort in the thought that it need not be made in a whisper in either Germany or France?

R.—And yet you make your headquarters in this country?

Dr. M.—For obvious reasons; the right of association is here an established thing. It exists, indeed, in Germany, but it is beset with innumerable difficulties; in France for many years it has not existed at all.

R.—And the United States?

Dr. M.—The chief centres of our activity are for the present among the old societies of Europe. Many circumstances have hitherto tended to prevent the labor problem from assuming an all absorbing importance in the United States. But they are rapidly disappearing, and it is rapidly coming to the front there with the growth as in Europe of a laboring class distinct from the rest of the community and divorced from capital.

R.—It would seem that in this country the hoped for solution, whatever it may be, will be attained without the violent means of revolution. The English system of agitating by platform and press until minorities become converted into majorities is a hopeful sign.

Dr. M.—I am not so sanguine on that point as you. The English middle class has always shown itself willing enough to accept the verdict of the majority so long as it enjoyed the monopoly of the voting power. But mark me, as soon as it finds itself outvoted on what it considers vital questions we shall see here a new slave-owner's war.

I have here given you as well as I can remember them the heads of my conversation with this remarkable man. I shall leave you to form your own conclusions. Whatever may be said for or against the probability of its complicity with the movement of the Commune we may be assured that in the International Association the civilized world has a new power in its midst with which it must soon come to a reckoning for good or ill.

R. Landor

THE PARIS COMMUNE AND MARX'S CONCEPTION OF THE DICTATORSHIP OF THE PROLETARIAT

Monty Johnstone

The Paris Commune occupies a central position in Karl Marx's political thought. Already in his first draft of his *Address on the Civil War in France,* started in the middle of April 1871, he described it as "the initiation of the social revolution of the nineteenth century" which, whatever its fate in Paris, would "make *le tour du monde.*"[1] It represented for him the first experience of the working class holding political power,[2] albeit extremely briefly and under exceptional circumstances in one city.

Since he had always refused on principle to follow his Utopian predecessors in "playing with fantastic pictures of the future structure of society,"[3] the Commune provided Marx with the only opportunity in his lifetime to discuss in any detail the characteristics of the transition period that he believed lay between capitalism and a classless Communist society. Above all, a study of Marx's writings on the Commune is essential for an understanding of that part of his thought that has for a century aroused more bitter controversy than any other: his conception of the dictatorship of the proletariat and its relationship to democracy. This article limits itself to considering this one aspect of Marx's connection with the Commune.

Concept of Working Class Hegemony

From the autumn of 1870 Marx and Engels had opposed on tactical grounds any attempt at a rising in the French capital.[4] However, as soon as they saw rebellion sparked by Thiers' attempt to seize the artillery of the National Guard, they declared their support for the Parisians.[5] In a private letter to Ludwig Kugelmann in Hanover on 12 April 1871, Marx expressed his admiration for the "elasticity, historical initiative and capacity for sacrifice" of the Paris revolutionaries. The Commune, he wrote, was "the most glorious deed of our Party since the June insurrection in Paris" in 1848.[6] The term "party" is used here in the "great historical sense," in which he had spoken in his letter to Freiligrath of 29 February 1860,[7] to denote the movement of the workers as an independent class, as an expression of which he was now forcefully identifying the Commune.[8] In another letter to Kugelmann, on 17 April 1871, Marx was even more enthusiastic. "The struggle of the working class against the capitalist class and its state has entered upon a new phase with the struggle in Paris," he wrote "Whatever the immediate results may be"—and already on 6 April in a letter to Liebknecht he had expressed himself very pessimistically on these[9]—"a new point of departure of world historic importance has been gained."[10]

It does not fall within the scope of this article to consider whether or not Marx was right in his view of the proletarian character of the Commune. What it is my intention to establish—for this is also in dispute—is that this was indeed his view not only as expressed in his famous *Address on the Civil War in France,* issued in its final form just after the crushing of the Commune, but also on all other occasions.[11] Dr. Shlomo Avineri's assertion[12] that "the various drafts of *The Civil War in France* offer clear evidence that Marx considered the Commune not a working class affair, but a petty-bourgeois, democratic-radical émeute," does not stand examination. Marx's drafts in fact emphasize again and again his view that "the red flag, hissed[13] by the Paris Commune, crowns in reality only the government of workmen for Paris!" and that "the workmen's revolution" had delivered "the true elements of the middle classes . . . from their sham representatives."[14]

In this last-quoted statement is expressed the essence of Marx's concept of proletarian hegemony, which occupies an important place in his theory of Socialist revolution.[15] "For the first time in history," he wrote, "the petty and *moyenne* middle class has openly rallied round the workman's Revolution, and proclaimed it as the only means of their own salvation and that of France! It forms with them the bulk of the National Guard, it sits with them in the Commune, it mediates for them in the Union Republicaine." Only the working class could rescue them from financial ruin, as well as converting "science from an instrument of class rule into a popular force" and "the men of science" (i.e. the intellectuals) "into free agents of thought." Indeed, the "principal measures" that the Commune had taken after its establishment were "for the salvation of the middle class—the debtor class of Paris against the Creditor class!"[16] A five-page section of Marx's first draft is devoted specifically to the peasantry.[17] The main lines of its argument are incorporated in the final *Address,* which represents the Commune's victory as the peasants' only hope of freedom from debt. A Communal Constitution for all France would bring "the rural producers under the intellectual lead of the central towns of their districts, and there secure to them, in the working men, the natural trustees of their interests."[18]

The concept of working class political power did not therefore presuppose the necessity of the proletariat as the majority of the population.[19] Writing three years after the Commune Marx explained:

"Where the peasant exists on a mass scale as a private property owner, where he constitutes a more or less substantial majority, as in all the states of the Western European continent . . . the following occurs: either he prevents, wrecks every workers' revolution, as he has done up till now in France; or the proletariat (for the peasant proprietor does not belong to the proletariat and even where, according to his position, he does belong to it, he does not believe that he does) must as a government take measures through which the peasant finds his position directly improved and which thus win him for the revolution."[20]

Such a working class government would be based on an alliance with other classes which accepted proletarian leadership and gave it majority support in the country. Despite efforts to do so, which were made neither consistently nor early enough, the Paris workers did not succeed in persuading the peasant majority in the French provinces that it was the champion of their true interests. In the capital itself, however, Marx saw "the working class . . . openly acknowledged as the only class capable of social initiative, even by the great bulk of the Paris middle class—shopkeepers, tradesmen, merchants—the wealthy capitalists alone excepted."[21] With such a conception of hegemony in mind, he went on to declare: "If the Commune was thus the true representative of all the healthy elements of French society, and therefore the truly national government, it was at the same time, as a working men's government, as the bold champion of the emancipation of labour, emphatically international."[22] There was for him no contradiction whatsoever in speaking of a "workmen's revolution" as a "people's revolution"[23] and the "working men's government" that it established as "a government of the people by the people."[24]

The Dictatorship of the Proletariat

M arx did not actually use the words "dictatorship of the proletariat" to describe the Paris Commune. It was a term that he used synonymously with such expressions as "the rule of the proletariat" or "political power held by the working class," which occur much more frequently in his works.[25] One would hardly expect him to use such a phrase in his one work on the Commune, the *Address on the Civil War in France*, since this was not written in his own name but on behalf of the General Council of the First International with its British trade union members, to whom it would have been unfamiliar and potentially alarming.[26] If, however, we compare the way in which he characterizes the Commune with his description elsewhere of the function of the dictatorship of the proletariat, the identity becomes apparent.

Engels noted in 1872-73 that "the views of German scientific socialism on the necessity of political action by the proletariat and its dictatorship as the transition to the abolition of classes and with them of the state . . . had already been expressed in *The Communist Manifesto* and since then on innumerable occasions."[27] In 1848, in the *Manifesto,* the conception of the dictatorship of the proletariat (though not yet the term, which is first found in Marx in January 1850[28]) is put forward as follows: "The first step in the revolution by the working class is to raise the proletariat to the position of ruling class, to win the battle of democracy. The proletariat will use its supremacy to wrest, by degrees, all capital from the bourgeoisie, to centralize all instruments of production in the hands of the State, i.e. of the proletariat organized as the ruling class."[29] In 1852, writing to J. Weydemeyer, he emphasized as something new in his theory, his belief that "the class struggle necessarily leads to the *dictatorship of the proletariat''* and that "this dictatorship constitutes the transition to the *abolition of all classes and to a classless society.''*[30] There is no record of Marx using the term again till 1871, four months after the end of the Commune. Then, at a dinner attended largely by Communard refugees, after referring to the Commune, he noted that, before it would be possible to eliminate the basis of class rule, "a proletarian dictature would become necessary.''[31] His best-known formulation of this idea in this period was made in 1875 in his *Critique of the Gotha Programme,* where he wrote: "Between capitalist and communist society lies the period of the revolutionary transformation of the one into the other. There corresponds to this also a political transition period in which the state can be nothing but *the revolutionary dictatorship of the proletariat.''*[32]

All these quotations make it clear that for Marx the dictatorship of the proletariat did not denote a classless society with a fully Socialist economy. It was to be a prolonged transitional phase, in which political power had passed to the workers, who would use it to destroy the economic basis for the existence of classes.[33]

This corresponds to his description of the Commune as precisely such a transitional regime already in the first draft of his *Civil War.* It was "the political form of the social emancipation, of the liberation of labour from the usurpations (slaveholding) of the monopolists of the means of labour.''[34] In the final *Address* this becomes the well-known statement that the Commune "was essentially a working class government . . . the political form at last discovered under which to work out the economical emancipation of labour. . . The Commune was . . . to serve as a lever for uprooting the economical foundations upon which rests the existence of classes, and therefore of class rule.''[35]

It is, in my opinion, anachronistic to argue that Marx made a distinction between a workers' government and the dictatorship of the proletariat, in the way that has at times been done by some twentieth century Marxists.[36] Nor do I find it plausible that Engels, whose agreement with Marx on all fundamental political questions is recorded in their correspondence over four decades, should have interpreted either the Commune or the concept of proletarian dictatorship differently from his great co-thinker. And Engels was to write quite unequivocally in his 1891 Preface to Marx's *Civil War:* "Dictatorship of the Proletariat. . . Do you want to know what this dictatorship looks like? Look at the Paris Commune. That was the Dictatorship of the Proletariat.''[37]

Was the Commune Socialist?

In 1881, in an atmosphere very different from that in which, ten years earlier, he had produced his memorable vindication of Paris' March revolution, Marx wrote in a letter to the Dutch Socialist F. Domela-Nieuwenhuis that the Commune "was merely the rising of a city under exceptional conditions, the majority of the Commune was in no wise socialist, nor could it be."[38] I do not think that this statement invalidates the contention that Marx saw the Commune as a dictatorship of the proletariat, at least in embryonic form, although it may at first sight appear to do so. Already during its existence he had recognized how limited were the opportunities for it to realize its potential. Thus, in the first draft of *The Civil War,* he wrote: "The actual 'social' character of their Republic consists only in this, that the workmen govern the Paris Commune! As to their measures, they must by the nature of things, be primarily confined to the military defence of Paris and its approvisionment."[39] There was "nothing socialist" in any of the Commune's decisions "except their tendency," he said, and he proceeded to welcome the fact that the "real conditions of the movement are no longer clouded in Utopian fables."[40] Similar points were made in the *Address,* which declared that "the great social measure of the Commune was its own working existence."[41]

The *Address* itself did however go farther than this by projecting into the future the tendencies that Marx believed to be expressed in the Commune's decision of 16 April in favour of the surrender to associations of workmen of all closed workshops with some compensation for their owners.[42] Thus Marx concluded that "the Commune intended to abolish that class property which makes the labour of the many the wealth of the few," aiming at "the expropriation of the expropriators" and leading to Communism.[43] This placing of "the *unconscious* tendencies of the Commune . . . to its credit as more or less conscious plans" was in Engels' view "justified and even necessary under the circumstances."[44] In doing so, Marx was anticipating the socialist measures that his class analysis of society (as well as his knowledge of the socialist trends and demands in the Paris labour movement) led him to expect sooner or later from a workers' government. "The political rule of the producer cannot coexist with the perpetuation of his social slavery," he wrote in the *Address.*[45] Such a concept was nothing new for Marx: it belonged to the heart of his dialectic of social development. Already in 1844, in *The Holy Family,* he and Engels had written: "The question is not what this or that proletarian, or even the whole of the proletariat at the moment *considers* as its aim. The question is *what the proletariat is,* and what, consequent on that *being,* it will be compelled to do."[46] In the first draft of *The Civil War* he wrote: "The Commune does not (do) away with the class struggles, through which the working classes strive for the abolition of all classes . . . but it affords the rational medium in which the class struggle can run through its different phases in the most rational and humane way."[47]

The Paris Commune represented for Marx a rudimentary form of working class rule, of the dictatorship of the proletariat. If he could welcome in it a high level of *Selbsttätigkeit* (initiative, self-activity) on the part of the Paris workers, he had no illusions about their comparatively low level of *Selbstbewusstsein* (consciousness), related to the inade-

84

quate level of development of industry and of an industrial proletariat.[48] He saw this reflected in the ideologies of Proudhonism and Blanquism, which he had criticized over the years and which predominated in one form or another among the largely semi-artisan Paris workers of that period. There was hardly a Marxist in the Commune.[49] The Paris members of Marx's own organization, the International Working Men's Association, the First International, came from the Proudhonist school of socialism. Contrary to the stories of the anti-Communard press of the period, Marx was neither able nor wished to dictate policy to them.[50] Above all, there was in Paris no working class party, such as Marx had long believed necessary for success and to the creation of which, in one country after another, he and Engels devoted themselves particularly actively after the defeat of the Commune, influenced by its weakness in this respect.[51]

Despite all these limiting factors, Marx expressed confidence in the Socialist tendencies that he believed inherent in the French working class to "work out their own emancipation" in the course of "long struggles . . . transforming circumstances and men."[52] These would doubtless include the formation of their own political party as a vital factor in raising the level of consciousness and cohesion.[53] Marx's whole conception rejected any sort of paternalist tutelage. As Engels expressed it in his 1890 Preface to the *Communist Manifesto:* "For the ultimate triumph of the ideas set forth in the *Manifesto,* Marx relied solely and exclusively upon the intellectual development of the working class, as it necessarily had to ensue from united action and discussion."[54]

What the Commune added to Marx's Theory

There has been much controversy as to whether Marx understood the dictatorship of the proletariat as "a social description, a statement of the class character of the political power"[55] or as a description, in addition, of the political power itself.[56] My own reading is that the concept was expressed by Marx first as the former: the rule of the working class, with its interest in the socialist transformation of society, directly counterposed to "the dictatorship of the bourgeoisie" by which he designated capitalist rule. Later, however, after the experience of the Paris Commune, he added a general indication of the type of state and the forms of government that he considered in keeping with its function of creating the basis for a classless and stateless society. These are suggested broadly in his description of the Commune as "the reabsorption of the State power by society as its own living forces instead of as forces controlling and subduing it, by the popular masses themselves, forming their own force instead of the organized force of their suppression—the political form of their social emancipation, instead of the artificial force . . . of society wielded for their oppression by their enemies."[57]

To achieve this, presupposed smashing the "bureaucratic-military machine" of the capitalist state rather then transferring it into other hands.

This, wrote Marx, was "the preliminary condition for every people's revolution on the continent."[58] Such a conception was not to be found in the *Communist Manifesto,* which, Marx and Engels now appreciated, had "in some details become antiquated." They therefore incorporated into their Preface to the German edition of 1872 the statement from their *Address on the Civil War* that "the working class cannot simply lay hold of the ready-made state machinery, and wield it for its own purposes." This point, they believed, had been "proved by the Commune."[59]

The old bureaucratic state structure was to be replaced by "really democratic institutions,"[60] reflecting "the people acting for itself by itself."[61] This meant that universal suffrage, "instead of deciding once in every three or six years who was to misrepresent the people" in a parliamentary talking shop, would be extended to give the people real control over administration at all levels.[62] "The Commune was to be a working, not a parliamentary, body, executive and legislative at the same time," wrote Marx. "Instead of continuing to be the agent of the Central Government, the police was at once stripped of its political attributes, and turned into the responsible and at all times revocable agent of the Commune. . . From the members of the Commune downward, the public service had to be done at *workmen's wages.*" The first decree of the Commune was the replacement of the standing army by the armed people, comprising the National Guard, the bulk of whose members were working men.[63]

Marx emphasized every anti-bureaucratic measure envisaged by the Commune. "Like the rest of public servants, magistrates and judges were to be elective, responsible and revocable," he wrote.[64] It was a question, as Engels was to point out in his 1891 Preface, of the need for the working class to "safeguard itself against its own deputies and officials, by declaring them all, without exception, subject to recall at any moment."[65] All public functions, whether administrative, political or military, were to be made into *"real workmen's functions,* instead of the hidden attributes of a trained caste." The Commune pointed the way for getting rid of "the whole sham of state-mysteries and statepretensions" (sic).[66] It did not "pretend to infallibility" but published its doings and sayings and "initiated the public into all its shortcomings."[67]

Repressive Measures

These predominantly "libertarian" prescriptions are not contradicted by Marx's criticisms of the Commune for "an excess of moderation" shown towards its enemies.[68] This was, in his view, the result of the Parisians' failure to recognize from the outset that Thiers had started a civil war against them, in which through "a too 'honourable' scrupulosity" they held back from taking the necessary initiatives.[69] In particular, he argued, they should have marched at once on Versailles after Thiers' forces had retreated there following the miscarriage of their attempt to seize the cannon at Montmartre on 18 March.[70] Instead of devoting themselves to mounting such an offensive, "they lost precious moments . . . by the election of the Commune."[71] It was not a question of opposing the election of a Commune, for which (as we have seen) he was full of praise as a model of democratic government, but of the inappropriate *timing* of these elections, which diverted attention from the urgent military task of the moment. As a corollary to this, the Central Committee "surrendered its power too soon" to the newly elected Commune,[72] at a moment when its undivided authority was needed to deal with the hostile troops preparing to attack Paris from without and their reactionary supporters organizing armed demonstrations within. Marx's criticisms were dictated by considerations of wartime emergency. It was also from this standpoint alone that he approved the Commune's suspension of hostile papers two weeks after the Versailles troops had started attacking the outskirts of Paris and bombarding the city. "With the savage warfare of Versailles outside, and its attempts at corruption and conspiracy inside Paris," he wrote, "would the Commune not have shamefully betrayed its trust by affecting to keep up all the decencies and appearances of liberalism *as in a time of profound peace?*"[73] And he stressed how "free from . . . acts of violence" the Paris proletarian revolution had remained from 18 March till the entry of the Versailles troops into Paris.[74]

If, for Marx, a proletarian dictatorship had to be prepared to have recourse to measures of coercion and repression, it should be solely against the minority of its active class enemies on behalf of the majority of the people, from whom it derived its mandate, and only under conditions of civil war.

The difference between such a mass democratic "dictatorship" and one by a small elite was brought out sharply by Engels in 1874 in his article, "The Programme of the Blanquist Communard Refugees." In it he contrasted the Marxist conception of "the dictatorship . . . of the whole revolutionary class, the proletariat" with "Blanqui's conception of every revolution as the *coup de main* of a small revolutionary minority." From the latter followed the necessity after its success of "the dictatorship . . . of the small number of those who carried out the *coup* and who are themselves already in advance organized under the dictatorship of one or a few individuals."[75]

In Marx's writings on the Commune, there is nothing to suggest that he would have favoured a one-party system or any sort of monolithic political structure, let alone a "personality cult." On the contrary, what emerges is a pluralistic conception of the Commune as "a thoroughly expansive political form, while all previous forms of government had been emphatically repressive."[76] In his first draft Marx quoted an extract from the London *Daily News,* which deplored the fact that the Commune was "a concourse of equivalent atoms, each one jealous of another and *none endowed with supreme control over the others.*" The last phrase was underlined by Marx, who noted that "the bourgeois . . . wants political idols and 'great men' immensely."[77]

87

Revolution & Reaction

An Alien Body in Marx's Thought?

It had been widely argued that the ideas developed by Marx in *The Civil War in France,* emphasizing destruction of the power of the centralized bureaucratic state machine, constitute an alien body in his thought.[78] In my opinion, this view is not borne out by an examination of his writings. On the contrary, from the early 1840s throughout his life, there runs the strong and continuous theme of the struggle against bureaucracy. Already in 1843 in his *Critique of Hegel's Philosophy of the State,* he was denouncing bureaucracy as "the 'state formalism' of civil society . . . a *particular, closed* society in the state" which "constitutes itself as an actual power and becomes its own *material* content." Its universal spirit was "the *secret,* the mystery sustained within bureaucracy itself by hierarchy and maintained on the outside as a closed corporation."[79] Opposing the monarchic rule favoured by Hegel, he argued for a democracy where "the *constitution itself* appears only as *one* determination, and indeed the self-determination of the people . . . based on its actual foundation, on *actual man* and the *actual people,* not only implicitly and in its essence, but in its *existence* and actuality."[80] The "atomization" of bourgeois society "in its political act" resulted directly from the fact that "the community . . . , in which the individual exists, is civil society separated from the state, or the *political state* is *an abstraction* from it."[81]

In 1852, in *The Eighteenth Brumaire of Louis Bonaparte,* Marx denounced the executive power of the French state "with its enormous bureaucratic and military organization" as an "appalling parasitic body which enmeshes the body of French society like a net and chokes all its pores." All revolutions hitherto had "perfected this machine instead of smashing it."[82]

Marx took up these themes and developed them, often in very similar terms, in *The Civil War,* presenting the Commune as "the direct antithesis" of the Second Empire with its "State power, apparently soaring high above society."[83] What the Commune envisaged, he wrote, was to "restore to the social body all the forces hitherto absorbed by the state parasite feeding upon, and clogging the free movement of society."[84] These last words were quoted and underlined by Bakunin's Comrade-in-arms, James Guillaume, as "a remarkable passage . . . where Marx seems to have abandoned his own programme."[85] Even Lenin, copying out Marx's reference to the "destruction of the state power" as "a parasitic excrescence"[86] alongside the copious other extracts from *The Civil War* in his famous "Blue Notebook," was led to exclaim: "By calling 'the state' a parasitical excrescence, Marx 'almost' speaks of the abolition of the state." He added, however, in my opinion correctly: "The point, of course, is not the term, but the *essence.*"[87] It is easy to "discover" any amount of verbal contradictions if quotations from Marx and Engels are viewed in isolation. From the context in this case, it is clear that the state power that Marx wished to destroy was specifically "the State power which claimed to be the embodiment of (a national) unity independent of, and superior to, the nation itself."[88] This state, acting as "the master instead of the servant of society,"[89] served "full-grown bourgeois society" as "a means for the enslavement of labour by capital."[90] The Commune stood for the destruction of *such* a state and its replacement by one of a new type, in which "the merely repressive organs of the old governmental power were to be amputated," whilst "its legitimate functions were to be wrested from an authority usurping preeminence over society itself, and restored to the responsible agents of society."[91]

Centralism and Local Autonomy

Did Marx's *Civil War in France* represent theoretically "a partial retreat of Marxism in the face of Proudhonism"?[92] Was Marx now championing the standpoint, which he had opposed in the International, of the French Proudhonists who wanted "everything to be dissolved into small 'groups' or 'communes,' which in turn form an 'association,' but no state"?[93] A close examination of the text does not support such a conclusion despite its superficial plausibility.

In his first draft, Marx showed that in a France "organized into self-working and selfgoverning communes" the "state-functions" would not disappear but would be "reduced to a few functions for general national purposes."[94] In the *Address* he emphasized:

"The few but important functions which would remain for a central government were not to be suppressed, as has been intentionally mis-stated, but were to be discharged by Communal, and therefore strictly responsible agents. The unity of the nation was not to be broken, but, on the contrary, to be organized by the Communal Constitution."

And, in case there should still be any doubt, he went on: "The Communal Constitution has been mistaken

for an attempt to break up into a federation of small States, as dreamt of by Montesquieu and the Girondins, that unity of great nations which, if originally brought about by political force, has now become a powerful coefficient of social production. The antagonism of the Commune against the State power has been mistaken for an exaggerated form of the ancient struggle against over-centralization."[95]

Moreover, Marx made it clear that "united co-operative societies are to regulate national production upon a common plan,"[96] thereby securing the centralization of the economic system to which the *Communist Manifesto* had attached so much importance.[97]

Marx had always been and remained a centralist. However for him, as for subsequent Marxists, the issue was not one of centralization versus decentralization, but of finding the right balance between the two. The equilibrium was inevitably a shifting one, varying from one country to another and as between different historical periods. In 1848–50, he saw the strongest possible centralization as the *sine qua non* of the bourgeois-democratic revolution in Germany directed against the feudal absolutism entrenched in its petty principalities.[98] In France, in 1871, the problem was of the opposite character. Already in 1852, in his *Eighteenth Brumaire,* Marx had pointed to "the most extraordinary centralization" of the French bourgeois state which found its counterpart "in the helpless dependence, in the loose shapelessness of the actual body politic."[99] Even "a bridge, a schoolhouse and the communal property of a village community" were "snatched from the activity of society's members themselves and made the object of government activity."[100] One can hardly charge Marx with inconsistency for not putting forward the same demands in a proletarian revolution directed against such bureaucratic-capitalist overcentralization as he had in a bourgeois democratic revolution against feudal particularism!

The democratic transformation initiated by the Commune demanded forms of local self-government that would make possible the greatest measure of initiative and popular participation at grass-roots level, whilst preserving a united republic with a central authority. The programme of the Commune—the Declaration to the French People of 19 April—incorporated both these elements.[101] (The fact that the Commune adopted it unanimously minus one vote bears out Engels' point, in his 1891 Preface to *The Civil War,* that in the course of the revolution the Proudhonists evolved from their hard anti-centralist and the Blanquists from their supercentralist positions.)[102] Marx felt able to write approvingly of this "rough sketch of national organization which the Commune had no time to develop,"[103] despite its ambiguity on the nature of the relationship between "the absolute autonomy of the communes" and "the great central administration."[104] This indefiniteness is reflected in Marx's account in *The Civil War,* which he did not think was the place to subject these proposals to detailed critical examination.[105] The more so because he considered the broad outlines of the suggested Communal Constitution as justified by its social essence: the superseding of the old governmental machinery "by real self-government, which in Paris and the great cities, the social strongholds of the working class, was the government of the working class."[106] Except on this condition, "the Communal Constitution would have been an impossibility and a delusion."[107]

Marx spoke favourably of proposals for a national structure whereby the rural communes, which were to be established even in the smallest hamlets, would "administer their common affairs by an assembly of delegates in the central town" of each district. "These district assemblies were again to send deputies to the National Delegation in Paris, each delegate to be at any time revocable and bound by the *mandat impératif* (formal instructions) of his constituents."[108] Nowhere, however, did he try to present this particular method of indirect election as the only possible system for a working class administration, and he was in fact never to refer to it again. What was of lasting importance for him in this connection was that future society should develop organs of local self-government with a large measure of autonomy and scope for initiative from

90

below.[109] Thus in 1874 or 75, in his notes on Bakunin's *Statism and Anarchy,* he meets Bakunin's challenge: "The Germans number about forty million. Will, e.g. all forty million be members of the government?" with the comment: "Certainly! Since the matter begins with the self-government of the commune (*Gemeinde*)."[110] Similarly, twenty years after the Commune, in his *Critique of the Social Democratic* (Erfurt) *Draft Programme,* arguing for a unitary rather than a federal republic in Germany, Engels demanded within it "complete self-government in province, district and commune (*Gemeinde*) through officials elected by universal suffrage."[111]

Conclusions

Marx on the Commune reveals no dramatic turn in his political thought. Paris' spring revolution did however provide the experience, of international relevance, that crystallized into positive forms the attitudes inherent in his long-standing criticisms of the political alienation in capitalist and feudal states. With this, as I have argued, he added a new dimension to his concept of the dictatorship of the proletariat. This entailed a thoroughgoing participatory democracy, combining direct democracy at the base with the election at regional and national levels of delegates operating under continuous control and briefing from below. Such forms were necessary for the adequate expression and safeguarding of the class character of the new transitional regime, which would begin to transcend the divorce between state and civil society that Marx had deplored as early as 1843, and to prepare the way for a classless and stateless society.

The Commune, in the seventy-two days of its existence, could but suggest the first steps to be taken along this road, and Marx felt himself obliged to extrapolate some of the others from the tendencies that he perceived in it. His views were therefore only a first outline, derived from this particular "model,"[112] which reflected a localized experience in France of 1871. It could not be more than the initial stage of a proletarian dictatorship, neither fully developed nor nationally based, whose days were probably numbered from the start. Much of Marx's exposition was consequently sketchy, tentative and in need of development in the light of subsequent revolutions. These never came in his own lifetime, but there has been no lack of revolutionary experience for Marxists to scrutinize and generalize from in the last fifty years. It is a weakness that they have not adequately done so, in order to carry much further forward the analysis of post-capitalist societies in the light of these subsequent events.

Yet, even after a hundred years, Marx's deeply democratic, anti-élitist, anti-bureaucratic *Civil War in France* retains its relevance as the starting point for such theoretical elaboration. Its basic ideas, reflecting his horror of giant state bureaucracies alienating man politically, depriving him of effective control of his society and constricting all his activities, have a highly topical ring. So do the ideas that he counterposed, under the inspiration of the Commune, for "the self-government of the producers,"[113] with "the haughteous masters of the people" replaced by "their always removable servants . . . continuously under public supervision."[114]

REFERENCES

[1] K. Marx, *The Civil War in France* (Peking, 1966), hereafter *C. W. F. P.*, p. 166. This edition carries the two preliminary drafts in Marx's original English, previously published only in *Arkhiv Marksa i Engelsa* (Moscow, 1934), Vol. III (VIII). [2] Preface to the 1872 German Edition of *Manifesto of the Communist Party*, in K. Marx/F. Engels, *Selected Works* (Moscow/London, 1950), hereafter *S. W.*, I, 22. [3] K. Marx to F. A. Sorge, 19 October 1877, *Selected Correspondence* (Moscow/London, 1956), hereafter *S. C.*, p. 376. See, also, *Manifesto, S. W.*, I, 58-59. [4] K. Marx, *The Civil War in France, S. W.*, I, p. 451; Marx to Engels, 6 September 1870, in K. Marx/F. Engels, *Werke* (Berlin, 1956–68), XXXIII, 54. [5] Minutes of Meeting of General Council of 21 March 1871, in *Documents of the First International* (Moscow/London, n.d.), IV, 160–162. [6] *S. C.*, pp. 318-319. [7] *Werke*, XXX, 495. [8] It was in the same sense that Engels was to speak of the Commune, in his letter to Sorge of 12–17 September 1874, as "without any doubt the child of the International intellectually, although the International did not lift a finger to produce it." (*S. C.*, p. 350.) [9] *Ibid.*, p. 317. [10] *Ibid.*, p. 320. [11] At least from 12 April, by which time he had had an opportunity to form a well-grounded impression of the situation in Paris through the reports of couriers, letters and newspapers. He filled two notebooks with extracts about the Commune from French and British papers. The first, with extracts from 18 March to 1 May used for writing *The Civil War in France* and containing some marginal comments, was published in *Arkhiv Marksa i Engelsa*, III (VIII). The second, with extracts from 1 April to 23 May and not used for any of his works, is published in Vol. XV (1963) of the *Arkhiv*. [12] In his erudite, stimulating, but frequently highly contentious *Social and Political Thought of Karl Marx* (Cambridge, 1968), p. 247. [13] This is, of course, a gallicism: *hissé*-raised. The sometimes bizarre English in the preliminary drafts is due to the fact that they were only notes often drawing on material from the French press. [14] First Draft, *C. W. F. P.*, pp. 182, 178. Similar statements in the first draft can be found on pp. 136, 160, 166, 168, 170 and 171, and in the second draft on pp. 216, 218, 227, 232, 237, 244 and 247. [15] Marx already formulated this idea in his *Class Struggles in France* (1850), in which he used the expression "dictatorship of the working class" for the first time. "The French workers could not advance," he wrote, "until the course of the revolution had aroused the mass of the nation, peasants and petty bourgeois, standing between the proletariat and the bourgeoisie, against (the bourgeois) order, against the rule of capital, and had forced it to attach itself to the proletarians as their protagonists." (*S. W.*, I, 137.) See, also, his *Eighteenth Brumaire of Louis Bonaparte* (1852): "The peasants find their natural ally and leader in the *urban proletariat*, whose task is the overthrow of the bourgeois order." (*Ibid.*, p. 306. Emphasis in original.) [16] First Draft, *C. W. F. P.*, pp. 178-9. The Union Républicaine was a bourgeois organization formed in Paris in April 1871, which aimed peacefully to abolish the Commune and end the civil war by mediating between Versailles and Paris. This draft contains a section entitled "Measures for the Working Class" (pp. 150–152), followed by one headed "Measures for Working Class, but mostly for the Middle Classes" (pp. 152-153). [17] *Ibid.*, pp. 173–177. [18] *S. W.*, I, 473, 476-477. This passage should not be taken to imply that he and Engels favored a dictatorship of the city over the countryside. They disagreed in particular with the prevalent Blanquist idea of a dictatorship of Paris. See F. Engels to K. Marx, 6 July 1869: "It is a strange idea that the dictatorship of Paris over France, on which the first revolution foundered, could come about once again without further ado and with a different outcome." (*Werke*, XXXII, 336.) [19] Such a viewpoint was attributed to Marx particularly by German Social Democratic theorists. See, e.g., H. Cunow, *Die Marxsche Geschichts-, Gesellschafts- und Staatsauffassung* (Berlin, 1920), p. 329: "In Marx's view the proletariat will only come to rule when it already comprises the great majority of the population." In his *Dictatorship of the Proletariat* (Manchester, 1919), Karl Kautsky wrote:

"The dictatorship of the proletariat was for [Marx] a condition which necessarily arose in a real democracy, because of the overwhelming numbers of the proletariat." (p. 45). However, he modified this on the next page, where he stated that "as a rule the proletariat will only attain to power when it represents the majority of the population, or, at least, has the latter behind it. . . This was the opinion of Marx and Engels." [20] *Marginal Notes on Bakunin's "Statism and Anarchy," Werke,* XVIII, 630–633. [21] *S. W.,* I, 475. [22] *Ibid.,* 477. [23] *S. C.,* p. 318. [24] *C. W. F. P.,* p. 182; *S. W.,* I, 478. [25] See H. Draper's extremely well-documented study, "Marx and the dictatorship of the proletariat," in *Cahiers de l'Institut de Science Economique Appliquée,* Série S, *Etudes de Marxologie* (Paris, 1962), No. 6, pp. 5–73. [26] Whilst it is true that two British trade union leaders, Odger and Lucraft, repudiated the *Address* anyway, 19 other British members of the General Council appoved it. (See K. Marx, "A Reply on the First International," 1878, in *Labour Monthly,* London, September 1954, p. 420.) [27] F. Engels, *The Housing Question, S. W.,* I, p. 555. Engels' statement stands in contradiction to—one might say in refutation of—those attempting to present the dictatorship of the proletariat as an incidental or subsidiary element in Marx. Among them Karl Kautsky, who referred to it as a *"Wörtchen"* that Marx used once "in a letter in 1875" (K. Kautsky, *Die Diktatur des Proletariats,* Vienna, 1918, p. 60), and Karl Diehl for whom "the demand for the dictatorship of the proletariat, as well as the word itself, only play an insignificant role in the works of Marx and Engels." (K. Diehl, *Die Diktatur des Proletariats und das Rätesystem,* Jena, 1920, p. 44). More recently, Shlomo Avineri (*Social and Political Thought of Karl Marx,* p. 204) contrasts the passage in the *Communist Manifesto* (see my Note 29 below) to the "dictatorship of the proletariat," which term Marx allegedly "does not use more than two or three times in his life, and then always in what is basically a private communication." [28] In the form of "dictatorship of the working class," in *The Class Struggles in France* (*S. W.,* I, 149). In his article (see my Note 25 above), H. Draper attacks "the myth that Marx took the term . . . from Blanqui," showing that there is no recorded use of the term by the latter (pp. 15–19). [29] *S. W.,* I, p. 50. [30] *S. C.,* p. 86. Emphasis in original. [31] Reported in *The World* (New York), 15 October 1871, and reproduced in *New Politics* (New York), II, Summer 1953, 132. (A German translation appears in *Werke,* 17, p. 433.) [32] *S. W.,* II, 30. Emphasis in original. [33] See, e.g. Marx's comment on Bakunin's statement that the Marxists "console themselves with the thought that this dictatorship will only be ephemeral and short": *"Non, mon cher!* The *class rule (Klassenherrschaft)* of the workers over the strata of the old world struggling against them must last for as long as the economic basis of the existence of classes is not destroyed." (*Marginal Notes on Bakunin, Werke,* XVIII, 636. Emphasis in original.) cf. K. Diehl, *Die Diktatur,* p. 45, who asserts that Marx saw the dictatorship of the proletariat as "only a short ephemeral state of emergency." [34] *C. W. F. P.,* p. 171. Emphasis in original. [35] *S. W.,* I, 473-474. [36] Notably in June 1922, when the Communist International advanced the slogan of a "workers' government," seen by many of its leaders as a stage preparatory to, and separate from, the dictatorship of the proletariat. The resolution of its enlarged Executive Committee on this occasion cited the Paris Commune in support of this conception as "a workers' government, a bloc of the working class parties and groups opposing the bourgeoisie . . . a stage on the road to the establishment of Socialist rule." (See A. Reisberg, "On the Workers' Government Slogan in 1922," in *Beiträge zur Geschichte der deutschen Arbeiterbewegung* (Berlin, 1967), IX, 1035-36, 1040.) This approach is reflected in the later Hungarian Marxist historian Erik Molnar, who considered that "a working class government is not synonymous with dictatorship of the proletariat" and that Engels' characterization of the Commune as the latter was at variance with Marx's description. In his view the Commune "did not arrive at the stage of the dictatorship of the proletariat, it did not go beyond that of the democratic revolution and . . . the concrete definition that one can give of the Commune is that it was a democratic dictatorship of the working class and the petty bourgeoisie, under the leadership of the former." (E. Molnar, *La Politique d'Alliances du Marxisme,* 1848–1889, Budapest, 1967, pp. 217–219.) [37] *S. W.,* I, 440. [38] *S. C.,* 410. This passage has been widely quoted as "Marx's final verdict on the Commune" (G. Lichtheim, *Marx-*

Revolution & Reaction

ism, London, 1961, p. 121), which "contradicts both the express statements and the entire spirit of Marx's *Civil War in France."* (B. D. Wolfe, *Marxism,* London, 1967, p. 147.) [39] *C. W. F. P.,* pp. 182-183. [40] *Ibid.,* pp. 183-184. [41] *S. W.,* I, 478. [42] The decree to set up a commission to prepare for this is reported in the first draft (*C. W. F. P.,* pp. 150-151) and summarized in the *Address* (*S. W.,* I, 478). Its full text is given in Jacques Rougerie's new book on the Commune, along with some very interesting supplementary documents on its economic policies. He insists on the Socialist spirit and perspectives that animated them. (J. Rougerie, *Paris libre 1871,* Paris, 1971, pp. 173-190.) [43] *S. W.,* I, 474. [44] F. Engels to E. Bernstein, 1 January 1884, *S. C.,* p. 440. Emphasis in original. [45] *S. W.,* I, 474. [46] K. Marx/F. Engels, *The Holy Family* (London, 1956), p. 53. Emphasis in original. [47] *C. W. F. P.,* p. 171. [48] For this reason Marx had written in 1870 that England, rather than France, was "for the present the most important country for the workers' revolution and moreover the *only* country in which the material conditions for this revolution have developed to a certain degree of maturity." (K. Marx to F. S. Meyer and A. Vogt, 9 April 1870, *S. C.,* p. 287. Emphasis in original.) [49] Perhaps only A. Serraillier, Elizabeth Dimitrieva and Leo Frankel could be called Marxists, though not at the time themselves very developed ones. (See, e.g. Marx's criticism of Frankel's misunderstanding of his theory of value, *Werke,* XXXII, 474.) [50] See Marx's second draft indicating that neither "the Paris, or any other branch of the International received its *mot d'ordre* from a centre." (*C. W. F. P.,* p. 244.) His private letter to Frankel and Varlin of 13 May 1871 bears this out. (*S. C.,* p. 321-322.) There is no record here or elsewhere of his attempting from London to satisfy Frankel's request for advice on reforms to be introduced by the Department of Public Works, for which he was responsible. (See F. Mehring, *Karl Marx,* London, 1948, p. 449.) This is in keeping with his criticism of those, like Lassalle and Proudhon who instead of basing themselves on "the genuine elements of the class movement, . . . wanted to prescribe the course to be followed by this movement according to a certain doctrinaire recipe." (K. Marx to J. B. Schweitzer, 13 October 1868, *S. C.,* pp. 257-258.) For Marx, "every step of real movement is more important than a dozen programmes." (*Critique of Gotha Programme, S. W.,* II, 15.) [51] Even before the Commune, impressed particularly by the electoral successes of Liebknecht's and Bebel's German Social Democratic Workers' Party (founded at Eisenach in 1869), Marx and Engels were anxious that the International should promote such parties, as is shown by Engels' letter of 13 February 1871 to the Spanish Federal Council of the International (*S. C.,* pp. 314-315). After the Commune this became a central question for them and was reflected in the famous Resolution IX of the London Conference of the International in September 1871, incorporated into the latter's General Rules, which saw the "constitution of the proletariat into a political party" as "indispensable to ensure the triumph of the social Revolution and of its ultimate goal: the abolition of classes." (*S. W.,* I, p. 352.) For a discussion of how Marx and Engels conceived of such a party in differing historical contexts, see my "Marx and Engels and the Concept of the Party," in *The Socialist Register—1967* (London), pp. 121-158. [52] *S. W.,* I. 474. [53] The organizations and groups from out of which such a party could have been formed already existed in the various Paris workers' organizations (especially the branches of the International), Socialist political clubs, neighbourhood vigilance committees, *Union des femmes pour la défense de Paris et des soins aux blessés* etc. (See E. W. Schulkind, "The Activity of Popular Organizations During the Paris Commune of 1871," in *French Historical Studies,* 1960, 394–415; J. Rougerie, *Paris libre,* pp. 73-81: "Vers la formation d'un 'parti' socialists révolutionnaire;" J. Bruhat, E. Tersen et. al., *La Commune de 1871,* Paris, 1960, pp. 153, 162 ff.) [54] *S. W.,* I, 30. [55] H. Draper, "Marx the Proletariat," p. 66. Draper appears to have modified this subsequently. More recently he has written that for Marx and Engels "the idea of the Commune state, any genuine workers' state, is not merely a state with a different class rule but *a new type of state* altogether." ("The Death of the State in Marx and Engels," in *The Socialist Register—1970,* p. 301.) [56] This is the view of Ralph Miliband "Marx and the State," *Socialist Register— 1965,* p. 289. [57] First draft, *C. W. F. P.,* p. 168. [58] K. Marx to L. Kugelmann, 12 April 1871, *S. C.,* p. 318. [59] *S. W.,* I, 22. [60] *Ibid.,* 473. [61] First draft, *C. W. F. P.,*

94

p. 141. [62] *S. W.*, I, 472. [63] *Ibid.*, pp. 470-471. Emphasis in original. [64] *Ibid.*, p. 471. [65] *Ibid.*, p. 438. In his *Marxism: a Re-examination* (Princeton, 1967), Irving M. Zeitlin refers to this passage as "almost a verbatim anticipation of Michels' thesis on the 'iron law of oligarchy.'" (p. 151.) It should, however, be stressed that for Marx and Engels such bureaucratic dangers did not constitute an "iron law" but a *tendency* that should and could be overcome. [66] First draft, *C. W. F. P.*, p. 170. Emphasis in original. [67] *S. W.*, I, 479. This was not fully implemented in practice, in common with certain other features or intentions of the Commune cited by Marx. [68] Second draft, *C. W. F. P.*, p. 223. [69] Marx to Kugelmann, *S. C.*, p. 319. [70] *Ibid.* [71] K. Marx to W. Liebknecht, 6 April 1871, *Ibid.*, p. 317. [72] Marx to Kugelmann. [73] *S. W.*, I, 478-479. My emphasis. Marx's comment refers only to the suppression of "Party-of-Order" (i.e. right-wing, reactionary, anti-Communal) papers and not to the banning by the Committee of Public Safety in the last days of the Commune also of some critical revolutionary papers. (See F. Jellinek, *The Paris Commune of 1871*, London, 1937, pp. 295-296.) [74] *Ibid.*, p. 463. [75] *Werke*, XVIII, 529. [76] *S. W.*, I, 473. [77] *C. W. F. P.*, p. 157. [78] This argument was advanced first by Bakunin and his followers. See J. Guillaume, *L'Internationale: Documents et Souvenirs* (Paris, 1907), II, 191-192. [79] *Writings of the Young Marx on Philosophy and Society*, translated & edited by L. D. Easton and K. H. Guddat (New York, 1967), pp. 184–186. Emphasis in original. [80] *Ibid.*, p. 173. Emphasis in original. [81] *Werke*, I, 283. [82] *S. W.*, I, 301. [83] *Ibid.*, p. 470. [84] *Ibid.*, p. 473. [85] Guillaume, *L'Internationale*, II, 191-192. [86] *S. W.*, I, 472. [87] V. I. Lenin, *Marksizm o Gosudarstve* (Moscow, 1958), p. 90. This is the notebook that Lenin took into hiding with him in the summer of 1917 and which he used for writing his *State and Revolution.* [88] *S. W.*, I, 472. [89] First draft, *C. W. F. P.*, p. 167. [90] *S. W.*, I, 470. [91] *Ibid.*, p. 472. [92] A. Rosenberg, *Democracy and Socialism* (London, 1939), p. 204. This viewpoint was strongly advanced in 1898 by Eduard Bernstein in his well-known *Voraussetzungen des Sozialismus* (English edition, *Evolutionary Socialism*, London, 1909, pp. 156 ff.). Lenin replied to it in *State and Revolution* (Moscow, 1965), pp. 47–50 in the section entitled "Organization of National Unity." [93] K. Marx to F. Engels, 20 June 1866, *S. C.*, p. 216. [94] *C. W. F. P.*, p. 171. [95] *S. W.*, I, 472. [96] *Ibid.*, p. 474. [97] *Ibid.*, pp. 50-51. [98] See, e.g. K. Marx/F. Engels, *Address of the Central Committee to the Communist League*, March 1850: "The workers . . . must not only strive for a single and indivisible German republic, but also within this republic for the most determined centralization of power in the hands of the state authority. They must not allow themselves to be misguided by the democratic talk of freedom for the communities, of self-government." The France of 1793 was cited as an example of such strict centralization. In a note to the 1885 edition, Engels indicated that this passage "was based on a misunderstanding" of French revolutionary experience: local authorities had acted with complete freedom, which had served as a most powerful lever for the revolution. And he drew the general conclusion that "local and provincial self-government" did not stand "in contradiction to political, national centralization." (*S. W.*, I, 106-107.) [99] *S. W.*, I, 258. [100] *Ibid.*, p. 301. [101] See full text in Rougerie, *Paris libre*, pp. 153–156, and Rougerie's rejection of the interpretation of it as a "Proudhonist" text (pp. 156-157). [102] *S. W.*, I, 437-438. [103] *Ibid.*, pp. 471-472. [104] Rougerie, *Paris libre*, p. 154. [105] Although he does make some criticisms of Communal weaknesses in it, *The Civil War* was written primarily as a *"Kampfschrift"* (Mehring), in which Marx saw himself acting as the *"Ehrenretter"* of the Commune. (K. Marx to F. A. Sorge, 9 November 1871, *Werke*, XXXIII, 314.) [106] Second draft, *C. W. F. P.*, p. 232. [107] *S. W.*, I, 473-474. [108] *Ibid.*, p. 472. [109] In 1850, in the March Address, Marx and Engels had put forward a perspective of dual power, whereby alongside new official bourgeois democratic governments, the workers would "establish simultaneously their own revolutionary workers' governments, whether in the form of municipal committees and municipal councils or in the form of workers' clubs or workers' committees." (*S. W.*, I, 104.) Now, on the basis of the experience of the Commune, Marx was envisaging that in the cities such local organs of working class power should become basic units of a proletarian state. [110] *Werke*, XVIII, 634. [111] *Ibid.*, 237. [112] See, e.g., Second draft, *C. W. F. P.*, p. 232: "As Paris was the initiator and the model we have to refer to it." [113] *S. W.*, I, p. 471. [114] First draft, *C. W. F. P.*, p. 169.

MARX, ENGELS, AND THE BRITISH
RESPONSE TO THE COMMUNE

Royden Harrison

T hese misguided Communist Republicans of Paris," observed *The Reformer* of Edinburgh, "are doing what they can to throw back the index on the dial of time another century. . . . We have even less sympathy with the wealthy monopolists. . . But we have even less sympathy with the socialist sentiment which would confiscate the property of the industrious, well-doing artisan for the benefit of his lazy and profligate fellow-labourer."[1] Before the fall of the Commune, *The Reformer* discovered some virtue in the demand for Communal liberties and dissociated itself from abusive references to the Communards, but its attitude towards events in Paris lends support to the view that the British workmen were a world away from the attitudes and ambitions of the Parisian wage-earners.[2]

According to Engels, the English working class disgraced itself terribly during the Paris Commune. While their Parisian brothers fought upon the barricades the English displayed a disgraceful apathy and indifference.[3] His charge may be made to seem eminently plausible. Who were the defectors from the General Council of the I.W.M.A. who did not dare to append their names to the 'Address' on the *Civil War in France?* Why, those champions of the London proletariat, George Odger and Benjamin Lucraft. And who came to the comfort and aid of Odger and Lucraft but those heroes of 'advanced thought' (as it was understood in England)— Bradlaugh and Holyoake. Where was the schoolmaster of London Trades Unionism, T. J. Dunning of the Bookbinders? Why, he was proving that the Communards must be mad since they contemplated the abolition of rent and God knows what other immutable economic categories![4] As for George Potter, who had so recently appeared as Ogre Extraordinary to the whole of bourgeois society, he was helping Baron Rothschild to raise money to help get the Paris workers' tools out of pawn:—and doing this just at the moment when the Parisians were abolishing the pawnshops![5] What a superb illustration of Marx' contention that the English workmen had all the material condition required for the social revolution, but were woefully deficient in the capacity for generalization and in revolutionary ardour![6] Yet, Engels was mistaken. The English working class responded to the events in Paris in a manner which was clearly distinct from that of all other social classes.

During the year of the Commune there was one, and only one, explicit and direct discussion of the response of English workers.[7] It appeared in *Frazer's Magazine* for July 1871 and it came from the pen of Thomas Wright, the "Journeyman Engineer." Thanks to his book *Some Habits and Customs of the Working Classes* (1867) Wright had established himself as an authority on labouring life. He was soon to consolidate his reputation with a second volume, *Our New Masters* (1873). Both these books are regarded as useful sources by historians of mid-Victorian society.

According to Wright: "the working classes of this country did sympathise with the Commune, though not upon strictly Communistic grounds." He acknowledged, as clearly as Marx, that English workmen "have not the type of mind for which theoretical or philosophical politics have fascinations, or the habits of life which lead to the interchange of political ideas and the keeping alive and intensifying of political feeling." He insisted upon the reality and importance of the Labour Aristocracy. At the head of the "working classes" there stood a stratum which was more skilled, more prosperous and better organized and better educated than those in the strata beneath it. This 'aristocracy,' he explained, believed that Communism "would make the skilful and thrifty workman suffer for those who are neither. There are thousands of well to do workmen, men who own houses, have shares in building societies, and more in banks; men also who, by reason of the 'push' and energy which have, as a rule, enabled them to accumulate money or property, are among the most influential of their class, and these men are keenly opposed to anything that tends to trench upon the 'sacredness' of individual property, or about which there is any savour of the levelling doctrine."

While Wright believed that the presence of the Labour Aristocracy constituted a formidable barrier against the progress of Communism, he did not suppose that it eradicated the sense of class identity. It was the instinct of class, found in all the components of the working classes, which attached them to the cause of the Commune. They saw that the Paris Revolution was a conflict between those who 'want' and those who 'have.' They thought that the Commune meant bettering the position of the workman in relation to capitalists and the non-productive classes.

To this instinctive feeling was added the observation that the Communards were true republicans and patriots. The English workmen wanted nothing more themselves than to "unhorse monarchy" and they saw that Thiers stood at the head of a monarchist assembly and they suspected that he was nothing but the instrument of monarchistic intrigue. Moreover, they were "unreservedly" and "emphatically" in sympathy with the internationalist character of the Commune and its avowed desire to extinguish national rivalries. According to Wright, this was not because they shared the sublime ideals of international brotherhood entertained by some continental workmen, but because they had a shrewd understanding of the working of the market. They knew that a successful struggle to raise wages in England required the development of fraternal relations with their opposite numbers abroad. Beyond all these considerations which tended to produce sympathy with the Commune, Wright found another one: the regard which workmen felt for fair play; "When Paris was taken there was the most passionate indignation among the working classes of this country at the manner in which Communist prisoners were butchered by the mercenary soldiery. . . ." The greatest contempt was felt for a press which displayed its partisanship when it raised a great howl about the shooting of hostages by the Parisians while condoning the massive butchery authorized by the men of Versailles.

Wright's testimony is a valuable introduction to an appraisal of English working class opinion. However, it is open to two objections: it was interested and it was impressionistic. In 1871 the "Journeyman Engineer" was himself on the way out of the working class and was soon to find salaried public employment. In the meantime he had to cater to his middle class readers by simultaneously assuring them about his own probity while arousing a discreetly regulated anxiety concerning the class in which he affected to be a participant observer. The anxiety had to be 'discreetly regulated,' for if he pretended that there was no danger he would be uninteresting, while if he suggested that there was a great deal of danger he would not be believed. His assessment exactly matched the conditions of his own employment. Wright furnished no documentary evidence in support of his conclusions. He pretended to know what was being remarked around "the workshop breakfast stoves" in the Metropolis, the Black Country, the Tyne, the Clyde and the manufacturing towns of Lancashire: but it is highly unlikely that he had any first-hand knowledge of what was being said in more than a localized part of one of these regions during the ten weeks of the Paris Revolution.

It follows that little reliance can be placed upon Wright's testimony unless it can be supported by outside sources.

One of the curiosities of his piece is that he makes no reference to the working class press. He contents himself with remarking that: "Anyone taking the general tone of English public opinion from the 'organs' which are popularly supposed to embody it would have been led to the conclusion that horror and reprobation were the universal feelings in regard to the Commune." This is perfectly correct so far as the middle class press is concerned. The *Daily Telegraph* dismissed the revolutionaries as "assassins" and "convicts." The Tory *Standard* described Paris as a Red Republic "dominated by thieves, rowdies and demagogues." The Liberal *Daily News* characterized the Communards as "cowardly ruffians" and affirmed that "the most humane among us would not be too scrupulous about the repressive measures which might be necessary." When the *semaine sanglante* duly arrived many a correspondent on the spot drew back before the horror, but the *Army and Navy Gazette,* anticipating some of the values of our own century, called for the vivisection, without anaesthetic and in the interests of science, of the captured roughs of Paris. But the journals which can properly be described as 'working class' held to a very different language. If Wright chose not to refer to them it could only be because he wanted to maintain that they were not representative and that he alone could furnish a reliable guide to plebian opinion.

Reynolds News, founded by the old Chartist, G. W. M. Reynolds, was by far the most widely read workers' paper. Ten years before the Commune it had attained a circulation of over 350,000 and there is no reason to believe that it was not still one of the most widely read weeklies. Reynolds had indeed been the first English journalist to discover and exploit the possibilities of a new commercial radicalism. He created a paper which was proudly plebian: stridently democratic and spiced with salacious tit-bits—preferably concerning instances of moral laxity among the upper classes. *Reynolds* gave its unreserved support to the Commune which it regarded as a model of economical republican and democratic Government. The great point about Paris was that: "we find those clever-headed, noble-hearted men—Assi, Pyat etc.—disdaining to plunder the public, awarding themselves the very modest sum of twelve pounds per month for their services—or less than a clever journeyman's wages. What a contrast does this conduct present to that of all monarchical and imperial rulers who by revolution or succession come to the throne!" Reynolds held it perfectly just and equitable that tenants should be granted a deferment of rents and that the palaces of France should be sold so as to pay off the debt and get rid of the foreigner. The shedding of blood was to be deeply deplored, but the blame for it rested with Thiers and the Orleanists. "There is scarce a Court in Europe that is not terrified at the existence of a democratic Government, fulfilling some of the noblest missions of democracy—or, in other words, preventing the rich and the powerful from plundering the poor and the helpless, asserting the rights of labour to enjoy the wages of its industry, without being diminished to almost nothingness, in order to support herds of harpies that, clad in imperial purple, in lawn sleeves, in ermined gowns, with coronets on their heads, in broadcloth, with no other title to consideration than their bank-books— harpies such as these that have spread themselves over the face of Europe like a flock of locusts, to eat up the production of the labouring mass. Such as those are the curse of humanity, the affliction of the world. The time must come when like vermin, they will be extirpated; and the time has come when the eyes of the English, and other working men, are being opened to the fact that kings, princes, nobles, prelates, and millionaires are not needful to the good government of a nation. . . ."[8]

In the pages of the *Republican,* which was addressed exclusively to politically conscious workmen, the threatening tone was given a still sharper edge. On 1 May 1871 it carried an article by James Harvey entitled: "Paris To-Day: London To-Morrow." Harvey maintained that "the claims of property and the claims of labour, i.e. the creator of all property are totally opposed—so opposed, that, as the present state of Paris shows us, there is war to the knife between them." Was London, he asked, not in the same situation as Paris? "Have we not money-lenders, bill-brokers, capitalists, loan societies, pawnbrokers, all screwing usurious interest from the debtors? It only wants a combination of circumstances— say a bad harvest, and a run for gold to bring the battle between property and labour to the same issue in this country."

If Harvey saw the Commune as a momentous chapter in the history of class struggle, he still thought of the propertied primarily in terms of 'Landlords and the money-lords': of the propertied classes as "the creditor interest" and the working class, not so much as the producing class, as "the debtor class." Other contributors to the *Republican* were equally ardent in their support of the Commune even if they understood it in different terms: what one called "a transcendental poetry" and what another saluted as the highest expression of *la solidarité humaine*. Nor were more practical spirits entirely absent. J. Johnson, identified in the bourgeois press as "the Marat of Walworth Common," tried to raise a British battalion to join the Parisians on the barricades: evidently with but limited success.

Harvey's "Paris To-Day: London To-Morrow" took the form of an open letter to Samuel Morley, M.P. Morley was a great employer, a man who turned philanthropy into a system of business, the chief procurer of labour leaders for Mr. Gladstone. Marx believed that Morley controlled the *Bee-Hive*, the weekly paper which had, off and on, the closest ties with the trade unions and the organized labour movement. Marx was not entirely mistaken. Morley did, indeed, give some money to the paper. However, the striking fact was that during the Paris Revolution the *Bee-Hive* kept its pages open to both the friends and the enemies of the Commune. Each week, so long as the Commune lived, it published an impassioned defence by Marx' Positivist friend, Edward Spencer Beesly, Professor of History at University College, London. Beesly had a real and an acknowledged claim to the affection and respect of his working class readers for he had risked his career and reputation for the cause of organized Labour. However, it may be safely assumed that the *Bee-Hive* published Beesly's articles, not only because he was a trusted adviser, but because working class opinion would no longer stomach the goody-goody mish-mash which it had served up to its readers during 1870 when it had been controlled by the Unitarian minister, Henry Solly. The growth of militant republicanism had made that policy inconsistent with the paper's[9] continued existence.

Beesly began by alleging that the ordinary English newspapers were in a conspiracy of misrepresentation with respect to the Commune.

"On the miserable petty questions of party warfare, on a quarrel at the Admiralty, on a squabble about pebble gunpowder, they are some check upon one another; and from a comparison of their recriminations the truth may be made out. But when it is a question between poor and rich, between genuine Republicanism and the manifold forms of privilege, they all sing the same song, which they know will please the upper and middle classes. . . . First then, I warn my readers not to believe that Paris is in the hands of what our journalists are pleased to call a 'rabble of roughs'. The Revolution is supported by two hundred and fifteen battalions of the National Guard. It is supported by the whole artisan population; and if the engineers, masons, carpenters, painters, bricklayers, tailors and shoemakers of Paris are 'roughs', what are you my readers? But further, it is supported by the lower middle class. A great part of the industry of Paris is in the hands of small masters, employing five or six workmen, as is the case at Birmingham. These employers are all with the movement. So are the small shop-keepers. Whatever opposition exists is to be found among what the *Times* calls 'the best blood of Paris', the wealthiest citizens, the friends of order, waving their shiny hats with delicately gloved hands. We thus begin to understand what journalists mean by 'roughs'. They are men whose hands are not delicately gloved—working men in fact."[10]

Week by week, Beesly did his best to arouse and sustain the class feelings of his readers. On 15 April he wrote:

"One at least of the shameful insults heaped upon the workmen of Paris by our middle class press has been effectually silenced by the events of the last fortnight. For six months it has been diligently impressed upon us that the sons of the men of '48 are cowards, and the middle-class soul throughout Europe has been cheered by the belief that no example of manhood and generous devotion would ever again fix the eyes of the suffering proletaries of all countries upon the Metropolis of the West. So fully persuaded of this was respectable society that it treated the guard of the cannon of Montmartre as a farce, and enjoyed by anticipation the ludicrous figure which the 'Belleville poltroons' would cut when a few regular soldiers should come to disarm them. For there was one thing which it desired more earnestly than the defeat of the working men, and that was their dishonour. It desired they should discredit themselves and their class before the world, and be taught not only that they were slaves, but that they deserved to be slaves—of which the labouring class of other countries might take note.
This idiotic cackle has died away into blank and chop-fallen dismay."[11]

For a moment John Ruskin identified himself with the Commune and proclaimed: "I too am a communist: reddest of the red." But Ruskin swiftly withdrew his support when he believed that the workmen were destroying the public buildings and art treasures of Paris.[12] Beesly never pretended to be a communist, but he, too, was momentarily deceived by the extravagant reports of the work of *les pétroleuses*. (In general he showed an uncanny sense for the proportion of events and for the tendencies which were present). Still more than Ruskin he had a truly religious reverence for the inheritance bequeathed by past generations to present and future ones. Yet even now he would not flinch. "It is," he wrote,

"indeed a lamentable disaster, this conflagration, not to us alone, but to posterity. But I must avow that it is not the uppermost thought in my mind, this terrible

Thursday, 'Blighted be the tongue' that can only prate of bricks and stones when the blood of brave and devoted men is flowing, and the curtain is following on the first act of the most momentous historical drama of modern times. There is something in Paris nobler than her palaces, more precious than her monuments; it is her breed of men, which even the National Assembly cannot utterly exterminate. . . .

"I know the howl which is going up today from the class in this country who think that not Paris alone, but all creation, exists simply for their pleasure and amusement. But I am writing for workmen, with whom life is very far from being a pleasure and amusement; and I think that they will distribute praise and blame with a more even hand."[13]

Beesly was no communist nor was he a democrat in the manner of *Reynolds News.* He held that: "Parliaments of all sorts inevitably govern in the interests, not of the people, but of the propertied classes."[14] He congratulated the Communards on being done with democratic dogmas about universal suffrage and proportional representation. He saluted the Communists whom he identified as leaders of an insurrection which was supported by most workmen on other grounds. But whether in his private correspondence with Marx[15] or in the pages of the *Bee-Hive* he made no secret of his differences with Communism. "I have already said that there are among the leaders of the Commune men whose ulterior aim is to abolish private property. While respecting the sincerity and earnestness of those men (who are probably much more free from personal selfishness than the capitalists and economists crying for their blood), I reject their doctrines. I believe that comparatively few of the Parisian workmen would support them if they attempted to carry out their doctrines. But that does not alter the fact that they are defending the cause of labour. The immediate aim is to preserve the Republic, to secure Municipal Government for Paris, to exclude a paid soldiery from the city, to repeal their Combination Laws, and to withdraw state support from religious sects. In fighting for these objects they are fighting the battle of labour all the world over, and however it may turn out, they will have deserved the gratitude and veneration of all working men."[16]

In the *Bee-Hive* for 3rd June, Beesly concurred with the arguments of Marx;

"If the Commune had marched at once on Versailles, Thiers and his Assembly would have vanished without a blow. But by a fatal moderation, Paris for once renounced her claim to act for France." Later he remarked: "The party of blood, whether in France or in England (for we have it here, too, and in great force), endeavours to treat the slaughter of the hostages as a set-off against that of the workmen of Paris, but *we* will not forget that there were sixty-four of the one class, and many thousands of the other, and that the workmen did not take a life except in fair fight until they had been persistently refused all quarter."[17]

Beesly's fellow Positivist, Dr. J. H. Bridges, also contributed to the *Bee-Hive* in the interests of elaborating upon these arguments. "I have yet

102

to learn," he wrote with reference to the responsibility for the death of the Archbishop and other hostages, "in what respect Mr. Karl Marx is wrong."[18] The Commune, Bridges insisted, defended the cause of "the Republic," protested against the spirit of national vainglory, and showed that workmen, when the need came for it, could govern. "They failed, not from attempting too much, but from attempting too little. Immediately after the 18th of March, the very day after, they should have marched upon Versailles, where they would have found no resistance of any importance." But Bridges was not content merely to follow Marx in those matters in which Beesly had already anticipated him. He discovered a further failing of the Commune, and in doing so might almost be considered to have anticipated Lenin. "The Communals of Paris," wrote Bridges,

"shared with the whole revolutionary party throughout Europe, the grand want of definite convictions of a Social Faith. And the inevitable results of that want followed: doubt and mistrust of one another among the leaders; anarchy and insubordination among the ranks. The aspirations of the Commune were most noble. But the clear insight, the sure guidance and the prompt obedience, without which failure was certain, were not there. . . . Take the essential question, the question of capital and labour. Some of the Communals were Communists; some were not. . . . Until men are agreed on this essential question, no great success can be achieved in the cause of labour. . . . The Revolutionist of France or England has yet to learn a lesson from the Prussian soldier and from the Jesuit priest. His faith is nobler than theirs, for his rises above the narrow spirit of nationality, and he prefers, or, at least, is ready to prefer, the religion of humanity to the religion which confines salvation to a single sect. But the Prussian soldier has learnt how to obey. The Jesuit has learnt how to sacrifice his personal vanity to the cause which he serves. Let Republicans learn these lessons."[19]

Despite—indeed, partly thanks to their extraordinary crotchets—the English Positivists were peculiarly well equipped to lead the English defence of the Commune. The pedantic detail with which their master, Auguste Comte, had mapped out the future course of human development seemed to be confirmed by events. Comte prepared them for Paris and its workmen to set themselves in the van of human progress. He encouraged them to expect that she would combine Republicanism with decentralization and even with the temporary dictatorship of a great proletarian Governor. He knew that the intellectuals (positivist Priests) must align themselves with the proletariat against the capitalists, not to establish communism, but rather the "moralization" of capitalism.[20]

It was this theoretic standpoint, together with the special information which was supplied to him by his co-religionists within Paris, that allowed Frederic Harrison to write an 'instant' history of the Commune which has still much to be said for it when it is compared with the conclusions of later-day scholars. (Harrison was the architect of the Trade Union Act of 1871 and had, perhaps, still greater claims upon the regard of workmen than Beesly or Bridges.)

"This struggle" asked Harrison,

"of the capital against the provinces, of the great cities against the country, of the Republic against the Monarchy, of communal against Parliamentary government—what does it mean?" And he answered "There is one thing which inspires and causes these. That one thing is the struggle of the workman against the capitalist. It is because the workmen in the great cities, and especially in Paris, by their numbers, by their intelligence, by their social unity and intensity of purpose, are strong enough to insist on a government in their own interest, that the capital represents the cause of the workman, as the peasants of the country, whom the fatal blunder of the Revolution converted into proprietors, represent the cause of wealth. So, too, the Republic has become the symbol of government in the interest of the people, as Monarchy is the symbol of government in the interest of the privileged orders and proprietary classes. And the Commune represents responsible action in the interest of the public, as the Assembly represents artificial administration and rivalry of 'interests'.

"And so all these contrasted systems virtually spring out of the grand contrast of all society, those who live by their labour, and those who live by accumulated capital. And the transcendant importance of the crisis is this—that for the first time in modern Europe the workmen of the chief city of the Continent have organised a regular government in the name of the new social order."[21]

Of course, for "les bougres de bourgeois,"[22] as Harrison privately described them,

"The old familiar world has been suspended; but was not dead. It was about to restore its wonted triumph; and whilst the poor struggled for bread and life, Competition and Riot should renew the spectacle of selfish and pitiless ostentation.

"And this, the workmen of Paris, with arms in their hands, this, they said, should not be for ever. Little knowing how to end it or what it might be that could save them they have thrown up this wild veto on the absolute reign of capital. . . . Their great political programme is effectually founded in France; is sufficiently suggested to Europe; and the bloody vengeance of the Monarchists will not blot it from the memory of the future."[23]

How does Engels' condemnatory judgment stand-up to this sort of evidence? Retreat was not among the favoured strategies of "the General" and we may imagine that he would have been unimpressed by the facts arrayed against him. One can imagine him muttering that Thomas Wright remains an interested and impressionistic witness and complaining that *Reynolds* and the *Republican* express the shallow sentiments of a minority of workmen: their tone is at best reminiscent of George Julian Harney in his character of 'Citizen Hip, Hip, Hurrah'. As for the *Bee-Hive,* if it gave space to Beesly and Bridges, it took good care to exempt itself from the reproaches of Mr. Samuel Morley by including the most abusive personal attacks upon them and the vilest slanders against the Commune.[24] Besides, who were these Positivists? As Engels had warned the General Council of the International, the Positivists were not properly speaking a working class party at all, but middle class men whose highest ambition was to 'moralize' the capitalist: who believed in no religion but Comte's:

104

and who imagined that France ought to rule the world.[25] Doubtless Beesly had spoken up bravely for working men and doubtless he made a courageous attempt to keep English workers right on the Commune; but could he be said to have succeeded? Beesly himself, after the fall of the Commune, had contributed an article to the *Bee-Hive* in which he complained about the apathy and narrow-mindedness of London workers. He wrote:

"The man whose nature prompts him to think of something beyond his own personal satisfaction, and who in France or Germany would turn his attention to the larger interests of his class and his country, in England stops short at the interests of his own particular trade. The energy and devotion, which assuredly are not more rare qualities among English than among Continental workmen, are here wasted upon petty and subordinate movements. It might easily be shown that this is a short-sighted policy, even from the Trades Union point of view; witness the contemptuous refusal of Unionist demands in the present session of Parliament. But this is far from being the worst result. The intellects of our workmen are cramped and their sympathies narrowed. With all their advantages of free public discussion, a free press, and right of association, they are less thoughtful, less informed, less earnest and less united than the artisans not only of Paris and Lyons, but of Berlin and Vienna."[26]

One can well imagine how Engels would have enjoyed using this passage! The very man who has been used to rebut the charge of English working class apathy and inadequacy explicitly affirmed something like this characterization! But suppose that he had not done so, would that have impeded the German Socialist or discouraged him from bringing his charges? One may conjecture that it would not. Engels was concerned, not with what Thomas Wright said or with what *Reynolds* said or with what Beesly said, but with what the English workers *did:*—or rather failed to do, in relation to support for the Commune.

However, the implication that the English workers did nothing in the way of meetings and demonstrations is not justified. To be sure, they did much less than they had done for the Republic of September 1870. Then they had raised a loud and powerful cry for the Recognition of France. But their very enthusiasm, shallow and uninformed as it was, now presented itself as a barrier to a whole-hearted defence of the Commune. Men like George Odger had made it impossible for themselves to champion the Commune because of the elaborate greetings and expressions of confidence which they had earlier conveyed to Jules Favre. Nevertheless, on Clerkenwell Green—'our own Belleville' as the bourgeois press anxiously described it—workmen met on behalf of their brothers in Paris. In the middle of April 1871 they marched from the Green to Hyde Park headed by a brass band and the large red flag of the International Democratic Association. The flag was surmounted by the red cap of liberty while the marchers carried other banners bearing such inscriptions as 'Vive La Commune' or 'Long Live The Universal Republic, Social and Democratic." Despite the most appalling weather a crowd of some seven thousand people listened to speeches and endorsed an 'Address' which was sent to Paris. James Murray, once a Chartist, soon to figure in the socialist revival, presided. He said: "It was because the ruling classes of the world wished to live as giants by dwarfing their fellow men—because they wished to live in affluence without working or thinking, that they were opposed to social justice being done, and opposed therefore to revolution." The Address from the people of London to the Commune greeted them in the name of "the Universal Republic." It read, in part:

"We salute your proclamation of the Commune, or local self-government, as the resurrection of the glorious era of the first French Republic, which, in the Constitution of 1793, Article 58, 59 and 60, placed direct legislation by the people into the hands of the then existing Communes. . . . We quite approve your project for liquidating the heavy war indemnity by selling the palaces and appropriating the Crown lands to national purposes; and we can only regret that our fellow countrymen are not yet sufficiently educated to imitate your noble example. . . . The 'Government' of Versailles, if Republican in name, has evinced its monarchical predilections. . . . We mourn with you the loss of the brave Florens. . . . It remains now for us to abjure the impious lies concerning you, and the motives of your enemies, promulgated by our venal and corrupt press, which is the instrument of despotisms that thrive on monopolies of all kinds, and interested in the subjugation and exploitation of the wealth producers of all countries. . . . We, the people of London, believing you to be fighting for the liberty of the world, and the regeneration of mankind, hereby express our profound admiration for the grandeur of your enterprise, and tender you the honest, uncompromising hand of friendship and fellowship."

The proceedings ended with three cheers for the Universal Republic: and the Singing of the Marseillaise.[27]

The International was associated with this demonstration, but the General Council had to impose its will on Engels who was against having anything to do with it.[28] Throughout the entire lifetime of the Commune the English members of the General Council expressed their wish for some initiative, some gesture, some 'address', on its behalf. The task was entrusted to Marx. He nobly celebrated the dead, but he was unable to supply any support for the living. Engels and he maintained the most complete public silence until the fall of Paris. Under these circumstances it was not surprising that some English members of the International indignantly repudiated Engels' condemnation of their class.[29] After all, the International was the obvious agency through which to organize and express the English workers' support for the Commune. It was Marx and Engels who were most directly responsible for the failure of the International to perform this function.

This sin of omission has plainly got a bearing on the showing of the English working class. Engels continually referred to Marx' ill health as explanation for the failure to produce an Address. However, Marx was perfectly capable of writing. During the Commune he collected a large amount of material, wrote vigorous and excited letters to Beesly and

106

Kugelmann about events in Paris, and actually managed two long drafts which anticipated, in some respects both the form and the content of *The Civil War in France*.[30] H. Collins and C. Abramsky in their *Karl Marx and the British Labour Movement* (1965) tried to explain the silence of Marx by reference to his conviction that Paris was doomed to defeat. In the *Second Address on the Franco-Prussian War* the International had clearly cautioned the workmen of Paris against Revolution. As Collins and Abramsky point out, Marx subsequently held that with a modicum of common-sense the Communards could have reached a compromise with Versailles which would have been of advantage to the whole body of the people. Since he had counselled against a rising and since he knew that it could not succeed, Marx was disabled—so the argument runs—from publicly championing the Commune during its lifetime.

This hardly does justice to Marx' quality as fighter and Promethean. Beesly had also cautioned against a rising. Moreover, he was, as a matter of general principle, opposed to the use of force in effecting the Social Revolution. Yet these considerations did not inhibit him from championing the Commune and trying to arouse sympathy for it among his English working class readers. It seems more likely that Marx found himself unable to offer a confident characterization of the nature of the Revolution: or of its probable outcome: or of its location in relation to the modern labour movement which the International aspired to direct and organize. The Inaugural Address of 1864 differed from the *Communist Manifesto* in more respects than style and scope. Each document anticipated the crises of 'democracy', but those crises were of a profoundly different order matched by a shift in the meaning of the concept of 'democracy' itself. The *Manifesto* appeared on the eve of a round of popular revolutions intent, albeit vainly, on imposing from below the 'principle of nationality' and the rule of "the Democracy," the rule of all the poor and all the oppressed. The 'Address' appeared on the eve of the triumphant achievement of the Liberal Democratic State and the consolidation of the modern nation state system in Western Europe and North America. These achievements were the result of various conjunctions of forces working from 'above' and from 'below.' Given this perspective, the Commune might be regarded as either the revival of an essentially archaic movement or as an anticipation of proletarian Revolution without benefit of any prior experience of the Liberal Democratic State and without any exploitation of its opportunities. Was it dusk or dawn? The evidence of the two unfinished drafts of *The Civil War in France* suggests that Marx was torn between these possibilities. Only when the complex nature of the Commune was obscured beneath the wash of blood; only when the immediate issue was no longer in doubt; did he categorically affirm that this was a revolution of a new kind: the first of a new round of revolutions rather than the last episode in the tradition of 1793. In his early drafts Marx attended to the French Revolutionary tradition and to the role of the middle class and the peasantry far more assiduously than he did in the final version. The Commune appeared, not so much as the definitive conquest of political power by the proletariat, as the discovery of a new form within which a more rational and humane solution to the conflicts of modern society might be worked out. Anti-statism and opposition to over-centralization were accorded a still greater prominence than that allotted to them in *The Civil War in France*. But this could not be published. He could not declare, "this is the Socialist Revolution," without making himself answerable for its future conduct: about which, in fact, he was intelligently agnostic. He could not risk the dismissive assertion "this is the heroic last stand of *The Democracy*" without thereby separating himself from 'proletarian' practice and without running the risk of diminishing what he regarded as genuinely world historic departures latent within it.

Accordingly, Marx was obliged to be silent and Engels was obliged to offer a string of defensive excuses and apologies. Further, Engels' condemnation of the English working class must be placed in the context of the opposition which Marx had put up against the demand for an English Federal Council of the I.W.M.A. What Marx had said in confidential circulars concerning English "backwardness" now had to be blurted out to the English themselves. Understandably they found it curious to be reproached with their want of initiative when they had been so long denied the institution which they believed would make that initiative possible. The London Conference of the I.W.M.A. held in September 1871 duly authorized a British Federal Council. If it arrived *post festum,* no one was more to blame for that than Marx and Engels.[31]

To sum up: the available evidence (and there is need for more) supports Thomas Wright's contention that the English Working Class, unlike all other social classes and their 'organs' of opinion, sympathized with the Paris Commune. (This was not true of the "Irish element": at any rate, not after the execution of the Archbishop. Irish hostility was certainly regarded as a difficulty in the way of organizing pro-Communard demonstrations.)

The sources of pro-communard sentiment were most various. In this respect they may be said to have almost matched the diversity within the Commune itself. Its English sympathizers defended it as a protest against privilege and monopoly, as well as a working model of cheap Government. Some saw it as the defence of the Republic against the sham Republicans at Versailles, while others thought of it as the full realization of a Republicanism which was "social" as well as political. It was admired for its patriotism by those who were alarmed by the new ascendance of Prussian militarism in Europe and for its internationalism by those sickened by dynastic wars. The Positivists saw it as a dramatic moment in the breakdown of the "metaphysical" world view and a brilliant confirmation of the insights of their "Master," Auguste Comte. Perhaps most universally the supporters of the Commune regarded it as a rejection of over-centralization and as a recognition that popular government could only realize itself in political units smaller than nation states.

Few of those who championed the Commune were members of the International and membership of the International by no means signified "Marxism" or a standpoint which was recognizably that of modern socialism. Thus, Thomas Smith, Secretary of the Nottingham Branch of the I.W.M.A. and a self-taught working man, contributed a series of letters to the *Nottingham Daily Express* which were later published as a pamphlet. Smith interpreted the Commune in terms of his own "historicist" theory: the law of the Revolution. As 1789 had inaugurated the Political Revolution, so the Commune inaugurated its complement, the Social Revolution. Thus, the complement of the rights of conscience and free enquiry was universal education. The complement of personal freedom and the rule of law was the emancipation of women: "the equality of all classes and both sexes." If 1789 "emancipated the land", 1871 meant the emancipation of labour: making capital the servant of labour rather than the other way round. If the Political Revolution meant the right of national self-determination, the Social Revolution meant the end of the dominance of race over race and nation over nation: and, he insisted, a federalism sufficient to protect the "rights of minorities."[32] Other English members of the International were less original thinkers than Smith, but they were rarely closer to the ideas of Marx and Engels. For example, when William Harrison Riley projected "Our Commune" in the pages of the *International Herald* it turned out to be no more than a programme for community building on something resembling the old Owenite lines.[33] The one great common sentiment which united all the English supporters of the Paris Revolution was *class feeling*. The middle class had taken its side; the workers and their allies must take theirs. But in England violence was not 'agenda.'

Despite the large sales of *The Civil War in France*, it was not until the eighteen eighties that any large number of English workmen came to see the Commune in Marxist terms. The pages of *Justice* and the *Commonweal* were full of reports of meetings or of processions to Marx' grave to commemorate the Commune. There was no "confusion" any longer between the Commune and experiments in community building. "We prefer," declared *Justice,* perhaps with an unconscious irony, "to stick to the hard truths of historical, social and economic development, rather than to imagine petty paradises flopped about here and there all over the universe."[34]

The recovery of the memory of the Commune came too late (and came too much in Marxist terms) to console some of those English workmen who had spoken up for it at the time. Thus Daniel Chatterton, who had been associated with the *Republican* and who had followed up his defence of the Commune with a pamphlet on the *Revolution in the Police and the Coming Revolution in the Army and Navy,* produced in the eighties *Chatterton's Commune.* Seemingly half-demented by disappointments and

long isolation, his demands amounted to little beyond the physical extermination of the bourgeoisie to the last man, woman, and child. The case
was better with Adolphe Smith, otherwise known as Headingly, who had
served with the Commune in Paris. He was sought after as a speaker at
commemorative meetings where his presence may have given an added
truth and immediacy to the words of William Morris:

Yea and we were a part of it all, the beginning of the end,
That first fight of the uttermost battle whither all the nations wend.[35]

REFERENCES

[1] *The Reformer,* Edinburgh, 25 March 1871. [2] The present writer himself tended
to endorse that view: *Before the Socialists* (1965), p. 232. I underestimated the
British workers' sympathy with the Parisians and overestimated the socialist content
of the Commune. [3] Minutes of the General Council of the I.W.M.A., 8 August
1871: Documents of the First International, IV, p. 256 (Moscow and London)
n.d. [4] R. Harrison, *Before the Socialists* (1965) p. 233. [5] *Ibid.,* p. 233. [6] K. Marx,
Letters to Kugelmann (1936), p. 107. [7] This work, like all other major sources referred to, will be found, reprinted in full, in my forthcoming: *The English Defence of the Commune* (Merlin Press), 1971. [8] Gracchus' column, *Reynolds Newspaper,* 9 April 1871. [9] For Morley see R. Harrison: *Before the Socialists* (1965).
For the *Bee-Hive* see S. Coltham: "George Potter and the *Bee-Hive* Newspaper":
International Review of Social History (Amsterdam) X (1965), Pts. 1 & 2.
[10] Professor Beesly on the Paris Revolution, *Bee-Hive,* 25 March 1871. [11] "The
Poltroons of Belleville," *Bee-Hive,* 15 April 1871. [12] J. Ruskin: *Fors Clavigera:*
Letters to the workmen and labourers of Gt. Britain, Letter July 1, 1871, p. 4.
[13] "The Fall of Paris," *Bee-Hive,* 27 May 1871. [14] "The Paris Massacres," *Bee-
Hive,* 3 June 1871. [15] R. Harrison, "E. S. Beesly and Karl Marx," *International
Review of Social History* (Amsterdam), IV, Pt. 2. [16] Professor Beesly on the
Defence of Paris, *Bee-Hive,* 20 May 1871. [17] "Comparative Atrocity," *Bee-Hive,*
10 June 1871 (Emphasis in the original). [18] "Dr. Bridges on the Commune of
Paris," *Bee-Hive,* 8 July 1871. [19] "The Late Commune of Paris," *Bee-Hive,* 22
July 1871. [20] The most convenient source for the study of Comte's attitude towards
the Labour Movement is R. P. Lopez (Editor), *Auguste Comte: Le Proletariat
dans la Societé Moderne,* (Paris 1946). [21] F. Harrison, "The Revolution of the
Commune," *Fortnightly Review,* May 1871. [22] In his letters to John Morley: See
Before the Socialists, p. 234 *et seq.* [23] F. Harrison, "Fall of the Commune,"
Fortnightly Review, August 1871. [24] However, while Beesly was attacked in
articles by middle class correspondents, he was supported in *letters* from working
class readers. [25] Minutes of the General Council of the I.W.M.A., 31 January 1871,
op. cit., iv, 113. [26] E. S. Beesly, "London Republicans," *Bee-Hive,* 24 June 1871.
[27] *Reynolds,* 23 April 1871. [28] Minutes of the General Council, 11 April 1871, *op.
cit.,* pp. 20, 173. [29] *Ibid.* [30] *Archiv Marksa i Engelsa,* CXI (Moscow), 1934.
[31] For the struggle over the question of a separate British Council see Collins and
Abramsky, *op. cit.,* pp. 24, 221-223. [32] T. Smith: *The Law of the Revolution*
(Nottingham), 1872. [33] *International Herald,* 18 January 1873. [34] *Justice,* 27
March 1886 (I am indebted to Anna Davin for this reference). [35] W. Morris:
"Pilgrims of Hope," *Commonweal* (1885).

FROM A LETTER

W. J. LINTON ON FRENCH COMMUNISTS

NATIONAL STATESMAN, APRIL 15, 1871

These objectionable French Communists are, it seems, notable for holding with some force two prominent dogmas of Christianity: community of goods and a spirit of self-sacrifice. They may not have much else that is Christian: but surely more enlightened Americans of Boston and New York will not damn them as "lunatics and rascals" for the Christianity that they have?

I am not a Communist. I have spent a great part of my life in combating what seems to me to be the Communist error, however respectable its source. I mean the error of seeking to abolish private property. I do not therefore think that I should join in pelting them with the stupidity of opprobrious names. I know their Christian orthodoxy on this point of sacrifice is rendered somewhat less orthodox by their carnal disposition to fight. And I allow also that fighting is very wicked, that they ought to submit to being quietly crucified, according to the Gospel of the Poor Man, between two thieves. Now-a-days Wealth and Power are the thieves, and the impenitent one is Wealth. Forgive so much heresy (theirs and mine), since it is not quite orthodox for the thieves to be the crucifiers.

Yet "they shoot generals." Innocent generals, whose business is to shoot them! "And if they do pillage?" That is just the point. There is no proof yet of even a disposition to pillage, for all the ages of provocation. Pillagers! What do you exactly mean? Do these communists hold land-grants from Washington, or stock in Erie; or are they among the annexers of Santo Domingo?

There may be pillagers and assassins among them. Some respectable anti-communist communities can match them there. But on the ground of christian and heroic life can you outnumber them? The communist Barbes is worthy to stand beside your best—John Brown. "Ah yes! John Brown was a Bad Republican."

I have said, I think their communistic principle a mistake; and on that ground the Republican party in Europe is opposed to the Communist. We Republicans do not want to abolish the institution of property, to reduce all men to a mere brute level. On the contrary we want to make property available for all men, so that none shall be reduced to brutishness through being robbed of their birthright (whether by landlords or capitalists, kings, presidents, or shopkeepers), none too poor to grow to the utmost capacity of their manhood. But we agree with Communists, or Christians, so far as wanting some better social ordering than that of the Bonapartes and the Fisks. *And it was because they knew this that the brigands flung out this epithet of* RED REPUBLICANS, *which men who would not ally themselves with brigands are yet foolish enough to pick up against us.*

IMAGES OF THE PARIS COMMUNE IN CONTEMPORARY CHINESE MARXIST THOUGHT

Maurice Meisner

On the 21st of May 1968, 700,000 Chinese demonstrated in Peking in support of rebellious French students and striking French workers who had paralyzed the Fifth Republic of Charles deGaulle. Over the next week, according to Chinese Communist reports, 20,000,000 people marched through the streets of various Chinese cities ("in the spirit of proletarian internationalism," it was said) to express their solidarity with "the revolutionary struggles of the people of France."[1] It perhaps was not without some sense of historical irony that the Peking correspondent of the Agence France Presse noted that the most prominent slogan of the Chinese demonstrators was "long live the revolutionary heritage of the great Paris Commune."[2]

The Paris Commune of 1871, half-forgotten by Marxists in France, long has been celebrated by Marxists in China—and in recent years with a very special enthusiasm. In 1961 the 90th anniversary of the Commune was commemorated in China by the holding of academic symposia and public meetings and by the publication of a multitude of books and articles devoted to explaining the historical significance of the Commune and the theoretical significance Marx attributed to it. In March of 1966, the 95th anniversary of the Paris uprising was marked by the opening (first in Peking and then in Shanghai) of an exhibit of historical documents of the Commune. And despite the Maoist aversion to specialization, Chinese newspapers reported on the work of "Chinese scholars specializing in the study of the Paris Commune."[3]

At the same time—and the time, significantly, was the eve of the Great Proletarian Cultural Revolution—Chinese Marxist theorists were writing lengthy articles discussing the contemporary relevance of the Commune and the revolutionary lessons it had bequeathed. These lessons soon were to become intimately involved in the turbulent events of the following years.

That the Marxist interpretation of the Commune was deemed relevant for the revival of revolution in China was a view officially put forth in the Famous "Sixteen Points" of August 1966. And Red Guard manifestoes of the time attributed to Mao Tse-tung a statement to the effect that the "Peking People's Commune" was a 20th century version of the Paris Commune and they proclaimed (among other things) that it was now the "true proletarian revolutionaries" of China who were the legitimate bearers of "the red banner of the Paris Commune."[4] In the ensuing months, ideas, images and concepts derived from the Parisian events of 1871 (or, more precisely, from Marx's recreation of those events) played a prominent role in the Maoist call for the masses to rebel against existing organs of state and party and replace them with genuine forms of "proletarian dictatorship." Ch'en Po-ta and others close to Mao frequently and explicitly suggested the Paris Commune as the revolutionary model to emulate. And an article in the August 1966 issue of *Red Flag*, the major Maoist theoretical journal, elaborating on one of the "Sixteen Points," proclaimed the universal validity of the Commune's electoral system and indicated the need for its immediate application. It was the people's right to elect, supervise and immediately recall officials that allowed the Commune to realize the Marxist goal of transforming the state "from the ruler into the public servant of society."[5]

This is not the place to attempt to relate the complex history of the Cultural Revolution. Here it need only be noted that the use of the Paris Commune as the model for the reorganization of political power culminated in the abortive "Shanghai People's Commune" of February 1967, an attempt by more radical Maoist groups to establish "proletarian dictatorship" wholly in accordance with the revolutionary principles Marx announced in his analysis of the Parisian events in 1871. The demise of the Shanghai Commune after a hectic two-week existence signalled the beginning of the retreat from the more utopian experiments of the Cultural Revolution and the beginning of a long process of restructuring Chinese political life on the basis of "revolutionary committees" representing new mass organizations, old (but pro-Maoist) Party cadres, and the army. Although the Marxist description of the Paris Commune no longer served as a literal guide for political action after the early months of 1967, many of the concepts and much of the revolutionary imagery of the Commune remained to influence significantly the new organizational structures which emerged during the Cultural Revolution. And it remains a prime article of the Maoist faith that "the principles of the Paris Commune are eternal" and that only true Maoist proletarian revolutionaries are capable of understanding and defending them.

The special Chinese interest in the Commune, and its political use in recent years, is one of the more intriguing features of contemporary Maoist thought and action. Today's China and 19th century France, after all, are separated by more than time and space; the Chinese Cultural Revolution and the Commune of Paris are products of vastly different processes of historical development and radically dissimilar social and political circumstances. Whatever else they may have been, the Red Guards were not the Parisian Communards reincarnate and the People's Liberation Army of Lin Piao is hardly the historical resurrection of the proletarian battalions of the popularized National Guard of Paris.

Why, then, do Chinese revolutionaries look back across so much history to the Paris of 1871? Why did Red Guards and "revolutionary rebels" of recent years adopt the names, the slogans and the political forms of the workingmen of Paris of a century ago, or, at least, the slogans and forms that Marx attributed to them? Why do Chinese Marxist theorists insist that Mao Tse-tung has inherited (and also "developed and enriched,") the experience of the Paris Commune? If China is a blank sheet of paper on which the most beautiful new revolutionary words can be written—as Mao Tse-tung has said and has so often been repeated—why then is it necessary to look back to historical precedents, and ones which are so distant in historical time and space? And if the Cultural Revolution was a completely new, original and unprecedented phenomenon in human history—as we are constantly reminded (and who can deny that it is true)—then why did the actors in this contemporary drama attempt (in part) to model their actions, and to justify them, by reference to what happened at a very different time in a very dissimilar place?

It is not difficult to offer cynical answers to these questions. And a convenient one is suggested in an historical essay by Karl Marx. Commenting on Hegel's remark that all great historic facts recur twice, Marx observed (with reference to Napoleon III) that Hegel forgot to add: "Once as tragedy and again as farce." If the Paris Commune of 1871 was a tragedy, was the Shanghai People's Commune merely a farce? Did Red Guards who imitated the Parisian Communards make history or merely act out an historical parody? Was the Cultural Revolution really a revolution or only a caricature of revolution?

For the spectator, it is tempting to view the Cultural Revolution as a gigantic farce; so much the easier, then, to dismiss the whole business as a case of mass hysteria. Not history, some might suggest, but an historical parody played out by madmen in Peking under the supervision and direction of the Marquis de Mao. A farce need not be taken seriously and thus there is no need to seriously inquire into the motivations of men who take part in so bizarre a play.

There are, of course, less cynical ways to view the Cultural Revolution and more serious approaches to why revolutionaries who attempt to achieve a radical break with the present look back to precedents of the past. One such approach is suggested in another well-known passage from Marx:

"At the very time when men appear engaged in revolutionizing things and themselves, in bringing about what never was before, at such very epochs of revolutionary crisis do they anxiously conjure up into their service the spirits of the past, assume their names, their battle cries, their costumes to enact a new historic scene in such time-honored disguise and with such borrowed language."[6]

There is a sense of historical parody implied here, but more importantly a sense of the real drama involved in the way in which men make history, how men use the past—and at the same time how they are restrained by a need to retain forms and concepts inherited from the past—in their attempts to create a new future. In the following pages, I shall attempt to

114

suggest some of the reasons why contemporary Chinese revolutionaries use notions taken from a Marxist European past in attempting to bring about "what never was before" in China.

II

This is not the place to reproduce Marx's well-known analysis of the Commune or attempt to trace its complex and controversial role in Marxist thought and movements. Suffice it to note that for "orthodox" Social-democratic Marxists, Marx's *Civil War in France* has tended to be seen as something of an utopian aberration, an unfortunate regression to what was regarded as the outmoded Jacobin revolutionism of 1848. While appropriate lip service was paid to what inevitably became a canonical Marxian text, the entire notion of the "dictatorship of the proletariat"— and especially the utopian revolutionary definition Marx gave it in 1871— proved largely and logically irrelevant to the historically deterministic Marxist theory and reformist political practice of the "maturing" democratic socialist labor movement. For Kautsky, and orthodox Marxists in general, the Paris Commune was an heroic event of a revolutionary past, but one safely buried in the past; it was to be commemorated on appropriate occasions, to be sure, but no longer really relevant to contemporary political needs. As Martin Buber once observed: "What Marx praised the Paris Commune for, the Marxist movement neither wanted nor achieved."[7]

With Lenin one enters a much more complex realm of affairs, for what Lenin apparently wanted from Marx's interpretation of the Commune he obviously was unable (or perhaps unwilling) to achieve. Lenin, of course, in reviving, as he partly did, the revolutionary utopian strains of original Marxism, made frequent and glowing references to the Commune as the model for the dictatorship of the proletariat, reiterated the major themes of the *Civil War in France* in *State and Revolution,* and described the Soviets as identical with the Commune "in their social and political character." Yet nowhere is the gap between Leninist theory and practice more glaring than between the classic Marxian revolutionary principles so passionately proclaimed in *State and Revolution* and the actual policies Lenin pursued during the course of the Bolshevik seizure of power and in the years that followed. It was by no means accidental that the increasingly repressive and bureaucratic character of the new Soviet state was accompanied by the virtual disappearance of references to the Paris Commune in Lenin's writings and speeches after mid-1918. And it is entirely consistent with familiar patterns of post-revolutionary institutionalization that the revolutionary model of the Commune, along with ultimate Marxian goals in general, should have become ritualized in Stalinist and "post-Stalinist" Russia. For the purpose of the present discussion, it need only be observed that *State and Revolution* (however little it had to do with

115

actual Soviet political practice) became a central doctrinal text in the evolving Marxist-Leninist orthodoxy and thus served to transmit to other lands Marx's model of the Commune and the utopian revolutionary imagery associated with it.

Since Marxist theory defines the Paris Commune as the historical model for the dictatorship of the proletariat, it is rather paradoxical that this notion should have assumed special prominence in the thought and writings of Marxists in China who led a revolution in which the proletariat was only marginally involved. And it is even more curious that it was not before, but more than a decade after, the revolutionary victory of 1949 that the Paris Commune model became a truly dynamic factor in Chinese Communist politics.

While the Marxist interpretation of the Commune was known to China's first converts to Marxism in the early 1920s, there is little in the general history of Chinese Marxist thought—and even less in the history of the Communist revolution that Mao led—which foreshadows the very special importance Maoists now attribute to it. To be sure, *State and Revolution* was one of the most influential of "Marxist-Leninist" writings from the very beginning of the Communist movement in China and it was by way of Lenin's famous pamphlet that Chinese Marxists were introduced to Marx's description of the Commune. The notion of the Paris Commune became part of the Chinese Communist ideological heritage and was duly celebrated in standard Marxist-Leninist fashion over the years, but prior to very recent years there is nothing distinctive about Chinese Marxist comments and commentaries on the subject. Indeed, one searches in vain for even passing references to the Paris Commune in *The Selected Works of Mao Tse-tung*.

Given the nature of the revolutionary situation in China, there is, of course, no particular reason why Mao should have been drawn to the writings of Marx and Lenin on the Commune. For the Maoist strategy of mobilizing revolutionary peasant armies in the countryside to surround and eventually overwhelm the non-revolutionary cities, nothing could have been less relevant than the classic model of urban proletarian revolution presented in *The Civil War in France*. The faith in the revolutionary self-activity of the urban proletariat which Marx so passionately praised in his description of the Paris Commune was totally incongruous with Mao's ardent faith in the revolutionary creativity of the rural masses and his long-standing distrust of the revolutionary capacities of the Chinese urban working class—and incongruous with his powerful anti-urban biases in general. Moreover, in 20th century China (unlike 19th century France or Czarist Russia), there was no powerful, centralized bureaucratic state to destroy; rather the revolutionary task in China, as Mao perceived it and practiced it for two decades, was to build new military and political organizational nuclei in an historical situation characterized by incredible political disintegration and fragmentation—and to do so in a process of

116

"protracted revolutionary warfare." Thus the central theme of Marx's interpretation of the Paris Commune—the need to "smash" the existing centralized bureaucratic-military state apparatus and replace it with an entirely new form of political organization (the proletarian dictatorship) which would return to society as a whole the powers which had been usurped by the state—was simply largely irrelevant to Chinese historical conditions prior to 1949.

Nor did Marxist-Leninist writings on the Paris Commune provide even ideological support for the Chinese Communist revolution or the post-1949 Chinese People's Republic. Whereas the Marxian significance of the Commune was that it was the model for the dictatorship of the proletariat, in Maoist theory (until recent years) proletarian dictatorship was explicitly rejected as an unsuitable revolutionary formula for a country characterized by "semi-feudal" and "semi-colonial" conditions—and, in fact, was proclaimed to be unnecessary for the eventual achievement of socialism and communism. According to the Maoist modification of the Leninist notion of a "two-stage" revolutionary process for "precapitalist" lands, the Chinese revolution was to result in the establishment of "a new-democratic state," a "joint dictatorship" based on an alliance of the four "democratic classes" of workers, peasants, petty bourgeoisie, and national bourgeoisie. While this alliance of classes was to be led by the "proletariat," i.e. the Chinese Communist Party, Chinese historical conditions dictated, according to Mao, "a particular form of state and political power," a system of "new democracy" that was to be "different in principle from a socialist state under proletarian dictatorship" and one "distinguished from the Russian system."[8]

These views about a distinctively Chinese form of state, suggested in Mao's writings between 1939–1945, were reaffirmed and summarized in 1949. With the revolutionary victory of that year, and on the eve of the formal establishment of the People's Republic, Mao proclaimed not the inauguration of "the dictatorship of the proletariat" but rather "the people's democratic dictatorship," a term which became duly enshrined in the Constitution of 1954. What is noteworthy about Mao's well-known essay on that topic, and generally characteristic of Maoist theoretical writings until 1956, is the view that a socialist society could be built in China without the necessity of the dictatorship of the proletariat. While Mao, in 1949, presented the classical Marxist vision of an eventual classless society, the achievement of which meant that "parties and the state machinery" would "lose their function, cease to be necessary (and) therefore gradually wither away and end their historial mission," this Chinese road to socialism and communism was to be travelled through "the people's dictatorship," not the dictatorship of the proletariat.[9] But the road to socialism and communism was to be a long one, Mao implied, and the immediate needs of the time (as opposed to "the long-range perspective of

117

human progress") were political order and economic development.[10] In the increasingly institutionalized social and political conditions which resulted from the pursuit of these two tasks, the revolutionary utopian themes of Marx's interpretation of the Commune struck no particularly responsive chords. Although the anniversary of the Paris Commune was one of eight official holidays decreed in the Constitution, this ritualistic observance was no more than merely *historically* significant (to borrow Joseph Levenson's suggestive phrase),[11] no more than part of the general historical and ideological legacy handed down from one generation of Marxists to the next.

What made the Marxian concept of the Commune (and the revolutionary imagery it conveyed) *really* historically significant and a truly dynamic factor in Chinese communist thought and politics was the unique Maoist attempt to forestall the bureaucratic degeneration of the revolution. The upheavals which have kept Chinese society in almost continuous revolutionary ferment over the past decade and a half are matters too complex to discuss in any systematic fashion here. But specifically "Maoist" policies and efforts of the last fifteen years have shown an increasing distrust of working through formal state and party institutions and a growing faith that the more or less spontaneous activities of the masses (and especially the peasantry) could effect the radical social transformations Marxists envision. The tendency to bypass official bureaucratic channels by direct appeals to the masses (and to celebrate their inherent revolutionary creativity and socialist strivings) is apparent in the accelerated drive for agricultural collectivization in 1955-56 and especially in the communization program of the Great Leap Forward period. Behind this tendency lay a Maoist perception that existing state and party organs were no longer effective to achieve Marxian socialist ends—and a Maoist fear that the works of the revolution were threatened by an increasing institutionalized state apparatus which stood above society and by the entrenchment of new bureaucratic elites (governmental administrators and a technological intelligentsia) separated from the masses and potentially alien to Marxist goals and Maoist values.

It was by no means entirely coincidental that the growing Maoist suspicion of existing state and political organizations was accompanied (in the realm of theory) by an increasing Maoist emphasis on the notion of the dictatorship of the proletariat. Whereas it had been standard Chinese Marxist theory that peculiar Chinese historical conditions permitted the attainment of socialism and communism through a "people's dictatorship" (which, as we have noted, was explicitly distinguished from the concept of "the dictatorship of the proletariat"), in 1956 and after it became a standard Maoist canon that the "dictatorship of the proletariat" was essential to the achievement of Marxist ends—a view that was to become the central ideological theme of the Cultural Revolution. The distinctively

Maoist treatise of 1956 "On the Historical Experience of the Dictatorship of the Proletariat" proclaimed both its universal validity and its particular Chinese historical necessity.[12] Since original Marxist theory identifies the Paris Commune as the model for the dictatorship of the proletariat, it is hardly surprising to observe a growing Chinese interest in Marxist writings on that particular historic event over the past decade and a half. Nonetheless, the question of what constitutes "proletarian dictatorship," and the particular form that it would or should take in China, remained (and indeed remains) highly ambiguous.

III

It is of some interest here to take note of certain political implications of the people's communes. In examining the theoretical literature on the communization movement in 1958, it is difficult to escape the impression that Maoists originally conceived the communes as organs of "proletarian dictatorship," albeit *sans* urban proletariat. The communes were to be not only more or less self-sufficient socio-economic units (combining industry with agriculture and education with productive activities—two of the classically-defined functions of the "transition" period), but they also were seen as organs of revolutionary political power. The noted Maoist theoretician Kuan Feng, for example, interpreted the commune's appropriation of the administrative function of the *hsiang*[13] as making the commune not only a new form of social and economic organization but, more importantly, a political unit "performing the functions of state power" and "the most desirable organizational form" for the period of the transition from socialism to communism.[14] At the same time, editorials in both *Hung-ch'i* (Red Flag) and *Jen-min jih-pao* (People's Daily) stressed that the communes were not mere productive organizations but rather ones which "combined economic, cultural, political and military affairs,"[15] and merged "workers, peasants, merchants, students and militiamen into a single entity."[16] Special emphasis was placed on the political role of the commune, the "merging" of the basic economic organization of society with the basic "organs of state power,"[17] and on the crucial role of the commune in carrying out the "transition from socialism to communism," a process during which the internal functions of the state (now theoretically assigned to the commune) would gradually disappear.[18] Indeed, the Maoist vision of 1958 saw the people's commune as the agency to perform all the social and political tasks which Marxists traditionally have identified with the "transition period" of the "dictatorship of the proletariat"— everything from the abolition of the distinctions between town and countryside, between mental and manual labor, between industry and agriculture and between workers and peasants to the very "withering away" of the state itself. The commune was to be "the organizer of living" as well as the organizer of production; it was conceived as the means to realize

119

ultimate communist ends as well as the embryonic social unit of the future communist utopia.[19]

Quite apart from other similarities, there is a rather striking affinity between this Maoist scheme for the decentralization of political power in the People's Communes and Marx's "federalist" inclinations in the writings on the Paris Commune. The Commune, Marx had observed, was not to be a centralized, Jacobin-type dictatorship over all of France but rather was to serve as a model for more or less autonomous communal units in the rural provinces as well as for the secondary industrial centers; the old centralized form of government would "have to give way to the self-government of the producers" in the local areas. "In a rough sketch of national organization which the Commune had no time to develop," Marx writes with apparent approval, "it is clearly stated that the Commune was to be the political form of even the smallest country hamlet" and "the rural communes of each district were to administer their common affairs by an assembly of delegates in the central town."[20] Moreover, the decentralization of administrative functions into the hands of the actual producers was not relegated to some distant future communist society but was seen as an integral part of the revolutionary process itself, a process in which the Commune (and the communes) would function as political organs for revolutionary social change at the same time they threw off their purely political character. While Lenin later insisted that Marx showed no "deviation" from centralism in his conception of the dictatorship of the proletariat, it is interesting to note that Engels (certainly given more to centralist proclivities than Marx) praised the Commune's plans for a "free federation" of local communes as opposed to "those agencies of oppression in a centralized government."[21] And in his well-known critique of the 1891 Erfurt program, Engels criticized German centralist tendencies by pointing to earlier French revolutionary precedents where "every French department (and) every parish" possessed "complete self-administration."[22]

The extent to which the Maoist conception of the decentralization of political power in the "people's communes" was influenced by earlier Marxian writings on the Paris Commune is problematic. The similarity, however, did not go unnoticed at the time. A Chinese Marxist theoretician writing in September of 1968, for example, observed that "the integration of the *hsiang* with the commune will make the commune not very different from the Paris Commune, integrating the economic organization with the organization of state power."[23] More important than the possible influence of Marxist precedents is that the political function which Maoists originally assigned to the communes posed a fundamental challenge to existing party and state bureaucracies. Had the people's communes actually developed in the manner Maoists first envisioned, centralized political power in China would have been gravely undermined—much in the way in which Marx attributed to the Paris Commune the potentiality

120

to restore to the producers those social powers which had been usurped by the state. As matters turned out, the economic and organizational chaos of 1959-60 (which Mao later attributed to the resistance of a conservative bureaucracy) gravely undermined Maoist plans for the people's communes—and the latter emerged only in modified and disfigured form.

The problem (for Maoists) became acute—and acutely political—with the forced retreat from the radical socio-economic policies of the Great Leap Forward period and the reassertion of the power of state and party in the early 1960s. However one assesses the social results of these policies, they clearly failed to reverse the general process of bureaucratic institutionalization. While Mao remained the master of ideology, others paying little more than lip service to Maoist notions and slogans were the masters of political and economic organization—and of science and technology. While Maoists were proclaiming the theory of "permanent revolution," Chinese society was dominated by the seeming permanence of bureaucracy. At no time in the history of the People's Republic was the gap between theory and practice so great and so glaring.

IV

That most extraordinary historical phenomenon known as the Great Proletarian Cultural Revolution which burst forth in the spring of 1966 was (among many other things) a dramatic attempt to close the gap between radical social theory and conservative bureaucratic social and political practice. One of the most striking features of the Cultural Revolution was the most remarkable charge that not only the state but also party organizations (in large measure) had fallen into the hands of "counter-revolutionary revisionists" and authorities "taking the capitalist road," who, it was alleged, had betrayed the "dictatorship of the proletariat," established organs of "bourgeois dictatorship," and were preparing the way for the restoration of capitalism.

No less remarkable were the proposed remedies. Presumably degenerate state and party bureaucracies were not to be reformed from within—or rectified by other bureaucracies from without—but rather were to be overthrown by mass revolutionary action from below. To the masses came Maoist directives that "to rebel is justified" and to "struggle to seize power." And as the Cultural Revolution turned increasingly political, one of the most celebrated slogans of the time was "the Marxist principle of smashing the old state machinery."

It is beyond the scope of this essay to inquire into the validity of the Maoist analysis of the Chinese political condition or the nature and results of Maoist-inspired political activities during the Cultural Revolution. While much of what was specifically said and done was questionable and often bizarre, there is nothing surprising about the general phenomenon of post-revolutionary bureaucratic institutionalization. It is something of a

121

truism, after all, that the general revolutionary process of social leveling creates fertile soil for the growth of bureaucracy and for the rise of a new and repressive state power. What is surprising—in the Chinese case—is that this common post-revolutionary phenomenon was so explicitly recognized and that the response to it assumed an entirely non-Leninist character. Nothing could have been less Leninist than the unprecedented Maoist call for the masses to rebel against the Communist Party. However that may be, the point to be noted for the purposes of the present discussion is that in the early phases of the Cultural Revolution existing state and party organs were seen (and described) as conservative and potentially counter-revolutionary structures opposed to the general interests of society—and the presumably revolutionary masses were encouraged to "seize," "overthrow," and "smash" them and in their place establish true forms of "proletarian dictatorship." It was in this political and ideological context that the example of the Paris Commune was removed from the museum of Marxian historical exhibits and deemed relevant to the making of history in the present. In the chaotic political struggles of the Cultural Revolution, the "Paris Commune" was invoked as the model for the restructuring of political power and the revolutionary battle cries that Marx and Lenin attributed to the Communards were heard throughout the land. A celebrated Marxist interpretation of a long-past European historical event came (for a time) to be celebrated as a guide for contemporary Chinese political action.

To return, then, to a question which was posed earlier: why did the example of the 19th century Paris Commune assume such prominence in the 20th century Chinese Cultural Revolution? One answer, of course, is that the immediate Maoist political purposes were served. If the Chinese Communist state and party had fallen into bourgeois hands and were becoming parasitic bureaucratic structures, as was alleged, then revolutionary Marxism demanded the destruction of these oppressive forms of political power. The Commune provided an historical example and a source of revolutionary inspiration for the masses to rally to the Maoist call for a rebellion to return political power to true "proletarian" revolutionaries. And it provided Maoists with the theoretical support of the classic Marxist model of proletarian revolution.

Yet the Chinese revival of the original Marxist view of the Paris Commune was not simply a matter of immediate political utility and ideological convenience. More interesting and important than the role of the Commune model in the politics of the Cultural Revolution are notions and ideas in Marxist writings on the Commune which Maoists found (and still find) intellectually attractive as well as politically useful. Indeed, it is precisely because there are striking affinities between basic tendencies in Maoist thought and themes which Marx announced in interpreting the events of 1871 that the Marxian model of the Commune acquired its particular Maoist political utility in recent years—and it is this broader

122

realm of intellectual affinity which makes the matter more than one of purely transient interest.

Although a detailed analysis of Chinese Marxist writings on the Paris Commune cannot be undertaken in this space, several of the more prominent themes should briefly be noted. First and foremost, Maoists draw from the original Marxian interpretation of the Commune powerful support for their profoundly anti-bureaucratic impulses and their general hostility to formal state organizations and representative institutions. What is especially noteworthy here is that Maoist writings not only stress the standard Marxist-Leninist formula that the old state machinery must be destroyed and not simply taken over (although that particular "lesson" of the Commune invariably appears) but also place special emphasis on the general Marxist notion that a true "proletarian dictatorship" must be "a basic negation" of state power.[24] A recognition of the need to "smash" what Marx referred to as "the ubiquitous organs of standing army, police (and) bureaucracy" is accompanied by a general concern with the question of the nature and organization of political power in the "post-revolutionary" era and a deep anxiety that a new parasitic bureaucracy can all too easily once again rise to stand above society. The crucial question posed in Chinese Marxist literature on the Commune—and especially at the time of the Cultural Revolution—is, as it typically is put, the question of "how to prevent state organs under the dictatorship of the proletariat from degenerating into the opposite of what they were intended to be," to forestall the threat of state "changing from the servant to the master of society."[25] (The latter phrase is borrowed from Engels' words in his Introduction to the 1891 German edition of *The Civil War in France*.) And the measures which Maoists proposed to deal with this problem are precisely those anti-bureaucratic safeguards which the Communards introduced and which Marx hailed with such great enthusiasm. In order to restore political power to society, the producers were to be organized in working (and not parliamentary) bodies which combined executive and legislative functions; these were to be organs of social and political action which were to carry out the tasks of revolutionary socialist transformation. Such administrative functions which were socially necessary were to be performed not by appointed officials but by those selected from and by the masses, persons who were to be directly responsible to (and constantly supervised) by the people, and who were subject to immediate popular dismissal and replacement. And those performing public service were to do so at ordinary workingmen's wages and were not to be granted special privileges or status. Such are some of the more practical political "lessons" which Maoists derive from Marx's description of the Paris Commune. The importance of these measures is emphasized time and again in Chinese writings on the Commune, for they are in accord with the long-standing and extraordinary tradition of Maoist hostility to bureaucracy and are in resonance with the ideal patterns of political organization drawn from Chinese Communist revolutionary experience.

The powerful anti-bureaucratic and egalitarian impulses which characterize Marx's description of the Commune—and which receive special attention in Maoist commentaries on the subject—are closely related to another Marxian theme which Maoists prize: a faith in the spontaneous revolutionary creativity of the masses. The non-bureaucratic picture of proletarian dictatorship that Marx drew rested on the creative and heroic qualities of the Parisian workers which he so eloquently praises in the *Civil War in France*. Nowhere does he discuss the role of "parties" or even say much about "leaders." The entire emphasis is on the initiatives undertaken by the workers themselves—for in the Commune, Marx above all found historical confirmation of his original confidence in "the revolutionary self-activity" of the proletariat. It is this that Maoists find so attractive in quoting from (or paraphrasing) Marx's account, even though it is the revolutionary spontaneity of the people in general (rather than that of the urban proletariat in particular) that is celebrated. And thus when Chinese writers characterize the Paris Commune as "a crystallization of the creativity of the masses" and argue that it was "the activism and initiative of the masses which was the source of the strength of the Commune,"[26] they both reflect and reinforce Mao Tse-tung's own long-standing (and non-Leninist) faith in "the inherent socialist activism of the masses."

v

Several other aspects of Marx's analysis of the Commune—largely neglected in Western Marxist interpretations but highly important in Chinese Communist perceptions—deserve brief mention. Of particular interest is the manner in which Marx blends nationalist and internationalist themes. Although the Commune, as the product of a genuine proletarian revolution, was necessarily basically internationalist in character and purpose, the Communards nonetheless were the true defenders of the French nation against foreign invaders. The workingmen's government was "emphatically internationalist," yet at the same time, Marx declares, the Commune was "the true representative of all the healthy elements of French society and therefore the truly national Government" in resistance to the Prussian army.[27] By contrast, bourgeois counter-revolutionaries are seen as being driven by their class interests into becoming national traitors: in the conflict between national duty and class interest, "the Government of National Defense did not hesitate one moment to turn into a Government of National Defection."[28] Thiers, the epitome of bourgeois class corruption, is the leader of bourgeois national capitulation to the foreign enemy—the instigator of a civil war carried on "by the special permission of Bismarck," the solicitor of "the immediate occupation of Paris by Prussian troops," and the leader of "a slaveholders' rebellion protected by

124

foreign invasion."[29] Whereas the history of the Commune proved that the bourgeoisie—by recognizing Prussia as "the supreme arbiter in internal French politics"—was no longer capable of disguising class rule "in national uniform,"[30] the Parisian workers proved to be the defenders of French national integrity as well as the harbingers of international proletarian revolution. From Marx's comments on the Paris Commune, it is easy enough to derive the notion (as Chinese Marxist writers do) that there is nothing inconsistent between a national war against foreign aggression and the international character and mission of the working class. The picture of bourgeois class rule taking on a reactionary and spurious "international" character while proletarian revolutionaries become genuinely "national" in pursuing genuinely internationalist aims is highly attractive to Maoists—for it provides a Marxist sanction to reconcile their strongly Chinese nationalist impulses with their internationalist claims and aspirations.[31]

Another theme of special contemporary Chinese relevance is the anti-traditionalist strain in Marx's analysis of the Commune. For Marx the Commune was not only a revolutionary break with the old socio-economic and political order but also a radical break with the burdensome social traditions, habits and values of the past in general. While in the French situation the focus was on the destruction of the repressive "spiritual force" of the Church and "parson-power," this was to be accompanied, Marx observed, by the freeing of science and education in general from "the fetters which class prejudice and governmental force had imposed" upon them.[32] In the original Marxian conception of proletarian revolution, it was presupposed that the emergent new society would radically devaluate all of traditions, beliefs and values associated with the doomed old society. This anti-traditionalist impulse which Marx attributed to the Commune is frequently noted in Chinese Marxist writings, for it is very much in accord with the general Maoist belief that "material" social and economic change must be accompanied by a "spiritual transformation" which will bring forth "new men" freed from the burden of old habits and ideas. And it was particularly relevant to the era of the Cultural Revolution when the call for "proletarian revolution" was accompanied by a fiercely iconoclastic assault on all traditional values and beliefs.

There are many other themes in Marx's description of the Commune which Chinese Marxists emphasize. The acts of revolutionary heroism and the ascetic values of devotion and self-sacrifice for which Marx so ardently praised the Communards are no less fulsomely reproduced and celebrated in contemporary Maoist accounts. Many of the grandly heroic characteristics of the Commune which Marx extolled are precisely what Maoists prize in their own revolutionary history and what they now celebrate as the spirit of "revolutionary romanticism." Marx's description of simple workingmen efficiently performing the tasks of displaced bourgeois officials and experts nourishes the general Maoist distaste for occupational specialization and fortifies the Maoist faith in the "self-reliant" masses who are capable of mastering all specialized technological knowledge as well as basic administrative functions. Particular attention is given to Marx's comments about the necessity of proletarian revolutionary violence to counter inevitable bourgeois violence (thus reaffirming the well-known Maoist maxim that the masses must recognize "the importance of taking weapons in their own hands") and, as the suppression of the Commune proved, the need for constant revolutionary vigilance and even ruthlessness in the fact of the "savagery" and "barbarism" of the forces of counter-revolution (thus offering Marxist historical testimony to the Cultural Revolution slogans that "the revolution must be carried through to the end" and that "the enemy must be given no breathing spell"). And Marx's general picture of the Commune (and therefore of the "dictatorship of the proletariat") as a community of armed workingmen is reproduced to support Maoist notions that proletarian revolution necessarily involves the militarization of the masses, the Maoist emphasis on the importance of the people's militia, and the Maoist distrust of a professionalized standing army.

VI

There is of course much (and much that is crucial) which separates contemporary Maoism from classical Marxist theory. Marx's faith, after all, rested with the actual proletariat as the agent of universal human liberation and the dictatorship of the proletariat was, if anything, the agency by which that specific (and all-important) social class would carry out its appointed historical mission. For Maoists, "proletarian dictatorship" is not exercised by the proletariat as such but rather simply by those deemed to possess "proletarian consciousness." While the cluster of beliefs and values which constitute this "consciousness" may be defined (and redefined), its particular social carrier is not so easy to identify. "Proletarian consciousness" is neither an attribute of a specific social class (as Marx believed), nor, for that matter, does it reside in a specific institution (the communist party, as Lenin insisted). Although it is claimed that Mao has developed and enriched the experience of the Paris Commune, the social and political content of the Maoist version of the "dictatorship of the proletariat" remains vague and unfulfilled.

While one may ponder the implications of the Maoist use of the ambiguous term "dictatorship of the proletariat," there can be little doubt that Maoists look to the rural people's communes as the basis for revolutionary social and economic transformation. Here one observes another obvious departure from classical Marxism. Whereas Marx assumed that the proletarian revolutionary process necessarily would bring "the rural producers under the intellectual lead of the central towns," as he put it in his report on the Paris Commune, Mao's revolutionary hopes still rest on a faith in the creative energies of the peasantry. In Maoist eyes, it is the com-

126

munes of the countryside that will determine the question of the survival and continuation of the revolution.

On the most fundamental issue raised in Marx's analysis of the Commune—the relationship between state and society—the Maoist view is rather equivocal. While the Maoist orientation is profoundly anti-bureaucratic and exhibits a good deal of hostility to centralized state power, Chinese Marxist theorists are reluctant to fully and explicitly accept the original Marxist proposition that all political power is a form of alienated social power—just as they fail to confront the problem of human self-alienation in general. There has been, to be sure, a greater concern with the question of the relation between state and society than generally has been the case with Marxists in power and Maoists explicitly have rejected the Stalinist (and typically conservative) notion of an organic, non-antagonistic relationship between state and people. Yet there remains an unresolved tension between Leninist and Stalinist conceptions of the leading role of a strong state in promoting post-revolutionary social and economic development, on the one hand, and a general populist-type distrust of the state on the other. The latter tendency is reinforced by quotations from Marx on the alien nature of state power as such, but the discussions of this matter are much too brief (and usually much too superficial) to determine whether the question is one of genuinely serious theoretical concern.

Despite these obvious differences (and others), many aspects of the original Marxian conception of proletarian revolution strike responsive chords in the Maoist mentality. The utopian strains in Marx's description of the Paris Commune have been revived and popularized because they are intellectually and politically conducive to promoting that "uninterrupted" process of radical social transformation which is seen as essential for the survival of the revolution. In China the revolution continues and the thrust is still to change the world in accordance with the Maoist vision of ultimate Marxist social goals and not to fall victim to what is called the "typical pragmatic fallacy" of "adaptation to reality." The concepts and images derived from the model of the Paris Commune serve as a stimulus for change and as a barrier against tendencies to institutionalize existing social and political reality. Although there is some evidence to indicate that these concepts have had a significant influence in molding the character of the new forms of political organization built during the Cultural Revolution,[33] it is perhaps premature to undertake any general evaluation. Indeed, the nature and significance of the general political and social changes wrought by the Cultural Revolution is a matter that still awaits serious investigation.

Yet quite apart from the organizational and ideological role it may have played—and may yet still play—in internal Chinese political life, the Maoist celebration of the Paris Commune has a broader historical significance. The appeal to the classic Marxist model of the dictatorship of the proletariat was not only one way Maoists used to reassert their political and ideological authority in China; it was also, at the same time, a way to reaffirm Mao's claim to be the true heir of Marx. For when Chinese Marxists invoke the revolutionary tradition of the Paris Commune, as that tradition was created by Marx, they look across Russia to the "working-men's Paris" that Marx proclaimed would be "forever celebrated as the glorious harbinger of a new society." And in looking across Russia to Paris, they implicitly reject much of the Russian revolution, or at least (and less implicitly) they condemn the contemporary results of that revolution. It is rare to find a recent Chinese commentary on the Paris Commune that fails to point out that the Soviet Union presents a "negative example" in the history of the dictatorship of the proletariat. And thus the assertion that only Maoists are capable of exercising "proletarian dictatorship" according to the principles of the Commune supports the larger claim that Mao has raised Marxism to a "higher stage" by resolving the theoretical and practical revolutionary problems which the Russians proved incapable of solving. Unlike "Soviet revisionists," Maoist revolutionaries have both the will and theoretical understanding to prevent "the restoration of capitalism," build and maintain genuine forms of "proletarian dictatorship," and therefore, for the first time in history, they have prepared the way for the transition from socialism to communism.

Much more is involved in this grandiose claim than the desire to score political points in anti-Soviet polemical battles. Also very much involved is a universal human need to feel part of a living historical tradition that establishes some coherent relationship between past, present and a conception of a future that is to be. Having rejected both traditional Chinese and modern Soviet precedents, Maoists attempt to fill the void by searching for roots in original Marxist sources, by tying Mao to Marx in an uncorrupted and universally valid tradition of Marxist revolutionary history. Chinese pronouncements that they have inherited and enriched Marxian concepts of the Commune reflect this search for a link to a viable and useful past and this is one reason why Maoists feel the need to "conjure up into their service the spirits of the past" and use "borrowed language" to enact new revolutionary dramas.

Thus the Maoist search for roots in the Marxist tradition has an important psychological dimension as well as political and ideological implications. For, as E. H. Carr has suggested, those who believe that they are going somewhere in history must believe that they have come from somewhere as well.[34] Maoists would like to believe that they come from the revolutionary Marxist tradition, for that is a tradition which not only sanctions, but also demands, radical departures from the present in order to create a radically new future.

128

REFERENCES

[1] For a description of the demonstrations, see *Peking Review* (May 31, 1968), pp. 9–17. [2] *The New York Times*, May 23, 1968, p. 15. [3] "Exhibition on the Paris Commune Opens in Peking," *Survey of the China Mainland Press* No. 3671 (March 30, 1966), pp. 39-40. [4] For a sampling of typical references to the Paris Commune in the literature of the period, see K. H. Fan (ed), *The Chinese Cultural Revolution: Selected Documents* (New York: Grove Press, 1968), esp. pp. 161–196, 239–258. [5] Liu Hui-ming, "The General Election System of the Paris Commune," *Hung Ch'i* (Red Flag), August 21, 1966. Translated in *Selections from Chinese Mainland Magazines*, No. 543 (August 21, 1966), pp. 1–3. [6] Karl Marx, *The Eighteenth Brumaire of Louis Bonaparte* (Chicago: Kerr, 1919), pp. 9-10. [7] Martin Buber, *Paths in Utopia* (Boston: Beacon Press, 1958), p. 98. [8] Mao Tse-tung, *On Coalition Government* (Peking, 1955), pp. 55-56. See also Mao Tse-tung, *On New Democracy* (Peking, 1954), passim. [9] "On the People's Democratic Dictatorship," *Selected Works of Mao Tse-tung* (Peking, 1961), Vol. IV, p. 411. [10] *Ibid.*, p. 412 ff. [11] On the utility of the distinction between the "merely *historically* significant" and the "historically really significant," see the fascinating discussion in Joseph Levenson, *Confucian China and Its Modern Fate*, Vol. III (Berkeley: University of California Press, 1965), esp. pp. 85–125. [12] *On the Historical Experience of the Dictatorship of the Proletariat* (Peking, 1959). The document appeared originally on April 5, 1956 as an editorial in the *People's Daily*. [13] The *hsiang* is the basic and lowest unit in the state administrative structure, generally encompassing several villages and a local market town. [14] Kuan Feng "A Brief Discussion on the Great Historical Significance of People's Communes," *Che-hsüeh yen-chiu* (Philosophic Research), 1958, No. 5. [15] *Jen-min jih-pao* editorial, Sept. 3, 1958. [16] Wu Chih-pu, "From Agricultural Producer Cooperatives to People's Communes," *Hung Ch'i* (Red Flag), 1958, No. 8. For a translation see *SCMM* No. 147, pp. 1–10. [17] *Ibid.*, p. 5. [18] Kuan Feng, *op. cit.* [19] See Wu Ch'uan-ch'i, "Communism Seen Through People's Communes," *Jen-min jih-pao* (Oct. 1, 1958), *SCMP*, No. 1887, pp. 9–13, for a typical example. [20] Karl Marx, "The Civil War in France." From the 1902 translation reprinted in *The Paris Commune* (New York: Labor News Co., 1965), pp. 75–77. [21] In his Introduction to the 1891 German edition of *The Civil War in France, The Paris Commune, op. cit.*, p. 17. [22] Karl Marx and Friedrich Engels, *Werke* (Berlin: Dietz, 1963), Vol. XXII, p. 236. [23] Wu Chih-pu, "On People's Communes," *Chung-kuo ch'ing-nien pao*, September 16, 1958. *SCMM*, No. 524, p. 5. [24] Liu Hui-ming, *op. cit.*, p. 1. [25] Chen Chih-ssu, "Great Revelations of the Paris Commune," *Hung Ch'i* (Red Flag), 1966 No. 4 (March 24, 1966), *Joint Publications Research Service*, No. 35137 (21 April 1966), pp. 14–17. [26] Chen Chih-ssu, pp. 12, 14. [27] "The Civil War in France," *op. cit.*, p. 84. [28] *Ibid.*, pp. 47-48. [29] *Ibid.*, pp. 51–59, 69. [30] *Ibid.*, pp. 95, 104. [31] It is interesting to observe that it is this "nationalist" aspect of proletarian revolution which was emphasized in perhaps the earliest Chinese commentary on the Paris Commune—by Li Ta-chao (the first Chinese convert to Marxism) in 1923. "The people of Paris," he stressed, "rose up to resist a traitorous government." "I-pa-ch'i-i nien ti Pa-li 'K'ang-miao-ssu' " (The Paris 'Commune' of 1871), *Li Ta-chao Hsüan-chi* (Selected Writings of Li Ta-chao) (Peking, 1959), pp. 447–456. The general theme reappears in most recent Chinese Marxist literature on the Commune. [32] "Civil War in France," *op. cit.*, pp. 74-75. [33] Jan Myrdal has provided a rare first-hand account of changes brought by the Cultural Revolution at the village level. Comparing his observations on life in a village in northern Shensi in 1962 with those made in the same village on a visit in 1970, he notes that in the former year there existed a relatively complex administrative structure with clearly defined functional differentiations. On the basis of his 1970 study he observes: "During the cultural revolution this structure had been transformed into a unified and directly elected management: the Revolutionary Committee, which worked under permanent supervision from public meetings and public discussion." Jan Myrdal and Gun Kessle, *China: the Revolution Continued* (New York: Pantheon, 1970), p. 23. [34] Edward Hallett Carr, *What is History?* (New York: Vintage Books, 1967), p. 176.

CASTAGNARY'S
A PLEA FOR A DEAD FRIEND (1882)

GUSTAVE COURBET
AND THE DESTRUCTION OF THE VENDOME COLUMN

Edited and trans. by
Alda Cannon and Frank Anderson Trapp

During the days of the Commune of Paris, the city actually suffered fewer artistic losses than might readily have proven the case. This is not to overlook the razing of the Tuileries Palace, the ransacking of the Palais Royal, or the gutting of the Hôtel de Ville, which deprived the world of the murals painted for that interior by Delacroix and Ingres. These and other losses scarred Paris under the Commune. Yet the treasures of the Louvre went unmolested, and likely targets for populist resentment, such as the Cathedral of Paris, escaped serious abuse. The Arc de Triomphe and Napoleon's Tomb at the Invalides were spared, despite the surge of pacifist and egalitarian feelings, for which those grandiloquent, Bonapartist monuments served as a goad. It might be said that Baron Haussmann's long efforts to render Paris at once more beautiful and more governable by force, if need be, showed greater callousness toward historical association and artistic merit than the destructions attributable to the Communards—whether accidental or deliberate. Of all of these incidents, the one which aroused the greatest notoriety was the demolition on May 16, 1871 of the Vendôme Column—a Napoleonic monument of marginal artistic significance, which might be all but forgotten today, had the incident not involved one of the greatest artists of the era, Gustave Courbet. In 1875, the column that had only recently been hauled down, to the victorious outcry of ardent witnesses, was reconstructed as it now stands.

At the time Courbet was drawn into partisanship with the Communards, he was still in the prime of his creative powers, if anything, invigorated by the controversies aroused by his much-publicized Realist doctrines. Courbet's socialist convictions, nurtured by his friend, the late Pierre-Joseph Proudhon, had become integral with his artistic radicalism, so his attraction to the Communard cause was natural. But once the fall of the Commune left him vulnerable to prosecution, so publicized a figure as Courbet provided a welcome target for the leaders of the Third Republic, bent on·repressing radical sentiment. For his part in the demolition of the Vendôme Column, Courbet was tried and convicted of a crime against the State. First imprisoned, then brought to new trial and burdened with an irreparably huge indemnity for restoration of the column, Courbet finally made his way to exile in Switzerland, where he died in 1877.

Castagnary's Plea for Courbet

Castagnary's small volume, written in the effort to rehabilitate Courbet's reputation, was published after the painter's death, when the political climate of France had greatly changed from the reactionary, punitive ethos of the "Moral Order" under Marshal MacMahon and his ministers. Early in the administration of Jules Grévy (MacMahon's liberal successor), former Communards were granted amnesty and released from indemnities.

As an open-minded, younger critic, Jules Antoine Castagnary had expressed his admiration for Courbet in his first salon review, written in 1857. Three years later, the two men finally met, and a close friendship rapidly formed. In 1861-62 Castagnary served as Courbet's aide in establishing his short-lived "Realist Academy," and thereafter acted as the painter's chief spokesman and confidant. He was appointed to several high official posts during the more liberal years of the Third Republic. Under Gambetta's short administration, he rose to the rank of cabinet minister. At the time of his death, in 1888, he was Director of the Ecole des Beaux-Arts. He left uncompleted his biography of Courbet. However, his devotion to Courbet's memory shines through the pages of his defensive pamphlet. What follows is a translation of essential excerpts from Castagnary's plea.

F. T.

A PLEA FOR A DEAD FRIEND

PREFACE

I have asserted that contrary to widely held opinion, the painter from Ornans had nothing to do with the leveling of the Vendôme Column on May 16, 1871, and I pledged to prove it.

Today, I am redeeming that pledge. I know about the existence of a decision of the Military Court of the Third District, which condemned Courbet to six months' imprisonment and a fine of 500 fr. . . . I know that other decisions from the Civil Court of the Seine, based upon this first sentence, have condemned the artist to pay the State the sum of 323,097 fr. 68 c., representing the entire cost of reconstructing the destroyed monument. But I also know that court decisions do not bind the historian. . .

Let us leave aside, then, what might have been thought, said, or printed before. Let us start from scratch, as if looking at things for the first time. . .

September 9, 1882

CHAPTER I

*The Vendôme Column on
September 4, 1870*

When a dynasty is overthrown, it is only natural for its emblems to disappear with it. Hence, in a time of insurrection, some destruction is allowed— even ordained.

In this respect, September 4, 1870 could not have differed from July 29, 1830 or from February 24, 1848.

I can still see the national guardsmen on the step of the Assembly, wrenching the imperial eagles from their helmets and, to the applause of the crowd, casting them to the ground. A few hours later, on Rivoli Street, along the path of the cortège which was taking Jules Favre to the Hôtel de Ville, merchants hurrying to pledge allegiance to the new regime were smashing the imperial insignias at their doors. With the same scene being reenacted all along the way, by the end of the day the symbolic destruction was complete.

Those first reactions were too harmless for the crowd. When a Paris which had forgotten the Prussians for twenty-four hours awoke to the next day's reality and foresaw the immensity of the disaster into which the nation would be plunged, there was a redoubling of anger toward the author of the war. The idea that his image or that of his family could survive in our public squares, in our streets, or on our monuments, became unbearable. The authorities foresaw excesses. They understood that to avoid them they must control the movement, and in order to control it, lead it. By their orders, Barye's bas-relief of Napoleon III on horseback was dismantled from the tympanum of the Caroussel Arch and relegated to a warehouse. Seurre's statue of Napoleon I in a gray frock coat, which stood in Courbevoie Square, was taken by night to the Neuilly Bridge and thrown into the Seine. And the memorial to the Prince Eugène Beauharnais was, in turn, removed from its pedestal and replaced by a statue of Voltaire.

There remained the Arch of Triumph of l'Etoile, the Tomb of Napoleon I at the Hôtel des Invalides, and the column at the Place Vendôme.

Not a voice was raised against the Arch of Triumph or Napoleon's tomb—an obvious proof that monuments free of politics are safe from the anger of revolutions. On the other hand, protests against the Vendôme Column were numerous and so violent that at one point it seemed to rock on its base.

Let anyone who may be surprised at such an outburst be reminded that the Vendôme Column has always been more a Napoleonic monument than a national one. Erected by Napoleon I, to his own glory, and restored by Napoleon III in its pure character of family glorification, on September 4, 1870, it evoked and honored the memory of the two men who had done the most harm to France, freedom, and progress.

This was not enough to protect it!

To be sure, it did commemorate the Grande Armée and in that sense, the whole nation; but what an indirect homage! Look at the ribbon of soldiers that winds around the bronze shaft. You immediately feel that they are there less for themselves than as an escort for the invincible Emperor.

[Castagnary here cites documents reviewing the project for the column and insists upon the intentions implied by it: the Minister of the Interior maintained that it would satisfy popular will to substitute a statue of Napoleon for the one of Charlemagne, at first intended as the crowning feature of the column. Castagnary concludes:]

The meaning of the monument is the Apotheosis of Napoleon I. . . . In its character of apotheosis, the column is vulnerable: any change is threatening to it; any revolution can be deadly for it. . . . Upon the return of the House of Bourbon in 1814, the statue of Napoleon was removed and broken up. By an irony of fate—makers of images, take notice—parts of it were melted down to make the equestrian bronze of Henri IV, now on the Pont Neuf.

[Under Louis XVIII, the statue was replaced by a French flag; but under Louis-Philippe, a new statue of Bonaparte was erected, in response to a popular resurgence of Napoleonic sentiment. Castagnary points out, however, isolated protests, including those of the poets Barbier and Lamartine, along with the injunction of Auguste Comte: that it was the duty of all philosophers to oppose the rehabilitation of the man who had "organized the most sweeping political retrogression that mankind had ever to lament."]

Among writers of his time, Comte was the one most irritated by the Vendôme Column. He considered it an insult to humanity. Its presence in one of our public squares seemed to him the very negation of progress. As early as 1848, in his course at the Palais Royal, he was asking for its demolition. He reiterated this demand in the fourth volume of his *Positivist Politics*, published in 1854, in which he proposed replacing "this unworthy parody of a

Roman trophy" with a statue of Charlemagne, "the highest representative of the Middle Ages." He maintained the necessity "for the human metropolis [Paris] to purge itself of an oppressive monument, incompatible with its surroundings [the nearby Rue de la Paix], which conjure the advent of enduring peace."

Napoleon III had used the Place Vendôme as the seat of a veritable cult, with its altar, rituals, processions—all that a god requires. . . .

[Castagnary then points out that the deification culminated in the replacement of the Bonaparte in a frock coat with Dumont's image of Napoleon as a triumphant Caesar.]

CHAPTER II

Petition for the Demolition of the Vendôme Column

Thus, in the wake of the defeat at Sedan, a rumbling storm against the column was gathering.

The most moderate, among them M. Ernest Picard's newspaper, *The Free Voter*, asked for the removal of the statue, which only recalled a hated memory. Others, finding fault with the monument itself, wanted the elimination of so obvious a symbol of twenty years of slavery. Yet others, thinking about the approaching Prussian army, proposed to melt the bronze to make cannons. This notion especially worked upon the proletariat and found echo in the patriotic press. It assumed its most practical form in a report from the Munitions Committee of the 6th District of Paris.

[Castagnary's excerpt from the Committee's report includes the following recommendation:]

Art. 6 The Municipality of the 6th district proposes that the material for the cannons be taken, first, from the column honoring Napoleon I on the Place Vendôme. Apart from the material advantage of this measure, it would be of immense moral advantage to rid Republican France of

an odious image, which outrageously evokes the execrable and accursed race which brought our homeland to the brink of ruin. . . .

The Committee's proposal was picked up in a widely circulated petition, which was immediately covered with signatures.

The undersigned, in agreement with the wishes of the Municipality of the Sixth District, urgently request that the Government of National Defense remove at once the statue of Napoleon and the column still standing on the Place Vendôme, and assign them to the manufacture of the cannons needed to regain national independence and the political rights of France, twice destroyed by the Bonapartes.

And so the fate of the Vendôme Column was debated in public. . . . In a way, it was an open question, and each said his piece. How could the Commission of Artists, charged with the protection of our artistic treasures not have made known its position? . . .

The Commission of Artists, over which Courbet presided, had been elected in a meeting, held at the Sorbonne on September 6, 1870. M. Jules Simon, Minister of Education and Fine Arts, had given it an official mandate. . . . The Commission visited the museums, investigated the archives, took steps to protect the Louvre, to insure the safe-keeping of our masterpieces in case of bombardment. The Vendôme Column could not have been left out of its deliberations. Motions were being made against the structure. There was talk of its disappearance. This raised an artistic question, one upon which artists were most competent to decide.

Has the Vendôme Column artistic value and is there any reason for preserving it? These, then, were the questions posed to the artists' commission.

Courbet's opinion was a mystery to no one. He had little taste for military monuments. Except for the pedestal he found it all bad. "It's the sculpture of a child," he later said. That evening, he probably developed his ideas with his habitual colorfulness and fantasy, and then opened the floor to those who wished to speak. They unanimously agreed that the column was artistically worthless.

However, does it follow that a monument must be destroyed because it lacks artistic value? Courbet was far from thinking this. "It is not for the artist, whose mission is essentially creative, to destroy a work of art, however bad it may be," he said. "The reason is simple: if we sacrifice one monument to a particular esthetic today, we would in time be led to sacrifice all monuments to satisfy the tastes of everyone. We should not, then, destroy but relocate. The column on the Place Vendôme is not where it should be. Its historical value is not apparent enough there. What should be done? Transport it to more suitable surroundings, amongst other souvenirs of war—to the Invalides, for example, where live the descendants, at least, of those who won the cannons from which the column was made." This is what Courbet later repeated before the Military Court: "On the Place Vendôme the column is an unhappily pretentious work of art which makes the foreigner laugh; at the Invalides it would be just another military memento, and nobody could object to it." This argument prevailed, and the Assembly accepted the idea of relocation.

We may think what we will of these artists locked in discussions of a monumental esthetic question, while a beleaguered Paris shook with indignation and grief.

Such was the origin of Courbet's petition to dismantle the monument. The reactionary press has carried the text, but always in mutilated form. I reproduce it in full, after the Official Transcript of the Municipality of Paris.

CITIZEN COURBET,

President of the Fine Arts Commission in charge of the conservation of the National Museum and its collec-tions, after nomination by the general assembly of artists;

Whereas, the Vendôme Column is a monument devoid of any artistic value, and one which perpetuates the ideals of war and conquest espoused by the Imperial dynasty, but rejected by a republican nation;

Whereas, this monument is therefore antipathetic to the genius of our modern civilization and the ideals of universal Fraternity which must prevail among the nations from now on;

Whereas, it offends the nation's legitimate sensitiveness and makes France seem ridiculous and odious in the eyes of European democracies! Sets forth the following wish:

That the Government of National Defense kindly authorize the Commission to have the column dismantled or take upon itself the initiative by entrusting this task to the administration of the Museum of Artillery, and by having the components taken to the Hôtel de la Monnaie. He also wishes that the same measure apply to the relocated statue, now standing at Courbevoie, Avenue de la Grande Armée.

Finally, he wishes that names of these streets, which for some evoke victories, and for others, defeats, be stricken from our capital and replaced by the names of benefactors of humanity or by names referring to their topography.

GUSTAVE COURBET

Here is Courbet's real crime. On September 14, 1870, under the shock of Napoleon III's treasons at Châlons and Sedan, while thousands of angry Parisians are demanding that the column be demolished and made into cannons, he sets forth the three wishes that we have just read and which are, we must admit, those of a true conservative. He took seriously his duty as President of a Fine Arts Commission charged with the protection of works of art, and, naïvely, voluntarily, he undertakes to save the Vendôme Column and the Courbevoie statue, which was equally threatened. A Republican, who suffered from the Empire all his life, he intervenes to preserve these mementos of the Empire. And it is this very man who will be later regarded as the destroyer of the column: what an irony! . . . .

Thus, Courbet's intentions are clear. . . .

I concede to his adversaries that he may have gone farther. I admit that under the cover of words, he may actually have envisaged the destruction of the column. For what would he be culpable? How would he have exceeded his rights? He was in the situation of a citizen addressing his government, requesting something which he deemed reasonable and useful. This citizen is mistaken, his demand is absurd or illegal: of what is he guilty? It is for the government to evaluate his request, and to accept or reject it. In this particular case, Courbet's petition had no sequel. The wish of the Commission's President ended up in the Minister's wastebasket, along with the notion of the Munitions Committee of the Sixth District—and doubtless, many other proposals.

[Castagnary here proceeds to argue that Courbet had not pressed the subject of his petition and had the column not been destroyed, the whole matter would have remained forgotten. He then goes on to discuss the fate of the column under the Commune.]

Under the Commune there was less noise and more action. On April 12 [1871], the decree of demolition, on May 16, the overturning. Here, we are no longer dealing with a citizen's wishes or petitions, but with a government which gives orders and finds the agents to carry them out. The time when people talked of making cannons with that bronze or relocating the column at the Invalides is over. Eight months have passed since then—eight months filled with the siege of Paris, the organization of the National Guard, the inertia of General Trochu, the despair of the Parisians, the surrender, then the legislative elections, the Commune, the civil war—a long series of extraordinary events mixed with tragic anxieties and inexpressible sorrows. The present situation is unprecedented. Men, feelings, and aims are different. This time, the column is hauled to the ground with neither petitions nor oratory.

The question remains: to learn whether Courbet was involved in this second affair. . . .

CHAPTER III
Courbet's Denials

First, Courbet repeatedly denied the charges against him.

Before, during and after the military trial where he was condemned he always maintained that he was innocent of the destruction of the column. On May 20, 1871, the day before the entry of the armies into Paris, he handed Mr. Robert Reid a letter which he asked him to forward to the London *Times*. Its object was to answer the stupid accusation, brought against him by the British press, of his having by his own hand destroyed many works of art from the Louvre collection. Here is the text of this first protestation.

Paris, May 20, 1871

Not only did I not destroy any of the art objects of the Louvre, but on the contrary, I took care to gather and restore in their proper place in the museum all those works which had, under different ministers, been dispersed among the various government offices of the capital. The Luxembourg benefited from the same measure.

It is I who preserved and catalogued all the art works which had been taken from M. Thiers.

I am accused of having destroyed the Vendôme Column, when it is patently evident that the decree ordering its demolition was voted on April 12 and that I only became a member of the Commune after the election held on April 16, that is, ten days later [*sic*]. I warmly recommended the preservation of the bas-reliefs and proposed to install them as a museum display at the Invalides.

My motives are pure, but it has been my fate to take upon myself all the difficulties that arise from a regime such as the one bequeathed to us by the Empire.

G. COURBET

[Among other documentary evidence, including excerpts from Courbet's testimony before the Military Court, Castagnary includes the text of a letter Courbet wrote him from prison.]

September 23, 1871

My Dear Friend,

I have been at Sainte-Pélagie Prison since yesterday. They insisted on treating us like common criminals, not like political prisoners. We are among thieves; and so, when you come to visit me, I shall only be able to see you in the visiting room. . . .

Ulysse Parent must have told you how much we have suffered. This is a peculiar reward for all my services to the public good, and the government has its own way of paying me its debts of gratitude.

One must make allowances for injustice in life, but in this case they could have chosen someone else to satisfy the public.

In spite of my efforts, those of my co-defendants, and those of my lawyer, the tribunal decreed that I was the author of the column's fall. This fate has been arbitrarily assigned to me, despite the evidence. I have the column as my lot. This error is given credence by the public, and I am defenseless.

G. COURBET

CHAPTER IV

About Courbet's Non-Involvement in the Decree Ordaining the Demolition of the Vendôme Column

Time had passed. There was no longer a Government of National Defense. Against the Assembly at Ver-sailles, which was Royalist and pro-clerical, stood the revolutionary and atheistic Commune. The adversaries were at grips with each other. The old motions against the column and the column itself had been forgotten when, one day, Paris learned in the morning press that the municipal council had just ordered its demolition.

That measure had been taken during the meeting of April 12, 1871:

The Commune of Paris,

Considering that the Imperial Column of the Place Vendôme is a monument to barbarism, a symbol of brute force and fake glory, an affirmation of militarism, a denial of international rights, a permanent insult inflicted by the victors on the vanquished, a perpetual assault upon one of the three great principles of the French Republic, Fraternity.

Decrees simply:

The Column of the Place Vendôme will be demolished.

Who had taken the initiative for this proposal?

Eleven years ago [1871], amidst arrests, condemnations and tortures, there was only one answer to this question: it is Courbet! Nobody knew, but everyone said: it is Courbet! . . . Eventually, even the walls spoke; accusatory *graffitti* could be read, from one end of Paris to the other. "Courbet, the *colonnard*." "Courbet, the *déboulonneur*." [The bronze plates of the column had **been** **bolted** together. *Déboulonner* means, to unrivet or unbolt.]

Well, the walls were mistaken and mouths lied. It was not Courbet. . . . But if it was not Courbet, who was it? . . . I might well not answer that. I took it upon myself to prove Courbet's innocence, not to say who did topple the column. But there is a public document; even one which has been published to aid in Courbet's acquittal: I am authorized to use it.

[Castagnary here includes the full text of a long letter to the London *Times*, dated June 24, 1874. It was written by Félix Pyat, former member of the Executive Commission of the Commune. The following paragraphs are of special relevance to Castagnary's representation of Courbet's cause:]

"The Commune decreed the fall of the column for exclusively political reasons. Rightly or wrongly—let History be the judge—in my capacity as a member of the Commission, it was I who initiated the measure, without consulting Courbet and without regard for his feelings as a creative artist *vis-à-vis* that Roman pastiche. I stated the reasons for the decree in purely democratic terms. [With slight differences, the previously given text of the decree follows.]

"Not the least artistic consideration! The artist [Courbet] did not inspire nor, I may add, even vote on this "Socialist" decree, for as you can see, it was voted on April 12, and the artist became a member of the Commune only on the 20th, following a supplementary election.

"Finally, if on the 27th, the Commission had entrusted the artist with executing the decree, it was precisely to salvage whatever might be of artistic interest. He intervened, then, only to preserve.

"I must not let the responsibility for the destruction fall on Courbet; and for whatever it may be, I lay legitimate claim to it."

FELIX PYAT

CHAPTERS V-VI

[In Chapter V, Castagnary insists that Courbet was unaware even of preparations for the demolition of the Vendôme Column, and cites numerous official documents to corroborate this assertion. They add little new substance to the arguments already presented. In Chapter VI, he similarly treats the question of Courbet's involvement in the actual destruction. Once more, he concludes that Courbet was innocent.]

CHAPTER VII
Another Testimony

[A letter to Castagnary from another former member of the Commission, Paschal Grousset, then (April 7, 1878) living in London confirms the information previously provided by Pyat and adds several items of interest. He observes, for example, that "when the moment came for the Master of Ornans to answer this fantastic accusation, I did what anyone would have done in my place. I asked to speak and declared that Courbet had absolutely nothing to do with the toppling of the column. . . . By an odd coincidence, the estimate [for the demolition] prepared by the engineer was among the documents in my court files . . ." Grousset continues:]

"Admire, here, the justice of politics. All the reactionary newspapers ignored my protest, as though word had been passed among them. Courbet was troubled by this and brought that anomaly to the attention of the Court. The President of the Court told him to pay no attention to what was or was not printed by the press, because it had no bearing on the Court's mind.

"I shall not pause to explore what is monstrous about this concerted omission. The press of those wretched times surpassed anything I could say about this kind of operation.

"These hearings, which were monotonous even for us, went on for three or four weeks.

"Finally, the day of the verdict arrived.

"It would seem that after my formal declaration, I could expect to find myself indicted for the destruction of the column, and Courbet acquitted.

"Not at all. While unanimously finding me guilty of treason against the Versailles government, the Court found me innocent of the deed in question. As for Courbet, he was found guilty, with attenuating circumstances, and condemned to six months in prison.

"Was it that the Court deemed it necessary to render this satisfaction to public opinion, and to a press which had made Courbet's participation in the overthrow of the column an article of faith? Did the Court simply wish to punish a lack of taste—one especially deplorable in a great painter? Had Courbet's blasphemies against the masterpiece in the Place Vendôme offended the artistic convictions of the army officers who were judging us? I don't have to dwell upon these points.

"In any case, Courbet was duly convicted of having demolished the column. This judgement served as the basis for the State's legal claims for damages, which in turn resulted in the confiscation of most of Courbet's small estate, accumulated over thirty years of work. . . ."

PASCHAL GROUSSET

This letter closes the debate. It confirms my arguments. I shall not insist upon it further, but will instead hasten to my conclusion.

CONCLUSION

Courbet, Victim of the Moral Order

Condemned to six months in prison and to a fine of 500 francs for complicity in the overthrow of the Vendôme Column—which he had opposed and considered impossible—Courbet did not appeal the verdict. Those who recall this sinister era can easily guess why. The penalty was relatively light. As one facing prosecution at the same time for treason against the government and for usurpation of office, he had run graver risks. Once he learned his fate, he felt it prudent not to reopen the question. Thus, accepting his judges' decision, his only thought was to serve out his term. He was sent to the Sainte-Pélagie Prison. He was temporarily released to undergo a painful operation at the Duval Clinic. Then, after serving his sentence and having personally borne the full expenses of a common suit [he chose not to claim reimbursement from his thirteen co-defendants],

he returned home, cleared of all his debts to the State and only aspiring to get back to his painting [March 2, 1872].

Cleared and free! In the eyes of the government of that time, Courbet had paid his debt to society. There had been no suggestion of financial compensation in the hearings before the Military Court. The prosecutor had entered no qualifications regarding monetary restitutions. And surely, had one spoken with M. Thiers about a series of civil suits following a series of criminal suits, the head of the executive branch, who had political sense, would have rejected any such monstrosity by saying: "In times of trouble, the best suits are those which are dispatched quickly and do not crop up again."

Thus, as long as M. Thiers remained in power—fifteen months longer—the notion of bringing claims against those condemned as Communards for damages to monuments that had been burnt or otherwise destroyed, appeared nowhere. The reconstruction of the Hôtel de Ville was budgeted by the City of Paris. The restoration of the Pavillon de Flore, the Pavillon de Marsan, and the Palais-Royal was begun by the government. The rebuilding of M. Thiers' residence was done at public expense. All this was undertaken with no mention of reparation from anyone.

So openly vindictive a project could only take shape after May 24, 1873 and the fall of M. Thiers.

Thus, like Mssrs. Ranc, Rochefort, and so many others, Courbet fell victim to "the Moral Order"; and in Courbet's case he succumbed to persecution.

The decree for the reconstruction of the Vendôme Column was a rallying point for Courbet's enemies—and we know that they were numerous. No painter ever collected so many.

First, there was the majority of his professional colleagues: this was almost by law of nature. Those painters could not forgive his manner, his quips, his jovial banter, his high opinion of himself, his small esteem for others. While he was still under indictment, I pro-

GUSTAVE COURBET *Bust by* Jules Dalou

DEMOLITION OF VENDOME COLUMN AND BURNING OF THE TUILERIES
Etching

FELIX PYAT *Caricature*

RAOUL RIGAULT *Photograph*

PASCHAL GROUSSETT *Photograph*

LA COMMUNE HINDERED BY IGNORANCE AND REACTION
Gravure by Georges Pilotell

posed to Daubigny that the artists present a petition to M. Thiers, seeking his good-will toward Courbet. "We will obtain three signatures," Daubigny replied, "mine, Daumier's, and Corot's— not one more." Daubigny was not far wrong. The artists' feelings were vividly revealed at the first salon, following the Commune: the jury, arrogating to itself a right which it did not possess, expelled Courbet as unworthy. Of the twenty participating members of the jury, only two protested: M. Larrieu, a Deputy, and the venerable Robert-Fleury.

After the professional colleagues, there were the political partisans. If the Royalists loathed this painter of democratic subjects, it can be said that the Bonapartists were infuriated at the mere mention of his name. The man who had insulted the moribund Empire by refusing the Legion of Honor and who was held responsible for leveling the Vendôme Column seemed to them some kind of monster, lacking in any moral sense and estranged from civilization.

Finally, as if this was not enough, Courbet had aroused the antagonism of the clergy by painting what he called the morals of the clergy. *The Return from the Conference* was a sample of this kind of painting. The artist had many other such subjects in mind, and in time, he would have carried them out. He joked about them with his friends, and usually concluded with a quip: "At last, the clergy has found its painter!"

On May 24, [1873] the keepers of all these grudges and all these hates rose to power.

The decree concerning the column was formally considered on June 30. Discussion was brief. Everyone was of the same mind—both the government and the Assembly. It had been agreed beforehand that the statue of Napoleon should be restored to its place.

[Castagnary here traces the evolution of these events. The initial intention had merely been to restore the column as authentically as possible, in the interest of its value as an historical object. However, this did not satisfy the Bonapartists, who finally got their way. Twenty days later, the Minister of Finance, "an inveterate Bonapartist," ordered the attachment of all Courbet's possessions, both in Paris and at Ornans. A complicated legal tangle ensued. Eventually Courbet became so apprehensive about his freedom itself that he took exile in Switzerland. Finally, on May 4, 1877, a judgement was levied, fixing the sum Courbet was due to pay: 323,091 fr. 68 c., which represented the estimated cost of the prospective restoration. It also ordered that beginning January 1, 1878, he should pay 10,000 fr. per year in semi-annual installments.

On November 26, 1877, two of Courbet's paintings (an equestrian subject and his famous portrait of Proudhon and his daughters), impounded from his dealer, Durand-Ruel, were put on auction at the Hôtel Drouot, along with other forfeited objects taken from his studio. To end his plea, Castagnary uses the text of the last letter he received from Courbet and brief mention of a hopeful change.]

"And now, my dear Castagnary, I take leave of you and express, as much in my own name as in those of others forced into exile, the wish that our unhappy land will soon emerge from the crisis it is now suffering through. One might blush to be French on foreign soil but for the burning conviction that the last word will belong to Right and Justice."

He dictated these words on December 12 [1877]. At 6 A.M., on the 31st, he died. In the meantime, Marshal MacMahon [President of the Republic] had finally conceded to parliamentary procedure and given up *coup d'état* cabinets. Thus before his death, Courbet had the supreme joy of greeting this triumph of Right which so engrossed him and witnessing the rout of the "Moral Order" that was killing him. . . .

139

BRESDIN TO REDON

two letters 1870, 1871

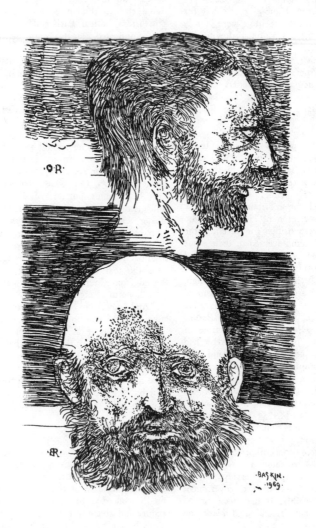

13 rue de Launoy Levallois-Perret February 26, 1870

My Dear Shark:[1]

If all of Homer's heroes had suffered all the storms and shipwrecks I have, and if they had enjoyed as many welts and bruises, had got knocked about as much as the undersigned, and if they had had as much resignation—I should say instead of resignation endurance, which is a practical philosophy—they would not have remained eternally demi-gods, but would instead have advanced in one fell swoop after their deaths to the status of gods.

The only reason for this not happening is probably because humanity already suffers quite enough from one god and from all the evil done in his name. What would it be like if there were gobs of gods?

My dear old friend, I think I've already written and asked you but do try again to find out chez la cavallerie[2] whether the drawings have been found, and try to make her understand that they can't have been lost. If you feel bold enough to see M. de Blangis, who has some of my engravings and was supposed to send me some money I would be very grateful. I have written to him, as well as to Oré of the prefecture, the doctor who also has some of them and quite a few at that, but have had no answer. So let me hear from you; above all, come to see me if you come to Paris.

My best to your brother.[3]

My greetings to your father.

Warmly, and with regards from my wife.

Bresdin[4]

---

[1] In February 1869, driven by poverty, fearing to become blind, Bresdin had left Bordeaux and settled in Paris with his family under the most precarious material conditions. (See letter of March 28, 1869 by Bresdin to Justin Capin, published by Fourès, 22-23.) [2] M. Cavalier(?), M. de Blangis and Dr. Oré were among the few people of Bordeaux who were interested in collecting Bresdin. [*Chez la cavallerie:* this obscure remark may refer to the cavalry depot—with a misspelling; or it may be a pun to suggest M. Cavalier's wife. tr.] [3] The musician, Ernest Redon. [4] Several weeks after this letter, early in April 1870, Bresdin was hospitalized at Necker. A benefit for him was arranged for April 27 in the Sorbonne gymnasium, under the chairmanship of Courbet.

Paris December 30, 1871

*. . . God is great, God is very great, there are no other gods than God.
And many cads, who think themselves prophets, are only poor slobs. Alla,
Allah, alha, 'allo, amen. O my dear friend, I don't dare say my pupil,
for I have contributed too little to your technical, artistic and 'aquatic'[5]
development to believe that I molded you and had a pupil. Nevertheless,
I should be flattered to have at least one, and since I last saw you
you must have become of a size to fill the shoes of a Titian, of a Poussin
or of a Caravaggio.*

*Please believe, my dear friend, in my sincere wishes for it to be so
and that I wish you, your brother and your dear ones, health, joy, and
prosperity in the New Year.*

*Remember me to Clavaud[6] and all our friends. I shan't try to tell you
everything I, my wife and children suffered through from all the sieges
of Paris.[7] I myself, my wife and my children came close to croaking.
I have had partial attacks of paralysis in all four paws, the result of the
trade of warrior which I pursued with a conscientiousness worthy of a
better fate and of a better country, lying in mud, in melted or frozen snow,
in rain, in wind, with no food but a licorice stick most of the time—
but with rage in my heart sustaining me, at seeing the enemy invade
our poor country with nothing being done to stop them. Instead, all doors
were opened to them. Cowards, cowards, cowards, cowards, double, triple,
quadruple cowards. Sons of bitches, drunks, traitors, bastards, disbelievers,
sluts, whores, corrupt, degraded, sold out. That's what most of the efforts,*

---

[5] The French for "etching" is *eau-forte*, i.e., strong water or acid. [tr.] [6] Armand
Clavaud. Francis Jammes, on the basis of the memories of Clavaud and of Redon,
has depicted the gatherings of friends at Bordeaux in Bresdin's studio, near the
Chartreuse cemetery "where Goya rested." (*Feuilles sous le vent*, Paris, 1913, 197-
198.) [7] Cladel has related his meeting with Bresdin in May 1871, a few days
before the Versailles troops entered Paris on May 21: "Toward nightfall, near the
Pont Royal, a battalion of Communard soldiers [*Fédérés*] passed by. Bresdin, his
pipe in his mouth, his Chassepot rifle on his shoulder and with a sprig of lilac in
the barrel of the gun, was among these citizens armed for the defence of the
Republic and of their city." (*Raca*, 279.) Bresdin had a very narrow escape from
the reprisals against the Republican soldiers.

of the results, of the expedients have given us, what the herd of sheep
of the Empire and the Monarchy have been able to come up with, after
fifty years of exploitation, of moralizing and of perfecting—and yet how
many homilies, confessions, te deums, processionals, religious displays by
their-Honors, how many conversions, decorations, destructions. . . Since
those days, ugh! I am feeling better, my wife not much better, the children
well enough. Thanks to a will of iron, backbreaking work and the
protection of the God of honest men, I am beginning to manage, I have
just sold six Samaritans for 300 francs.

Cordially, with our warm affection and hopes for a visit from you.

100 rue Assas (formerly rue de l'Ouest)   *Bresdin*
behind the Luxembourg [Gardens], Paris

These letters are from the Gehenna Press edition of *Bresdin to Redon: six letters 1870 to 1881,* edited by Roseline Bacou and translated with additional notes by Seymour S. Weiner. The double portrait of Bresdin and Redon is reproduced from an etching by Leonard Baskin. A notable section on Rodolphe Bresdin with seven lithographs and two drawings, including a full-size reproduction of Bresdin's work, *The Good Samaritan,* appeared in the *Massachusetts Review* for Autumn, 1960

THE PARIS COMMUNE
AND THE ARTISTS

Jeffry Kaplow

The Paris Commune was both an end and a beginning and must be analyzed and celebrated with that dual character in mind. The king is dead, long live the king, one is tempted to cry. The old king was radical democracy on the Jacobin model: a society of small property holders and republican virtue supported, if need be, by the terror of the Committee of Public Safety. The heir apparent was the socialism of the working-class movement. The first belonged to the petite bourgeoisie, the artisans, shopkeepers, public servants, petty intellectuals, to whom the Great Revolution of 1789, and even more that of 1793, had promised much that had not been delivered. The second belonged to the newly born proletariat, still very much an infant whose period of gestation in France had been particularly long, and whose participation in the struggle was accompanied by all the problems to be expected from a royal minority. In other words, Jacobinism and socialism were the twin aspects of the Commune, but a Jacobinism and a socialism of 1871, appropriate to the situation of the classes whose ideologies they were: a Jacobinism on the decline but still capable of rallying great numbers of people in the defense of fatherland and freedom and the interests of the little man; a socialism more Proudhonian than Marxist and more Blanquist than Leninist, whose watchwords were federation and cooperation, rather than planning and expropriation, which reasoned in terms of eternal verities rather than dialectical truths, and spoke too much of the time of an undifferentiated people rather than of the working class. Regrettable perhaps, inevitable beyond the shadow of a doubt, the conflicts within the Commune—liberty versus authority, centralism versus local initiative, the existence of the state versus anarchy, patriotism versus internationalism, reform versus revolution—were the result not only of the fact that individual actors were marked by contradictory ideas, but even more the result of the interpenetration of whole movements, explicable only in terms of the incomplete differentiation of petite bourgeoisie and working class in the France of 1871. Historical movements have a tendency, Marx noted in his *Eighteenth Brumaire of Louis Napoleon,* to dress themselves in the clothing of the past (which is what the majority of the Commune did in May by decreeing the creation of a Committee of Public Safety, and with results no less disastrous than Louis Napoleon's exhumation of the Napoleonic legend). He might have added that the same movements

144

sometimes appear in the clothing of the future; the tendency then is to waddle in badly fitting shoes and to trip over pants' legs, a tendency that will persist until the wearer grows into his chosen garments. To pursue the metaphor, one might say that the working class movement then still in diapers was by the pressure of circumstance forced to put on long trousers. All things considered, it wore them rather well, although they were not the clothing that was required at that time. But as Marx also said, it would be easy to make the revolution only at such times as success was assured.

The actors may have had inappropriate costumes, but the play went on. Despite the repetition of elements borrowed from the past, it was not a farce. Nor can it be called a tragedy, although there were indeed some fatal flaws in the character of the hero. The Commune went down to defeat because of its mixed character, true, but it is more proper to place the emphasis upon another aspect: the Commune failed because the Parisian—in fact, the French—working class was neither sufficiently numerous, strong, nor conscious to carry the day against the combined forces of reaction of the French bourgeoisie and the German Empire.

The Commune living and dying contained within itself the germ of every movement, every theme of subsequent social struggles; and this heritage far outweighs the temporary disadvantages of defeat, the killings, the deportations, the intense human suffering, the destruction of proletarian organizations. As each issue is raised anew, its presence in embryo in the Commune is rediscovered and emphasized. Thus, the aspect of popular spontaneity and the revolution as an unleashing of joyous energy noted by the situationists and Henri Lefebvre, the celebration of libertarian and decentralizing tendencies by the latter-day disciples of Bakunin, the participation of women now rediscovered by militant feminists. Above all, the Commune as the first assault on heaven by the modern industrial working class: "essentially a working class government . . . the political form at last discovered under which to work out the economical emancipation of labour . . . the Commune was . . . to serve as a lever for uprooting the economical foundations upon which rests the existence of class, and therefore of class rule."[1] In short, the first stages of a dictatorship of the proletariat neither bureaucratic nor repressive and peculiar to the moment in history when, in Vaillant's words, "Paris did not have to undertake . . . a particularly socialist program: or rather her socialist program was to call up the revolutionary power of the workers against reaction for the first time."[2] Not, perhaps, the dictatorship we are used to in the form of single parties and massive bureaucracies, but closer no doubt to what Marx himself had in mind.

145

Revolution & Reaction

Now artists are like other people but more talented. Or, for one reason or another, they have had the chance to express their talent better. They have eyes to see and hands to draw with, have they not also organs and dimensions, brains to think with? The changes rung here on Shylock's questions are not so out of place as one might imagine, for there is an unfortunate tendency abroad among art historians to treat their subjects as disembodied machines for the production of works of art or, contrariwise, as tumultuous, flighty, emotional, not to say irrational, dreamers to whom politics are about as meaningful as the latest theorem of nuclear physics. In short, the Artist, capital *A,* and all the familiar images the word conjures up. In direct opposition to this point of view, it is our contention that artists were attracted to the Commune for political reasons; the word political, in this context, being understood to embrace matters relevant not only to the choice of government or regime, but also to the organization of society, to the texture of living, to individual life styles. If the artists were confused or, better, contradictory in the position they took, they were at worst no more so than anyone else and at best more consistent in their theory and action. They were, of course, led to the Commune by their experiences as artists; and they tried to act as a corporate body to better their condition, whilst at the same time making art more available to the public at large. How silly it would be to use this evidence to argue that they were, on this account, any the less political. It would be like maintaining that an industrial worker who joins a revolutionary movement under the pressure of a fall in wages is not engaging in a political act, or that he necessarily has no larger vision of what he is about.

So much for the myths. If we wish to discover the why and wherefore of the artists' participation in the Commune, we must look at the role they played—or were expected to play—in contemporary French society.

The official art world was closely ruled by the Académie des Beaux-Arts of the Institut de France, the equivalent in the fine arts of the Académie Française in literature but in fact more powerful. A writer needs a pencil and paper (and leisure to use them) but learns his grammar in school. The plastic artist needs not only canvas and paint, or marble and a chisel, but also models and, above all, the skill, in large measure acquired, to use them. The young man desirous of becoming an artist studied in a master's studio, sketched from life at a drawing academy, and hoped to pass the entrance examination of the École des Beaux Arts, which was controlled by the Académie. If successful, he con-

146

tinued his work, passing through a series of *concours,* or competitive examinations, in order to become eligible for the contest whose reward was the Prix de Rome, which was a scholarship to study in the Eternal City for a period of three or four years. The *cursus honorum* of the academic artist could then be expected to include a certain number of state commissions and purchases, and the exhibition of his works at the salons organized on an annual basis from 1831. If, in fact, only a small percentage of all artists, even those trained at the École, could expect to scale the heights and draw a regular source of recognition and income from state patronage,[3] exclusion from the salon, again decided upon by a jury controlled by the Académie, could be disastrous in terms of both notoriety and income. There were few artists fully prepared to go it alone in defiance of official doctrines and sanctions, and even independent men like Manet and Courbet continued to show their canvases in the salons when allowed to do so. Economic conditions being what they were, one cannot blame them at all.[4]

The message of the state-sponsored art establishment to the artist was clear: behave, paint well and truly, and, above all, don't rock the boat. But what did that mean precisely? The academic and official style(s)—if they were distinct from one another, they were only marginally different —required a concentration on drawing and draftsmanship, a close attention to detail, and the division of the process of pictorial composition into distinct preliminary and finishing phases. The limits on the exercise of artistic imagination within the prescribed framework were narrow, not only as regards color and line, but subject matter as well. In fact, the artist was educated to be a craftsman whose primary function was to manufacture goods for a bespoke market. His training took place within a hierarchical atmosphere which prepared him for submission to the hierarchy of official recognition. Like all dutiful journeymen, he was allowed his rituals within the studio and occasional outbursts of bohemian enthusiasm on the streets, but his product was supposed to be kept free of any such taints.

The rigidity of the artisanal system was becoming more and more anachronistic in an era when the increase in the number of consumers, the development of a bourgeois buying public, created the conditions for the artist to emerge as a free professional selling his own commodities in the market place away from official sanctions. This liberation was slow to come about and by no means was a matter of linear progress, both because the number of artists competing for custom increased throughout the nineteenth century, and, above all, because the taste of the customers had itself been so largely formed by academic precepts. But the *grandes*

147

machines of academic history painting were clearly on their way out (bourgeois houses didn't have as much wall space as aristocratic mansions), and genre painting was on the way in. The still life, animal pictures, and interior scenes continued the tradition of adjusted elegance and a kind of studied unreality that kept this decor, the only expression to which the title of Art could properly be applied, above the world of the common herd.

It has been said that this painting for a bourgeois public was one in which subject matter was more important than esthetic values.[5] If the statement were amended to read "personal esthetic values of the painters," it might make some sense. Otherwise, it is like saying that academic painting was bad art, and that judgment can only be made with great difficulty to apply to Ingres or Delacroix or even Horace Vernet, however much he may not speak to our present sensibility. What can be said is that this painting, and the esthetic it carried, were appropriate to the public it served and whose values informed it. It may be argued that this sort of art became increasingly sterile, imitative, and lacking imagination; as time went on and new styles appeared, men of genius were attracted to them. The historian is not in the business of giving out gold stars for artistic excellence nor demerits to those who fail to conform to his own standards of beauty.

This brings us to the question of style. The word is used in so many different ways that it would take more space than we have available here just to catalogue them. A definition is nonetheless required. My own conforms to that given by Nicos Hadjinicalaou, continuing in the Marxist tradition of Frederick Antal. In terms of style, there can be no distinction between form and content, because both contribute to the definition of the whole. Style is not mere form nor a technique of execution, but an *idéologie imagée,* a pictorial ideology, "in each case a specific combination of thematic and formal elements of a picture, a combination which is one of the particular forms of a global ideology of a social class."[6] There is, then, no such thing as the style of an individual painter, although his work partakes of one or more styles toward which he may adopt a critical attitude. The art of the *juste milieu* that emerged as official art during the July Monarchy adopted elements of both classic and romantic styles and as such, I would argue, corresponded to a certain balance of class forces in postrevolutionary France. Which is not to say that its appearance was absolutely determined, nor that it had, in some metaphysical sense, to take the form it did; but only that it can, indeed must, be understood in class terms.

Now, this style held a monopoly on social recognition, that is, it was the equivalent in the fine arts of a dominant ideology. Moreover, it was enforced upon the artists under penalty of exclusion from the Pantheon of Art. Because of the close association between the academic system and the style, their rebellion against the one necessarily brought the other into question. Both sorts of revolt were made possible by the developing market place, and in particular by the presence on that market place of a fraction of the bourgeoisie hitherto excluded from the establishment and open at the very least to the world view pictorially expressed by the painters. The best known example of this relationship is no doubt Courbet's friendship with Bruyas, a provincial millionaire. In a more general way, the fact that realist art has seen service in the cause of proletarian class interests should not blind us to its essentially bourgeois character in the nineteenth-century context.

The realists' rebellion against previous conventions is often spoken of as a development of spontaneity and expressiveness, which is just another way of saying that it broke the rules. What Boime has called the triumph of the sketch over the *fini* [7] was for the artist the right to say when a painting was finished, instead of conforming to imposed norms. It may be argued that this self-assertion would never be sufficient to overcome the alienation inherent in the production of a work of art for the capitalist market place. The enemy, that which limited the artists' freedom, was for the moment not the market in the shape of the dealer-critic system. On the contrary, it was the means to a partial liberation.

It is against this background that Courbet's art should be seen and his declarations read. His *Burial at Ornans* (1849), *Stonebreakers* (1849), and even more the *Return from the Conference* (1863) were so many bricks heaved at the windows of conservative taste. What he was doing was to challenge every assumption of the official school with its flight into the past and its search for bourgeois respectability. He made a radical choice for contemporaneity and the suitability of all themes in painting, including the life of the peasantry, the world of labor, and even movements of revolt (the latter to be found mainly in his portraits of *inter alia* Proudhon and Vallès). Fould, the spokesman for Second Empire reaction, wrote in 1857, "art is very near to losing itself when, abandoning the high and the pure regions of the beautiful, and the traditional paths of the great masters to follow the teachings of the new school of realism, it seeks for nothing more than a servile imitation of the least poetic and elevated offerings of nature."[8] The words "purity," "high," and "elevated" appear in this sort of commentary continually, for it is the task of art to relieve us after our daily contact with this sordid world, as well as to distract our attention from problems that are not esthetic. But for Courbet, the beautiful exists everywhere in nature, that is, in real life; and the role of the artist's imagination is to render it. As early as 1855, he explained what he was about in a text written to accompany the exhibition of his *Painter's Studio.*

> I studied both ancient and modern art without any sort of system or set intention. I no more wanted to imitate the former than copy the latter; neither was I interested in the futile idea of "art for art's sake". No! All I wanted to do was to be able to draw on the whole of our artistic tradition in order to find the appropriate expression of my own individuality.
>
> My idea was to develop my practical capacity through knowledge. My aim is to render the customs, the ideas and the appearances of my age according to my own feelings, in short, to create a living art.[9]

By 1862, his position had undergone further development.

> I cannot teach my art, nor the art of any school, since I deny that art can be taught, or as I maintain, in other words, that art is strictly individual and is for each artist precisely the talent resulting from his own inspiration and from his own studies of tradition. I add that art or talent according to me should be for each artist only the means of applying his own faculties to the ideas and things of the epoch in which he lives.
>
> The art of painting especially should consist solely of the representation of objects visible and tangible to the artist. Any epoch should be reproduced only by its own artists, I mean to say, by the artists who have lived in it. I hold the artists of one century radically incompetent to reproduce the things of a preceding or future century, or otherwise to paint the past or the future.
>
> It is in this sense that I deny historical art applied to the past. Historical art is in its essence contemporary. . . .
>
> I also hold that painting is essentially a *concrete* art and does not consist of anything but the representation of *real* and *existing* things. It is a completely physical language using for words all visible objects. An abstract object, one which is invisible, non-existent, is not of the domain of painting.
>
> Imagination in art consists in knowing how to find the most complete expression of an existent thing, but never to suppose or create that thing.

Beauty is in nature and is found in reality under the most diverse forms. After it is found there it belongs to art, or above all to the artist who knows how to see it. Rather, beauty is real and visible, it has in itself its own artistic expression. But the artist has not the right to amplify that expression. He cannot touch it without risk of changing its nature and consequently weakening it. The beauty given by nature is superior to all the conventions of the artist.

Beauty, like truth, is a thing relative to the time in which it is seen and to the individual fit to conceive it. The expression of beauty is in direct ratio to the power of perception acquired by the artist.[10]

The independence and refusal to conform could not be better stated. It would, however, be wrong to take Courbet's arguments against high-flown historicity for an affirmation of art as photography. The artist is most definitely not a camera. Gauss is mistaken in declaring that the "realist artist seeks to omit the subjective and to reproduce the world as seen. He is a descriptive artist who states without comment."[11] From the moment that beauty is stated to be dependent, at least partially, on time and the artist's perception, the door is opened to subjective interpretation, to personal vision. Although it is clear that Courbet was no friend to abstraction in painting, he erected no barrier against it, except perhaps his own scorn. The rights of nature (the object to be described) and of the artist to assert his personality are in a delicate balance here, but the groundwork is already laid for Zola's definition of a work of art as "a corner of creation seen through a temperament."[12]

In regard to the central function of art, Courbet by no means broke from the ambitions of the past. He, too, was concerned with beauty and the appearance of beauty, but above all with art as a means for moral regeneration of mankind. The crucial difference was that those means were to be found in man himself, rather than as transcendent qualities outside of man, in the past, or on Olympus. The reference is no longer to classical or Christian epics, but to everyday life. Art is to be brought down to earth. The critic Théophile Thoré summed it up in 1870.

[Art is changing in subject from the traditional spirit to the] free inspiration of the individual, [and in its object from] divine myths and historical epics [to the] interpretation of man and nature.

Art has beauty and not an idea as its object. But through beauty it must make people love that which is true, that which is just, that which is fruitful for the development of man. . . . Everything which expresses in thoughtful form, a profound characteristic of man or nature, encloses the ideal since it leads to reflection on the essential points of life.

Formerly art was made for god and princes. Perhaps the time has come to make an art for man.[13]

Here again we have an unresolved tension between ideas and esthetic values which are similar to the one found in Courbet between nature and her portrayers. It was perhaps to be expected that artists and critics, deeply influenced by tradition and their expected role as beauty merchants, should continue to hold to a reified conception of the quality they had to sell, whilst at the same time they tried to make art play a social role. For a man like Proudhon, who was no artist but to whom all looked for guidance, the problem was a less thorny one. He was certain that "in painting, neither more nor less than in literature, and in everything, thought is the principal thing, the dominant one, . . . and the question of content is always more important than that of form, and . . . in every creation of a work of art, before judging the matter of taste, the debate on the idea must be settled."[14] Art and beauty, like the esthetic faculty through which we perceive them, are secondary to ideas of *"justice and truth, conscience and science, law and knowledge,* complementary terms [that are] correlative and adequate, and which express the two great functions of human life, to the service of which, I repeat, art and industry are, *ex aequo,* subject."[15] Art is defined in terms of its purpose: "an idealistic representation [idealism: that which is destined to heighten thought, to give it more strength, relief, interest . . .] of nature and ourselves, with a view to the physical and moral perfection of our species."[16] Art left to itself is sterile and immobile. What is asked of the artist is not that he give us his impressions, but our own. "It is not for themselves that they paint, sing or play their instruments, it is for us. From which it follows that what causes them to be admired and applauded, what makes them famous does not come from them; they are only its faithful and resounding echoes; what creates the miracles of poetry and art is the idealist faculty, not of an individual but of a collectivity. If this obedience displeases artists, if they claim to sing and paint for their particular needs and their own glory, we will not stop them; only they ought not to be surprised to see themselves abandoned and to [be obliged to] listen to themselves in the wilderness. Some amateurs of their persuasion may perhaps give them the charity of a compliment; the masses will pass by, not seeing them, and they will die out in obscurity."[17]

For Proudhon, the art produced in contemporary France was bad, at least in part because the artists had "lost the power of collectivity which had raised earlier talents so high." They had lost touch with the aspirations of the times, which it was their task to express. They could play their role once again by assimilating current (Proudhonian?) ideas and denouncing the decadence of present society, so as to clear the way for the creation of a new one.[18]

Proudhon and the realist artists had in common a protest against the loss of community, the debasement of art in the service of a hostile ideal and of the ruling bourgeoisie, and the futility of art for art's sake. Proudhon the positivist theoretician saw his arguments vitiated by the assumption of an eternally valid truth and justice, a moral purpose to be derived from the observation of objects in the real world. Like the partisans of "scientific history" a generation later, he made purpose emerge from the chronicle without appearing to exercise any influence on its ultimate determination. Applied to art this meant, if pushed to a logical conclusion, that the artist was to be a translator, rather than a creator, although there might be a grey area in which the two functions merged. The artists would never fully accept this limitation on their freedom. They would serve the community (the people, if not a specific class) and derive sustenance from it, but they would set the ground rules for so doing themselves.[19]

II

No sooner had the Republic been declared on 4 September 1870 than a group of artists formed themselves into a committee to defend their professional interests. Courbet was, as usual, the leading light. That he should have assumed the role is not astonishing, given his status in the arts and the gregarious force of his personality; a *force de la nature* if ever there was one. But the committee he headed, although recognized rather much against his will by Jules Simon, the minister of public instruction of the Government of National Defense, could do little more than make propaganda for the freedom of art and attempt to exercise a more or less inefficacious surveillance over Parisian museums.[20] When one thinks not only of the repressive nature of the official world of art, but also of specific incidents such as the government's refusal to allow the exhibition of Manet's *Execution of the Emperor Maximilian,* it is easy to see that there was work to be done and difficult to imagine that much might be accomplished short of some radical alterations in class relationships.

This was the promise of 18 March. And once again it was Courbet who seized the initiative. No doubt the most consciously ideological of the artists (he later explained to his accusers, "He [Courbet] is absolutely for the French Federation . . . because he, like everyone, sees that the time of men who govern as masters, like that of absolute authority and of arbitrary rule, is past"), he issued the following call to his confrères.

Revenge is taken. Paris has saved France from dishonor and disgrace. Ah! Paris! Paris in its genius has understood that it could not fight a backward enemy with its own arms. Paris has chosen its own terrain, and the enemy will be defeated as it has been unable to defeat us. Today, Paris is free and belongs to itself, and the provinces are in bondage. When federated France includes Paris, Europe will be saved.

Today, I call upon the artists, I call upon their intelligence, their feelings, their gratitude; Paris has fed them like a mother and has given them their genius. The artists must, at this hour, bend all their efforts (it is a debt of honor) to the reconstitution of its moral state and to the reestablishment of the arts, which are its fortune. Consequently, it is most urgent to reopen the museums and to plan seriously for an exhibition in the near future; let each one from this moment on set to work, and the artists of friendly nations will answer our appeal.

Revenge is taken, genius will flourish: for the real Prussians are not those who attacked us at first. The Prussians helped us, by causing us to die of hunger physically, to reconquer our moral life and to raise up everyone to human dignity.

Ah! Paris, Paris the great city has just shaken off the dust of all feudalisms. The cruelest Prussians, the exploiters of the poor, were at Versailles. Its revolution is so much the more equitable as it comes from the people. Its apostles are workers, its Christ was Proudhon. For 1800 years, sensitive men have died sighing; but the heroic people of Paris will defeat the mystifiers [*mistagogues*] and the tormentors of Versailles, man will govern himself, [the idea of] federation will be understood, and Paris will have the greatest share of glory history has ever recorded.

Today, I repeat, let everyone set disinterestedly to work: it is the duty we have to our soldier brothers, those heroes who are dying for us. Right is on their side. . . .

Yes, each man following his genius without let or hindrance, Paris will double its importance, and the international European city will be able to offer to the arts, to industry and to commerce, to all sorts of undertakings, to visitors from every country, an im-

154

perishable order, an order by its citizens, which no longer may be interrupted by the monstrous ambitions of monstrous pretenders.

Our era is about to begin; curious coincidence! Next Sunday is Easter; is it on that day that our resurrection will take place?

Adieu to the old world and its diplomacy![21]

This curious mixture of appeal and panegyric, of municipal pride and federative zeal, had the desired effect. More than four hundred artists—painters, sculptors, architects, but also commercial designers—gathered in the amphitheater of the medical school on 14 April to adopt the statutes of the Fédération des Artistes de Paris and to elect a committee and an executive. The committee formed was to include sixteen painters, ten sculptors, five architects, six engravers and lithographers, and ten members "representing the decorative arts, improperly called industrial art." The inclusion of the latter was a conscious attempt to create ties of solidarity with the working class and at the same time to affirm art as a necessary part of everyday life. There is, however, no proof of the assertion made after the fact by anticommunards that the industrial artists "may be considered as having been the soul of the committee of the Fédération des Artistes."[22] This in itself would be of no particular importance were it not for the fact that the statement reads like an accusation, as if the reactionaries were trying to establish that no serious artist would have been mixed up in so disreputable an enterprise.

The bases of the Fédération were declared to be three in number: (1) the free expansion of art, relieved of all government tutelage and of all privileges; (2) the equality of rights among all the members of the Fédération; and (3) the independence and dignity of each artist placed in the safekeeping of all by the creation of a committee elected by the universal suffrage of the artists.

As we have already noted, the largest possible participation was invited (artists were those who had exhibited their work or who were otherwise known to work at the trade), and the statutes provided for all of the usual democratic safeguards (rotation in office, right of recall). This "government of the world of arts by artists" was to undertake three tasks: the "conservation of the treasures of the past; the creation and exhibition of all the elements of the present; the regeneration of the future through education." The museums and galleries were to be opened to the public and maintained in proper condition. Regular exhibitions of new work were to be arranged, to the absolute exclusion of "any commercial exhibit tending to substitute the name of the publisher or manufacturer for that of the true creator." No prizes might be awarded. And work for the Commune was to be alloted by vote of the artists, commissions for special projects to be determined by competitions. And education in techniques of execution as well as in esthetics and the history and philosophy of art was to be developed to the fullest possible extent. The committee might act, upon request, to arbitrate disputes between individual artists and would act as an arbitration council on all matters of "principle and general interest." Finally, the committee would seek to encourage "progress in art, the moral and intellectual emancipation of artists, and the material betterment of their situation." The Commune, individual citizens, and public opinion were called upon to aid the artists in this work of renovation and development. In a word, "by word, pen and pencil, by popular reproduction of masterpieces, by intelligent and moralising pictures that can be distributed in profusion and posted in the town halls of the humblest communes of France, the committee will contribute to our Regeneration, to the inauguration of communal luxury and the splendour of the future, and to [the creation of] the universal republic."[23]

An ambitious program, indeed, and one that was destined to remain unfulfilled for lack of time. But the generosity is there, the antiauthoritarianism and individualism to be expected from men too long kept under odious restrictions. What is equally remarkable is their implicit assumption that the best guarantee for the free flowering of the arts is popular support and education, together with liberty of creation and judgment. It was no doubt this shared principle that was responsible for overcoming potential conflict between the Fédération des Artistes with their demand for freedom above all, and the Commune, which in the person of Vaillant, the delegate responsible for public instruction, felt that a government "that called itself the Commune," that is, was of the people, could legitimately demand certain services of the artists, however much to do so would be to infringe upon their jealously guarded autonomy. The conflict, which here remained latent, is one that has faced every popular government from that day to this.[24]

The Fédération's role during the Commune had principally two aspects: to propose reforms in conformity with the demands of its program, placed under the sign of antielitism, freedom, and equality;[25] and to watch over the museums. And watch over them they did, despite the opposition of the regular administrators like Barbet de Jouy at the Louvre, who refused to recognize the authority of the Commune. The caricaturist André Gill at the Luxembourg, the painters Hereau and Courbet himself, among others, at the Louvre took their missions seriously and did their best, but with little success, to reopen the museums even as the fighting drew nearer to the center of the city and fires raged all around. That fire was not allowed to spread from the Tuileries to the Louvre is in no small measure due to the vigilance of the Communards. Under the circumstances, only the rankest sort of class prejudice, such as that which created the legend of the *pétroleuses,* could give rise to accusations like the one made by Cham in his lithograph (one of a series called the *Follies of the Commune*) bearing the legend, "The Administrator of the Museums of the Commune Receiving the Insignia of His Office," in which a bearded fanatic hands that shocked public servant a can of gasoline and a torch. But then right wing calumny knew no bounds in the months and years after the defeat of the Commune.[26]

The membership of the committee of the Fédération des Artistes was a kind of broad popular front, ranging from the highly politicized and very committed Courbet, Pichio, Dalou, Gill, Pottier (the designer on porcelain who went on to write the words of the *Internationale*), and the grand old men like Daumier and Corot, to the less overtly political Manet and the darling of the salons, Feyen-Perrin.[27] What they had in common was their republicanism and their determination to save themselves and their beloved city from the stigma of ignominious defeat. Lest this be taken as proof of the nonsocialist character of the Commune, let it be said that individual political propensities of those who participated in or who were merely in sympathy with the Commune proves nothing at all about the movement as a whole. At most, it may be said that most of the artists elected to the committee of the Fédération were not ideological socialists but had rather a visceral identification with the Parisian masses and their hatred of the Empire, their desire for some kind of vague, but nonetheless real, emancipation whose instrument would be the Republic, universal if not always social. Nor should inactivity in the common cause be taken as necessarily the reflection of conservative tendencies. Manet was away from Paris in late March and April, returning only in time to bear moving witness to the *semaine sanglante.* Bracquemond refused to serve on the committee but nonetheless found it expedient to spend a few months in London after the defeat. Amongst the more militant, Dalou remained in exile until 1879; Courbet served six months in Sainte-Pélagie, was ruined by the condemnation to pay the costs of rebuilding the Vendôme Column, and emigrated to Switzerland where he died in 1877; Lançon spent six months in prison at Satory before being acquitted by a court martial. Unlike the literati, few artists were militantly against the Commune. The only ones whose names come to mind are the caricaturists Nérac and Cham (whose real name was Count Amadeus de Noé) and Gustave Doré, and even the latter's position was somewhat ambiguous.

157

III

There were precious few works of art produced during or immediately inspired by the Commune. Before we try to understand why this should have been the case, let us look for a moment at what was, in fact, produced.

It was in caricature and drawing that production was greatest. This was to be expected not only because of the immediacy of both arts— paper, pencil, and perhaps access to a lithographic press are all that is needed for their execution—but also because, in the case of the former, there already existed a well-established tradition of its use for political purposes, despite the censorship imposed by various regimes. One has only to think of the extraordinary impact of Daumier from the days of the July Monarchy onward and of the contributions of the epigoni like Gavarni. The enormous (and international) popularity of Doré was also part of this same development.[28]

The caricaturists had never been tender towards Louis Napoleon and his family, and the fall of the Empire gave them free rein to declare their venom. The anonymous compositions showing the Empress in a variety of compromising poses, or the work by Ed. Renaux or Stick linking her sexually to Emile Ollivier are excellent examples of the genre. The Emperor's liaison with Marguerite Bellenger was often exploited, and he was frequently shown as the king of the cuckolds ("O, Badinguet, si tu n'es plus empereur des français, tu restes toujours le roi des c——").[29]

The siege of Paris was equally a field day for the caricaturists, who commented on all manner of things from strategems employed to find food to the valor (or lack of it) displayed by leading generals. If Jules Renard drew bad pictures about the high cost of living, the bombardments, and the vagaries of the National Guard (e.g., a National Guard is billeted in a lady's apartment. *She*: I've only one bedroom. *He*: That's quite enough),[30] this sort of boulevard humor and gauloiserie, happily, held no monopoly. The art of satire was very early applied ferociously and with great effect to Bismarck and the Kaiser and very rapidly thereafter by artists like André Gill, Faustin Betbeder, and Moloch (Alphonse Hector Colomb) to the lachrymose Jules Favre and the vicious Thiers. As the struggle turned from a war against the Prussians to a civil war, caricature became increasingly political. Thus we have Pilotell showing the allegorical female figure of France, her left arm covering her eyes, her right arm being amputated by Thiers and Favre, her blood flowing into a Prussian helmet. On the left, bags of money remind us of the war indemnity to be paid, whilst in the right background a rising sun

158

bearing the legend République Sociale spreads the light of better days to come. Moloch's best known contribution is called *Attempted Rape* and shows Thiers stamped with the fleur-de-lis being repulsed by France, while his accomplice Favre holds a candle for him to see by.[31]

The examples of politically committed caricature which is directly hostile to the Government of National Defense and thus at least implicitly favorable to the Commune are numerous. But few can compare in bitterness or brilliance with Daumier's compositions. This is incidentally the place to dispose once and for all of the legend that makes of Daumier a passive witness to the Commune. If it is true that his frame of reference was more the Revolution of 1848 than the political movements that would characterize the Left after 1871, it by no means follows that he made no choice between the Commune and the reactionaries. Quite to the contrary, he early and vigorously took a position. Always an enemy of the Empire, his pre-Commune lithographs can obviously be read as mainly republican in content and nothing more. Thus, the *History of a Reign* (12 September 1870) showing the bound figure of France standing between two cannon, one labeled Paris 1851, the other Sedan 1870. Or, again: *Ceci a tué cela,* published on 9 February 1871, showing France pointing to the bodies of the soldiers of the Franco-Prussian War whose death annulled the effects of the yes votes cast in the recent plebiscite. But the later prints leave no doubt in one's mind as to where the artist stood. On 16 February he published his view of the Bordeaux Assembly, showing the members surveying the prostrate body of France laid out as upon a slab at a morgue, with the legend, Who Will Take the Knife? On 30 March the allegorical figure of Paris is depicted showing a field of graves to a Versailles bourgeois and saying, "You see, Monsieur Réac, there are enough of them." And perhaps the finest of all (difficult though it is to choose among so many masterpieces): the piles of rent receipts raining down on a working woman, a result of the Commune's decree suspending payment.[32]

Beyond the field of caricature, we have the sketchbooks of artists such as Daniel Vierge, Doré, and Courbet (done while he was in prison after the Commune). There exist also the two extraordinary lithographs of Manet, *The Barricade* and *The Civil War,* which bear witness to his engagement on the side of the Commune. Renoir drew a picture of an amazonlike woman at a barricade, and another of the summary execution of a woman, her right arm lifted as if to welcome death, no doubt crying, "Long live the Commune."[33] In short, art of the kind that could be produced on the spot, art that chronicles and takes an immediate political position flourished under the Commune. It would not, I think, be going too far to compare this outburst of productivity in the visual arts to the sudden deluge of newspaper and pamphlet literature that inundated Paris in 1789, lithography having been invented in the meantime.

So much as lithography and drawing participated in the Commune, so little were painting and sculpture influenced by it. Pierre Joly has suggested that the reason for this is that great art doesn't grow up in a few weeks' time.[34] But what precisely does that mean, if it is not to be understood simply to refer to the amount of physical labor required to make a painting as opposed to a sketch. What, after all, was to prevent the artist from taking the time, after the Commune, to complete such work as he might have had in hand? There is, to be sure, the discouragement that follows on defeat and, for some of the artists concerned, the material impossibility of carrying on their trade while in prison or exile. Still, I would suggest that the answer lies elsewhere.

At times a revolutionary situation may produce "great art," works which are of particular merit because they express an especially strong sentiment in the pictorial-ideological terms appropriate to the continuing revolution. An example of this is David's *Marat*. When this happens, it is a wholly exceptional, truly privileged moment. In the case of David's painting, perhaps it was the result of the long and slow development of bourgeois consciousness, the already long existence of the Revolution by 1793 and hence its ability to reinforce that consciousness by creating a style appropriate to a bourgeoisie consciously avid of classical culture as both model and legitimation of its rule. David, who in his person combined both political and painterly roles, was in a sense only giving expression (of a genius, to be sure) to an already extant world view. Perhaps Courbet or another might have done the same for the Commune had it lasted a bit longer, which is to say had it been at least partially successful. Then and only then would there have been the opportunity for the working class socialist element in the Commune to emerge as dominant. Then and only then might a liaison have been effected between painters striving to free themselves from academic conventions, and an ideology clear and strong enough to support their experiments. As it was, no junction was made between painters and proletariat, and the Commune no more created an artistic style than it did its own specific ideology. In so far as the experience of the Commune contributed to the subsequent development of a socialist movement, it provided the subject matter for the compositions of certain artists like Steinlen and Luce, whose work belongs to the pictorial ideology of the working class. But in that case it is more proper to speak of the influence of socialism in general rather than of the Commune itself.

160

This is not to say that there are no contemporary paintings of the Commune. A few do exist, but only one or two of them at best make the kind of statement we may associate with revolutionary art; only one or two can claim to be in the same category as the paintings of David cited above. The series of large canvases by Didier and Guiaud portraying Paris during the war and the siege, together with Boulanger's paintings showing Versailles troops attacking barricades during the *semaine sanglante* are *grandes machines* of the historical type clearly intended for display in public buildings and presenting some marginal interest as documents expressive of the values of patriotism, duty, and conservation. G. A. Guillaumet's *Line in Front of the Butchershop during the Siege* is a competent, if wholly unmemorable, exercise in genre painting, if that word may be used to describe the portrayal of ordinary mortals in nonnoble situations. Henri Motte's *Execution of Hostages in the Court of La Roquette Prison* is a rather insipid depiction of how to die like a good bourgeois or priest, a moral lesson for our times. Jules Girardet painted a sketch of *Paris on Fire during the Night of May 28,* a landscape in which his use of patches of color gives it a certain distinction.

Of the paintings that may properly be termed communard, several are examples of good but uninspired craftsmanship. These include Jules Riou's *Quand Vous Voudrez,* a family of communards about to be put to death by a Versailles firing squad; and Alfred Roll's *Execution of a Bugler during the Commune,* a young man in a blue greatcoat, red scarf serving as a belt, bugle slung over his back, standing against a wall preparing to die. In the foreground, two bodies, one showing the feet only, the other the head and torso with clenched fists. In both cases, the defiance of the victims is clearly expressed, but neither painting succeeds fully in evoking an indignant or emotionally involved response from the viewer.[35] In the same vein but much more striking is Ernest Pichio's *Le Mur des Fédérés,* sometimes known as *The Triumph of Order.* Pichio, who, Bénézit writes, "was much concerned with politics" without further precision, had participated in the salons from 1864 to 1870 and had already acquired a certain notoriety with his protest painting of 1869 entitled *The Death of the Deputy Baudin on the Barricades of the Faubourg Saint Antoine* (in December 1851). Baudin is seen in heroic pose, book in hand, mounted on a sort of dais directly behind the cannon at a breach in the barricade. A young worker stoops to pick up a rifle, while a woman holds another. The crowd represents the "people," an undifferentiated mass drawn from all the classes, and it would seem that a municipal counselor wearing his scarf of office is haranguing the troops on the other side of the barricade. This is the perfect Jacobin painting:

the solidarity of the people opposed to the oppression of the military. If it had not been painted before the fact, it might almost be taken as showing the circumstances under which Delescluze went to his death in the Commune. *Le Mur des Fédérés* makes no partisan choice among the members of the Commune, but its somber tones do communicate the pathos of defeat.

Courbet's realist portraits of Vallès and Proudhon together with the canvas portraying Proudhon and his family, all done before the Commune, convey with great mastery the burning determination of the former and the reflective tranquillity of the latter, in addition to the affection the painter bore them. Curiously, the single oil done by Courbet apropos of the Commune, his self-portrait at Sainte-Pélagie, is marked by a certain primitivism that recalls the later manner of the Douanier Rousseau. Courbet in a beret and smoking a pipe sits calmly, in marked contrast to his usual bluff self, a wry comment on his enforced impotence. Among the other portraits, Louis Tinayre's *Louise Michel* does little, it seems to me, for its subject, whose expression remains resolute but impenetrable. Eugene Carrière's *Blanqui* is by far more successful. The anguished eyes, the flowing hair and beard blending into one another make for a mixture of determination and despair wholly appropriate to this leader of failed revolution. The brush stroke is smeared, as though just touching the canvas, creating an extraordinary sense of movement, a kind of swirl out of which the figure emerges in bust, the head set off by the firm stroke of black representing the ascot and underlining the firmness of chin and lip.

Last but not least, we come to Manet's *Execution of the Communards* that hangs now in the Folkwang Museum at Essen. Like the lithographs cited above, it is testimony to the defeat of the Commune, but also, I think, a clear affirmation of the painter's commitment. On the extreme left, Versailles soldiers are barely seen firing on a group of National Guards who occupy the entire pictorial space. Behind them is a cloud of white powder smoke, and in the foreground the cobbles provide contrasting color. Ten figures are seen in various stages of death and dying. From left to right their hands are particularly expressive: first on the head, then in the air, then at the heart before the body lies lifeless on the ground. The variations of light are less important than the mobility of line and the use of color which transmit the same sense of indignation, of revolt, as Goya's *The Third of May* on which it is modeled. Manet had made reference to this work before in his *Execution of the Emperor Maximilian*. But if it is true, as Linda Nochlin has argued, that the latter painting refuses to judge the event it chronicles, limited by good

162

realist principles to concrete description[36] (and I have great doubts about the entire thesis), still it is evident that the impact of the Commune made Manet throw such caution as he may have had to the winds. He sought and found, in the manner of his great predecessor adapted to his own genius, the expression of his revulsion. The shocked faces and, above all, eyes of the victims; the blood they vomit which flows over them counterpointing the red stripes in their trousers as they fall into death can have no other meaning. This is, I think, truly revolutionary art: uncompromising and unsentimental, politically committed and expressive of the artist's personality, and with the touch of greatness that combines esthetic satisfaction with the power of reflection.

IV

The amount of significant art produced in the Commune outside the field of caricature and lithography was, then, extremely limited. It remains clear, however, that the anticommunard lucubrations of a museum administrator like Darcel, who spoke of the "debauchery" of art and the reign of "licence," are totally unfounded, the purest calumny in defense of the bourgeois idea of beauty.[37] Even Courbet was, I think, rather too pessimistic when all he could find to say in his own defense was that "the arts are in the same state as on September 4."[38] Besides guarding the artistic heritage and attempting to make it available to a large public so as to maintain a continuity between the old and new societies (for the historian, this must appear as a doubly positive achievement: if only someone had thought to protect the archives at the Hotel de Ville), the artists affirmed their liberty, their social responsibility, and the necessity of art.

To be sure, official art went on in the salons. Charles Blanc, the director of fine arts in the newly launched Third Republic, expressed the traditional view in 1874.

In painting, what is being obliterated today, what is disappearing is precisely tradition: some don't want to learn it, others don't want to remember it. Art in the hands of the majority [*grand nombre*] is becoming a trade. . . .

In sum, painting in France is now, of all the arts, the one most soiled with heresy, the most delinquent. The strong side of the school is landscape. Our superiority is shown therein, but so also is our inferiority betrayed. When landscape takes over the first rank, one can say that painting falls into second place. May it not displease those critics in love with equality in art, and those who affirm with

163

serenity that there is no hierarchy of the beautiful, that one masterpiece is worth another, and that a pot of jam painted to absolute perfection by Chardin can equal the *Last Supper* of Leonardo or the *Saint Peter* of Titian; may it not displease them, but it is impossible not to admit some gradation in the realms of nature. Even supposing that the goal of art is to express life—which is precisely the definition they give—the human figure is the highest image the artist may propose, since it manifests the highest degree of life, which is thought.

Style is no more found in the countryside than eloquence is in the dictionary. Both come from the bottom of the human soul. The beautiful adolescents who besport themselves with so much candor and grace in the pastoral of Longus and in the admirable landscape of Français, cannot show themselves nude in the trees of Bas-Meudon. If reality mixes in, if the landscape is only a faithful study instead of being conceived by the soul or idealized by memory, I am no longer transported to the Island of Lesbos; Chloe is called Thérèse or Madeleine, and her nudity in the suburbs is no more than an indecent liberty.

Style! It is also truth, also life, but truth a hundred feet above the passers-by, life at the level where one breathes essences, where the species dominates the individual, where type dominates incident, where human beauty, imperishable beauty passes before those so-called Parisian beauties who, each year, show their charms in the salon under the borrowed names of Revery, Sleep, Spring, and whose address is whispered to the elegant and corrupt barbarians. Ah! Never would Athenians have asked the address of Venus Anadyomene. Everyone knew that she lived on Olympus, and if the Venus of Gnides, who was a marble Phryne, inspired impure passion in all of Greece, it was because style had already declined, the ideal had paled; and decadence was hurrying on its way.[39]

Ah, purity, where is thy sting? No doubt in the salons, even if the most conservative of traditionalists remained dissatisfied. While Courbet was refused admission to the salon of 1872 on the initiative of Meissonnier, a false archaism, a harking back to earlier styles reigned supreme. This could be seen in subjects ranging from the *Electra* of F. J. Barrias to *The Cinderella by the Fireside* of J. Bertrand, not forgetting the exotic exemplified in *The Young Arab Girl* by C. Brun and *The Turkish Barber* of L. Bounat (the latter may also be interpreted as a manifestation of patriotic, colonialist fervor in art). The war scenes were numerous by

A. M. de Neuville and L. Perrault, among others, too many others. And if Alsace was lost in real life, the artists spared no effort to affirm its appartenance to the national patrimony. Thus F. Lix in *Adieu to the Fatherland* shows Alsatians preferring France. And G. Doré in *Alsace,* portrays a woman standing against a wall, her eyes closed, grasping flags close to her in obvious mourning; while another woman, equally miserable, holds on to a child. The use of light to induce a sense of separation and alienation is expert.[40] Like everything else in France, from the construction of the Sacré-Coeur to the popularity of the Alsatian women in the whorehouses, salon painting was marked by reaction to the war and the Commune. It was characterized by its frightful mediocrity and a liberal dose of hypocritical pornography under the guise of moral lessons.[41]

The effect of the Commune upon art, even as upon the history of France in general, is to be sought in the long term through the development of the socialist movement and the emergence of a working-class culture and ideology. In terms of the role of its members as producers in society, the failure of the Commune meant that the conditions for the radical liberation of the artists from the constraints of the Academy and, even more, those of the dealer-critic system could not even be envisaged. And yet, the role of the Academy was never to be the same in the Third Republic as it had been in the Second Empire and before. The movement of revolt against its authority had started much before the Commune and was now taken up by numerous apolitical artists; men like Bastien, Worms, Butin, and Firmin-Girard who were not radical innovators but did obtain, with the foundation of the Société des Artistes Français, the right for artists to elect the members of the salon jury starting in 1881. In 1889, a new salon group called the Société Nationale des Beaux Arts was formed by Carrière, Puvis de Chavannes, Carolus-Duran, Raffaelli, Roll, Rodin, and Bracquemond; and its statutes were remarkably similar to those of the Fédération des Artistes, with the significant difference that it could not hope to exercise state power in favor of the arts.[42] This striving after liberation by the artists was not part of any larger contestation of social values, which is perhaps why it succeeded. The bourgeoisie could drop some part of its philistinism and could afford to recognize a certain kind of innovation in art, provided that those changes did not presage a revolutionary challenge to class relationships. The state could accept the impressionists (after how long a time!) because most of them were apolitical.

Some artists made no secret of their political sympathies. Camille and Lucien Pissarro, Seurat, Steinlen, Signac, and Luce were all sympathetic to anarchism and often expressed their feelings in their graphic art. In painting, the junction between art and politics (in the largest sense of the term) that did not come to pass during the Commune remained unestablished in the following generation. Painterly problems tended to become more abstract, less socially anchored, and artists felt their isolation. Henceforth, they might attempt to overcome that solitude by joining a movement or a party, but in their art they resigned themselves to believing what Signac put into words, "the anarchist painter is not he who does anarchist paintings but he who without caring for money, without desire for recompense, struggles with all his individuality against bourgeois or official conventions . . . basing his work on the eternal principles of beauty which are as simple as those of morality."[43] Of course, it is not a question of judging whether he was right or not. The important thing to note is that his remarks mark the end of an era when art was supposed to have a direct moral purpose. The artist gains in freedom what he loses in control over the destinies of men, what he abandons as the exponent of their concrete needs and desires. The engineering of the human soul would have to wait.

REFERENCES

[1] Karl Marx and Frederick Engels, *Selected Works* (London, 1970), p. 290. See above Monty Johnstone, "The Paris Commune and Marx's Conception of the Dictatorship of the Proletariat," and *Massachusetts Review* 12, no. 3 (Summer 1971): 447–62. [2] Maurice Dommanget, *L'Enseignement, l'enfance et la culture sous la Commune* (Paris, n.d.), p. 156 (my translation). [3] Harrison C. and Cynthia A. White, *Canvases and Careers: Institutional Change in the French Painting World* (New York, 1965), p. 53. [4] On French painting in the nineteenth century, see Albert Boime, *The Academy and French Painting in the Nineteenth Century* (London, 1971); Charles Edward Gauss, *The Aesthetic Theories of French Artists, 1855 to the Present* (Baltimore, 1949); and Joseph C. Sloane, *French Painting between Past and Present: Artists, Critics and Traditions from 1848 to 1870* (Princeton, 1951). [5] Boime, *The Academy and French Painting*, p. 14. [6] Nicos Hadjinicalaou, *Histoire de l'art et lutte des classes* (Paris, 1973), p. 103 (my translation). [7] Boime, *The Academy and French Painting*, p. 87. [8] Cited by Sloane in *French Painting*, pp. 44–45. [9] Cited by Teddy Brunius in *Mutual Aid in the Arts from the Second Empire to Fin de Siècle* (Uppsala, 1972), pp. 31–32. [10] Cited by Gauss in *Aesthetic Theories*, pp. 10–11. [11] Ibid., p. 11. [12] Brunius, *Mutual Aid in the Arts*, p. 71. [13] Cited by Sloane in *French Painting*, pp. 63–64. [14] Pierre-Joseph Proudhon, *Du principe de l'art et de sa destination sociale* (Paris, 1865), p. 14 (my translation). [15] Ibid., p. 44. [16] Ibid., p. 43. [17] Ibid., p. 123. [18] Ibid., pp. 181–83. [19] It seems to me that Proudhon's formulations are more congenial to the imposition of a single style of painting—socialist realism, to name names—than anything found in Marx. It is worth noting that in France, between 1885 and 1920, plastic artists were more likely to be attracted to anarchism than to socialism. Eugenia W. Herbert in *The Artist and Social Reform: France and*

Belgium, 1885–1898 ([New Haven, 1961], 208ff.) argues that this was due not only to anarchism's emphasis on creative liberty, but also to the socialists' failure to allay artists' fears of "collective constraints" being imposed upon them by a socialist regime. If this is so, would it be too much to suggest that the cause of the failure lies in the survival of the Proudhonian tradition? [20] Other members were the painters Daumier, Veyrassat, Feyen-Perrin and Lansyer; the sculptors Ottin, Moulin, Le Véel, and Geoffroy Dechaume; the printmaker Bracquemond; and the designer of jewelry, bronzes, and bookbindings Reiber. See Alfred Darcel, "Les Arts et les musées pendant le siège," *Gazette des beaux arts,* 29 (1 October 1871): 285–306, and (1 November 1871): 414–29. [21] *Réimpression du Journal officiel de la Commune* (Paris, 1872), p. 178 (my translation). [22] Alfred Darcel, "Les Musées, les arts et les artistes pendant la Commune," *Gazette des beaux arts,* 30 (1872): 51 (my translation). [23] *Journal officiel,* pp. 273–74. [24] On the question of liberty of artistic expression, see *Le Père Duchêne,* no. 31 (26 Germinal an 79): 4–5: "Toute oeuvre d'art, par cela même qu'elle est une oeuvre d'art, est morale, et le bon bougre Proudhon s'est absolument foutu dedans quand il a dit que l'art devait avoir pour lui de moraliser les patriotes! Ça n'est pas vrai! Si vous voulez faire un traité de morale, ne faites pas un tableau, mais une déclaration des droits de l'homme. Une oeuvre d'art est morale quand elle est bien faite; Car si elle est bien faite, elle sert la morale, soit par l'horreur, soit par la sympathie qu'elle excite, Et il n'y a pas autre chose à faire! En art, c'est comme en chimie: Il n'y a pas de corps sales! Le Père Duchêne, qui a tripoté dans toutes les drogues, sait bien qu'on ne doit pas avoir de préjugés! Il faut laisser la liberté à tout le monde!" [25] *Journal officiel,* pp. 523–24. [26] For a hostile but not totally unfair account of this matter, see Darcel, "Commune," *Gazette des beaux arts,* 30, pp. 41–65, 140–50, 210–29, 398–418, and 479–90. [27] For a list of the members of the commission, see Archives Nationales, F 17 2685 (1). [28] Arwed D. Gorella, "Zur Geschichte der Politischen Karikatur Frankreichs im 19 Jahrhundert," in *Pariser Kommune 1871: Eine Bild-Dokumentation* (Berlin: Neue Gesellschaft fur Bildende Kunst, 1971), pp. 138–50. [29] Susan Lambert, *The Franco-Prussian War and the Commune in Caricature* (London, 1971), especially figs. 17–26. [30] Draner (Jules Renard), *Paris assiégé: scenes de la vie parisienne pendant le siège* (1871), and *Souvenirs du siège de Paris: les défenseurs de la capitale* (1871). [31] Lambert, *Caricature,* figs. 98 and 99. [32] *Pariser Kommune,* pp. 48, 54–56, 95–99. See also A. Dayot, *Histoire de France par l'image: l'invasion, le siège (1870), La Commune (1871)* (Paris, 1901). [33] Georges Bourgin, *La Guerre de 1870–1871 et la Commune* (Paris, 1939). *Iconographie de l'époque réunie sous la direction de Max Terrier,* pp. 303, 353. [34] Pierre Joly, "La Culture," in *La Commune de 1871,* 2d ed., ed. J. Bruhat, J. Dautry and E. Tersen (Paris, 1971), pp. 212–16. [35] The paintings mentioned here are reproduced in Terrier, *Iconographie.* [36] Linda Nochlin, *Realism* (London, 1971), pp. 31–33. [37] Darcel, "Commune," p. 488. [38] *Bulletin des amis de Gustave Courbet* (Paris and Ornans, 1971), No. 45. [39] Charles Blanc, "De l'état des beaux arts en France à la veille du salon de 1874," *Le Temps,* April 7, 1874. [40] Anon., *Salon de 1872* and *Salon de 1873* (Paris, part of a series published each year by Goupil and Compagnie). [41] Paul Vogt, *Was Sie Liebten. Salonmalerei im XIX Jahrhundert* (Cologne, 1969). [42] Boime, *Academy, passim.* [43] Herbert, *Artist and Social Reform,* p. 190.

RIMBAUD AND THE COMMUNE

Wallace Fowlie

Beyond the purely literary influences that help explain the writings of Arthur Rimbaud, two very different kinds of influence, prior to his meeting with Verlaine in September 1871, count in the development of his personality and his work: the role of his mother in his life and that of the Commune of March 1871. But these two influences, the one maternal and lifelong, and the other political and limited to two months, are extremely difficult to evaluate and even to describe.

What was the Commune? When Paris surrendered to the German invaders in 1870, a revolt was organized against the new conservative French government. It was a revolt of workers in Paris, small artisans and shopkeepers, who elected their representatives on March 26, 1871, at the Hôtel de Ville, and carried off a successful insurrection. The members of the government took refuge in Versailles and were called the Versaillais. Two months later, on May 21, the Versaillais returned to Paris. At the end of eight days of massacres and destruction of the city by fires, the Commune was put down, bringing to an end the revolutionary movement. Karl Marx, in London, called la Commune a communist uprising. He repeated this claim many times. Later, Lenin made the same claim. Their French disciples today look upon the Commune as a French pre-socialist uprising.

Ernest Delahaye, a close friend of Rimbaud in Charleville, wrote one of the first books on the poet, which he published in 1923. In it he says that he and Rimbaud were together in March, in the Ardennes, and discussed with enthusiasm the Commune which they interpreted as the advent of socialism in France. This much of Delahaye's account is probably accurate. But he goes on to say that Rimbaud participated in the actual fighting of the Commune. And this part of his account is impossible to prove in the light of documentation available today. Rimbaud's sister Isabelle claimed it was not true, that if her brother had made such a statement, it would have been a form of bragging.

In February 1871, Rimbaud was in Paris—on his third escape from home. When his money gave out, he returned to Charleville on foot, in March. He was certainly in Charleville soon after the middle of March. After that date the real facts of Rimbaud's actions are not certain. It is possible that he went to Paris at the end of April, joined up with the *corps francs* of the Commune and spent some time in one of the barracks (*la caserne de Babylone*). It was from Charleville, however, that he wrote the two famous letters of the 13th and 15th of May, in which he says that in eight days he will be in Paris. He makes no reference to any recent sojourn there. It is possible that Rimbaud saw Paris at the time of the Commune. But absolute proof of this is lacking.

Rimbaud and the Commune

One important fact is certain. During that spring of 1871, an inner turmoil or revolution was going on in Rimbaud that corresponded to the political revolution of the Commune. He felt in sympathy with the Commune politically and emotionally. The two letters of the 13th and 15th of May are documents on this double turmoil. They are more than a system of poetry, more than a literary manifesto.

These two letters, and especially the second, addressed to Paul Demeny, and usually referred to as *La Lettre du Voyant,* were written at a moment of great exuberance when, in every sense, literary as well as political and sociological, Rimbaud was expecting a new age to begin. He obviously was looking upon himself as one of the founders of the new age.

In the first of the two letters, the one to his teacher Georges Izambard, Rimbaud berates Izambard for his fidelity to the teaching profession in a time of revolution, and says, ironically, of course, *On se doit à la Société* ("We owe everything to society"). Rimbaud contrasts Izambard's routine profession with his own hope of becoming a worker (*Je serai un travailleur*). This idea, he writes, holds him back (in Charleville) where the anger he feels urges him on to the battle in Paris (*les colères folles me poussent vers la bataille de Paris*). This would seem to indicate that Rimbaud had not been in Paris late April and early May. With a sense of guilt in not being there, he speaks of Paris as that place where workers are dying at the very moment he is writing his letter to Izambard.

Everything in the letter testifies to Rimbaud's break with society and with the conventions of society. He castigates his teacher for staying in the "ruts" (*ornières*) of these conventions. The new life the poet has chosen to lead has to be scandalous and unruly. *Je m'encrapule le plus possible,* he writes to Izambard. The problem of Rimbaud's participation in the Commune is stated here in the reference to Paris. On the one hand, he refuses to go to Paris because that would mean his integration in Parisian society, in the sense that he would be a worker (*travailleur*), and on the other hand, he feels the communard spirit urging him to go to Paris to help *les travailleurs,* to help those who are dying in the battle of Paris.

Of the four poems inserted in the two letters, *Le coeur supplicié,* attached to the letter of the 13th of May, is the most important for an elucidation of Rimbaud's relationship with the Commune. The text will be called later *Le coeur du pitre,* and finally *Le coeur volé.* It is a poem of confession in which Rimbaud seems to be describing a violent kind of sexual initiation. On the literal level (as analyzed by the Belgian critic Emilie Noulet), it is the confession of a boy (Rimbaud was sixteen and a half) degraded and nauseated by orgies in which he was forced to participate. By using such a word as *ithyphalliques,* Rimbaud alludes to priapic debauchery. Other critics refuse to read the poem literally because Rimbaud made no reference to such an experience in his letters to Izambard or Demeny. Still other critics point out that perhaps such letters were written but have been lost. The controversy has no easy solution.

169

Whether *Le coeur volé* is based on the disorder and rowdiness that Rimbaud had witnessed at *la caserne de Babylone,* or whether it is based on the poet's imagining of what a barracks' scene would be like in May 1871, the vital significance of the text is the expression in it of Rimbaud's disgust with society. Some of its nautical vocabulary: *poupe, gouvernail, flots* points the way to *Le Bateau Ivre,* his most famous poem, written probably in the summer of 1871, on the escape from the familiar world and the conventional society of Charleville. Such words might lead one to think Rimbaud had in mind the image of a boat rather than that of a barracks. The poet's reaction to the scene he observes is both physical (nausea) and moral (disgust). Without any doubt, Rimbaud felt at the time that he belonged to the masses (*le peuple*). At least morally speaking he was a communard.

The conclusion of the poem, its last line,

Comment agir, ô coeur volé?

translates an experience that is both physical and moral. It is the impossibility of taking any action.

The poet's suffering comes from his inability to carry out his actions of a poet and a visionary (*voyant*). This is more clearly stated in the *Lettre du 15 mai.* The second poem, included in this second letter, is *Chant de guerre parisien,* and testifies to Rimbaud's fury against the Versaillais. He calls it a springtime poem,

Le Printemps est évident

and alludes to the month of May,

O Mai! quels délirants culs-nus!

Rimbaud is in close touch with the events as they are happening: Thiers' flight to Versailles on the 18th of March, the Commune's taking over the power, the bombs from Versailles that fell on the outskirts of Paris.

In the fifth stanza, a typical line clearly indicates Rimbaud's attitude toward the Versaillais:

Au pétrole ils font des Corots.

The landscape is lit up with the petroleum bombs and takes on the ruddiness of a Corot painting.

The defeat of the Commune inspired Rimbaud's most revolutionary poem: *L'Orgie parisienne ou Paris se repeuple.* One of the literary sources of the poem is a piece by Leconte de Lisle, *Le Sacre de Paris,* which by its date January 1871, indicates that the subject is the Paris siege by the Germans at the end of 1870. Rimbaud's poem describes the return

170

to Paris of those Parisians who had taken refuge in the country during the Commune. It is too pompous in tone to rank among Rimbaud's major poems, but in it the poet lucidly affirms his faith as a communard. In strong almost obscene language he castigates the Versaillais. The *vainqueurs* are those who give themselves over to gourmandizing and debauchery. Paris is the whore (*la putain Paris*) depraved by the bourgeois in Thiers' party. Throughout the poem (and one of its weaknesses) the tone and vocabulary of Hugo's *Les Châtiments* are too much in evidence.

Of all the Rimbaud poems directly inspired by the Commune, *Les Mains de Jeanne-Marie* is perhaps the most successful and the most moving. In it Rimbaud describes the struggle of the communards with the Versaillais, and recalls the action of women from the working class who literally fought in the streets during the terrible week of May 21–28, when they helped defend the barracks on the Place Blanche, the Place Pigalle and the Batignolles. The poet contrasts the beautiful delicate hands of women in love, as celebrated by various parnassian poets (cf. *Etudes de mains* by Théophile Gautier) with the rough hands of women who fought in the streets of Paris. Rimbaud is intent upon exalting revolutionary violence and he does it by pointing out this contrast between the white hands of noble ladies and the dark hands of the typical communarde women.

The last three stanzas of *Les Mains de Jeanne-Marie* contain very precise allusions to the Commune and especially to the repression that followed the "bloody" week of May 21–28. The hands of the communards are apostrophized as being sacred: *ô Mains sacrées*. The "chain" named in the next-to-last stanza is undoubtedly a reference to the long line of communard prisoners who were sent to Versailles, and who numbered from one hundred and fifty to two hundred each day. They were bound hand to hand, in ranks of four. On the way they were insulted and derided by the crowds watching them. The last line of the poem,

En vous faisant saigner les doigts

indicates that those insults were often physical which bruised the chained hands of the prisoners to such an extent that they bled.

These three poems, then, *Chant de guerre parisien, Paris se repeuple* and *Les Mains de Jeanne-Marie,* are ample proof that Rimbaud's heart was with the Commune. His personal youthful revolt in which his vocation of a writer was clearly affirmed, coincided with his almost sudden awareness of the political and social problems of the moment. In earlier poems of 1870, he had spoken out against the concept of the Empire (*Morts de quatre-vingt-douze*), and against all tyrants in one of his best poems, *Rages de Césars*. At the time this sonnet was written, Napoleon III was a prisoner of the Germans. But Rimbaud put his title in the plural, *Césars,* in order to show that Napoleon III was merely a symbol designating all oppressors of the people.

171

EDMOND DE GONCOURT AND THE
PARIS COMMUNE

Richard B. Grant

The literate public which knows anything at all about the Goncourt
brothers thinks of them primarily as novelists and perhaps also as
the authors of the *Journal: Mémoires de la vie littéraire*,[1] that vast and
precious storehouse of history and anecdote, insight and prejudice. What
is perhaps less well known to this public is the fact that after Jules' death
in 1870, Edmond witnessed the siege of Paris and the days of the Commune (late February to late May, 1871) and wrote about these events in
his *Journal*.[2] Edmond's reportage is of particular interest today, not only
because of his undoubted mastery of words, but because although hostile
to the socialistically oriented Commune, he was an artist deeply dedicated
to his calling, a man who despised propaganda and sought truth. To
watch a man torn between his class prejudices and his innate desire for
honesty can be a salutary lesson for those caught in the same position a
century later.

Although the nobility of the Goncourt family was only as old as the
eighteenth century, Edmond and Jules always gave the impression of belonging to the old landed aristocracy. It was the younger of the two,
Jules, who wrote to his friend Louis Passy in 1848 when he had earned
his baccalaureate degree: "I have made a firm resolution and nothing will
make me change it, neither sermons, nor good advice . . . *I shall do
nothing.*" The pose of an aristocratic idler with a vast fortune was fraudu-
lent, of course. What Jules meant was a life dedicated, not to commerce,
but to art. Edmond shared these views.

The reason for their lofty attitude was not only the result of a natural
elitist temperament, but a consequence of the historical direction that
modern Europe was taking. The Revolution of 1848 showed the depths of
popular ferment, not in France alone, but all over Europe. Edmond, now
twenty-six years old, served in the National Guard which put down the
popular Parisian uprisings in June of that year, and he did so in the belief,
as he wrote shortly afterwards: "Yes, it was necessary to be severe with
the ringleaders; yes, it was necessary to be pitiless towards the perpetrators
of atrocities that brought dishonor on their party." But he was a realistic
conservative, and he judged the reprisals to be excessive, if only for reasons of expediency: "Is it not an established fact that ideas are more formidable when they are watered with the blood of their martyrs?" But
however much they disliked what they chose to call mob rule, they were
not blind to the defects of the old nobility and the reigning bourgeoisie.
Edmond opined that "socialist ideas, however absurd they may appear . . .

172

[are] the bases on which a new society replacing the old, will be established." In this new mass society, he felt, the artist could never be understood, and like many sensitive writers of their generation, he and Jules withdrew from the political scene: "The artist, the man of letters, the scholar should never get involved in politics, which is a storm that they ought to let pass beneath them."

Their views were, therefore, fixed by the mid-1850's, when they decided to become historians of the upheavals of the French Revolution. In 1854 they published *L'Histoire de la société française pendant la Révolution,* and the following year *L'Histoire de la société française pendant le Directoire.* As historians, they were serious about their work. They consulted original documents in great quantity (diaries, correspondences, newspapers, and the like), which they purchased along the Paris quais. They sought to go beyond the "public and exterior acts of a state or social system" and write that history "which had been disdained by political history," as they put it in their preface to *Les Maîtresses de Louis XV.* But their a priori hostility to the French Revolution and to its doctrines of progress and stated egalitarianism warped their views. They avoided using pro-Revolutionary material and were unwilling to admit that their own favorite sources could be heavily biased. For these reasons, as well as for their inadequacies in economics, critics were not kind to their volumes, and it was no doubt because of the cool reception that they abandoned formal history (they had planned a volume on the Empire) and turned to biography, which has a much narrower scope. Until the Franco-Prussian War, their energies were devoted to art history, biography, and the novel.

The year 1870 was a crucial one for Edmond de Goncourt. Jules, only forty-eight years old, died of syphilis on June 20. Edmond was disconsolate: "I am sad, broken, obliterated," he wrote in the *Journal* that day, and he had to struggle to keep the diary going. However, private misfortune was swept away by public events, for during the summer France embarked upon the disastrous war that was to topple the Empire and create the Commune. As Edmond walked the streets of the capital in an effort to shake off his personal grief, he found himself observing the changes in the city that had been brought on by the outbreak of hostilities. Little by little he recorded in his *Journal* vignettes of a nation at war.

When early enthusiasm disappeared with the onset of military reverses, the scenes that Edmond witnessed appealed to that aesthetic sense in him which relished the spectacle of disintegration: "I find at the St. Lazare Railroad station a group of some twenty Zouaves, the remnants of a battalion that had gone into action under MacMahon. Nothing is so beautiful, nothing has so much style, nothing is so sculptured, so pictorial as these exhausted refugees from a battle. They bear on themselves a weariness comparable to no other weariness and their uniforms are worn, faded, as if they had drunk the sun and rain of years" (Aug. 23). This paragraph is fairly typical: what begins as detached—even inhuman—

173

aesthetics gives way to compassion, for essentially, there was little lofty detachment about his reportage. Edmond was an ardent nationalist, and he could become more than a little annoyed at the Olympian views of his acquaintance Ernest Renan, the great historian, who seemed to be above national prejudices, and spoke in the name of all humanity. Edmond suffered keenly at the presence of German troops on French soil and, like everyone else, had conclusions to draw. He blamed the failures of the French on the lack of discipline in the working class, and saw this slackness as having been fostered by the moral laxity of the Empire, but he avoided the simplistic polemics of those who blamed it all on the private excesses of Napoleon III.

Edmond's success in capturing kaleidoscopic scenes brought about by the upheavals of war led him to write more and more extended descriptions, and by September 19, when the Germans completed the encirclement of the capital, Edmond had clearly undertaken the task of a responsible reporting of the total picture, in an effort to penetrate the hypocrisy of war and politics. He was acutely conscious of the illusions of his compatriots and he sensed irony even in the weather: "Nature seems to enjoy the contrast that novelists like for their intimate catastrophes. Never has the decor of September been so laughing, never has the sky been so pure, the weather so beautiful" (Sept. 26) as the disaster loomed. This illusion was reflected in Edmond's opinion by the political "changes" that occurred when the Republic was declared. On September 21st, on the anniversary of the proclamation of the First Republic, there was a parade in honor of liberty. Edmond was furious at what he considered play-acting, convinced that the Republic gave no freedom and merely shifted power from the hands of one set of adventurers to another. Illusion was even more obviously a factor in the press, for to sell their newspapers, sensational news items were cynically fabricated. "Journalists of the present hour are robbing the public," declared Edmond on October 16 in scornful anger. He was disgusted by euphemistic military bulletins that labeled retreats as "offensive reconnaissances" (Oct. 20), and by the invention of nonexistent victories. Even when reporting was honest, the constant disillusionment of hope quickly destroyed by reality was a terrible and exhausting experience. Even Edmond's own self-centered world at times seemed unimportant: "I look at this house full of books, *objets d'art*, of engravings, drawings, which will create holes in the history of the French School if it all burns, and these things which were my loves . . . before, I don't have the energetic desire to save" (Aug. 25). (He even noted the fact that he had lost interest in buying old historical pamphlets.) There were times when he admitted his selfishness openly: "I desire peace keenly, I desire very selfishly that no shell fall on my house and bibelots" (Nov. 11), and on January 16, 1871, he worried again about their destruction, but the caricature of Edmond whose only concern in the war was his collection of *objets d'art* is unjust. As a patriot he railed at the

174

defeatists and grieved over the surrender. He had a truly lofty goal of being a responsible journalist, even a modern historian, who would tell the truth about the conflict. He chronicled all the daily miseries and examples of cowardice, the lack of leadership and discipline, the omnipresent concern for food as stocks dwindled. His conclusion is categorical: "Let posterity not try to tell future generations about the heroism of the Parisian in 1870. His entire heroism consisted in putting rancid butter on his beans and eating horsemeat instead of beef—and this last without being very aware of it, as the Parisian has little discernment about what he eats" (Nov. 12).

When the siege ended with the surrender of the French, Edmond—and Paris—felt a temporary sense of relief. The Germans were "correct" and Edmond could write in his *Journal* on January 24, 1871: "I was seized this morning by the desire to write *La Fille Elisa*. . . . I wrote a few lines on a piece of paper. It will perhaps become the first chapter." But history, which often disrupts human plans, forced another postponement.

Edmond was still jotting down in his diary what he saw when each day he left his home in Auteuil to prowl around Paris. On February 27, he commented on the somber, anxious faces of the Parisian population and noted, too, that National Guardsmen, who were supposed to keep order, had gotten out of hand. He saw some on parade, drunk and shouting "Long live the Republic." Two days later—March 1, the Prussians actually entered the city, but left on March 3, creating a power vacuum. On March 18, when Edmond went out to buy bread, he learned that fighting had broken out in the populous working class section of northern Paris—Montmartre. He was upset to realize that most people seemed indifferent to this turn of events; they had had too many months of anguish already. But he himself was full of the "most powerful forebodings" at this "terrible revolution," for as he walked around Paris, he observed that the swarming National Guardsmen had gone over to the Revolution and that barricades were being set up everywhere.

Edmond's nationalistic feelings had been outraged by the defeat in war; now his class feelings suffered. Weary at the changes that the modern world was bringing, he wrote on March 19: "A feeling of weariness at being a Frenchman; a vague desire to go look for a country where the artist's thoughts are tranquil and not constantly troubled by stupid agitation, the stupid convulsions of a destructive mob." This last phrase summarizes succinctly Edmond's dominant attitude toward the Commune, and he never was to make a serious, consistent effort to see the situation from the insurrectionists' point of view.

In that same entry, he elevated his class prejudices to the level of theory:

On the Boulevard Montmartre, I see the names of the men in the new government posted, names so unknown that it seems a joke. After [Adolphe-Alphonse] Assi's name the least unknown is that of [Ernest-Charles] Lullier, who is notoriously mad. For me this poster marks the permanent death of the Republic in France. The experiment of 1870, made with people from the top of the basket, was deplorable; this one, made with men from the very bottom, will be the end of this form of government. Decidedly, a Republic is a beautiful dream of minds that think in grandiose terms and are generous and disinterested, but it is not practicable in view of the evil, petty passions of the French populace. To them, *Liberty, Equality, Fraternity* means only the enslavement or death of the upper classes (p. 231).

A red flag was already flying from the roof of the City Hall.

Exasperated, Edmond lashed out at those who had—in his mind—encouraged this folly. He took the moderate Republicans to task for soft-pedaling the crimes of the Revolutionaries in order to curry favor with the mob. The bourgeoisie were, as a class, responsible in a deeper sense, he felt, for putting highest values on money rather than on sacrifice; the Empire, as he had made clear during the siege, had weakened patriotism and indirectly led to the present upheavals. Above all, the culprit was the doctrine of progress. On April 12, when the bourgeois government at Versailles had begun to attack the *communards,* he wrote: "When I woke up this morning, I saw that the Issy fortress, which I thought had been taken, still had the red flag. The Versailles forces must have been pushed back.

"Why this stubbornness, such as the Prussians never encountered? Because the idea of patriotism is dying. Because the formula 'All men are brothers' has made headway even in these times of invasion and cruel defeat. Because the International's doctrine of indifference to nationality has infiltrated the masses." When on the following day his friend Philippe Burty, the art critic, upheld the position that everything should give way to "the instinct of the masses," Edmond snorted: "That is like saying that the most stupid people are the most intelligent" (p. 253).

Like most people who see what they are looking for, he eagerly leaped upon tidbits that justified his view of the Commune as ignoble. On May 3, he observed three sailors turn away from an idealistic orator and he heard one say, "Shit on these *liberalistic* speeches. The important thing is to have eight litres of wine in our canteens [and] a four kilogram loaf of bread." Edmond concluded that this was indeed the materialistic attitude of the present revolution. So great was his hostility that when the killing was over, he could write with callous complacency on May 31:

It is good that there was neither conciliation nor bargaining. The solution was brutal. It was by pure force. The solution has held people back from cowardly compromises. The solution has restored confidence in the army, which learned . . . that it was still able to fight. Finally, the blood-letting was a bleeding white; such a purge, by killing off the combative part of the population, defers the next revolution by a whole generation. The old society has twenty years of quiet ahead of it, if the government dare all that they may dare at this time.

176

Edmond De Goncourt

Rather than condemn Edmond de Goncourt totally for this unfeeling hostility, one may rather admire that a man so hostile to a movement made at times a heroic effort to be impartial. As is usually the case in matters human, this fairness appeared whenever he became conscious of the immediate presence of human suffering. Edmond never let himself remain huddled in his home out in Auteuil, but as a realistic novelist felt the need to see for himself. He walked the streets disdainful of distant— or nearby—cannonading and rifle fire. Being under fire can draw even enemies together. On April 9 he wrote: "Having returned to Auteuil for a while after the horrible spectacle of the day, I am thrown into profound sadness by the fury of the continuing cannon fire. I feel a sort of tenderness over the fates of these brutes" (p. 251). And after the insurrection was over, Edmond overcame the horror he felt toward the survivors being led off to execution: "the sight of the lugubrious procession is painful" (May 28).

More significant were the following episodes, for these show that amid the condemnation of his deep-seated prejudices, he could at times understand another point of view. He was sincere in his desire for truth. He noted (April 21) that workmen talked sense about inflation and quotes a man who observed shrewdly: "What good does it do *me* for there to be monuments, café-concerts where I have never set foot because I don't have any money?" The worker went on to rejoice that henceforth there would be no rich people in Paris, so convinced was he that the gathering of the wealthy into one place raises prices. Edmond admitted that despite the worker's stupidity, he made good sense at times.

Edmond also obtained a first-hand view of the simple courage of the revolutionaries. His facile descriptions of the people as dirty, drunken bums dissolved before the poignancy of the following experience. On May 23, during the last agonizing days of the Commune, Edmond was trapped in a room with his friend Burty near the barricade of the Rue Druot. Just after the barricade fell, Edmond looked out the window and reported what he saw:

On the other side of the boulevard a man is stretched out on the ground; I see only the soles of his boots and a bit of gold braid. Two men, a National Guardsman and a lieutenant stand near the corpse. Bullets make the leaves of a little tree spreading over their heads rain on them. . . . The National Guardsman, with angry indignant gestures, shouting to someone off stage, indicates by signs that he wants to pick up the dead man. The bullets continue to make leaves fall on the two men. Then the National Guardsman, whose face I see red with anger, throws his rifle on his shoulder, butt in the air and walks toward the rifle shots, insults on his tongue. Suddenly I see him stop, put his hand to his forehead, for a second lean his hand and forehead against a little tree, then half turn around and fall on his back, arms outstretched.

The lieutenant had remained motionless by the side of the first dead man, calm as a man meditating in his garden. One bullet, which made a little branch fall on him close to his head, which he tossed off with a flick of the hand, did not rouse him from his immobility. He looked for a moment at his fallen comrade. Then

177

without hurrying he pushed his sword behind him with disdainful deliberation, then bent down and attempted to lift up the body. The dead man was tall and heavy, and like an inert thing evaded the lieutenant's efforts and slipped out of his arms to one side or the other. Finally, the lieutenant lifted him up and, holding him tight against his chest, he was carrying him off when a bullet, breaking his thigh, made them turn together in a hideous pirouette, the dead man and the living man, and fall on top of each other. I doubt that many people have been privileged to witness so heroic and simple a disdain for death.

Although at first Edmond saw the action as a play with a stage, illusion was dispelled by the reality of the action. There is no hint of condemnation.

Personal admiration is fine, but implies no necessary sympathy with a movement. But Edmond once had a glimpse into the ideal of the Commune, and even this crusty old aristocrat was deeply affected. On May 7 he had attended a Revolutionary club meeting at the Sainte Eustache church, and one of the orators—a cobbler named Jacques Durand—impressed him greatly. First the shoemaker expressed his disdain for "rolling phrases by which one wins easy popularity," an attitude that would surely appeal to the artist in Edmond, and then the orator reminded his fellow revolutionaries that there is no desire to confiscate property without payment, that the Commune is *not* intending to rob everyone, and most reasonably reminded his audience that the men of '93 had only military action to contend with, whereas those of '71 had far more complex problems. He voiced hostility to any reign of terror and concluded: "What do I care whether we are successful against Versailles if we don't find solutions for social problems, if workingmen remain in the same condition as before?" The author of *Germinie Lacerteux* could not fail to respond to this appeal to genuine working-class misery.

Despite these experiences, however, Edmond never changed his basic ideas. For the rest of his life he expressed sympathy with all the suffering but remained stoutly aristocratic in temperament and detached in his views, seeing in all political parties only stupidity, greed, and desire for power. His cynicism made him so pessimistic that he was incapable of political action, and forever reduced him to the role of spectator. The first lesson for today's citizen is to avoid being trapped into inactivity through excessive despair. But Edmond should not be scorned. The second lesson is that we need to be reminded that *all* forms of government, even—or particularly—idealistic ones, are imperfectly run by fallible men.

REFERENCES

[1] The standard edition is Edmond et Jules de Goncourt, *Journal: Mémoires de la vie littéraire*, texte intégral établi et annoté par Robert Ricatte (Monaco: Les Editions de l'Imprimerie nationale de Monaco, 1956), 22 volumes. [2] This section of the Journal has been recently published in English translation: *Paris under Siege, 1870-1871: From the Goncourt Journal*. Edited and translated by George J. Becker, with a historical introduction by Paul H. Beik. Ithaca and London, Cornell University Press, 1969. Despite the excellence of the translation, we have made our own for this paper.

TRAUMA AND RECOIL: THE INTELLECTUALS

W. M. Frohock

The general effect of the combined events of 1870-71 on the established liberal middle-class intellectuals was trauma under the first impact, then recoil, and finally a sort of sclerosis, not greatly different from rigor mortis, that became more and more evident as political attitudes stiffened and set. I say "general effect" and "combined events" because in this context the damage caused by the defeat can't be separated from that caused by the Commune. A structure of accepted myths collapsed and the center of French intellectual life moved to the Right, where it sat until the Dreyfus Case and perhaps until the end of World War I.

It is hard to speak precisely about such things. The surest way to confuse your reader, and make an ass of yourself at the same time, is to write about past political attitudes and events in terms that don't mean now what they meant then, or in terms that then didn't even exist. Before 1870 a man could think of himself as a liberal and still not make a sacred cow of Democracy. The noun "intellectual" came into use only with the Dreyfus Case, after 1895. And in 1870 "middle-class intellectual" was a tautology, since there wasn't anything much else for an intellectual to be, the working class having no education and the aristocrats, such as they were, not much more. Let it stand that I can't use any other formula that would fit men like Hippolyte Taine and Ernest Renan and mean much to us today.

Taine and Renan have to figure here both because they were widely-read and influential in themselves, and at the same time fully representative of the generation that was born in the 1820's, matured toward the end of the Bourgeois Monarchy; they were in their prime under Napoleon III—the less inventive and creative but infinitely brainy contemporaries of Flaubert and Baudelaire. They may be hard to differentiate today from the *salops* in Sartre's Sunday afternoon chapter in *La Nausée*, but this is simply a problem in perspective.

What happened to them in 1870-71 was not what happened in our time to the late John Dos Passos, or, earlier, to William Wordsworth, if it was really Wordsworth Browning had in mind in that poem about a handful of silver and a ribbon. Nothing in the story was as dramatic as that: in the aftermath of war and aborted revolution they began emphasizing beliefs which it seems they had always held but hadn't had any reason to emphasize earlier. This could happen to anybody, and still does. And so the ideas, or some of the ideas, of these men who still thought of themselves as liberals, could become cornerstones of the radical-reactionary ideology that Charles Maurras and the rest of the Action Française were still preaching up to the time they decided that the coming of the Nazis might be a Good Thing for France after all.

179

Taine and Renan had worked their way into international reputations—honorary doctorates from Oxford and that sort of thing—under the pussyfooting Empire of Little Napoleon, a ruler with a strong preference for subjects who didn't threaten to overturn applecarts. As a young man Taine had been assigned one of the least attractive teaching posts the Ministry could find, even though he had been the perennial head of his class at the Ecole Normale Supérieure, just because the ideas he had expressed in the competitive examination didn't conform with those of the official philosophers of the regime. One year of what he called "that provincial hole," Nevers, and he threw up the job to live by free-lance writing in Paris. Renan had lost his chair at the Collège de France all in one afternoon: his reference to Jesus as "that perfect man" (not God) had displeased the clerical party that supported the Emperor.

The regime had early revealed its preternatural inability to tell talent from obstructionism, and its quaking fear of possible radlibs. It had driven Victor Hugo, the historian Michelet, and the philosopher Edgar Quinet into exile, and dragged Flaubert and Baudelaire through the courts for endangering public morals. It feared ideas, especially new ones; and while what Renan and Taine wrote was too technical, scholarly, and other-worldly to be suspect of the degree of dissidence men were exiled for, both men had to suffer the kind of frustration that comes whenever aggressive mediocrity prevails over talent in public life. Even conservative and reticent old Sainte-Beuve, who was notoriously willing to keep the peace so long as he was not molested, finally took up the cudgels for Renan in a speech in the Senate that taxed the government for neglecting one of its really great men.

But if Renan and Taine had so little reason to love the Empire and Napoleon III, how explain their consternation to see both disappear? A case could be documented for ticketing them as early exemplars of what Julien Benda would much later call the *clerc,* the priest of the life of the mind who is supposed to be immune to political passion and to enter the hurly-burly only when eternal values are threatened. Taine, especially—Renan had too much sense of humor—may have seen himself in this light. But their private writings make such an explanation seem too fancy. The simple truth is that, even though Renan had allowed himself to stand for political office shortly before the war—and been convincingly defeated—both men had been politically apathetic.

In their early years their political attitude had been hard to distinguish from the stance of the Art-for-Art's sake poets, who had disdained political activity just because their elders, like Victor Hugo and Lamartine, had not. As much as Frédéric Moreau in Flaubert's *Education sentimentale,* they seem to have been permanently out for lunch during the Revolution(s) of 1848; they do not seem to have been perturbed when, for the first time, French troops fired upon French workers. The most they asked, one gathers, of the Second Empire, was to leave them alone. Thus, in our current Swahili, the defeat and the Commune "politicized" and "polarized" Taine and Renan, shook them out of their apathy, made them ask themselves what they did in fact think.

Renan and Taine got through both the war and the Commune without material or physical damage or even more inconvenience than was to be expected. But the jolt was hardly the less painful:

What a nightmare [Renan wrote when the crisis was over]. . . . The only ones who can enjoy the peace are those who didn't help bring on these horrors and who gained nothing from them. The harm is even deeper than we suppose. The revolt has been broken and the fires are put out, but hearts and minds are full of hate, envy, ignorance, and unreasonableness. It would take years of peace, good government, and solid education at all levels to cure these ills, if indeed they are curable. Who will give us those things? (To Princess Julie, June 15, 1871.)

Taine's distress was as great, but it would be unfair to quote him: even in his letters to his wife he is so ridden by the clichés of elevated style that after a century he sounds impossibly stuffy—death is in his heart, he is surrounded by madmen on a sinking ship, and so forth. He was never the stuffed shirt his language makes him seem, and from February 1871, when he first scented civil war, on into late Spring when he left to lecture at Oxford, his anguish increased daily. He hated disorder, and the Commune had brought nothing else.

Events had let the air out of two myths very dear to Renan and Taine.

Both men had bought the myth of a Germany that never was on land or sea. German philology and philosophy—both were, in their way, Hegelians—had been primary influences in their intellectual formation. Both their philosophy of history and their ideas of historical method were imports from across the Rhine. They had shared the prevailing French dream of a Germany full of music and poetry and intellectual accomplishment, the source of the world's future culture, and too pacific to be dangerous. How aware they were of the existence of William I, Bismarck, Von Moltke and the modernized Prussian army, before 1870, is moot.

Renan's trauma comes through eloquently in his letters.

Everything I had ever dreamed, desired, preached, turns out to be a pipe-dream. I had made the goal of my life to work for the intellectual, moral, and political union of Germany and France. And now the criminal madness of the government that has gone under, the political ineptitude of French democracy, the exaggerated patriotism of the Germans, and Prussian pride have opened a gulf that centuries will not heal. (To Charles Ritter, March 11, 1871.)

They had also bought the myth of inevitable human progress, which had been on the market since the French *philosophes* and had more recently had an assist from Hegel. Taine was so imbued with this persuasion that the final volume of his *History of English Literature* had put him in a real dilemma, because if his theory was right the nineteenth-century poets should somehow be superior in stature to Shakespeare, but he was too honest, and too good a critic, to swallow such nonsense. Similarly, Renan's interpretation of the emergence of Christianity in the history of the Semites made of it one step, among many, on the way to the perfection of the religious and ethical sensibility of the whole human race.

This myth collapsed as thoroughly as the other. Man should not have gone into the streets in 1871 to do the same things—and worse—he had done in 1783. Shooting Bishops and taking over private property! Who, after this, could believe in the perfectibility of the race?

This willingness to measure our course toward perfection by the standards of the middle class may seem incredibly narrow. Neither man was rich: Taine's father had been a minor civil servant, and Renan, the son of a Breton seaman, was from the working class if not from the urban proletariat. It never occurred to them that the interests of the intellectual were not always identical with those of the bourgeoisie. They were men of their time.

I don't mean to be quite so simplistic as to argue that the collapse of such myths, by itself, explains what they did in the aftermath of the Commune. But having to bear the specific humiliation of the intellectuals in addition to the one everyone else had to bear must have made a burden meriting some sympathy.

Their response to disaster, and the fine if naive faith in the intellect that it reveals, is touching. France was in deep trouble; the trouble could be remedied only if its sources were revealed; at a time when every Frenchman should assume personal responsibility, identifying the sources was the special responsibility of the intellectuals. They assumed it. It may have been characteristic that Renan's *Réforme intellectuelle et morale,* a 121-page prescription for putting the country back on its feet, went to press in 1871; the five volumes of Taine's *Les Origines de la France contemporaine* took him the rest of his life. (He died in 1893.) But each man was putting his talent in the service of his country.

Renan's book argues that universal direct suffrage had put too much power in the hands of the common man, and urges a return to parliamentary monarchy, with a bi-cameral legislature elected by indirect suffrage and the election laws so rigged that the "responsible element" will always be in control, especially of the upper house. He also advocates strengthening existing institutions: an aristocracy reinvigorated by recruiting men of established merit, a church with two degrees of membership—one for literal believers and one for the rest—so that France can be unanimously Catholic again, an expanded university system with increased prestige, a firm colonial empire which he justifies by a Kiplingesque racism. In these and similar ways, he says repeatedly, the damage that originated in the French Revolution must be repaired.

I can't find an idea in these pages that some French liberal or other had not suggested at some earlier time, but his whole intent is to make sure that the same lightning will not strike the same place again. It does not occur to him that in order to last a state has to be capable of adapting to new conditions. His reforms provide for no flexibility to deal with the unforeseen. He looks resolutely backward.

So does Taine. In the same way that he had looked, earlier, for the secret of genius in the "origins" of the individual, meaning his heredity and environment, he now looks for the causes of the recent debacle in remote history. Not unsurprisingly, he finds them in the French Revolution. Or rather, he had already found them there. Taine believed that his method was "scientific," detached, and completely objective, but actually it consisted, as it had always done, in hunting out documentary support for conclusions already formed. In 1908, when the old man had been dead for years, a Sorbonne professor named Aulard pawed through the National Archives and found that some of the old papers Taine had cited in support of his argument had never been out of their original wrappers. There were enough of these to make it clear that the *Origines* was much less a dispassionate demonstration than an immensely elaborate counter-revolutionary tract. More charitably, since Taine was unaware of its nature, it was a monumental piece of self-kidding.

Taine's deterministic positivism was not what blinded him. Emile Zola has been accused of half-understanding Taine's ideas, or of understanding them very crudely—as well as of being a remarkably unsubtle novelist. But he could see that the outrageous exploitation of the working class in France had created a problem of heredity and environment that would not be solved by mere suppression of uprisings like the Commune, or by trying to undo the work of the Revolution. His picture of the Second Empire agrees with theirs as to its frivolity, absence of seriousness, lack of contact with reality and delight in mediocrity, but he was far more aware than they were of the social and economic dimension. This is the whole point of novels like *Germinal* and *L'Assommoir*.

But Zola was a rarity. Most of the new generation scurried to safety on the Right, taking what ideas of Taine and Renan they could use to bolster their positions. Example, Paul Bourget.

What he had seen of the Commune as a young teacher fresh from the provinces had frightened Bourget to his boots. By the middle 1880's he would be the most brilliant essayist in France and a successful novelist; by 1900 he was ready for the taxidermist; he basked in the admiration of the snobs of the Faubourg Saint-Germain until his death in 1935. Knowing him as we do, mostly, from the cruel caricature in Gide's *Caves du Vatican*, it is hard to remember that he was not always a complete stuffed shirt.

But his two-volume investigation of the intellectual climate in France *circa* 1885 is serious, and anxiously open-minded. He is openly ambivalent about Taine and Renan, especially the former: the ethic implied by Taine's famous remark that "vice and virtue are chemical products like vitriol and sugar" strikes him as morally enervating, but he also sees Taine as a valuable partisan of his own traditionalism. In the novel, *Le Disciple,* a philosopher named Adrien Sixte, who holds Taine's views, is made responsible for the moral collapse of the hero. But in later novels, like *L'Etape*—thesis: it is dangerous for a man to move from his social class to a superior one—he is still leaning on Taine's ideas of heredity. He never got completely free of the incubus.

His more sensitive and subtle contemporary, Maurice Barrès, succeeded no better. His chapter on Taine in *Les Déracinés,* a novel about a group of young provincials whose lives are more or less corrupted by moving to Paris, is partly a declaration of independence. So, with respect to the other grand old man, was his skit-essay called *Huit jours chez M. Renan.* But Barrès' famous burden, "la terre et les morts," which informed his most effective books, was really a poeticization of Taine's prosaic *race-milieu-moment*—which makes Taine one of the sponsors of Barrès' militant, lyric nationalism, so popular in France up to World War I.

Barrès and Bourget are probably extreme cases, but it is easy to count the writers who, from the Commune to the Dreyfus Case and even later, did not follow the same general trajectory. After Rimbaud, about whose politics after 1873 we know nothing, few poets had much to do with the Left; the so-called *symbolistes* were, by and large, either conservatives or a-political, and among the prose-writers, Zola's mild socialism was exceptional. The working-class was understandably slow to produce men like Jules Vallès and Charles Péguy. It took the scandal of Dreyfus to start a realignment, and even then the number of consciences that were *not* outraged is startling: André Gide and Paul Valéry, among others, subscribed quietly to anti-Dreyfusard organizations. And on the eve of World War II there were still some sixty writers and intellectuals in France willing to sign a manifesto declaring that Mussolini was the savior of the West because he had invaded Ethiopia. Among them were the last survivors of the generation that had felt the influence of Taine and Renan.

But the position Taine and Renan took when the pressure was on them wasn't, given the political temper of the country as a whole, an extreme one. The Republic emerged because the various kinds of monarchists couldn't compose what today look like idiotically small differences. In such a situation, a dislike for unlimited democracy and a preference for preserving traditional institutions don't mark a man as a wild reactionary. This may be why, despite the efforts of the extreme Right to annex them and bask in their prestige, Renan and Taine finally had the best of both worlds—Renan in particular for excellent reasons being a hero for the anti-clerical Left.

184

FRENCH WRITERS AND THE COMMUNE

Henriette Psichari

The thunderbolt which struck out on March 18, 1871, the first day of the insurrection which marked the opening stage of the Commune, should have made the great intellectuals of that period quiver with emotion. How did they not realize that a new breath was blasting out from amidst the pave-stones and that a country is never at a loss as long as it has enough strength left to revolt against injustice and shame?

Because for France the Commune means nothing less than this. One may enumerate economic causes, make endless statistics, the truth remains that the French had had enough of civil or military treachery whether from Thiers or from MacMahon and that on March 18 the defence taken up by the Communards with the guns at Montmartre had crystalized in a tangible and bloody reality the opposing positions of the nation and the government. Yet thousands of people whether of good-will or bought over by propaganda refused to believe this. Many a great mind, however objective and liberal, closed their eyes to these generous ideas.

And so it is even now. If one were to open the history of literature written by Lagarde and Michard, which is the most considered amongst our older pupils in the final classes of secondary school in France, one would think that the writers of that period, from the least renowned to the greatest, passed by the Commune without noticing it. The fifty pages devoted to Victor Hugo make no mention of the *Année Terrible,* there is no extract from this work.

Addressing a different category of readers, the important work by René Dumesnil on *Realism* takes on an air sometimes of contempt, sometimes of painful modesty when speaking of the 1871 Revolution; so it is said that Goncourt on his long walks through Paris in its ruins suffered "at the sight of agonizing Paris." Poor man! But of Flaubert, Taine, Fustel de Coulanges and all the others, not a line is written about their attitude during the Commune.

More "in vogue" is the history of literature under the direction of Raymond Queneau (Pléiade). There is no mention of Jules Vallès other than in relation to naturalism. *L'Insurgé* is not even quoted. In this same work, there is the chapter written by Jacques Vier and devoted to journalism in 1870-71, there are indeed a few references to the role played by Vallès, but the word "Commune" is not even pronounced.

For Jacques Chastenet, a historian covered with all the academic Honors, the reasons for the Commune are only materialistic: too low wages, too high rents. He denies the fact that the Workers' International founded in London in 1864 had any influence at all. He even denies the fact that the Commune was a rebellion of the proletariat against the bourgeoisie. One seems to be in a dream.

Why this ostracism? Why this lack of good-will? Why these lies? The reasons become clear from the attitude of a few writers who lived through the Commune and who gave their testimony in their writings.

The quantity of writers at this time is no less important than their quality. Besides the great ones: Michelet, Renan, Flaubert, Baudelaire, many were the Goncourts, Dumas, Maupassants, Théophile Gautiers, who delighted the public, hungering for intellectual entertainment. Never had the small theatres been so full, nor journalists more listened to, nor serials more followed, nor public speakers more applauded. Except, however, at the Court, where, in spite of Mérimée, everyone was bored stiff. All that came from the Tuileries with its insane ostentation were attacks on freedom, and the covering-up of ideas. All the journalists and among the writers Flaubert, Renan, Baudelaire were merely innocent victims of it. Unfortunately too, Emperor, diplomats and generals were working together to stir up a war which, by a strange blindness, no writer, poet or philosopher had foreseen.

Let us then begin our review with the man who was in all his glory for the French, Victor Hugo. Back from his exile on September 5, the day following the proclamation of the Republic, he received such a popular and enthusiastic ovation that he could do all he wished. But he did not permit himself anything. Yet he was now in the circle of Louis Blanc, Rochefort, Schoelcher and received them continually in the Pavillon de Rohan, where he held his salon. Evidently he was not in the atmosphere of Paris. A twenty years' absence changes a man's judgment and induces a lack of understanding. Yet another misfortune befalls the poet; his son, Charles, dies, and it is on March 18 that his hearse traverses Paris. Rumours begin to go around: Victor Hugo is here, a friend of the people, republican without doubt, naturally a revolutionary, so they think. The crowd thickens about the procession and accompanies it up to the Bastille, where, spontaneously, a guard of honor is formed, guns are put down by the very ones who were to be shot during the days to follow. But whilst the revolution rumbled around him, Victor Hugo was thinking of the lines he was going to address to the people he loved: "Tu voyais devant toi se rouvrir l'ombre affreuse / Qui par moments devant les grands peuples se creuse. . ."

Civil war—that is what the terrible shadow is. A nameless horror for Victor Hugo, especially when it takes place "Devant l'éclat de rire affreux de l'ennemi." For he understood what others were unaware of or pretended not to see: the rebellion is the revolt of good French people who were opposed to the union of Thiers and Bismarck, to the remobilizing of the prisoners in order to fight against the Communards (which did in fact occur), to the bargaining done by Jules Favre with Bismarck in Ferrières: "God", shouted Victor Hugo, "do not let France fall into the abyss of this peace!"

186

French Writers and the Commune

A strange note by Victor Hugo was published in addition to the *Année Terrible;* it was an enumeration of what should have been, according to him, the arguments of the Commune. To quote more particularly, from him: "abolish the death sentence—proclaim an undenominational and compulsory education—declare absolute freedom for the press and public meetings—proclaim the inviolability of human life. . ." His programme was similar to that of the Communards. What, then, stopped him from declaring openly that he was with them and from acting in the same way as the revolutionaries?

Victor Hugo was now sixty-eight years old, was back in his defeated homeland, the outbreak of revolt irritated rather than surprised him.

"Has France not yet been killed enough?" he asked with anxiety when he saw the first flames from the fire of Paris, but he forgave the people because, for him, these people meant misery, ignorance, hunger.

> "Non ce n'est pas toi, peuple, tu ne l'as pas fait
> Non, vous les égarés, vous n'êtes pas coupables"

The culprits are those who formed part of the government, the Thiers and other Galliénis. On this point, Victor Hugo did not hide his ideas, he was even rather proud "of being accursed along with Barbès, with Garibaldi," all he felt for the repression of the Commune was disapproval: the massacres, Satory camp, shootings, exiles made him furious. Too late.

Somewhat similar to the feelings of Victor Hugo—although rather less well expressed—were those of George Sand. One should have expected from the person who had planted the Arbres de la Liberté at all the cross-roads in Nohant in 1848, from the one who, against all criticism, was spreading around the ideas of Leroux and Cabet as far as the threshold of the *Revue des Deux Mondes,* an outbreak of enthusiasm or at least an ideological admiration for the courage of the Communards. There was nothing.

Or rather a flow of words in her correspondence with Dumas or Flaubert—mere words. Mere, because after having declared in August 1870: "I belong to the reddest Social State, now as before," after having written on September 5: "What a beautiful thing, what a beautiful day!" she changed sides and decided that "we are threatened here by bandits and stealthy people who are more to be feared than the German soldiers." Then came with each day a series of the lowest insults against the Commune: *vomitting attacks—saturnalia of madness—ugly adventure*—at the head of the insurrection some are *insufferable,* the others are *imbeciles*— and as a conclusion she wrote to a friend on May 30, 1871, the day of the shooting of the Mur des Fédérés: "Thanks to God, the Luxembourg, the Odéon and the Panthéon have not been burned down and thanks to you all my little fittings are intact."

Let us be fair. George Sand had an excuse; at that time, she was under the influence of Flaubert whose attitude was similarly hostile towards the Communards. But this hostility, too, came as a surprise from the shrewdest of writers, from the man who had inveighed against "le bourgeois," and who had exposed the vices of conformism to the point of composing a dictionary on it.[1] That he should not have foreseen the war, such was the lot of all authors of that period, but his lack of political sense lay exposed even after the defeat.[2] He declared: "there will be no civil war, I believe the Social State will be put off for a long while." And with the end of the torment (June 1871): "one must resign oneself to living between imbecility and insanity." Such observations show that Flaubert did not understand anything of what was taking place. In the same way March 18 only produced from him a single remark: "stupid convulsions from a destructive mob." And so it is that we find the Commune with its doctrines, its men, its thinkers, its economists, its Louise Michels, its Blanquis and its heroic soldiers bundled up together in a literary formula!

What is to be said about the relationship between Maxime du Camp and Flaubert! It was a powerful friendship, a dangerous intimacy. Maxime du Camp—a mediocre writer in fact—was, in addition, brutal and uncouth. The main theme of his pamphlets in *The Convulsions of Paris* defines the Commune as a pack of murderers, criminals, debauched people and above all drunkards. We could disdain this flow of unpleasant words except that Maxime du Camp had close links with Flaubert, and through him, with various literary people, from Gobineau to Théophile Gautier, from Ludovic Halévy to Paul de Saint-Victor.

With this latter we arrive at the epitome of hate. Saint-Victor gives the reasons for this in his book, *Barbarians and Bandits* of which the title gives sufficient indication as to his feelings. According to him "the bourgeoisie, the family and industry (i.e. money), all these go together to make up the dignity and security of a people." And the insults for the Communards continue: *lewd revolution—red orgy—detestable rebellion—professional rioters—filthy men* . . . and many more. What does it matter, some might say, this writer left no trace in history. This is so, but he was a journalist and belonged to a profession which permits one to do the best or the worst and he used his power very badly.

The Goncourt brothers—important personalities and good writers in as far as their books on art are concerned—gave themselves a deplorable reputation with their *Diary*, now published in its entirety.

Edmond de Goncourt was one whom a war disturbs only in as far as his refined tastes and Japanese bronzes are threatened. Neither a historian nor a politician, he understood nothing of what was taking place, and however interesting his descriptions of Paris during the Commune might be, they are interesting only because he had the gift of making his impressions come to life. But he had not even tried to understand why things were happening the way they were. On October 30, the day of the Metz capitulation, he was astonished to hear cries of "Long live the Commune!" loud in the Town Hall square. As for the government of the Commune, it is composed of unknown names exclusively, "it is like a practical joke" and Goncourt adds this touch of irony: "Jules Vallès is Minister of Public Instruction. The bohemian of the café-restaurant has Villemain's seat!" (March 20, 1871). What then had Villemain, that eloquent speaker, done in favor of schooling? Jules Vallès, at least created undenominational and free schooling.

Goncourt, in spite of his preconceived ideas, sometimes showed good judgment. One day, on June 10, 1871, i.e. shortly after the bloody week, he dined with Flaubert. Flaubert would speak only about *la Tentation de Saint Antoine,* on which he was working, and Goncourt remarked: "this disaster took place around him without him lifting a hair from his calm and collected writing of the book." A good observation, which Goncourt might also have turned upon himself.

Goncourt is representative of the state of mind of the writers we have referred to, and of several others, rather less important. Straight away the following question comes to mind: how was it possible that a group of intelligent, thinking, talented and intellectually powerful men should be so badly informed as to what the Commune really was? To understand this, one must take a look a little further back in history.

The bourgeoisie, ascendent in the early 19th century, as one result of the 1789 revolution, were hard-working, clever, ambitious, and aware. They, and their values so dominated French teachers, writers, artists, scientists that they became catastrophically representative of the nation. No other social category was to count thereafter. The aristocracy was retreating of its own accord, the working class—essential to ensure that the work was done—was easy to manœuvre or at least so the bourgeoisie hoped.

Everything changed from the middle of the century onwards, with machinery and its direct consequence, the proletariat. But the habit of class division had been firmly established: there should never be any link, any contact between intellectuals and laborers. And in actual fact the wall between these two classes at the time of Goncourt or Baudelaire was erect, impermeable, solid. Neither of these authors knew what a factory or syndicate, or even a social law was.

Let us take Renan as another example. He spoke German fluently, knew Feuerbach, Hegel, and was well acquainted with Mommsen, Moritz Carriére, David Strauss; he was interested in politics, but was totally unaware of social problems. When publishing Renan's complete work, I made up the index of all the proper names quoted. . . It contains more than thirty thousand names for the fifteen thousand pages composing the ten volumes. Not once is the name of Marx mentioned.

And Renan was not the only one like this. Victor Hugo, very much attached to the people and their suffering, could only see a solution to their misery in pity and charity. George Sand only knew about the life of the peasants—that is quite a lot—but her idealistic dreams come to a halt when faced with the concrete solutions that the workers demanded. It is true that at that time the living standards of the working class—very badly clothed, badly educated—were very much inferior to what they are at present, which could excuse a little the remark made by Goncourt on March 20, 1871: "the cohorts of Belleville, opposite Tortoni, crowd our boulevard." Let us interpret the attitude this way: Belleville is the enemy, and Tortoni, the elegant café on "our" boulevard des Italiens belongs to us. Why are they coming to invade us?

This class division among the French still exists, but to a lesser degree. For the intellectuals in 1870, it originated mostly from their ignorance. Goncourt did not hesitate before writing: "the people no longer fight for a word, a principle, some sort of faith." So? Goncourt had not heard of Marx's *Manifesto* (1848)? Had he never thumbed through the *Vorwaerts* or the *Annales franco-allemandes* although both were published in Paris? Had he not seen on the walls the *Adresse* posted by the General Labourers' Committee, rejecting the thesis claiming the necessity for the security of Germany of the annexation of Alsace-Lorraine? Was he even aware that Victor Hugo used to see Louis Blanc, Schoelcher, Lockroy or Clemenceau often, and that they also brought him other information besides what took place at the Magny dinner?

This culpable indifference on the part of teachers or writers towards social problems, this hostility, created by the ruling class, continued until late in the century. When Zola wrote *Germinal* in 1884, he was only just becoming acquainted with the Workers' International founded in London twenty years earlier. We know this from his notes. Worse yet: it took the Dreyfus affair, at the end of the nineteenth century, to make teachers realize that they could do something more for their country besides explaining Virgil. Safeguarding a just idea should come before laboratory experiments, before career or money interests, and it was in this way that the Dreyfus affair gave a lesson to the world.

One must consider the government propaganda which spread with a horrid force, which, up to a point, is an excuse for those who did not understand. However, the writers were not all fanatics of Thiers, not by a long shot. The great majority of them condemned the bloody repression of the Communards and suffered because they did—even Goncourt to whom we are indebted for a few breath-taking pages on deportation, even George Sand and Flaubert. All the same, Thiers had gone too far!

A hundred years after these grave events we may judge the speed of the progress in improving the laborers' condition. Social advance, which everywhere is considered of prime importance, shows from day to day only a big step taken towards a still too timid equality. Compared to the

French Writers and the Commune

Second Empire, journalism in France today is almost completely free of censure; vote bulletins are the reflection of the most diverse opinions; the critical sense is sharper, and the demand for information is greater and greater. The bourgeoisie itself has to abandon its supremacy since the proletariat now takes care of its own defense. This wide-spread movement would have been far more rapid but for the mortal fall on France of three wars in a hundred years. Even so, the advance, such as it is, did not come about single-handed. Struggles, newspapers, books, meetings, brave men—were necessary. More still will be required in the coming generations to finish the building of a just and humane society, precisely that which the Commune of Paris had laid down as its ideal.

REFERENCES

[1] *Dictionnaire des Idées reçues.* [2] The surrender of Louis Napoleon to Prussian forces at Sedan in September, 1870. [3] Oeuvres complétes, T. I. (Calmann-Lévy).

BERTOLT
BRECHT

THE
DAYS
OF THE
COMMUNE

TRANSLATED BY
LEONARD LEHRMAN

PUBLISHED WITH THE PERMISSION OF SUHRKAMP VERLAG AND
© STEFAN BRECHT, SUHRKAMP VERLAG FRANKFURT/MAIN 1967

DRAMATIS PERSONAE

MADAME CABET, *seamstress* • PIERRE LANGEVIN, *her brother-in-law, Delegate to the Commune* • JEAN CABET, *her son, a young worker who drives a locomotive* • BABETTE CHERRON, *his girl-friend, a seamstress* • FRANÇOIS FAURE, *a seminary student, now a National Guardsman* • GENEVIÈVE GÉRICAULT, *a young teacher, roommate of Babette* • GUY SUITRY, *her fiancé, a lieutenant in the regular army* • PAPA, *a National Guardsman, fiftyish, a former watchmaker, his real name is Goule* • COCO, *his friend, a National Guardsman and former bricklayer* •

LOUIS ADOLPHE THIERS (1797—1877), *Chief Executive of the National Government (first at Bordeaux, then at Versailles)* • HIPPOLYTE, *Thiers' valet* • JULES FAVRE, *member of the French parliament, Thiers' envoy to Bismarck* • BISMARCK, *first Chancellor of the Prussian Empire* • LE MARQUIS HENRI DE PLOEUC, *Director of the Bank of France* • SERVANT, *to the Marquis* • MAYORS OF PARIS • MONSIGNOR BEAUCHAMP, *a fat priest, envoy of the Archbishop of Paris* •

DELEGATES *to the Commune (Proudhonian, Pacifistic, Violent, Humanitarian, etc.),* Vermorel, Chardon, Rogeard, Vallès, Arnaud, Avrial, Rastoul, Pindy, Durand, Jourde, Billioray, Dupont, Champy, Amouroux, Theisz • CHARLES BESLAY, *negotiator with de Ploeuc and the bank* • EUGÈNE VARLIN, *spokesman for the working class* • RAOUL RIGAULT, *director of police intelligence, advocate of force* • CHARLES DELESCLUZE, *venerable veteran in charge of War Command* • GABRIEL RANVIER, *a notable militant* • CAPTAIN ANDRE FARREAUX, *wounded officer of the National Guard, representative of General Rossel* • LEADER OF THE DELEGATION OF WOMEN, *from the Eleventh Arrondissement* •

A CORPULENT MAN, *in the Montmartre café* • A WAITER, *Emile* • KRAUS, *German prisoner, won over to the Commune* • TWO CHILDREN, *Jules and Victor* • BAKERY OWNER • JANITOR, *at the Ministry of Interior* • THREE SOLDIERS *of the National Guard, including a Sergeant* • EMPLOYEE *of the Railway Company* • OLD BEGGAR *from Auvergne* • STREET MERCHANT • TWO STRETCHER-BEARERS • REGULAR ARMY SOLDIER *disguised as a Nun* • DYING WOMAN • TAX COLLECTOR • TAX COLLECTOR'S WIFE • TAX COLLECTOR'S SON, *Alphonse* • CIVILIANS • BOURGEOIS WOMAN • NATIONAL GUARD SOLDIERS • DELEGATES *to the Commune* • REGULAR ARMY SOLDIERS • WORKING WOMEN *from the Eleventh Arrondissement* • ARISTOCRATS *(men, women, children)* •

NOTE

The American premiere of this play, translated and directed by Leonard Lehrman, took place at Sanders Theatre, Cambridge, Mass. March 17, 1971. For that production (but not included in the text printed here) Mr. Lehrman adapted six more songs by Hans Eisler which he added to those Brecht originally included. For a full text of both the Brecht translation and the various musical and dramatic adaptions Mr. Lehrman prepared for its performance see the DUNSTER HOUSE DRAMA REVIEW, X, 2. Persons interested in producing or reproducing Mr. Lehrman's translation and adaptions should consult directly with Leonard Lehrman, 10 Nob Hill Gate, Roslyn, New York 11576.

THE DAYS OF THE COMMUNE

SCENE ONE

January 22, 1871. A small café in Montmartre. The café has been transformed into a recruiting station for the National Guard. Seated at a table on the terrace is a Corpulent Man, in a heavy coat, busily talking to the Waiter. In front of him, two children are talking, while one of them holds a cardboard box. The thunder of guns is heard in the distance.

WAITER *(polite)*: Monsieur Bracque was here three times looking for you.

CORPULENT MAN *(very polite)*: Bracque? Here? À Paris?

WAITER: Yes, just for a little while. Here's a message he left for you, sir. *(Hands him a piece of paper.)*

CORPULENT MAN *(while reading)*: Paris is not a very good place to rest these days. Prices! Percentages! Provisions! Enfin, c'est la guerre! You do what you can. Dis-moi, *(as he gets out a tip and hands it to the Waiter)* would you know somebody who could run an errand for me—someone with courage, and whom I could trust?—the two qualities seldom go together, hé?

WAITER: We'll find someone *(as he accepts the tip)*. Does Monsieur really prefer to sit out here in the cold?

CORPULENT MAN: For a little while longer. The air inside is, uh. . . . *(makes a sign with his fingers on his nostrils to indicate disgust)*.

WAITER: *(looking at a poster which reads* CITIZENS, OUT THE PRUSSIANS! JOIN THE NATIONAL GUARD!*)* I know what you mean.

CORPULENT MAN: Do you? Well you know when I have got to pay eighty francs for my own déjeuner, I don't really appreciate the stinking smell of the slums of Paris shoved up my nose, hein? So would you be so kind as to try and keep those . . . vermin over there—away from me?

(A poorly dressed woman, Madame Cabet, and a young working man, her son Jean, have entered, carrying a basket between them. The Children move toward her, offering their wares.)

MADAME CABET: No, I'm not buying anything. Well, maybe later. Rabbit? Hmm, how about a nice Sunday roast, Jean?

JEAN: That's not rabbit, Mother.

MME. CABET: But it's only fourteen francs.

CHILD: And it's very fresh, Madame.

MME. CABET: First I've got to find out how much money we're going to get today. Wait a minute, children. I may take that meat . . . *(starts to go, some military emblems fall out of the basket)*. O! Better be more careful, Jean. I'll bet we lost quite a few of those on the way over here. Which means I'm going to have to do some fast talking, so they don't notice back at headquarters.

CORPULENT MAN: Business, business, business!—while the war goes on!

WAITER: Des petites et des grosses, Monsieur.

(Sounds of a large crowd and of marching steps in the background.)

CORPULENT MAN: What's that? *(to one of the Children:)* Hey, you, I'll give you five francs if you run over there and tell me what's going on. *(The Child runs off.)*

MME. CABET *(explaining to the Waiter, who has gone over to her, interrogatorily)*: We're selling emblems to the soldiers, Emile.

WAITER: Monsieur has a small errand for your son Jean, Madame Cabet.

MME. CABET *(to the Corpulent Man)*: Oh, that's so nice of you! It's been two months since Jean's had a job, you know. He's an engineer. . . . Well, he drives a big locomotive—only the trains haven't been running—Isn't that nice, Jean? . . .

JEAN: Mother, you know I don't like running errands.

MME. CABET: Please excuse that. My son takes after his late father—he's a good man, but he has . . . opinions. *(They carry the basket into the café.)*

CORPULENT MAN *(bored, to the Waiter)*: O, this can't last much longer. Believe me, Aristide Jouve was so right

194

when he said that all the profits that can be made from the war have already been made. "Il n'y a plus rien à en tirer."

(Down the street come three National Guardsmen, limping and battle-weary. The first, Papa, is a watchmaker, in his middle years. The second, Coco, is a bricklayer, and the last is a seminary student, François Faure, his wounded arm in a sling. In their midst is a dirty German Soldier they have taken prisoner, with a soiled bandage around his chin.)

CHILD: A Kraut! Hey, d'you get a bad beating, Kraut? *(to Papa:)* Can we have his epaulettes?

PAPA: Sure—help yourself. *(They do.)*

SECOND CHILD: Everything OK at the front?

PAPA: Yeah, for the damn Prussians. . . . !

FIRST CHILD: The Governor's not about to surrender, is he?

PAPA: No. Or at least not in front of the people of Paris, my son. Or else—how do you say it?—À bas le Gou. . . .

CHILDREN: . . . verneur!

PAPA *(to Waiter)*: Three glasses of wine!—no, four.

WAITER: All right, but, uh, the owner *(indicating the Corpulent Man)* insists that you pay in advance—that'll be twelve francs.

COCO: Hey! What's the matter with you! Can't you see? We're straight from the Front!

WAITER *(softer)*: Twelve francs, Monsieur.

COCO: You're out o' your mind!

PAPA: No, he's not out of his mind, Coco. We are. You've got to be out of your mind if you fight for a franc and a half a day. That'd pay for half a glass of wine here, wouldn't it. *(Takes out a pistol and holds it under the nose of the Corpulent Man.)* This is an old one *(indicating the pistol)*; from the '40's, but good enough for the most up-to-date battalions. When it was new it cost seventy francs; today it's worth two hundred. *(affectedly)* Guaranteed never to miss, Monsieur.

COCO: Get that wine out here right now, you bugger. Here we are defending Paris for you, and you suck us dry making money on your drinks! *(Waiter hesitates.)*

PAPA: *(to the Corpulent Man)*: Monsieur, do you think we wiped out the bosses, proclaimed the Third Republic, and formed the National Guard so that you could make a profit out of it!?

CORPULENT MAN: Voilà! Tu l'as dit: L'anarchie. You don't want to defend Paris—you want to conquer her!

COCO: You're quite right, you know. But then maybe it's because people like you *own* the place. *(to Papa:)* The fat man's got good things in him—or maybe it's the other way around: the good man's got fat things in him *(jabbing the Corpulent Man in the stomach, gently).* (To the Corpulent Man:) The siege hasn't been that bad for you, has it?

CORPULENT MAN *(trying to get away from him)*: You seem to have forgotten where the Front is, Messieurs. *(The Child that ran out before runs in.)*

PAPA: What do you mean? *(to François:)* François, he thinks you don't remember where you got that *(indicating the sling on François' wounded arm)*!

COCO: Monsieur *(meaning the Corpulent Man, but addressed to him:)* wants us to remember the Prussians when we can't have any wine. Kraut, what do *you* think about that? You're not exactly fat. *(to the waiter:)* Garçon! A glass of wine for Kraut! Or the whole place has *had* it. *(peremptorily:)* Four glasses of wine for two francs—you hear?

WAITER: Oh, all right, all right. *(Exits.)*

CORPULENT MAN *(to the Waiter)*: Just a minute. Wait! Stay here, you hear me!?

CHILDREN *(singing)*: Kraut is not exactly fat! Now what do you think of that!

CHILD WHO HAS RETURNED: O, Monsieur, what you heard is the 207th battalion. They are very discontented and are marching to the City Hall to hang the generals. May I have my . . . *(He is interrupted.)*

CORPULENT MAN: And this with the siege. . . . !

PAPA *(interrupts him)*: Yes, with the siege! Citizens, smash your chains and out the Prussians—and you'll be able to eat again! Now we see who the real enemy is. You. And your fellow fat men. Or was it the Prussians who raised the price of potatoes?

CORPULENT MAN: Messieurs! Discussing the price of potatoes while out there our men are fighting for. . . .

PAPA (interrupting again): You don't mean fighting but dying. Do you know what's been happening out there? Every night, we lie in the fields of Mont Valérien, in the mud and the rain. And me with my rheumatism. The attack starts at ten in the morning. (getting more and more animated) We storm the Redoute de Montretout, the parc de Buzenval. We take St. Cloud, move on to Garches. We've got 150 guns, but only 30 of 'em fire as we storm Garches with no artillery cover and send the Prussians back in a wild retreat and THEN (suddenly more slowly, bitterly) an order from the rear says "STOP!" We wait for two hours and the order comes: "RETREAT!" And Trochu leaves Montretout and all the positions we've won—undefended. How do you like that, Monsieur?

CORPULENT MAN: Your generals know where the enemy is concentrating his fire.

COCO: Oh, they know it only too well, Monsieur. That's where they always send the National Guard.

CORPULENT MAN (angrily): Now that's enough. Do you know what you're talking about? You dare accuse your commanders, the generals of France, of treason? Perhaps I might ask you to produce some proof?

PAPA: He wants proof, Coco. And we don't have any. Except death. We happen to be dying like flies. Well, so we die, eh, Monsieur Whoeveryouare? Will it please you to produce some proof that somebody hit you over the head, eh? (gesturing menacingly:) Just you say one word and we . . . open up the hearing.

Ah, you have nothing to say! I inquire politely as to how I may be of service, Monsieur Whoeveryouare, and suddenly you are silent.

CORPULENT MAN: We know all about your "services" and demonstrations at the Hôtel de Ville. It's the old blackmail of the Commune. . . . (Coco gets up. The Corpulent Man stops speaking.)

COCO: Oh, go right on. Please. We've got plenty of time before the 101st starts moving.

CORPULENT MAN: The truth is, you just don't want to pay your rents. While France is fighting for her very existence, all you care about are your pensions, and anything else you can get your hands on. (sardonically) "Butter is too expensive!" But watch out! The patience of Paris is at an end! (The National Guardsmen are silent.) You, you are the traitors! We're beginning to take less pleasure from your newspapers. Look out. We've just about had it with a certain class of people! Had it, I say! (The Waiter comes back with four glasses of wine and a casserole covered with a cloth napkin. The Corpulent Man motions him to shut up and go away.)

WAITER: Votre poulet, Monsieur.

COCO (mockingly): Monsieur, your chicken!

CORPULENT MAN: I'll see to it that you get such a. . . . You and your whole goddamn Guard. Of all the nerve. . . . You'll see. . . . (He exits hurriedly.)

CHILD: Monsieur! The five francs— you promised—(The children run after the Corpulent Man)

WAITER: Messieurs, I am privileged to invite you to some refreshments.

COCO (trying to give the German prisoner a glass): There you go, Kraut. Oh shit! You can't take it, you poor slob. Well, I'll drink to your health! (They drink. Out of the café come Mme. Cabet and Jean. She is still carrying the basket.)

JEAN (to the Waiter): Where's the man who wanted me to run an errand? (The Waiter motions for him to be silent. Then François recognizes the Cabets.)

FRANÇOIS: Madame Cabet!

JEAN: François!

MME. CABET: François, are you wounded? I must beg you to pay up your rent. You know the government is asking us to pay up on all back rents —and they're not buying any of my emblems in there (i.e., the café). I'm ruined. We'll be thrown into the streets!

FRANÇOIS: But Madame Cabet, I haven't received a single sou of my soldier's pay in three weeks. And I'm

196

also not feeling very well at the moment.

MME. CABET: Well, so when will you pay? *(to Coco, who is smirking);* Please don't laugh, Monsieur. He's my tenant.

COCO: Yes, François, when will you pay? Madame, we understand your problem. All we can do is tell you that two battalions have just returned from two days of battle, and are on their way to the Hôtel de Ville to ask the government a couple of questions.

PAPA *(elegantly):* And that one of those questions will be a moratorium on all rents. In the meantime, we can but offer you a small advance. Will you not accept this chicken a fat man ordered but ate not? *(They lead Mme. Cabet to the table on the terrace and proceed to serve her in a grand manner.)*

PAPA: Garçon, in the future, the owner might do well to ask his finer clients to please pay in advance. It might just happen that circumstances beyond their control would render it impossible for them to eat the food they order! Would that be difficult for you?

WAITER: Yes, it would, Monsieur. I would have to decide to join you. Perhaps the government would purchase the chicken for Madame Cabet? Two battalions of the National Guard should be enough to force through that demand.

COCO: À votre santé, Madame.

PAPA: Bon appétit! The 101st is honored, Madame, to have you as their guest.

MME. CABET: Messieurs, you're much too kind. It just so happens that I have very little in my stomach today. And chicken is my weakness. May I give my Jean a piece too?

JEAN: Perhaps it might interest these people why none of the soldiers in there wants to buy our emblems any more. The employees at the recruiting station anticipate new instructions that will end recruitment for the National Guard.

COCO: What's that? Did you hear that, Papa?

PAPA: Now don't get excited. She'll come *with* us to the Hôtel de Ville.

COCO: Did you get that, Madame? Papa wants you to come with us to City Hall and show them the emblems nobody wants to buy. Put the chicken in your basket.

FRANÇOIS: Here comes the 101st battalion!

(Behind the barbed wire the guard are seen passing by. Bayonets with loaves of bread speared on them are raised like flags. Papa and Coco help Mme. Cabet up and start to lead her away with them.)

PAPA *(pointing to Jean):* What's the matter with him? How come he isn't fighting? We aren't too *gauche* for him are we?

MME. CABET: Oh no, Monsieur. I think you're a little too *droite,* if you'll excuse me. He's a real radical!

PAPA: Ah!

JEAN: Messieurs, consider me one of you from now on, won't you? I've been wanting to ask the government some questions myself for quite a while. *(Papa takes François' cap and puts it on Jean's head.)*

PAPA: There!

FRANÇOIS *(to Jean, glad to have him along):* It's been deadly without you, Jean. *(They all leave—the Waiter throws his apron onto the table, turns out the lights, and is about to follow them when his glance falls on the forgotten German prisoner. He motions him away with his hand and pushes him after the guards.)*

WAITER: Come on now, Kraut. Let's go. Vorwarts! En avant!

SCENE TWO

January 25, 1871. Bordeaux. Conversation between Thiers and Jules Favre. Thiers is still in his bathrobe and is adjusting the temperature of the water in his bathtub, by having his servant pour in hot and cold water. He is extremely polite. So is Favre.

THIERS *(while drinking his morning bowl of milk):* The war has lasted long enough. Elle commence à devenir une montruosité! We 'ave fought it and we

197

'ave lost it, so now for what are we waiting?

FAVRE: Ah, but the demands of the Prussians! Herr von Bismarck is talking about an indemnité of five billion francs (!), plus the annexation of Alsace et Lorraine, plus the detainment of all French prisoners of war, *and* the occupation of all the forts until everything is settled to his satisfactión. C'est la ruine!

THIERS: And the demands of the Parisians—ça ce n'est pas la ruine also?

FAVRE: À coup sûr.

THIERS *(offering him some coffee):* Du café? Then milk, comme moi? No, not even that? Ah, Favre, if we only had the stomachs and the appetites we used to have! But back to Herr von Bismarck. Ein wahnsinnig gewordener Bierstudent! He makes his demands intolérable, knowing that we will have to accept them—every one of them.

FAVRE: But must we? Really? What about those iron and tin mines in Lorraine?—the future of French industry!

THIERS: And what about those police agents being thrown into the Seine? What good are those mines in a France under the Commune of Paris? Hein?

FAVRE: But five billion! That's our whole economy!

THIERS: That's the *prix courant de l'ordre.*

FAVRE: And the prédominance of Prussia for the next three generations.

THIERS: And the protection of our power for the next five!

FAVRE: We'll be a nation of peasants for the next hundred years.

THIERS: I count on those peasants. La paix se fait avec eux, n'est-ce pas? What does your Alsace-Lorraine mean to them? They don't even know where that is. You really should at least have a glass of water, Favre.

FAVRE: Is it really necessary, I wonder.

THIERS: A swallow of water is still life—even just the swallowing by itself. Ah, oui—But what is also necessary is the price of order.

FAVRE: These National Guards will be the death of France! We've made the patriotic sacrifice of arming the mob against the Prussians; so now they're armed against us! But, on the other hand, can they not be considered the defenders of Paris? After all, they want to fight. . . .

THIERS *(interrupting):* Mais mon cher Favre, qu'est-ce que c'est que ça, Paris? You speak of it as if it were something holy.—"Better for it to be burned to the ground than ever surrendered!" You forget that even Paris by itself has no value. The scum are ready to blow it all up—because it doesn't belong to them. They are screaming for gasoline! But for us, the authorities, Paris is not a symbol, but a property—to burn it is not to defend it.

(The sound of marching feet. The gentlemen suddenly become very nervous. Thiers, unable to speak, motions his servant to the window to see who is marching.)

SERVANT: Une compagnie de marins, Monsieur le Président.

THIERS: If you think I will ever forget this degradation. . . . !

FAVRE: But Bordeaux is quiet, is it not?

THIERS: What do you mean by quiet? Perhaps quiet is too quiet! Favre, we are going to have to make an example of these gueules crasseuses! Il faut les exterminer! Take them by the scruff of their filthy necks and smash their heads on the pavement in the name of civilisatión! Our culture was founded on the principle of private property, which must be protected at any cost. What!? —they dare to try and tell us what we can 'ave and what we can not 'ave!? Give me a sabre and a cavalry and if only an ocean of blood can cleanse Paris of this vermin, then let there be an ocean of blood! *(To Servant:)* Ma serviette! *(The Servant hands him a napkin and he wipes the foam from his mouth.)*

FAVRE: You get too excited. Think of your health! You are too important to us.

THIERS: And you have armed them! From this moment on I shall have only one thought: how to end this war, vite, immédiatement!

FAVRE: But unfortunately those Parisians are still fighting like the very devil. The good Trochu said it well:

The Nationalgarde will not be sensible until ten thousand of them have bled. *(Thiers expresses disbelief in his look.)* Oui, oui! And so he sends them into combat like cattle to the slaughter to calm their ambitions. *(Whispers something into Thiers' ear.)*

THIERS: No, it's quite all right if he hears us. Hippolyte is a patriote.

FAVRE: I can assure you, Monsieur Thiers, that on this point you will have Herr von Bismarck's complete sympathy.

THIERS *(dryly)*: I'm glad to hear that. It has come to my attention that he has been belittling my abilities. And this, after having seen me in person!

FAVRE: *That* is impertinénce, but it has nothing to do with his true opinion of you.

THIERS: I can say this about myself, mon cher Favre—that I am above such personalities. I am only interested in how Herr von Bismarck thinks he can help us.

FAVRE: He has made a personal offer directly to me, that the population of Paris, immediately after the armistice, shall receive a large delivery of food. Then, after a short period, he will reduce the amount of incoming food by one half, until all the weapons the people have accumulated have been returned to the authorities. He is quite certain that this will be far more effective than outright starvation.

THIERS: Not bad. We'll remind the Parisians what meat tastes like again! I never denied Herr von Bismarck was a man of talent.

FAVRE: He will even clamp down on the Berlin food companies who wish to do business with Paris.

THIERS: A part of his talent lies in his courage, eh, Favre? We will oblige the Prussians to occupy those suburbs in which the Nationalgarde have installed their cannons.

FAVRE: An excellent point. Splendide.

THIERS: There are, I believe, a few men of talent besides Herr von Bismarck. We, for example, will write into the capitulation agreement that the first payment towards the five billion will fall due only after the pacificatión of Paris. That will give Bismarck an interest in our victory. The word pacification should be used more frequently; it's one of those words which explain everything. Oh yes. The indemnity . . . *(to Servant:)* Hippolyte, vous pouvez nous laisser.

SERVANT *(bowing)*: Le bain de Monsieur le Président est prêt. *(Exit.)*

(Thiers nods and gets into the bath.)

THIERS: What do you think we can do to raise the money?

FAVRE: It has been proposed that the indemnity be financed by a few German banks, especially those of Herr von Bleichröder, Herr von Bismarck's personal banker. That's a provision we're going to mention. . . . O, naturally I had to turn down my commission as a member of the government.

THIERS: Cela va de soi. But did they name any figures? *(Favre writes some figures on a piece of paper. Thiers takes it and reads it.)*

THIERS: Impossíble.

FAVRE *(low)*: Comme je vous le dis.

THIERS: But we must have peace. France demands it. I only hope I'll have the strength to see her through it.

FAVRE: Your éléction is assured, Monsieur le Président. All the rural districts will vote for you.

THIERS: I will need that strength too. The powers of disorder are armed.

FAVRE: Monsieur Thiers, France worries about your health. You alone can save her.

THIERS *(modestly)*: Je le sais. I know. *That* is why you see me drinking this milk, which I absolutely abhor, mon cher Favre! *(A sardonic smile.)*

SCENE THREE

(Part I)

1:00 a.m. March 18, 1871. Rue Pigalle. In the middle of the street stands a cannon. François Faure and Jean Cabet are sitting on rattan chairs, keeping watch over the cannon. Babette Cherron gets up from Jean's lap.

BABETTE *(seductively stroking the shaft of the cannon)*: Bonne nuit, Jean.

(Goes slowly toward her house at the other end of the street.)

199

JEAN (satisfied with himself): There isn't a man alive who can get away with not giving his girl a present of some kind. Materialists, that's what they are! Used to be a mirror 'ould turn the trick. Now it's one of the cannons M. Thiers wanted Herr von Bismarck to have.

FRANÇOIS: And he'd have 'em too, if we hadn't gone and taken it away from 'em. (Looks hard at Jean.) Geneviève isn't a materialist.

JEAN (teasing): Geneviève Géricault, the little professeur? no, she's very pure and spiritual now, and that's why you'd like to go to bed with her. . . .

FRANÇOIS: I would not like to go to bed with her.

JEAN: Mmm! Babette says she's quite well developed.

FRANÇOIS: How can you talk with her about that?

JEAN: They live together, that's how. Besides, she's engaged. (François looks at him as if to ask, "To whom?") He's a lieutenant. Taken prisoner by the Prussians. . . . Her breasts are the best. . . .

FRANÇOIS: You're trying to make me angry.

JEAN: The way you talk about girls you wouldn't know you're from the provinces. Doesn't everyone there start at fourteen with a cow maid or a . . .

FRANÇOIS: You are not going to make me angry.

JEAN: Oh I told Babette to tell Geneviève you were . . . interested. It might perhaps amuse her to have a little priest to wrap around her finger.

FRANÇOIS: I'm a physicist.

JEAN: So much the better! Physics, doesn't that require a knowledge of bodies?

FRANÇOIS: But didn't you just tell me she's in love with a lieutenant?

JEAN: No, that she's engaged to a lieutenant.

FRANÇOIS (under his breath): C'est la même chose.

JEAN (laughing): You have such ridiculous ideas! You think that people only go to bed with each other when they're madly in love. The truth is that there's enough in front of you when you get up in the morning that says: today, I've got to have a girl. Eh? Why should it be any different with women? (singsong:) Necessity! Not necessarily watching for a particular pair of breasts, not that a particular pair might not suit you, but the same thing goes for les femmes aussi. Chercher—quand il fait chaud! The same for Geneviève.

FRANÇOIS: Not exactly. But I think I'm gonna hit the sack now. (Stands up to go, but turns back to Jean.) You know, I'm kind of glad my room is next to yours again.

JEAN (smiles, gets up too): I don't think we have to keep watch any more. Surprise attacks don't come at night. And in the morning I hear we're getting white bread. (Pause. They start to go.)

FRANÇOIS (stops): Say, Jean?

JEAN: Mmm?

FRANÇOIS: While we were talking about physics—I remembered that your uncle Pierre still has my microscope, and my volume of Lavoisier.

JEAN (embarrassed): My uncle? Langevin?

FRANÇOIS: Your mother gave them to him to keep for me. I only mention it 'cause I wish I had that Lavoisier here now.

(Jean smiles, nods. They both take their chairs into the house.)

SCENE THREE

(Part II)

5:00 a.m. A line of women, including Geneviève Géricault and Babette Cherron, in front of a bakery waiting for it to open.

FIRST WOMAN: White bread from Papa Thiers—so we can swallow down his peace treaty!

SECOND WOMAN: Paris for ten tons of flour!

GENEVIÈVE: You know, not one train has arrived, so the flour must have been here all the time!

THIRD WOMAN: My husband lost his leg just last week. Shrapnel. And they

200

were already negotiating the peace at the time! . . .

SECOND WOMAN: They must have some deal they're cooking up. They don't give away anything for nothing. The lady I do the washing for gave me a torn pair of pants, to try and keep me quiet after she'd turned in my Émile for making some remark or other.

THIRD WOMAN: "I'll take my leg home," my husband told 'em, "or they'll tell me at the pension office I only had one to begin with!"

FIRST WOMAN: Thiers'll get five billion from the Germans.

GENEVIÈVE: And how much from certain French, I wonder!

SECOND WOMAN: Why surrender while we've still got 300,000 National Guardsmen in Paris alone?

GENEVIÈVE: Because there are 300,000 in Paris alone!

FIRST WOMAN: And the Prussians won't return the prisoners of war until they're completely paid.

BABETTE: God damn this fucking war! It's only good when it ends.

FIRST WOMAN: Ah, but who pays for the peace?

BABETTE: We do, citizens. Who else? Those with nothing pay for the whole thing.

GENEVIÈVE: Oh we have nothing, Babette? We've got 200,000 bayonets. . . .

FIRST WOMAN: I tell you it's only a ceasefire and they won't get the suburbs, not the Prussians and not Thiers either.

GENEVIÈVE: That Herr von Bismarck doesn't dare show his face in Paris, does he? Paris is not for sale!

(A man with a poster enters.)

BABETTE: Well, you're up early old man. Your wife wanted to be alone, eh?

GENEVIÈVE: Maybe someone else should be putting up posters. *(The man pastes a poster on the wall and exits.)*

BABETTE *(going to the wall to read the notice)*: From M. Thiers! *(reads, gradually becoming sing-songy:)* "La paix, c'est l'ordre. Peace is order. Citizens of Paris: With commerce at a standstill, orders being cancelled, and capital leaving the city, there must be order! The guilty must be punished by the regular procedure. . . . la la LA la la la LA!" *(The woman who owns the bakery takes

off the iron grating from the door in preparation for opening the store. The Women on line now mimic the rich to each other:)

FIRST WOMAN: Did you hear, Madame Pullard? In spite of the war, business is bad!

SECOND WOMAN: How true! How true! Since last month I've been unable to sell all my locomotives!

GENEVIÈVE: Yes, and raising capital's impossible because of that disgusting National Guard!

SECOND WOMAN: You too, you too?

BAKERY-OWNER: What is this, another demonstration? I think the government's white bread speaks louder than you ever can, mesdames.

SECOND WOMAN: White bread and order!

FIRST WOMAN: Will Order pay the rent, eh?

BABETTE: The ink on this poster is still wet. They must've been in an awful hurry.

FIRST WOMAN: Farting comes from eating bread, right? Those bastards can't give us even a little bit of bread without farting about order, can they?

THIRD WOMAN: Now come on, watch your language. What does Mademoiselle Géricault know about farting? She's a school teacher.

FIRST WOMAN: Leave Mademoiselle Géricault alone—she's OK. After all, didn't she help the Cabets and Papa when they brought our cannon here from Clichy before the Prussians came?

SECOND WOMAN: Do you believe M. Thiers turned Clichy over to the Prussians 'cause our cannons were there?

GENEVIÈVE: Yes, citizen, I believe he did. The Central Committee of the National Guard received reports to that effect.

SECOND WOMAN: Oh! She's a regular politician!

FIRST WOMAN: What if she is? Does that prevent her from speaking the truth?

THIRD WOMAN: My husband says his leg wasn't ripped off by any weapon but by politics. And that's why he's reading *La Patrie en Danger* by Blanqui. *(A few infantry soldiers—at least two—, among them Philippe Faure, come into view and go directly to the cannon.)*

BABETTE *(wary)*: Ah, Philippe, you're back! Welcome home! Just in time; the bakery's about to open.

PHILIPPE: Shh, Babette. I'm not here to see the baker. *(He starts to survey the cannon.)*

BABETTE: What do you want with that cannon?

PHILIPPE: It's coming with us to Versailles. Orders.

BABETTE *(yelling to the Women)*: Hey! They're gonna steal our cannon!

SECOND WOMAN: What are you trying to do!

FIRST WOMAN: With a handful of guys?

GENEVIÈVE: Philippe! You should be ashamed of yourself!

BABETTE: They must have sent him 'cause he knows the area, having worked as the baker's assistant!

PHILIPPE: Why the devil are you all up this early in the morning? And what are you doing? Take it easy.

GENEVIÈVE: We're getting white bread from your leaders so you can steal our gun, like wool from the sheep. *(The Women run over towards the cannon.)*

BABETTE: Hey! This is ours, damn it! We paid for it—all of us, with our last sous!

PHILIPPE: But the war's over.

GENEVIÈVE: So you want to start one with us?

PHILIPPE: This cannon has got to be turned over to the Prussians.

BABETTE: Then let the Prussians come and get it! Take your hands off it! Don't you dare lay one finger on it, you shitheads. *(to Geneviève:)* Go wake the Cabets!

(Geneviève runs to the Cabets' house and knocks on the door. Mme. Cabet comes to the window.)

GENEVIÈVE: Get Jean! Quick! They're taking the cannon away! *(She runs back.)* It's not for the Prussians; it's for M. Thiers. He wants to turn it on us. Don't let him get it, citizens!

FIRST WOMAN: Hands off the cannon!

SECOND WOMAN: This is Madame Cabet's cannon!

(Jean comes running out of the house in pants and undershirt.)

BABETTE: Jean, they've come for the cannon. Philippe brought them here.

(From a nearby alley a loud noise is followed first by shots and then by the ringing of bells.)

GENEVIÈVE: There are cannons in the rue de Tabernacle, too. This is a surprise attack on the whole area. Now we know why the white bread. . . .

JEAN *(calling back to François)*: François, your brother's here—from Thiers!

PHILIPPE *(surrounded by the Women)*: No, no, no! Come on now. Out of the way. We're only obeying orders, my good women.

JEAN: Yes, out of the way so *we* can get at them.

FRANÇOIS *(running in, bayonet drawn; he too is only in pants and undershirt)*: Leave the cannon right where it is, Philippe. It doesn't belong to you.

BAKERY-OWNER *(from inside the shop)*: You carry out your orders, Philippe, or don't ever think you'll work in this bakery again.

PHILIPPE *(to François)*: Since when are you in the National Guard?

FRANÇOIS: The school's closed. Out of the way. *(The Women move out of the way. François cocks his gun.)*

PHILIPPE: Put that gun away, brother.

BABETTE: Shoot him down!

GENEVIÈVE *(throwing herself in front of Philippe)*: No violence!

JEAN *(dragging her out of the line of fire)*: You keep out of this. *(Philippe cocks his gun.)*

PHILIPPE: Put the gun down, little brother.

FRANÇOIS: Make one move and I'll pull the trigger. *(praying:)* Our Father, who art in heaven, hallowed be thy name. . . . *(Continues to pray while still aiming.)*

BABETTE *(to Philippe)*: You mean you'd massacre us, just 'cause your fucking generals ordered you to?

GENEVIÈVE: You poor bastards! You can't take our cannon away! We'll throw ourselves under the wheels!

PHILIPPE: I am going to count to three—One . . .

(Enter Mme. Cabet and Papa from the house.)

MME. CABET: Philippe! Put that gun down at once! You silly fool! How dare

202

you contradict your brother who has studied physics while you don't know nothing from nothing. *(holds out a bottle)* Here's some wine I brought for you. They sent you here without even giving you a good breakfast, didn't they?

PHILIPPE *(turns and looks at his comrades, who have not drawn their weapons, and slowly puts down his gun)*: But Madame Cabet, you are hindering me from carrying out my orders.

(The women laugh and then crowd around the Faure brothers.)

THIRD WOMAN *(to Philippe)*: Attaboy, baker!

GENEVIÈVE: They can't order you to kill your own brother, can they?

BAKERY-OWNER: Philippe, you're fired! I don't employ traitors.

BABETTE *(giving Philippe a kiss)*: This is what traitors get!

PHILIPPE: I'm no longer a brother or a baker, my good women. I'm in the service.

FRANÇOIS *(timidly, to Geneviéve)*: And what about me? Don't I get anything?

GENEVIÈVE *(gaily)*: To each according to his needs.

FRANÇOIS: That's not an answer.

(The Women are talking with the soldiers meanwhile, simultaneously.)

FIRST WOMAN: Aren't you ashamed of yourselves? Doing business with a woman without flirting with her?

SOLDIER: The war's over. We just want to go home.

SECOND WOMAN: Ooh la la, he wants to go home. Where are you from, my little son?

SOLDIER: From the Auvergne, and it's harvest time now. But you Parisiennes, you don't care about that.

THIRD WOMAN *(who has gotten wine from Mme. Cabet, which she had intended to give Philippe)*: Have a drink, soldier.

FOURTH WOMAN: Come on now, show us the other end of the pistol. Not the front with the hole. We've got holes in front, too.

SECOND WOMAN: Madame Cabet, bring a blanket! He's so cold, how could *anyone* make love in such a condition!?

GENEVIÈVE: This cannon belongs to the woman who lives here: Madame Cabet. It's as important to her as the pots she cooks in!

PAPA: Long live Madame Cabet, the only owner of a cannon in the rue Pigalle! *(He lifts her up on top of the cannon. To the soldiers:)* You see, all we've got to do is talk to each other. *(To the Women:)* Now you have it back. Guard it carefully. Don't let it ever leave Paris. Hold on to it; clutch it to your breast, where it won't be dangerous.

(From the side street, which has grown quieter, comes Pierre Langevin, a worker, followed by at least two Children.)

LANGEVIN: Hello, Papa. Have you finished them off? Without any violence?

PHILIPPE *(to his comrade)*: What can we do if they send us without any horses? We can't drag that thing by ourselves through all these women.

PAPA: Everything's OK here. How 'bout the other places?

LANGEVIN: The whole quarter is awake. Not a single cannon's been lost.

CHILDREN: They tried to steal our cannon at the Moulin de la Galette. And they shot down two of our people in the Rue Lepic.

MME. CABET *(to the soldiers)*: Gentlemen, this is my brother-in-law Pierre Langevin. He's a member of the Central Committee of the National Guard.

LANGEVIN: In the Rue Granot, General Lecomte ordered the soldiers to fire on the people. But his own men arrested him.

PAPA: Serves him right, the pimp. Paris knows how much blood was spilled on account of him! Where is he?

LANGEVIN: They took him to the guardhouse.

PAPA: But he'll escape! If he isn't shot in five minutes, he's a free man!

LANGEVIN: He will be turned over to justice, Comrade.

PAPA: But *we're* justice! *(Exits.)*

MME. CABET: Would somebody please help me down from this cannon?

LANGEVIN *(to the soldiers)*: What are you going to do with those rifles? Kill your own people?

SOLDIER: Shit. Against our own people! *(They put their rifles down.)*

GENEVIÈVE *(to the Children)*: You

can tear down those stupid signs they posted, if you want to. *(They start to do so.)*

JEAN *(to the Soldiers)*: Hey, let's help my mother down! And then we march straight to City Hall and arrest Thiers! Let him tell us what he was going to do with that cannon!

BABETTE: Three kisses for whoever gets Thiers alive!

SCENE THREE

(Part III)

8:00 a.m. The Bakery-owner closes the iron grating in front of the door again. Philippe Faure stands near her, unhappily, watching a stout woman, carrying a rifle, marching up and down in front of the cannon.

BAKERY-OWNER: Now I think we're going to have a riot. 'Cause if they declare Paris a Commune, like everybody's saying they're going to, that means only one thing: Everything'll be divided up and everyone'll get drunk. They'll drink it all down, and then divide it all up again. You! You're a traitor: you'll never work in my bakery again. And that brother of yours, the young priest! He's a traitor too!

PHILIPPE: He's only at the seminary 'cause he couldn't study otherwise.

BAKERY-OWNER: So he goes around stealing his lessons from the good brothers of Saint-Josèphe. He's just like you, you Communard! *(She goes back into her shop angrily. At the same time, Geneviève comes out of the house next door.)*

GENEVIÈVE: Bonjour, Philippe. How do you feel in this—new epoch? *(He grumbles.)* Violence is finished! We've got the cannon!

PHILIPPE: Yeah, it's a woman's world now. And if that's the "new epoch. . . ." *(curses under his breath. Geneviève laughs. As he goes into the Cabet's house, she gaily puts on her gloves. Then Papa comes down the side street with a somber look on his face.)*

GENEVIÈVE: Bonjour, Papa. . . . Oh Papa, weren't you at the Rue Granot when they took General Lecomte prisoner? What happened to him?

PAPA: He was shot, citizen.

GENEVIÈVE: But . . . who shot him?

PAPA: Who do you think? The people.

GENEVIÈVE: Without a trial?

PAPA: Of course not. . . . He was tried by the people.

GENEVIÈVE: And were you there?

PAPA: Everyone who was there was there. . . . Now don't you go worrying your head about the enemies of the people. *This* is what is to be done. *(He enters the Cabets' house, in a very bad mood. She is confused, and follows him with her eyes.)*

[*Projection: WHAT IS TO BE DONE*]

SCENE FOUR

March 19, 1871. Hôtel de Ville. The stairs leading to a meeting hall, where an assembly of the Central Committee of the National Guard is in session. In front of the door stands a Guardsman eating bread and cheese and checking passes at the same time. Papa, Coco, and Mme. Cabet stand waiting. Delegates are entering the hall. We hear the conversations of at least four of them.

PACIFISTIC DELEGATE: If we decide to have new elections, we'll have to discuss it with the mayors of the twenty arrondissements.

VIOLENT DELEGATE: No! No! No! What we need is a battalion to arrest them. They're crooks—all of them. Otherwise how could they have become mayors?

HUMANITARIAN DELEGATE: The main thing is that we gain an overwhelming majority, and all of Paris will go to the polls if the mayors join us. So let's welcome them.

PROUDHONIAN DELEGATE: For God's sake, no violence. If we want to win Paris over to us, we can't do it by terrorizing her.

PAPA *(to Guard)*: Good citizen of the Central Committee, could you tell Pierre

Langevin, inside, that we've got to speak with him. This is his sister-in-law. *(More directly:)* And could you also please tell us why all the people can't go in?

GUARD: The room is much too small. And don't forget, citizen, the enemy is listening.

PAPA: But more important is that the people are trying to listen. At least leave the door open. *(He does.)*

VOICE FROM INSIDE THE HALL: Urgent resolution of the 67th battalion: "Whereas the population of Paris spared neither life nor limb, nor blood, nor worldly goods in the defense of our country, be it resolved that there shall be distributed among the twenty arrondissements, by way of reparations, the sum of one million francs, obtained through the cancellation of all salaries due to officers of the government of treason."

VOICE OF THE PRESIDENT *(after counting hands)*: Adopted.

(The next four lines are simultaneous with the three following them.)

MME. CABET: Mm—they're really doing something today, aren't they?

PAPA: The important thing is to march on Versailles.

MME. CABET: Not only are we gonna get white bread, but I'll be able to buy it!

PAPA: But there won't be any white bread for anybody if we don't start marching on Versailles soon, Madame Cabet.

VOICE OF THE PRESIDENT *(in the hall)*: We now continue with the discussion of the question of elections. Delegate Varlin has the floor.

VOICE OF VARLIN: Citizens and fellow guardsmen! This morning, at approximately two o'clock a.m., the enemy tried to capture the cannons we refused to turn over to the Prussians.

VOICE: That's the second time they've tried to punish Paris. The first was when they tried to force that general on us.

([Georges Clemenceau and other] *Mayors, well dressed and with top hats, come to the stairs.)*

VOICE OF VARLIN: Citizens, why was this plot hatched against the people of Paris? To take the last weapons away from France, and hand her over to the iron will of Bismarck; and at the same time to make Paris, and Paris alone, pay for all that he demands of France. So that the perpetrators of this terrible war make those who suffered in it pay the cost of it! We who fought, and spilled our blood, will pay, so that those who made money from this war can go right on making it in peacetime. Citizens and guardsmen, we, the Commune, demand that the deputies, senators, generals, industrialists, landlords, not to mention the Church, in short, the people and the institutions responsible for this damned war should pay the five billion francs and that for this purpose all of their possessions be immediately confiscated and sold!

(Loud applause. The Mayors have entered the hall.)

VOICE: The Central Committee salutes the Mayors of Paris.

VOICE OF A MAYOR: This is the Hôtel de Ville, the City Hall of Paris. You have occupied it by military force. Will you kindly tell us, by what right?

VOICE: By the right the people gave us, Monsieur Mayor! Consider yourselves as the people's guests, and you'll be welcome here. *(Sounds of protest.)*

VOICE OF A MAYOR: Do you know what that answer means? That everyone will say, "These people want revolution."

VOICE: What do you mean "want"? This *is* the revolution! Look around you!

VOICE OF A MAYOR: Citizens of the National Guard, we, the mayors of Paris, are ready to transmit your wishes to the newly-elected National Assembly in Versailles. But what are your wishes? Will you be satisfied with a petition to the Assembly for a Municipal Council?

VOICES: No! No! No! An independent Commune! An autonomous Commune!

VOICE OF VARLIN: We don't want just the freedom to vote for a Municipal Council. We want real municipal freedom: the abolishment of the police force, the right of the National Guard to elect its own officers, the proclamation of the Third Republic as the legal government, the suspension pure and simple of all rents, the exclusion of the army from the territory of this city. In short, a free Paris!

VOICE OF A MAYOR: You are flaunting a red flag. Prenez garde! If you fly that flag over City Hall, the government will throw all of France into an attack on Paris, and there'll be bloody days in May. The people will not only avoid your voting booths like the plague, but use them very likely as a place to spit.

VOICE: The Committee will take that chance. Our confidence rests in the fact that the people not only have hands to work, but eyes to see. (Applause.)

VOICE OF A MAYOR: They will see a great deal. In any case, I will not run on an election slate with murderers. (Hisses and boos.) Your Committee has not protested the murders of Generals Thomas and Lecomte.

(Voices respond simultaneously:)

VOICE OF PROUDHONIAN DELEGATE: We had nothing to do with that!

VOICE OF VIOLENT DELEGATE: I protest the use of the term "murder" to describe the legitimate execution of the enemies of the people!

VOICE OF PROUDHONIAN DELEGATE: The Committee must disavow all responsibility for that!

VOICE OF HUMANITARIAN DELEGATE: Careful—if you disavow the people, beware of their disavowing you!

VOICE OF PACIFISTIC DELEGATE: Stop these slanders! The people and the bourgeoisie united when the Third Republic was proclaimed September 4th!

VOICE OF HUMANITARIAN DELEGATE: Right! And that unity must remain. Everyone must vote! So no threats! Until we have the full approbation of the people of Paris, we must consider the government at Versailles as the government of the State.

VOICE OF VIOLENT DELEGATE: Still, the National Guard is a Nation, armed in the face of the power of the State. (The Mayors appear in the door.)

A MAYOR (going back angrily into the hall): We note with great satisfaction that even among yourselves, you agree on nothing.

(Voices [from inside, restively] continue:)

VOICE OF PACIFISTIC DELEGATE: But we need the bourgeoisie so we can start producing again. . . .

VOICE OF VIOLENT DELEGATE: That's

right, abandon the people to save the bourgeoisie. . . .

VOICE OF HUMANITARIAN DELEGATE: No. The people will abandon us. (sarcastically:) And then you'll see how well you can make a revolution with the bourgeoisie!

PAPA: That's right.

VOICE OF A MAYOR: You have our best wishes. And we hope you will succeed in your great task. For us, it is a little too much to shoulder. (They leave.)

VOICE: The bourgeoisie departs from the hall! Good riddance!

PAPA (calling to the Mayors as they pass by): Bastards!

(Langevin and Geneviève emerge from the meeting hall and close the door behind them.)

PAPA: Pierre, we must make a motion immediately to eliminate the people who are protecting the generals. They must be shot like dogs—with no trial! All of them—at once! Otherwise you're lost.

LANGEVIN (interrupting): Now what do you have to do with shooting? Just take it easy.

PAPA (answering his question): Me? Nothing. What do you want me to do? The Committee's diddling around doing nothing.

LANGEVIN: Wouldn't you like to hear a little better? (Opens the door again.)

VOICE OF RIGAULT: Citizens and guardsmen, the only ones who should have the right to decide the fate of France should be those who have defended her. Which means the proletariat, that is, the two hundred thousand fighters of Paris. And their vote comes out of the barrels of their guns! (Unrest.)

VOICE OF PROUDHONIAN DELEGATE: Do you want to destroy the elections? That's anarchy!

VOICE OF PACIFISTIC DELEGATE: That'll mean civil war; And with the Prussian batteries from the Bois de Vincennes to the Bois de Boulogne!

VOICE OF HUMANITARIAN DELEGATE: Let's make it unanimous we hold elections!

GENEVIÈVE: We are not united. And it'll hurt us.

LANGEVIN (smiling): No, no, it's good for us. That's what the Movement is all about. First, though, what we've got to do is to find the right direction to go in. *(to Papa, Coco, and Mme. Cabet:)* But what brings you here?

PAPA: The 101st says the barricades aren't up yet. Our police, baggage and artillery have been lining up in the direction of Versailles all night, 'cause that's where Thiers is. And as soon as we get the signal, Langevin, we march.

GENEVIÈVE *(quickly):* But that would also mean civil war.

COCO: Twenty thousand men are now camping in front of City Hall, with their bread rations fixed to their bayonets. There are fifty cannons ready, and all you've got to do is open the window and shout "À Versailles!" and that whole mess'll be finished forever.

LANGEVIN *(slowly):* Maybe. But we need the approval of the French people, don't we?

PAPA: Good, so hold elections. But elections or no elections, what matters is that we destroy the enemy. Now.

LANGEVIN *(hesitantly):* The Commune is treading on very shaky ground at the moment. If we succeed in cementing our power base in Paris, then Thiers and his company will be seen as nothing but a band of robbers in the eyes of France. But I know what you're saying, Papa. And it's good that you keep pushing us the way you do. Give us no peace; keep us moving ahead. *(He exits quickly back into the hall.)*

PAPA: I guess we'll have to be content with that, Coco. *(They start to leave, then stop and hear the last part of Varlin's speech:)*

VOICE OF VARLIN: Citizens and Guardsmen: In spite of the desertion and the treason of the ruling classes, the proletariat of Paris, decimated on the battlefield by the bourgeoisie—by the Prussian bourgeoisie and by her own—, weakened by the hunger brought on by the Prussian generals and Parisian profiteers, rose up early this morning to defend their battered homes, and take their destiny into their own hands. Their destiny is the destiny of France. The self-styled Government of National Defense, formed by the bourgeoisie after the defeat, has been shown to be a Government of National Betrayal. The same people who called upon the Emperor to deliver them, deserting him as soon as they no longer had a use for him, now call upon von Bismarck to protect them and their property against those who created it, the proletariat. But the capital of France will vote against this band of criminals, overthrown by a legitimate popular insurrection. With a calm and steady voice, in possession of their armaments only for self-defense, the people will vote in their free and sovereign Commune and enjoin the other liberated Communes of the country to group themselves around the great Commune of Paris! *(Great applause. Shouts of "Long live the Commune! Vive la Commune!")*

GENEVIÈVE: This is one of the greatest days in the history of France.

PAPA: And at least part of its greatness will be that no one will be able to say the leaders of the people wanted civil war.

GENEVIÈVE: A new era, without violence.

SONG: RESOLUTION

So be it resolved: our weakness let
All your statutes make us slaves, since you were stronger.
But that law now is finished as a threat.
Be it resolved: that we're content to be your slaves no longer.

CHORUS: Be it resolved: though you use your knives
Or your cannons, chains or wage slavery,
We have all decided: no more wretched lives
And an end to misery.

So be it resolved: our hunger pains
All are caused by lack of food, which keeps you fed;
Just remember that it's only fragile window panes
That keeps us separate from all of that good bread.

207

CHORUS AS ABOVE.

So be it resolved: your mighty mansion
Just stands over there—an empty tomb,
So now we've decided to move in
Since you will find that in our holes there just is no more room.

CHORUS AS ABOVE.

So be it resolved: there's so much coal
And we're so cold—just frozen through and through,
So now we've decided heat is good for the soul,
So now we'll take all the coal we need from you.

CHORUS AS ABOVE.

So be it resolved: you'll never pay
Any decent wages, as you love to stuff
Your big bellies, so the factory's ours today.
Be it resolved: that without you we'll have enough.

CHORUS AS ABOVE.

So be it resolved: Your government of cheaters
And fucking liars we'll no longer trust.
We have all decided, under *our* leaders
To work to make our lives both good and just.

CHORUS: Be it resolved: since you will not speak
        Any other language but the one
        That's spoken in the jungle by the strong and weak,
        Our power's in the barrel of a gun!

SCENE FIVE

Gare du Nord, March 19, 1871. Everywhere there are posters saying "Vote for the Commune!" Rich, bourgeois families, nuns, and officials are fleeing in large numbers to Versailles.

NEWSPAPER VENDOR: Get your late news here! Elections for the Commune declared unconstitutional by the following papers, calling for a boycott of the polls!: Le Journal des Debats, le Constitutionel, le Moniteur, l'Universel, le Figaro, le Gaulois, la Vérité, Paris-Journal, La Presse, la France la Liberté, le Pays, le National, l'Univers, le Temps, la Cloche, la Patrie, le Bien Public, l'Union, l'Avenir, le Libéral, le Journal des Villes et des Campagnes, le Charivari, le Monde, la France Nouvelle, la Gazette de France, le Petit Moniteur, le Petit National, l'Electeur Libre, la Petite Presse. . . . *(A tax collector, entering with his family, buys a paper.)*
TAX COLLECTOR: What does that mean —"Le Comité n'est rien?" They have 215 battalions and can do whatever the hell they want. Alphonse, stand up straight! So where is Bourdet with that briefcase? Do I or do I not have a solicitor in this hour of danger?
HIS WIFE: Alphonse, you must stand up straight. If Bourdet doesn't come, Christophe, then you'll have to stay here, 'cause we can't do anything in that expensive Versailles without money. There are so many people there. . . .
TAX COLLECTOR: "You'll just have to stay here," oh, that's great. They could have me put up against the wall if that money were to . . .
HIS WIFE: Don't get so emotional. You're waiting for Bourdet. Alphonse, stop shrugging your shoulders.
(An aristocratic woman and her niece and servants enter carrying hat boxes and various and sundry other things.)
NIECE *(Philine)*: Who would have thought, Aunt Marie, that the first trains leaving Paris would witness such a sight! All of Paris is in flight!

AUNT MARIE: But not for long. . . .
(Enter Philippe and Jean, talking. Behind them enter soldiers, clad in regular army uniforms, led by an employee of the railway company. The soldiers are dragging an iron trunk. The employee's instructions to them come in somewhere during Jean and Philippe's dialogue.)
EMPLOYEE: No, not in the baggage compartment. That's the mayor's records and cash boxes you've got there.
PHILIPPE: It's your mother's fault I had to go back into the army. How could she take François' microscope and pawn it!? While he was busy fighting. Now I'll need every sou of my soldier's pay, and I still haven't gotten any of it. And if I'm court-martialed because of that damn cannon, it'll be your fault too.
JEAN *(absently):* We had to pay the rent, Philippe. As soon as we get your twenty francs, we can get it back. The important thing is that François doesn't find out.
PHILIPPE: His studies eat up everything. And if now he gets drawn into this Commune business, the good fathers will throw him out of the seminary. A priest? With the Commune? Hmm! You see how wrong your ideas are? François wants his microscope, right? Why? Because it's his. Every man wants his own property. Fini.
JEAN: Philippe, you have a head like a bakery—floury ideas, all mixed up together.
PHILIPPE *(defensively):* Not every bakery's like that.
JEAN: Look, that microscope is the main tool of his profession, isn't it? That's why he wants it. It means as much to him as a lathe in the locomotive works means to us. Compris?
PHILIPPE: So where do you want to go now?
JEAN *(suddenly giving him the sack that he's been carrying):* Wait! Look! They're taking away all the cash boxes! *(to the Soldiers:)* Hey! You! you can't take that! That belongs to the people! *(The Soldiers pay no attention to him. One of them kicks him.)* You fucking asshole! And there's nobody here to stop them!
(Jean runs off while Philippe shakes his head, exiting slowly. Re-enter Aunt Marie and Philine.)

AUNT MARIE: Watch out, Philine—don't crush that box. It's a hat from Farnaud.
PHILINE: We should have taken the carriage.
AUNT MARIE: So that they could steal the horses away and eat them? Don't be foolish. *(Enter DePloeuc.)* Ah, DePloeuc, comme c'est amiable à vous! It's times like these that teach us who our friends really are.
DE PLOEUC: I could not let you go without shaking your hand, my dear Duchess.
PHILINE: But must you really stay behind? Isn't that dangerous?
DE PLOEUC: Peut-être, but the Bank of France is worth the risk, Mademoiselle. *(to the Duchess:)* May I ask you to deliver a note in these flowers, Madame? *(Hands her flowers, concealing a letter inside them.)*
AUNT MARIE: But of course. We shan't forget. But then the curtain will ring down on this whole comédie after one week, I prédicte. À bientôt, Henri.
DE PLOEUC: À bientôt, Mesdames!
(The Newspaper Vendor across the street has sold only one paper all this while. A Street Merchant enters with his wares, opposite.)
NEWSPAPER VENDOR: Read an important statement by a high official in le Figaro! The murders of Generals Lecomte and Thomas. . . . The illegal occupation of the Hôtel de Ville. . . . Is the Central Committee in cahoots with the Prussians? Looting in the Rue Gras. . . . Terror of the mob. . . .
STREET MERCHANT: Belts! Suspenders! Buttons! Soap and toilet articles, cheap! Harmonicas! Bells from Tripoli! . . .
(Jean, his clothes torn, is brought in by Soldiers. A Sergeant of the Guard and some of his men stop them.)
SERGEANT: Just a minute! What are you doing with him?
SOLDIER: He was caught trying to jump a train.
SOLDIER: A saboteur, Sergeant.
JEAN: They're stealing our Treasury! We've got to stop them and arrest the whole bunch o' them!
SERGEANT: Easy, comrade. We have no orders to stop trains. Let him go.
DE PLOEUC: My good friends, I am the Marquis de Ploeuc of the Bank of France. You are quite correct, Sergeant: the executives have left no orders.

209

And as far as I know there is no civil war as yet. So, this being the case, that man is a criminal and must be apprehended at once.

JEAN: But where are they going to put me? Tell me that, eh?

(Silence)

SERGEANT: Well, you tried to hijack that train. *(to the Soldiers:)* Go on. Get out of here. *(to his Guards:)* Go get reinforcements. *(Most of them leave, letting Jean go. The Soldiers disappear, and DePloeuc exits.)*

SOLDIER: Just doing our job, *(sarcastically:)* comrade.

SERGEANT *(to Jean)*: You, my friend, were very lucky.

JEAN: And you let them go. Don't you see the writing on the wall? Let me tell you something, Sergeant. I'll vote. But not for your Commune. It will lose. *(Stumbles off.)*

SCENE SIX

Montmartre, March 26, 1871. The café terrace again. Mme. Cabet and her family— Jean, Babette, François, Geneviève—are busily cleaning up the place, which has been closed. They're opening window shades, putting chairs outside, hanging paper garlands, etc. The Waiter, wearing the uniform of the National Guard, and the wounded German Prisoner, wearing civilian clothes, are also helping out. Jean and Babette are working on a red flag inside. Music from offstage. Geneviève comes out of the café with a few bottles of wine, followed by the two Children in their Sunday suits.

FRANÇOIS *(carrying some cane chairs)*: The New Age! And the Commune, modern science, and Paris lead the way! The People voted "Yes"!

WAITER: The owner voted "No" and chose not to stay. So, a waiter *(indicating himself)* is now the owner. Make yourselves at home in my café.

GENEVIÈVE *(teasing François)*: Even the young priests greet the new dawn! *(She puts wine bottles in front of Mme. Cabet.)*

FRANÇOIS *(teasing her back)*: And our professeurs buy wine at the black market to give to widows *(i.e., Madame Cabet)*, as it says in our new prayer book, which begins "Whereas" and ends with "Therefore be it resolved"! *(The German Prisoner laughs as he pulls up the window shade. François embraces him.)* I embrace you, soldier, my new brother, deserter from the anachronistic robber band of Bismarck!

MME. CABET *(who has from the beginning of the scene been sitting in a chair in the middle of the street)*: And to think that all of this is free! *(calling:)* Jean! Babette!

FRANÇOIS: "Whereas: this war of devastation was inflicted on the people by a small minority—and it was totally unjust to place the blame on the majority, be it resolved . . ."—I learned that by heart, just like my Lavoisier!

JEAN *(looking out the window)*: Just a minute!

FRANÇOIS: And all the pawned possessions of the people are to be returned without payment, because "Be it resolved: that life is to be lived!"

MME. CABET: François, do you know everything? I had to learn how to steal now that everything's so expensive. That's why I asked for the rent; a little tactlessly I admit, but I wanted to redeem your pawned things for you. You need them. Doesn't he, Jean? Jean! *(to Child:)* Sit down, Victor. Eat a little bit before you drink your wine. Jean! *(Child sits stiffly; Jean looks out at her angrily.)* I want to tell Babette something if you don't mind. O, haven't you finished yet?

BABETTE *(sticking her head out the window, her hair a little mussed up)* Yes, Mama?

MME. CABET: Look what nice wine we have, Babette! *(Babette laughs and sticks her head back in.)* We've really got to watch it. Wine always goes too fast when you need it. I guess you could say it's radical! *(Smiles.)*

(Down the street come Papa and Langevin, who looks very weary. Papa carries a white Chinese paper lantern on his bayonet.)

PAPA: Madame, Mademoiselles, I bring you your dear brother-in-law, Delegate to the Commune from Vaugirard. I forced him to take some time off from work. They're driving themselves to death over at City Hall!

MME. CABET: Have a glass of wine, Pierre!

WAITER: The owner of the wine is in Versailles. So help yourself, Monsieur.

LANGEVIN: There are six thousand sick people taking it easy. So there's nobody to light the streets. Which means work. *(Jean and Babette go upstairs to mount . . . the flag.)*

PAPA *(to Babette)*: Ah, a glass to drink to beauty! the loved and the feared! the pursued and the fearful! . . . friends, who came together in the middle of the storm.

MME. CABET: Yes, the storm is what did it. Take some bread, Pierre, Papa, and where's Jules? The bakery-owner from across the street gave them a little sailboat when we placed the flags in front of the house. Yes, I remember. She was so mad, but she wanted so much for us to buy her bread! *(laughs)*

GENEVIÈVE: If everybody'll sit down, I'll sing you an old song about that: *(sings:)* Margot went to market today,
And how the drums did play!
She bought her meat upon the way
From a man whose hair turned gray:
The butcher's hair turned gray!
"The meat is twenty francs."
. . . "How much?"
"Well, Madame, five francs?"
Mm-hmm! Mm-hmm! Mm-hmm, mm-hmm.
And tonight do you know what our Margot's going to do?
She's going to ask the landlord, "Now what do I owe you?"
"Now what do I owe you?"
"The rent is twenty francs."
"Well, Madame, five francs?"
(They all sing with her): Mm-hmm! Mm-hmm! mm-hmm, mm-hmm, mm-hmm!

(Enter a group of Men and Women wearing emblems.)

MAN: Ladies and gentlemen, come one, come all to the Place Vendôme to hear Monsieur Courbet, the well-known painter who will speak on the topic: the need to topple the monument to Napoleon, the monument melted from twelve hundred conquered European cannons, the monument to war, a tribute to militarists and to barbarians!

PAPA: Thank you comrades! We support that project, and hope to see it done!

WOMAN: Then come with us for soup —free! in the Latin Quarter!

(A Man neighs like a horse.)

MAN: That was in memory of the five horses which provided the soup, Messieurs et Mesdames.

FRANÇOIS: Shall we go?

PAPA: But I'm very comfortable here.

FRANÇOIS: What about the soup?

MME. CABET: You want to go? Where are Jean and Babette? Oh, I know where they are.

PAPA: Monsieur François, I see you are quite suited for the priesthood.

GENEVIÈVE: Thank you comrades, but I think we'll stay here a little while.

MAN *(as the crowd exits)*: As you wish. But remember, the Commune invited you and you said No.

PAPA: *That* is what freedom means.

(Jean and Babette come downstairs.)

MME. CABET: You've been up there much too long, you two. And I'm mad at both of you.

JEAN: Mother, you're making Geneviève blush.

MME. CABET: I told you: you've got to act according to . . . the circumstances.

PAPA: But they are the best, Madame. Really the best. Paris has decided that everyone should live according to his own tastes. And that's why Herr Kraus *(indicating the German prisoner)* has decided to stay with us. No more class differences and no more boundaries between peoples!

JEAN: Babette, answer my mother. Defend me.

BABETTE: Madame, your son isn't driving his locomotive too fast.

(sings:) Père Josèph has got no roof, got no shirt.
And on her back his poor wife has got no skirt.
Yet each night she cooks him all she's got:
Something grand, something cheap—in a stolen pot.
And naturally Père Josèph likes to complain a lot:
"Mother, make it 'extra-exquisite' for me.
Nothing is too tasteless for us two.

211

Mother, think of every recipe
you ever knew.
Take your time . . . but wait!
Do not forget the garlic!
Take your time . . . but wait!
Please don't forget the gar-
lic!"
Père Josèph is now in the
Salpetrière.
For the parson's rosaries he
just can't feel,
But he spends enormous sums
of money there,
As if he were condemned and
ordering his last meal:
"Waiter, make it 'extra-ex-
quisite' for me.
Nothing is so tasteless it won't
do.
Children, think of every recipe
your mother ever knew.
But above all please, do not
forget the garlic!
I don't want to live, if I
can't have my garlic!"

PAPA: That's true, you know. What
does man live for? According to my
sister, the curé of Sainte Héloïse answers that question: "for the perfection
of himself." "So what does he need for
that?" I ask. Answer: Quail for breakfast!
(to one of the Children:) My son, we
all live only for something "extra" like
that. We've got to have it, even if we
can only get it by fighting for it with
cannons. Otherwise, why are we doing
all this? À ta santé! *(Drinks. To Mme.
Cabet:)* Who is this young man?

MME. CABET: Victor, go get a fork.
(The Child goes into the café.) His
father was with the 93rd regiment.
Killed—in the defense of our cannons,
on the 18th of March. He had opened
a little butcher shop—rabbits. *(Jean
raises his eyebrows.)* Be quiet, Jean.
I've sometimes bought things from him,
because of his . . . *(The Child comes
back with a fork.)*

PAPA *(stands up and raises his glass)*:
To your health! *(The Child drinks to
the health of Papa. Music next-door:
Jean and Geneviève begin to dance. So
do Babette and François, the Waiter and
Mme. Cabet. Exeunt.)*

PAPA: Things are going pretty well,
eh?

LANGEVIN *(smiles slightly)*: Are you
satisfied?

PAPA *(after a short pause)*: This is
what the city was built for, and what
it really needed. We'd neglected it because of the defeat. But now we've
brought it back to life again! What more
could you ask for?

LANGEVIN: Just one thing: sometimes,
I wonder if we could have used the time
better on the 18th of March, when the
question was elections or a march to
Versailles. The answer, of course, should
have been both.

PAPA: Well, so?

LANGEVIN: So. Thiers sits in Versailles
and assembles his troops.

PAPA: Bah! Fuck him! Paris will make
all the decisions. We'll guillotine those
old men like nothing! They're already
half-dead! And as for their troops, we'll
reach an agreement with them, just as
we did on the 18th of March—with the
cannons.

LANGEVIN: I hope so. They're all peasants.

PAPA *(drinks)*: À Paris, Monsieur!
*(The music over, the dancers return
and take up glasses of wine.)*

BABETTE: À la liberté, Jean Cabet!
À la liberté totale!

PAPA: À la liberté!

LANGEVIN: I'll drink to that—in part.

BABETTE: To liberty in love, then!

GENEVIÈVE: Why only in part, Monsieur Langevin? Because total liberty is
only an illusion?

LANGEVIN: Yes, when it comes to
politics.

BABETTE: François, you can dance. But
how will you dance? As a physicist, as
priest, or as a student?

FRANÇOIS: I'm not going to be a priest.
This is a new time, Mademoiselle
Géricault. I mean to study physics on a
scholarship!

BABETTE: Long live sharing! *(provoca-
tively:)* We have everything, so let's
share it!

GENEVIÈVE: Babette!

BABETTE: That'll teach you to dance
with my Jean tête-à-tête! *(Goes to
Geneviève.)*

GENEVIÈVE: I will not defend myself
against you, Babette.

BABETTE: Then take that! and that!
and that! *(They roll on the floor. Now
Geneviève does defend herself.)* Oh, so

212

you won't defend yourself against me, eh? What are you trying to do, scratch my eyes out, you bitch? *(Jean laughing, restrains François from intervening. Papa and the Waiter part the two fighting girls.)*

MME. CABET: You're both acting like you've got closets full of clothes! Tsk! Tsk! Tsk! I didn't think you were just mounting the flag up there, Jean. Boy she's a regular stallion, isn't she!

FRANÇOIS: A good Communard is not a jealous one, citizen.

BABETTE: Oh, so you don't believe in violence, eh?

GENEVIÈVE: No I do not. But I defend what I have. I'm so glad there were no bayonets around here, Babette. O hello, Philippe!

PHILIPPE *(entering)*: Hello, I'm back again. I was curious as to whether I'd find any of you here alive. According to the papers in Versailles, you've all been arrested and shot. Whoever doesn't cry "Vive la Commune!" before going to bed each night is denounced by his own wife and tortured in the latrine by the Communards until he confesses. Everybody knows that's how the Commune rules—by Terror. *(They all laugh.)*

PAPA: My friends, this is the first night of history. We live today in a Paris that knows no murder, no theft, no embezzlement, and no rape. For the first time, our streets are safe, and we have no need of any police force! The bankers, the thieves, the tax collectors, the factory-owners, ministers, whores, and priests have all gone to Versailles and made Paris livable again!

FRANÇOIS: À votre santé Papa! *(drinks)*

PHILIPPE: I also read in the papers about your orgies: THE SEXUAL ORGIES OF THE COMMUNE. The tyrants in the Hôtel de Ville have seven mistresses each!

BABETTE: Oh, but Jean only has two.

FRANÇOIS *(to Philippe)*: So why did you run away?

PHILIPPE: I'll tell you. Monsieur Thiers is really in trouble now. He can't pay his soldiers anymore. So they're all selling their rifles for five francs.

PAPA: I get my pay here.

LANGEVIN: Because you pay it to yourself; that's the difference.

PHILIPPE: Everybody's talking about the inefficiency of the Commune. I spent a whole day in the country, in Arles, with our parents, François. I told them you'd become a Communard—a devil, they call it. "They want to share everything!"

LANGEVIN: But how did you get through the front lines?

PHILIPPE: Nobody stopped me.

LANGEVIN: That's not so good. It's the carelessness of the Commune.

PAPA: Pierre, you overestimate those old bastards, Thiers and Bismarck. Welcome, Philippe. They're finished. Pierre, a newspaper! *(Langevin hands him one; he makes a paper policeman's cap with it and puts it on his head.)* I'm Bismarck. Jean, you're Monsieur Thiers! Take François' glasses and let's show Pierre what those two old has-beens'll be saying when we celebrate the first anniversary of the Third Republic September Fourth! *(They both strike an historical pose.)* My dear Thiers, I have just made einer dummkopf of ours into a Kaiser; vould you like to have one zu, vielleicht?

JEAN: Mon cher Herr von Bismarck, I 'ave already 'ad one. . . .

PAPA: I understand: since you have just had a Kaiser, you certainly don't want another one! Das ist all very well und gut—aber if you do nicht obey, you'll get your Kaiser oder *(how do you call it?)* you'll get your Empereur right back again! Und that is not just a threat, für I will do it zu! Oh by de way, would you vielleicht like to have a King?

JEAN: Herr von Bismarck, only a small number of my subjects would appréciate zat—a very small number. . . .

PAPA: Aber if you do not do as ve say, you vill get one. Oh also, what do your subjects want, I mean those uh, how do you say? Those who . . . pay their taxes . . . oh yes—*people!* Yes, what do they want?

JEAN *(looking around modestly)*: Me.

PAPA: Aber das ist ja vorzüglich! excellént! I'm as delighted with you as if you were a Kaiser or a King. So they don't want them, eh? Hah! Isn't that funny! *(laughs)* Where were we? Oh yes, in France.

JEAN: Herr von Bismarck, I've been authorized to turn France over to you.

PAPA: By whom, Monsieur Thiers?

213

JEAN: By France. I have just been elected.

PAPA: So have we! *(laughs)* Der Kaiser und I have also just been elected!

JEAN *(also laughs)*: Sérieusely, Herr von Bismarck, I feel a little insécure. I am not even certáin zat I will not be arrested.

PAPA: You know what? I will support you! I have five tausend cannons!

JEAN: Then I have only one wish, Herr von Bismarck, permit me to implore you: may I kiss your shoes? *(bends down and kisses his shoes)* What shoes! How good they taste!

PAPA: Only please don't eat me all up.

JEAN: And will you make me a promise, Otto, that with these boots, you will stamp it out once and for all.

PAPA *(pause)*: Oh, you mean the Commune.

JEAN: Don't say that word! Please! Don't say that word! You should know what it's like. You've got "Socialistes" and "Communistes" of your own—like Liebknecht and Bebel. *(The former German prisoner stands and lifts his glass.)*

PAPA: Um Gottes willen! Don't utter those names!

JEAN: Mais pourquoi-y *(why)* are you so frightened, Otto? How can you support me if you are so afraid? Now I am afraid too!

(They take off the paper crowns and embrace, laughing.)

BABETTE: Bravo, Jean! I think I see the flag isn't hanging right. Let's go fix it! *(Embraces him. Exeunt.)*

FRANÇOIS: Now I'm going to read you something. *(reading from a newspaper by the light of a Chinese lantern.)* "Tonight you drink wine that belongs to no one but yourselves. And in the morning,

The dawn, decked out in red and green dress,

Will slowly come up on the deserted Seine,

And somber Paris, blinking his eyes,

Will gather his tools like an old working man."

FORMER GERMAN PRISONER *(raising his glass)*: Bebel! Liebknecht!

WAITER: À la Commune!

FORMER GERMAN PRISONER: Die Kommune!

WAITER: To Bebel! To Liebknecht!

FRANÇOIS: To science!

GENEVIÈVE: To children!

SCENE SEVEN

(Part I)

Hôtel de Ville. Red flags flying. March 29, 1871. A room with blackboard on which the following is written:

1. *Right to Live*
2. *Freedom of Choice*
3. *Freedom of Conscience*
4. *Right of Assembly and Association*
5. *Freedom of Speech, Freedom of Press, and Freedom of Intellectual Expression in Any Form Whatsoever.*
6. *Free Elections*

BESLAY: Some claim that we should have agreed to comply with the elections to the National Assembly of the Republic. . . .

VOICES: That's what M. Thiers says! —against Paris!

BESLAY: But the liberation of the community of Paris means the liberation of all the communities of France. Our enemies claim we've been destroying the Republic. We've been destroying it the way the American Revolution destroyed America! *(Applause.)* The Republic of

1792 was a soldiers' state. The Republic of the Commune will be a workers' state. Above all, what we need is the freedom to make peace!

VARLIN: Our Republic, Communards, will give the workers' tools back to the workers, just as 1789 gave land to the peasants, so that social equality and political freedom can finally become a reality. *(Applause.)* I hereby propose the first new law: "Whereas: all citizens stand ready to defend our country, be it resolved: that the regular standing army, and all conscription thereto, are hereby abolished!" *(Loud applause as he continues:)* "Every true citizen is to be considered a member of the National Guard."

VIOLENT DELEGATE: Away with the generals, those overpaid pigs! And long live the People's Army!

PROUDHONIAN DELEGATE: No more classes! No more nations! Let's call upon the workers in the Prussian Army to come to the aid of the workers of France!

VARLIN: "This country, with its institutions, belongs to the people who inhabit it. Whereas: the State is the People, who will rule over themselves; be it resolved: that all public officials will be chosen each according to his abilities, to be paid each according to his needs. . . ."

PACIFISTIC DELEGATE: . . . which will be the same as any worker!

VARLIN: ". . . and will hold offices for a limited term, which may be terminated at any time! Whereas: no nation is greater than the poorest of its citizens, be it resolved that all education shall be free and available to all!"

HUMANITARIAN DELEGATE: But *feed* the children first! Education begins with a full stomach! You've gotta eat before you can worry about learning how to read! *(Laughter and applause.)*

VARLIN: "Whereas: the goal of life is the uninterrupted development of physical, intellectual, and moral capacities of man, be it resolved: that property is the right of every individual, according to his ability to work; and that every shop and every factory must be organized collectively." *(Applause.)* This, my friends, is the first law which must be enacted immediately. I hereby open the First Workers' Assembly of the Commune of Paris.

SCENE SEVEN

(Part II)

Ministry of the Interior. A janitor leads Geneviève and Langevin into one of the offices. It is raining.

GENEVIÈVE: You say not a single employee has been here in the last week?

JANITOR: Um-hm. And I should know. I'm the janitor.

GENEVIÈVE: How many people work here ordinarily?

JANITOR: Three hundred and eighty-four. Plus Monsieur le Ministre.

GENEVIÈVE: Do you know their addresses?

JANITOR: No.

GENEVIÈVE: How can we find out where the schools are in this district, where the teachers live, and where they keep the money for the salaries? They even took the keys with them!

LANGEVIN: You'll have to get a locksmith.

GENEVIÈVE: And you'll have to go buy me some oil for the lamps. *(Looks in her pocketbook for some money.)*

JANITOR: Do you intend to work nights, too?

LANGEVIN: Mademoiselle is the Delegate from the Commune in charge of Public Instruction.

JANITOR: That's all very nice, but it's not my job to go out and buy oil.

GENEVIÈVE: All right, but . . .

LANGEVIN: No, it's not all right. You will go and buy the oil after you've shown the Delegate where the registers and the maps of the schools in this district are.

JANITOR: All I can show you is where the offices are.

GENEVIÈVE: I'll have to ask the cleaning lady. Maybe she has children who go to school.

LANGEVIN: She won't know anything.

GENEVIÈVE: Well, let's go together and find out.

LANGEVIN: Maybe we should just start from scratch and build new schools. Then at least we'd know where they were. Things weren't so good before, so now everything has to be redone. That applies to the clinics as well as the street lights. How much are you paid for your services—uh, not including the buying of oil?

JANITOR: Seven francs eighty centimes per day. But the people don't pay for that; the State does.

LANGEVIN: Yes, that makes all the difference in the world, doesn't it! Delegate Géricault is running the whole educational system of Paris for eleven francs a day, if that means anything to you.

JANITOR *(shrugs)*: It's up to her.

LANGEVIN: You can go now, that is if walking is part of your work. *(Janitor walks away, dragging his feet. Geneviève opens a window.)*

GENEVIÈVE: Poor guy.

LANGEVIN: That's not what I think of him. You know it was probably a mistake to admit to him how low your salary is. Now he won't think much of you. He has no intention of bowing and scraping for a person who only makes a few francs more than he does. And he just doesn't know anything except how to bow and scrape.

GENEVIÈVE: But you know he didn't learn to do that by himself. What does he see? The ministers, administrators, secretaries—even the clerks—have all fled because the salaries are so low. All of the officials left Paris in the dark, leaving behind a population that's still in the dark, to make its way through filth and ignorance, without the indispensable professionals.

LANGEVIN: And that's the most annoying thing: That they really have made themselves indispensable. That's the way it's been for centuries. Our job is to arrange the work so it may be done by anyone. The simplification of labor. That is the work of the future. Oh! Babette!

(Babette enters with Philippe.)

BABETTE: Where have you been lately? And what's this in the *Officiel* that you've become a minister or something?

GENEVIÈVE: Who told you where to find me?

BABETTE: The janitor. Philippe took out a pistol, and . . .

LANGEVIN *(to Philippe)*: As Minister of Transportation, I hereby name you my assistant. The trains at the Gare du Nord depart, but do not return. And on them all the furnishings of the rich are being taken away. I shall have to confiscate the property of the railway company and bring its highest officials before the War Tribunal. That's how it is in Paris now. All the officials leave and send us saboteurs in return. But what brings you here?

BABETTE: Something must be done at once for the bakers.

GENEVIÈVE: But I'm the Delegate for Public Instruction.

PHILIPPE: So instruct us. Don't the newspapers say that the workers must study? Well how can I study if I've got to work nights? I've got to sleep during the day.

LANGEVIN: The Commune has decreed, I believe, that night work for bakers has been abolished.

PHILIPPE: But the bakery-owners haven't recognized that decree. And they say we can't call a strike because we're indispensable. But of course, the bakery-owner can close her store whenever she wants to. O, by the way: have a loaf of bread. *(Hands them a loaf of bread.)*

GENEVIÈVE: *This* is a bribe. *(Bites into it.)*

LANGEVIN: If she closes the store, we shall confiscate it and run it ourselves.

PHILIPPE: Taste good? From us you can accept bribes, but not from the owners, I hope. I'll tell them what you said at the union meeting. Otherwise, they may break the windows in the bakery tonight. Oh! Guess what happened to Babette and Madame Cabet! Their boss, M. Busson, the soldiers' tailor is back.

BABETTE: And now he only pays one franc per pair of pants. He says, "The National Guard only buys from the dealer with the lowest prices!"

(Pause)

GENEVIÈVE: Why are you looking at me, Pierre?

LANGEVIN: I want to hear what you say to those people, citizen Delegate.

GENEVIÈVE: Well look, we're trying to save the people's money.

BABETTE: But we *are* the people.

LANGEVIN *(to Geneviève, who is looking at him uncertainly)*: Learn, professeur.

BABETTE: If the Commune pays less than the Empire, what do we need it for? Jean is at the barricades risking his life to end just this sort of exploitation!

PHILIPPE: For the sake of saving money, you take it out on his mother and his girl friend. You've got to start. . . .

LANGEVIN: What do you mean "you"?

PHILIPPE: All right, we've got to. . . .

LANGEVIN: That's better.

PHILIPPE *(his train of thought lost):* So what have we got to do?

LANGEVIN: You're not a member of the tailors' union, are you? *That's* where the prices are determined; not in the pants factory of M. Busson.

BABETTE: How do you know?

GENEVIÈVE: I'm trying to organize schools where children can be taught that.

BABETTE: And where will you get the money for them, when you can't even pay a decent price for uniforms?

GENEVIÈVE: The Bank of France is just a couple of blocks from here. That's where the problem is. But the safes are all locked.

PHILIPPE: Well, we can break them open, can't we?

LANGEVIN: What, a baker willing to work as a locksmith!? It's looking better for the Commune already! Next thing maybe we'll even learn how to run a government! *(He has been winding up a standing clock and now gives the pendulum a small shove so that it starts swinging again. Everyone looks and laughs.)* Don't expect any more from the Commune than from yourselves.

SCENE EIGHT

Bank of France, Office of the Director. The Director himself, the Marquis De Ploeuc—whom we have already met—is talking with a fat priest, Monsignore Beauchamp, an envoy of the Archbishop of Paris. Outside it is raining.

DE PLOEUC: Please give the Archbishop my deepest thanks for relaying the wishes of Monsieur Thiers to me. The 10,000,000 francs will be sent to Versailles in the normal manner. What will happen to the Bank of France in the next few days, I do not know. I expect a visit from the delegates of the Commune at any minute, followed immediately by my own imprisonment. In our vaults are well over 2,180,000,000 francs, Monsigneur. That is our nerve center. If it is cut, those Communards will have won, whatever else happens.

SERVANT *(entering, announcing):* Monsieur Beslay, délégué de la Commune.

DE PLOEUC *(blanching):* Now, Monsigneur, comes France's heure de décision.

BEAUCHAMP: But how do I get out of here?

DE PLOEUC: Just . . . take it easy. Sang-froid. *(Enter Beslay.)*

DE PLOEUC *(introducing):* Monsignore Beauchamp, Procurateur de son Éminence, l'Archevêque de Paris.

BEAUCHAMP *(bowing):* May I be excused?

DE PLOEUC: I believe you will need the permission of Monsieur?

BESLAY *(giving him a card from his pocket):* Show the captain at the door this card. *(The gentlemen bow to each other and the priest exits.)*

BESLAY: Citizen, the paymasters of the National Guard battalions stand before a locked safe in the Ministry of Finance. But I am telling you that the wages of the people must be paid, or there will be no way to prevent the Bank of France from being looted. The people have wives and children.

DE PLOEUC: Monsieur Beslay, according to the statutes of your Central Committee, the employees of the Bank of France were to form one battalion of the Nationalgarde. Let me assure you that they too have received not one sou of their pay for the last two weeks, and that they too have wives and children. Now, Monsieur, you have come through the courtyard, and you have seen them armed, even the sixty-year-old men, and I can assure you that if anyone attacks the bank which is their trust, they will defend it.

BESLAY: That defense would last about two minutes.

DE PLOEUC: Perhaps only one. But what a minute in the Histoire de France!

BESLAY *(after a pause):* The Commune issued a decree saying all special battalions must be dissolved and reincorporated into the National Guard.

DE PLOEUC: I knew that you would say that, Monsieur. *(Picks up a scroll.)* May I show you a decree from the archives of this bank? It comes from the oldest revolutionary corporation of all, the Convention of the French Revolu-

217

tion, and is signed by Danton. It stipulates that all employees of this corporation shall consider their offices as fighting posts.

BESLAY: Monsieur le marquis, I have not come here to spill blood, but to insure the means by which Paris may be defended. The factories must be opened, so that the people will have work, so that the Commune can survive!

DE PLOEUC: Monsieur, do not think for a moment that I question the right of the Commune to survive. The Bank of France is not involved in politics.

BESLAY: Ah, now we're coming to the point.

DE PLOEUC: My most fervent wish, Monsieur, is that you of the Commune will recognize the rights of the Bank of France to survive as well—for she is non-partisan.

BESLAY: M. le marquis, you are not dealing with street thieves but with just men.

DE PLOEUC: I knew that, Monsieur, the moment that you entered the room. M. Beslay, help me to save the bank! It is the economy of your country, la fortune de la France!

BESLAY: M. le marquis, now don't get me wrong. We're all working like slaves down at City Hall, eighteen hours a day. Our beds are chairs, and we sleep in our clothes. For fifteen francs a day, we do what used to be done by three or four people, and which cost the public three times as much. There has never been a less expensive government. But now we must have ten million francs.

DE PLOEUC (painfully): Monsieur Beslay!

BESLAY: Monsieur le marquis, we have not collected any tax on tobacco or on food. But we must have money to pay our soldiers and the salaries of our government. We can't hold out any longer without them. (De Ploeuc is eloquently silent.) If by tomorrow we do not have at least six million francs, then. . . .

DE PLOEUC: Six million francs! I am not *authorized* to give you that kind of money! You talk about corruption in your Assembly. You accuse M. Thiers of breaking laws to obtain money, and now you come here for money without even setting up a Department of Finance! (appearing to hesitate:) If you had a Department of Finance, I would not ask any questions, but you have no signed paper that I can recognize!

BESLAY: But that'd take at least two weeks. Perhaps you are forgetting that we *have* the power. . . .

DE PLOEUC: No, but I know that on this question I am in the right.

BESLAY: How much money do you have in the coffers?

DE PLOEUC: You know it is my sworn duty to keep that a secret. Would you break the secrecy of bank transactions? Would you break the lawyer-client relationship? or the doctor-patient? Monsieur, such things are inviolable. May I remind you, Monsieur, that you too are dealing with a just man, an honorable man, and no matter what side we are on, let us work together! Let us reason together how we can best fill the needs of our great, beloved Paris—without breaking the infinitely complicated but absolutely necessary laws of our oldest institutions. I am for peace in Paris: through negotiations.

BESLAY: All right, M. le marquis, let's negotiate.

SCENE NINE

(Part I)

Hôtel de Ville. A meeting of the Commune. Beslay stands before a storm of outrage, tempered by weariness on the part of many.

HUMANITARIAN DELEGATE: This is treason!

VIOLENT DELEGATE: Worse, stupidity!

HUMANITARIAN DELEGATE: Our comrades go hungry, while we listen to this Bank Director talk about the "necessary formalities"!

VIOLENT DELEGATE: No more negotiations! Send a battalion over there!

BESLAY: Citizens. If you are not satisfied with my work, then I shall hand in my resignation. But don't forget: the economy of France is our economy too, and it must be spent as carefully as our father's life-savings.

VIOLENT DELEGATE: Is that you or De Ploeuc saying that?

BESLAY: I take pride in having brought this honorable, though perhaps somewhat pedantic man to our side, by appealing to his honor as a business-man and his ability to find a legal solution to the problem.

VIOLENT DELEGATE: We're not interested in appealing to him, but in arresting him!

HUMANITARIAN DELEGATE: Why must there be a legal solution for the people to get their own money?

BESLAY: Do you want us to go bankrupt? Do you want to destroy the statutes of the bank and make the forty million francs in it worthless? The value of money is dependent on trust.

PACIFISTIC DELEGATE: In whom? The bankers? *(laughter)*

PROUDHONIAN DELEGATE: These are delicate questions! You should all read Proudhon. . . .

HUMANITARIAN DELEGATE: We've taken over the state, so let's take over the possessions of the state!

VARLIN: For whom? This clearly shows that one can't just "take over the state". It wasn't built to serve our goals. So it has to be destroyed; and you can't destroy a state without violence.

PROUDHONIAN DELEGATE: No arrests! We can't start the new era with terror! Leave that to the old regime!

PACIFISTIC DELEGATE: Let's get back to peaceful work.

LANGEVIN: But that's what we're doing, comrade.

PACIFISTIC DELEGATE: Arrest the Director of the Bank and see what the newspapers say about that!

RIGAULT: The bourgeois papers? I've read them, and I don't understand why they haven't been banned yet!

BESLAY: Citizens, I move this be discussed in secret session.

LANGEVIN: I counter-move the previous question! We can't act as though we were infallible, the way every other government before us has acted without exception. All speeches and legislation

must be published. Let the public in on the secret that we aren't perfect. Then we'll have nothing to fear but ourselves.

PACIFISTIC DELEGATE: Don't forget that 200,000. . . .

LANGEVIN: Let me finish. I don't want to talk about the 200,000 francs that the Delegate of War used, to get 1000 cavalry horses from the Germans—they'll sell anything. But I return to the question of the soldiers' pay, and would like to try and shed some light on it by referring to another question. . . .

PACIFISTIC DELEGATE: Don't forget that 200,000 people and their families depend upon getting their salaries! Their rifles are their livelihood, and they must support their families.

RANVIER: I request that the military situation be discussed.

LANGEVIN: Instead of just keeping our military comfortable, when we get the money from where it is now, namely the Bank of France, let's stop chiseling on the wages that we pay the women in the factories. I move that all supply agreements with contractors who give low wages for the sake of competitive prices be declared null and void, and that contracts be made only with work stations under the guidance of the Workers Association.

PACIFISTIC DELEGATE: We can't discuss two issues at the same time! One thing at a time!

VARLIN: I support your proposal, Langevin. *(to Beslay:)* And I support the immediate occupation of the bank. For the same reason.

LANGEVIN: The former demands the latter.

RANVIER: We must also discuss the military situation. That makes *three* issues! You see? we have no time to lose! 'Cause what good is destroying the internal enemy today if it strengthens Thiers for tomorrow?

PACIFISTIC DELEGATE: And how do you think we're going to get all that strength? We don't have enough men to do that!

PROUDHONIAN DELEGATE: Why can't we discuss the needs of the people?

RIGAULT: We *are* discussing the needs of the people. Why don't you listen to the proposals? We all want decisions to be made immediately. Why don't we

219

trust this strength, this power, citizens? Some of us here still seem suspicious of it. I'm talking about the power of the people—the people who stormed the Bastille and began the revolution; who spilled their blood on the Champs de Mars and who conquered the Tuileries; who routed the Girondists, the priests, and Robespierre; who took to the streets in May, only to disappear for twenty years, but who surged forth again in the émeute of 1830; who awoke and broke the chains of 1848, four months later to grab the bourgeois republic by the throat and bring it down; so that 1868 finds it rejuvenated as it bursts again to shatter the Empire, offer it to foreign invaders, only to be rejected, until the 18th of March, 1871, when they finally smash the hands that bind them. What can we have against the personal intervention of the people? That means the immediate surrender of all businesses and banks to the new regime, and battles on every side; but first and foremost, a march to Versailles! For the power of the people! *(Great unrest in the hall.)*

PACIFISTIC DELEGATE: So! Civil War!?

VIOLENT DELEGATE: A bloodbath!

PROUDHONIAN DELEGATE: We've heard that word power so many times—watch it!

RIGAULT *(motioning with newspapers)*: Just listen to what they're saying in the streets of Paris! I'm quoting from the paper *La Sociale*, one of the few papers on our side: "Citizen-Delegates, march to Versailles! You have 220 battalions of the National Guard behind you, so what are you waiting for? You've been patient too long. March to Versailles! Depend on Paris, as Paris depends on you. March to Versailles, citizens! Let us expand our power by using it! *(The disquiet continues.)*

PACIFISTIC DELEGATE: You're quoting your own article! You irresponsible . . .

PROUDHONIAN DELEGATE: Socialism must march without bayonets!

RIGAULT: But the enemy's bayonets are pointed against us, citizens. The red flag flies over Marseilles and Lyon. But Versailles is armed and the ignorance and prejudice of the provinces are against us. Let us carry the flame of revolution into the countryside! Let's break the iron belt around Paris and liberate other great cities. *(The agitation continues.)*

PACIFISTIC DELEGATE: This is military adventurism!

VIOLENT DELEGATE: I move to close debate!

PROUDHONIAN DELEGATE: The Commune condemns civil war!

PACIFISTIC DELEGATE: I move this Assembly stop listening to bourgeois adventurism and take up its work for *peace!*

VIOLENT DELEGATE: Right. But first I move the confiscation of the following enemy newspapers; *Le Petit Moniteur, le Petit National, le Bon Sens, la Petite Presse, la France, le Temps.* . . .

HUMANITARIAN DELEGATE: Point of order! Point of order!

(During the confusion, the President is handed a message.)

PRESIDENT: Citizen-Delegates, I have just been handed a message that will give this Assembly a new direction.

SCENE NINE

(Part II)

Hôtel de Ville foyer. Delegates and military personnel are going into the Assembly.

NEWSPAPER VENDOR: Extra! Extra! *L'Officiel!* "Versailles moves to attack! The Zouaves of the Pope push into Neuilly! Women and children among the wounded! Mobilization of all citizens 17 to 30! Versailles regime attacks!"

AN OLD BEGGAR *(going over to the Vendor)*: Would you have any bread, buddy?

NEWSPAPER VENDOR: Don't you know that begging is prohibited? "Versailles starts civil war!"

BEGGAR: Can I prohibit my stomach from growling, hein?

(Delegates are leaving the assembly.)

DELEGATE *(to another Delegate)*: A surprise attack with so few troops is an act of desperation. The provincial elections must have gone very badly for M. Thiers.

BEGGAR *(going over to them)*: Mes-

220

sieurs, permit me to show you: there's a balloon leaving Paris—you can see it over the houses.

DELEGATE: Oh, you mean the balloon of *La Sociale?* Has it left already?

BEGGAR: With 10,000 copies of proclamations and declarations to drop in the provinces, giving the land to the farmers. I'm from the provinces myself, so I can tell you all about it. Look— I'll show you the balloon. *(The Delegates look out a window.)* Messieurs, the balloon!

DELEGATE: Are you a farmer, old man?

BEGGAR: From the Auvergne. Saint-Antoine.

DELEGATE: And what brings you to Paris?

BEGGAR: Look at me! Can I pull a plow? Nah. That's for men younger than me.

DELEGATE: So you came to Paris to see your relatives, eh?

BEGGAR *(nods)*: Unemployed.

DELEGATE: And what do you think of the Commune?

BEGGAR: Messieurs, I am at your service. Your hearts are in the right place, even if you are for sharing everything— God protect you. A look at the balloon, Messieurs, costs ten centimes.

DELEGATE: But why are you against sharing the land?

BEGGAR: Well, Messieurs, they take it away.

DELEGATE: But not from you? They'll *give* it to you.

BEGGAR: Excuse me, Messieurs, but they take it away. Do I still have my farm? Ten centimes.

DELEGATE: Your children have it, don't they?

BEGGAR: Ah, so you see.

DELEGATE: But this comes from your not owning enough land.

BEGGAR: May I please have the ten centimes, since I let you look at the balloon? It may disappear any minute.

DELEGATE: Do you have a big landowner in Saint-Antoine?

BEGGAR: Oh yes, M. Bergeret.

DELEGATE: Do you like him?

BEGGAR: Well, Monsieur, he minds his own business.

DELEGATE *(shakes his head and gives him the centimes. To other Delegate)*: C'est un ennemi. Beggar-stick in hand, he defends the interests of the thief who robs him. And to convince him would take years. *(They exeunt.)*

BEGGAR *(showing the Newspaper Vendor his ten centimes)*: Ten centimes to see the balloon! They must be imbeciles! They didn't have to pay me, they just had to look and see for themselves!

NEWSPAPER VENDOR: "Women and children among the wounded!"—*(to Beggar:)* Hey, come here. Why don't you stop begging and take a packet of papers and go stand in front of that stairway. Call out just like I do. You'll get one centime for every paper you sell. *(He gives him a bundle of the newspapers and the Beggar repeats after him.)*

BOTH: *L'Officiel!* "Mobilization of all citizens 17 years of age!"

SCENE NINE

(Part III)

Night Session of the Commune. Some Delegates are working on their papers. Others are in conference. One is advising a Woman with a Child.

PRESIDENT: In view of the fact that it is inadvisable for this assembly to interfere with military operations, despite the disturbing situation at the front near Malmaison, we shall continue debate. Citizen Langevin has the floor.

LANGEVIN: I move the following: "Be it resolved: that the primary principle of the Republic is freedom; and be it further resolved: that freedom of conscience is the first and foremost freedom, but that whereas the clergy is in complicity with the monarchy in crimes against freedom, the Commune therefore decrees the separation of Church and State." To this end, I hereby request that the Minister of Education have all teachers remove all crucifixes, Madonnas, and other symbolic objects from the classrooms and that these objects be melted down into metal or currency.

PRESIDENT *(After counting the raised hands)*: Motion adopted.

PACIFISTIC DELEGATE: We have com-

221

plaints that the Catholic sisters are not treating the wounded Communards well.

PROUDHONIAN DELEGATE: And whatever happened to the proposed reading rooms in the hospitals? For most workers, that's the only time they've got to study in!

PRESIDENT (reading from a statement that has been handed to him): Citizen-Delegates: Directly from the front, a wounded battalion-officer, André Farreaux, wishes to address you. (Farreaux, an officer of the National Guard, is brought in on a stretcher.) Citizen Farreaux, I turn the floor over to you.

FARREAUX: Citizen-Delegates, Asnières is in our hands. (Cries of "Vive la Commune!" "Vive le Nationalgarde!") Citizens, with the permission of the delegate from the War Command, and at a moment when my wounds have taken me out of combat, I wish to bring your attention to certain . . . inconveniences that make it difficult for our troops to operate, and make even our victories much too bloody. Our soldiers fight like lions, but with nearly complete indifference to the necessity of being armed. The rights of private property, added to the fact that batteries are formed by district, has left us only 320 of the 1740 cannons available for action.

VIOLENT DELEGATE: Don't forget that this is the uniqueness of our army! The only one of its kind in the world!

HUMANITARIAN DELEGATE: The people cast those cannons themselves, Citizen-Officer.

FARREAUX: But they did not *build* them themselves, Citizen-Delegates. And perhaps that explains why they don't know how to use them. Our cannons have either been used as rifles or not at all. Everybody wants to aim and fire them, but nobody wants to pull the baggage cars with the ammunition. And every-

one picks his own commander and his own fighting post.

VARLIN: What is your background, Citizen-Officer?

FARREAUX: I completed my studies at the artillery school at Vincennes, and am presently a Captain in the infantry.

VARLIN: Why are you fighting with the Commune?

ONE OF THE STRETCHER-BEARERS: He's for us.

VARLIN: Did you know that at least 48 hours ago the Commune decreed the abolition of all military ranks? (Farreaux is silent.) And I presume that you will propose that we turn over our command to trained officers?

FARREAUX: War is a profession, Citizen Varlin.

VARLIN: Are you doing this for the delegate from the War Command who has not deigned to appear here himself?

FARREAUX: And who is at this moment in combat at the front—against all the rules of warfare.

DELESCLUZE: Citizen-Delegates. I understand the views of this man: Before you can do away with orders, you've got to know how to give them. Citizen Farreaux, we wish you a quick recovery. Don't misunderstand the silence of this Assembly: the unteachable are not the only silent ones. Our difficulties are great, and though we can't solve them all, in time they shall all be overcome. The Commune thanks you for your report. (Farreaux is carried out.) Citizen-Delegates, you have had a victory and a true report. Make use of both. You have the troops; the enemy has the experienced officers. But he has no troops like yours. Overcome your legitimate mistrust of people you have never seen but with the enemy. Not all of them are against you. Add your knowledge to the enthusiasm of our Communards, and victory is assured! (Applause.)

SCENE NINE

(Part IV)

Session of the Commune.

PRESIDENT: Citizen-Delegates, I am interrupting this discussion of the report of the good results of the military operations at Neuilly, to read to you

what August Bebel said yesterday in the German parliament: "The whole European proletariat, and all who nurture freedom in their breasts, look to Paris.

The battle cry of the Parisian proletariat, 'Death to misery and idleness!', will become the battle cry of the entire European proletariat." Citizens, I request that you stand in honor of the German working people. *(Everyone stands.)*

VARLIN *(calmly)*: Long live the Internationale of the Working Class! Workers of the world, unite!

SCENE TEN

Frankfurt Opera House. A performance of Norma *is in progress. Outside the door of one of the loges, Bismarck, dressed in military uniform, enters with Jules Favre, who is wearing civilian clothes.*

BISMARCK *(lighting a cigar)*: I want to tell you something, Favre. Mein Gott, you've gotten pretty gray, haven't you, heh, heh? Well you are signing this peace treaty here in Frankfurt, aber what is going on in Paris? When are you going to remove the red flag from your Stadthaus? This schweinerei has cost me a few nights' sleep, let me tell you; and they are a verdammt bad example for Europe! They must be ausrotten *(makes sign of hand across neck, à la guillotine)* like Sodom und Gomorrah, mit feuer und brimstone, ja? *(Through the open loge door we can hear the music.)* Colossal, that Altmann! Und what a figure, ach! *(continues his pacing, followed by the servile Favre)*: You are a bunch of queer fish. You won't accept our arms, but you want us to liberate your prisoners of war immediately. I know, I know, you don't want to appear to have the aid of a foreign power. Like the old song: "O Theodore, you old flirt, do nicht in publik put your hand under my skirt!" *(He listens to the music for a moment.)* Now she dies. Epochal! Fantastic! . . . Oh yes, our riffraff in der Reichstag demand the extradition of Bonaparte, but, I can assure you, nothing will come of it. We won't show you what is up our sleeves, so we can always keep you on a string, eh? Ha ha ha ha. We will turn this dangerous man over to your "comrades" in Paris and let them cut his throat, ah? That will be a little surprise! War is war, aber there must be order. For that, I would even join hands with our arch enemy *(business)* . . . uh, on the forearm, Favre. But by now we must have freed over 200,000 of your prisoners. . . . Have you, uh, begun thinking about paying for them?

FAVRE: I can tell you now that that was our greatest worry, Herr von Bismarck. Mais, we 'ave found the money. La Banque France has come through only today—with 257 million francs.

BISMARCK: À la bonne heure! Just in time. Ah, but also, what guarantee have you that the soldiers will not fraternize as they did on the 18th of March?

FAVRE: We have been able to train very reliable cadres, Herr von Bismarck. People with conservative peasant backgrounds, you know. And furthermore, the propagandists were not able to reach the prisoners of war, n'est-ce pas?

BISMARCK: Gut. Well, vielleicht the worst is over. But as I say, the proof of the pudding. . . . I have agreed that reparations will only be paid to us after the pacification of Paris, but please hurry up! *(listening to the music:)* Ach, doesn't she sing fabulously! Oh yes, just so you don't make any more mistakes, Favre, remember the first check goes to Bleichröder. I have great confidence in him. He's my private banker, und I want to make sure that he gets taken care of. . . . O that Altmann is so schön! . . .

SCENE ELEVEN

(Part I)

Hôtel de Ville. Night. The hall is empty. Langevin, working late, is talking to Geneviève, who has come looking for him.

LANGEVIN: They complain that there's no money to feed their children. You know what Beslay got the Bank to give us for building barricades? 11,300

223

francs. What mistakes we're making! What mistakes we've made! Naturally, we should have marched on Versailles immediately—on the 18th of March. Oh, if we had only had the time! But the people never get more than one time. Too bad if they aren't ready with all their weapons, just at that time.

GENEVIÈVE: But what people! *(She speaks in admiration.)* Tonight I went to a concert for the ambulances in the Tuileries. Only a few hundred were expected, but tens of thousands of them showed up! I was right in the middle of that immense crowd, and not *one word* of complaint did I hear!

LANGEVIN: They're patient with us. *(Looks up at the blackboard, or screen. On it, as in Scene Seven Part One, are written:*

1. *Right to Live*
2. *Freedom of Choice*
3. *Freedom of Conscience.*
4. *Right of Assembly and Association*
5. *Freedom of Speech, Freedom of the Press, and Freedom of Intellectual Expression in Any Form Whatsoever.*
6. *Free Elections.)*

LANGEVIN: Number one: The right to live. That's good, but how? Look at the other points. They look very nice, but what do they really mean? Number two: Is that also the freedom to choose to be a businessman, to live off the people, to plot against the people, and to serve their enemies? Number three:

What does your conscience dictate to you? I'll tell you: whatever the rulers told you when you were a child. Number four: Does that apply to the stock exchange, and the scandal sheets of the yellow press—which is free, by number five, free to be bought. And what about those blood-thirsty generals and all their little leeches, who assemble with them in Versailles and issue "intellectual expressions" against us! Is the freedom to lie guaranteed? And in number six: do we permit the election of thieves to rule the people, disturbed as they are by school, church, press and politicians? And where is *our* right to occupy the Bank of France, which hides the fortunes we created with our bare hands!? With that money we could have bribed all the generals and politicians—M. Thiers' and Herr von Bismarck's. There should have been only one point: *our* right to *live!*

GENEVIÈVE: So why didn't we do just that?

LANGEVIN: Because we did not understand the true meaning of the word freedom. We were not ready, the way every part of a group that fights for its life must be, to give up any personal liberties until the freedom for all could be won.

GENEVIÈVE: Wasn't it just that we didn't want bloodshed on our hands?

LANGEVIN: Yes, but in a revolution there are either hands that are bloody or hands that are cut off.

SCENE ELEVEN

(Part II)

Session of the Commune. Members of the Guard are going in and out carrying messages. Hastily summoned meetings of delegates. All the signs of an overpowering fatigue. Sound of cannons in the distance.

DELESCLUZE: Citizen-Delegates: You are hearing the cannons of Versailles. The final battle has begun. *(Pause.)*

HUMANITARIAN DELEGATE: In the interests of security, I have authorized a delegation of women from the eleventh arrondissement to appear before you to present to you the wishes of the people of Paris at this time.

(Sounds of approval.)

DELESCLUZE: Citizens, you named me your delegate for the War Command. It has been an almost overwhelming task

to deal with the destruction of this war, which has changed from a national war to a civil war. There were, in addition, the tremendous and unforeseen problems created by the return of 150,000 prisoners of war to the ranks of the Versailles government, courtesy of Herr von Bismarck. These, and many other matters, have not left us enough time to strengthen the proletariat in skills and in leadership. We have tried generals of all kinds. The ones from below, from our own ranks, did not understand how

224

to use the new weapons. The ones from above, that came to our side, could not get used to our soldiers. Our fighting men and women, having just emerged from the wage slavery of the captains of industry, will not take orders like marionettes. Their inventiveness and daring are, to experienced officers, the same thing as simple lack of discipline. Our field commander, M. Rossel, demanded 10,000 men to defend the fort of Issy. Through the personal efforts of many of you, we managed to mobilize 7,000. M. Rossel, informed that he was 3,000 short of that round number, rode off on his horse, and thus permitted the forces of Versailles to occupy the fort, while we stood in the barracks ready to fight. What's more, M. Rossel has given a communiqué to the reactionary newspapers that all is lost.

RANVIER: You need a great surgeon to perform an operation. So what does he do? If he can't wash his hands in an antiseptic, he washes his hands of the whole thing.

DELESCLUZE: Well, so this is how things stand now: everything will be decided in this battle, in the streets. Now is the time for barricades, not military specialists. For it is the people of this city who will defend it, house by house. Citizen-Delegates, let us go into battle as we go to our work, and let us do it well. And should our enemies succeed, citizens, Paris will become a grave; but a grave for our bodies, not for our ideas. *(Great applause; many stand up. Enter at least three Working Women, from the Eleventh Arrondissement.)*

DELESCLUZE: Citizen-Delegates, the delegates from the Eleventh Arrondissement. *(The meeting grows quiet; though a few delegates rise and talk to the women.)*

DELEGATE: Citizens, you have brought life into this room again.

WOMAN: That's what women are for, citizen. *(The delegates smile.)* Citizen-Delegates, I have a message for you. It's short.

DELEGATE: It's only twenty pages long!

WOMAN: Sh! Quiet. These are only signatures. Five hundred and fifty-two of them. *(Laughter)* Citizen-Delegates, yesterday afternoon, posters were put up in our district, calling upon all the women of Paris to make peace with the so-called government at Versailles. We answer that there can be no peace between liberty and tyranny, between the people and their oppressors. The place of every working man, and of every working woman, is on the barricades. Just as we declared on the Fourth of September, when the Third Republic was proclaimed, "After our forts, the walls. After our walls, the barricades. After the barricades, our chests." *(Applause.)* But we've altered that a little bit: (if I may:) "After the barricades, our homes. And after our homes, our brains." *(Applause grows.)*

We appeal to you, delegates of the Commune, not to turn your spears and guns into pruning hooks. Four days ago, citizens, the munitions factory of the Avenue Rapp exploded into the air and over forty working women were badly injured; four houses were destroyed. The culprits have not yet been found.

But why isn't everyone allowed to leave their work and join the fight? Citizen-Delegates, this is not a complaint against you, please understand that, but as citizens we see this as a weakness of the members of the Commune . . ., excuse me, that's been changed, . . . as a weakness of certain . . ., excuse me, I can't read it—it's been crossed out; as a weakness of . . . damn it, as *our* weakness 'cause we couldn't get together on the wording! *(Laughter.)*

There we are: as a weakness of a few members of the Commune which is destroying our future. You promised to provide for our future, and for the future of our children, and I would rather see *my* children dead than in the hands of the government at Versailles. But we do not want to lose them because of our own weakness. Signed, five hundred and fifty-two women from the Eleventh Arrondissement. Thank you, citizens. *(The women leave.)*

VARLIN *(jumping to his feet)*: Citizen-Delegates, the wives and mothers of the soldiers in Versailles shed tears, but not ours, my friends! Would you deliver them, defenseless, to an enemy which does not shrink from violence? We were told a few weeks ago that no force, and no military operations were necessary;

that Thiers had no troops, and that this would be a civil war in the face of the need to confront the Prussian enemy. But our bourgeoisie, without even giving it a second thought, has been working with the enemies of our country—receiving troops from them, former prisoners of war, to fight a civil war against us—with peasants from the Vendée, well-rested soldiers who could not come under our influence. No conflict between two different bourgeoisies is too strong as to stop them from uniting to oppose the proletariat. Then we were also told this was a new time, and there was to be no more terror. Well, what's left of that new time? Versailles is using terror to prevent its ever taking place. If we are beaten, it will be because of our tolerance, which is another word for stupidity! Citizens, I beg you, learn from your enemies! *(Applause and restlessness.)*

RIGAULT: Citizens, if you would stop crying for "moderation" towards your enemies for a minute, you might hear the cannons outside! *(People grow quiet, and the cannons grow louder.)* You can be sure that the enemy will be absolutely ruthless. The moment the bloodbath begins, Paris will be overrun with agent provocateurs, spies and saboteurs. *(Removes a list from his pocket.)* I have here the names and I have offered them to you for many weeks. The Archbishop of Paris doesn't just pray. The director of the Bank of France knows another use for the people's money that he hasn't told you about. The fort at Caen was sold to Versailles for 120,000 francs. At the Place Vendôme, where we tore down the monument to militarism, our military secrets are being discussed openly. With righteous indignation, our women have been throwing the spies for Versailles into the Seine. Are we going to fish them out again? Meanwhile in Versailles, they've been shooting our prisoners like mad dogs—including the old, sick, and wounded!—two hundred and thirty-five of them! When are we going to begin retaliating?

PACIFISTIC DELEGATE: Citizens, we've talked enough about that. Time and again we have said, and we still say, that we refuse to do what our enemy does. *They're* not human, but we are! *(Applause.)*

VARLIN: The question of "humanity vs. inhumanity" is not at stake. The question: their state or our state.

PROUDHONIAN DELEGATE: No state! Down with oppression!

VARLIN: Their state or our state?

PACIFISTIC DELEGATE: How can we live with ourselves if we become oppressors too?

PROUDHONIAN DELEGATE: Our struggle is for liberty!

VARLIN: If you want to live at all, and if you really want liberty, then you must murder the murderers! And you must give up as much of your own personal liberty as necessary. At this point there is only one liberty left: the liberty to fight against your enemies.

RIGAULT: Terror against terror, kill or be killed. Destroy or be destroyed! *(Great commotion.)*

PROUDHONIAN DELEGATE: No, no!

PACIFISTIC DELEGATE: That means dictatorship!

PROUDHONIAN DELEGATE: And tomorrow you'll destroy us!

PACIFISTIC DELEGATE: First the execution of the Archbishop of Paris, then the shooting of anyone who opposed it!

PROUDHONIAN DELEGATE: He who takes up the sword shall perish by the sword.

VARLIN *(loudly)*: And what happens to those who do not take up the sword? *(Silence.)*

PROUDHONIAN DELEGATE: The ideals of the Commune will yet bear fruit!

BESLAY: Let it at least be said that once, back in THE DAYS OF THE COMMUNE, they burned the guillotine!

RIGAULT: And left the banks alone!? Ideals! Citizens, the Commune has decided to adopt all orphans, even those of the soldiers who fought for Thiers. We have been providing bread for the wives of ninety-two murderers. For widows, there is no such thing as a national flag. The Republic has bread for all in need, and kisses for every orphan. And rightly so! But what about our provisions for murderers?—the active side of the Commune! Don't tell me there should be equal rights for the soldiers over there as well as here!? The people aren't just fighting a boxing match with the bourgeoisie! Or like a nation which negotiates in the interests of its businessmen! The people are fight-

226

ing like a judge against a criminal, like a doctor against a cancer. I only ask for terror against their terror, knowing full well that only we have the right to use it!

PROUDHONIAN DELEGATE: That's blasphemy! Would you deny that those who use force lower themselves?

RIGAULT: No, I don't deny it.

PACIFISTIC DELEGATE: Don't let him speak! That's the kind of speech which discredits us! Look around you: there aren't as many of us here now as there were in March!

PROUDHONIAN DELEGATE: Delescluze, you speak!

ALL: Delescluze! Delescluze!

DELESCLUZE: Citizens, I am undecided, I confess. I too once raised my voice most solemnly, and long ago, against violence. "Justice needs no violence." That's what I used to say. "Let us have victory for once with our bare hands. Lies may be written with blood, but the truth only requires ink.: That's what I said. "In a few weeks the Commune of Paris has accomplished more for human dignity than all the other govern-ments of the past 800 years. Let us continue to bring order into human relations; peacefully; to bring an end to the exploitation of mankind; to better people's lives; and to devote ourselves to our working class. The working class who will help anyone who is not destructive," I said. "Those fifty or so exploiters in Versailles will see their multitude of lackeys melt away like snow in springtime. The pure voice of reason, used without anger, will stop all who practice violence. That simple sentence, 'You are a worker too!' will draw them to our breasts." That's what I said, just as many of you did. Can you or I ever be forgiven if we were wrong?

May I ask all delegates who are still opposed to violent retaliation to raise their hands? (*Slowly most hands are raised.*) The Commune speaks out again against violence. Citizen-Delegates: from the Commune: rifles. (*National Guardsmen enter with arms full of rifles which they distribute to the delegates.*) Citizen-Delegates, let us continue our work. The discussion was on women's education. . . .

SONG: *Keiner Oder Alle (No One or Everyone)*

Who, O slaves, is going to free you?
Those who stand in darkness near you
From the Lower Depths shall hear you—
In the darkness they will see you.
Other slaves are going to free you.
> Nothing or the whole thing!
> Everyone or none!
> Workers of the world, now you must choose:
> It's guns or chains that you must lose.
> Nothing or the whole thing!
> No one or everyone!
Who, O hungry ones, will feed you?
Starving hardly makes you younger.
Come to us. We don't like hunger
Either. Let us show you what to
Do! O, hungry ones, we'll feed you!
> CHORUS AS ABOVE
Who'll avenge your scars and bruises?
You on whom all France depended,
Fellow workers, all befriended,
Will decide who wins, who loses.
We'll avenge your scars and bruises.
> CHORUS AS ABOVE
Who will dare? you ask in sorrow.
We who hate our misery
Will join with you in unity
So that the needy can be cared for.

And we won't wait till tomorrow!
Nothing or the whole thing!
Everyone or none!
Workers of the world, now you must lose
Your guns or your chains, but you must choose!
Nothing or the whole thing!
Everyone or none!

SCENE TWELVE

Place Pigalle (Montmartre), Easter Sunday,1871. Jean Cabet, François Faure. Two Children are working on a barricade. Babette Cherron and Geneviève Géricault are sewing sandbags for it. Cannon fire in distance. Geneviève has been singing to the children, who are playing with spades in a wooden bathtub much bigger than they are. Actually, they're mixing mortar for the barricade.

CHILD: Please, Mlle., sing it again.

GENEVIÈVE: All right. But this is the last time. *(Sings):*
Easter means Nogent-sur-Seine
With Grand-pa-pa, Mommy and Dad;
Paint your new boats with a pen
And they'll be like those you once had.
We've got no Easter eggs this year,
But next year we'll have a whole bunch!
So let me give you a kiss dear
And try not to think of lunch.
Under the table on the floor
It's so much fun! Let's talk some more
Of how we would fish at Nogent-sur-Seine.
Next year, shall we go again?

CHILD *(singing with her):* O, how we fished at Nogent-sur-Seine. Next year shall we go again?

THE OTHER CHILD *(to Jean):* Do you and Babette sleep together?

JEAN: Uh huh.

THE SAME CHILD: She's gonna have a baby, isn't she?

JEAN: Um-hm. *(winking at Babette)* That's what you get for falling in love with me.

BABETTE: Now you fell in love with *me,* remember?

JEAN *(teasing):* Well, whichever way it was, you started it.

BABETTE: Me? I didn't say a word.

JEAN *(grinning):* No, but your eyes said it!

BABETTE *(smiling):* And yours? *(to François who is sulking):* What's the matter, François?

FRANÇOIS: I don't like what you said before: "Philippe ran away." You've got to look at it scientifically; that is, dispassionately. I think that the struggle seemed hopeless to him. So he left Paris.

JEAN: You mean he left us.

FRANÇOIS: No, not us. Just the hopelessness of our cause.

JEAN: Unfortunately, we can't leave Paris quite so easily. Why not? The leaves can't leave the tree; but the plant lice can. Your brother is a louse.

FRANÇOIS: I'm going to give it to you, Jean.

JEAN: Dispassionately, please.

FRANÇOIS *(helplessly):* O, Jean! We just don't know. *(Pause.)* Maybe what you're thinking could be expressed like this: Philippe is not a particularly courageous man, because he never learned to think for himself.

JEAN: Okay.

BABETTE: If I move in with Jean, will you be able to pay the rent by yourself, Geneviève?

GENEVIÈVE *(after a pause):* Yes, Babette.

JEAN: God damn it! Why do you women always have to talk about the future?

GENEVIÈVE *(softly):* She has to, Jean.

FRANÇOIS: One of our problems is that we're cut off from the provinces. We haven't been able to speak to all of France.

GENEVIÈVE: They'll have to learn about us by themselves.

JEAN: Babette, that reminds me, we'll have to bring our masterpiece out here. One thing's certain: if they attack, Paris'll be one big grave. Don't you agree, François? *(They continue to work on the barricade as Mme. Cabet enters.)*

MME. CABET: Forgive me, but I had a real need to attend Mass, so last night I saved four extra bags. Here are your Easter presents! (She gives François a small package.)

FRANÇOIS (opening it): My Lavoisier! And just when I wanted to look something up!

MME. CABET: Oh, Jules and Victor, you should have come first, forgive me. (Gives each child a roll.) Jean, here's a tie for you—I shortened the flag a little. Papa wasn't very happy about that, but I did it anyway! I don't have anything for you Geneviève, so let me give you a handshake. (She shakes Geneviève's hand.) It's always so painful when you don't have anything for a present, isn't it? (to Babette:) And this is for you, Babette, and for someone else too, you know what I mean? (She winks at the slightly pregnant girl.) Next year, he'll get one of his own.

JEAN: You . . . (They all laugh.)

MME. CABET: And now I would like you all to come up to my place. I still have a little wine left. (They all leave with her except for Geneviève—as she gets up, two Nuns approach her.)

NUN (in a whisper): Geneviève.

GENEVIÈVE (runs to her and embraces her): Guy!

GUY: Sh! Not so loud, dearest. Has it been really bad?

GENEVIÈVE: But why are you in this habit, Guy!? Seven months. . . !

GUY: Couldn't we go somewhere else —like to your room? You live alone; don't you? And could you get me a razor? This damned beard. . . . !

GENEVIÈVE: But why all this secrecy? Now you're here, safe and sound. You escaped. . . . ?

GUY: No, no, I'll tell you everything up in your room.

GENEVIÈVE: But I don't live alone anymore. Babette's with me, and's liable to come in at any moment. I don't know why you don't want anyone to see you, Guy. Guy, you're not here to work against the Commune, are you? You're not for Thiers!?

GUY: Oh you're still for the Internationale! Despite all the horrors!

GENEVIÈVE: What horrors!?

GUY: The hell with that. Look, the time for revolutionary and humanistic declarations is finished. Seriously. All France has had enough looting and violence.

GENEVIÈVE: And so you've become a spy for that butcher, Thiers!

GUY: Geneviève, we can't discuss this in the street! I've been recognized—I didn't want to involve you, only this damned beard forced me to! We are engaged—or we were. You can't throw me to those bloodhounds, and the sisters of Saint-Josèphe mustn't be involved either. I thought you were a Catholic. Or is that over too?

GENEVIÈVE: Yes, it is, Guy.

GUY: Well, that's a fine state of affairs! And all this in the street!

GENEVIÈVE: The street's a good place. We've just begun our last stand in the streets.

GUY: This is absolute insanity! Versailles has three army corps outside the city. If you think you can deliver me over to those Communards, I'll . . . (reaches under robe for a pistol).

PAPA (who, along with Coco, has entered and heard his last words along with seeing his last action): Just a minute, Monsieur. (He cocks his rifle and aims it at Guy.) Mademoiselle, you have very interesting friends.

GENEVIÈVE: Monsieur Guy Suitry, my fiancé, Papa. (The Nun who came with Guy starts running away.)

PAPA: Stop her, Coco. Or maybe it's a him. (to Geneviève:) Explanation.

GENEVIÈVE (while Coco goes after the other Nun): Monsieur Suitry was taken prisoner by the Prussians, and has come to Paris for some business on behalf of Monsieur Thiers.

GUY: Geneviève!

PAPA: Oh dear. That's too bad. Sorry, Geneviève.

COCO (returning): No breasts, but very feminine. Up against the wall! And then a little visit to the convent at Saint-Josèphe (He pushes Guy with his bayonet towards the barricade.) Turn around.

FRANÇOIS (entering): Geneviève, where are you? Oh! What's going on here?

PAPA: Geneviève's Guy is back. Bismarck returned him to Thiers so he could come and spy on us. And the nuns of Saint-Josèphe made him a religious convert. (To Guy): Turn around!

FRANÇOIS: You can't do that. You can only arrest him.

PAPA: So that he can go to the Petite Roquette and eat lambchops with the Archbishop? We Communards try to compete with Saint-Josèphe in forgiveness, but unfortunately we're up against the wall ourselves at the moment. *(to Guy:)* No, you won't be doing any more spying after today, M. Suitry. Nor you either.

FRANÇOIS: Now cut it out, Papa.

PAPA: What do you mean cut it out? General Gervais sells one of our forts to Versailles, but I have to cut it out, eh? I'll tell you what I'm going to cut out. Maybe you think I'm getting too old, so I lose my cool every once and a while. *(To Geneviève:)* But I remember one morning when you couldn't sleep, and we had a little discussion.

GENEVIÈVE: Citizen Goule, I've learned since then what "Nothing or the whole thing, No one or everyone" means. And even if it were only to defend you, I would not leave this barricade.

PAPA *(unsurely):* I think I understand.

FRANÇOIS: Madame Cabet will not allow it, Papa. . . . Let Geneviève decide, and don't do anything too quickly. Geneviève, tell them you don't want them to do it. You needn't think we'll believe it was because he was your fiancé. Tell them Geneviève. *(She is silent.)*

PAPA: Good, Geneviève. Now go back into the house.

COCO: You, turn around! *(Enter Mme. Cabet with the Children.)*

MME. CABET: Jean and Babette wanted to be alone. Ah, l'amour, l'amour! Love is so much nicer than sewing sand bags! What are you doing?

COCO: This nun, Madame Cabet, is Geneviève's fiancé. A spy.

MME. CABET: Why is he standing in front of the wall? He's not very happy there, don't you see? *(They are silent.)* No! Don't do it! Not on Easter Sunday! And in front of the children! You can't do it in front of the Children! Hand him over to the police. That'll be bad enough for Geneviève! Now you come with me and have a good drink, you can use it. Don't do anything stupid!

PAPA *(with regret):* O, go to hell! We'd be wasting powder on you anyway, you bastards. March, you son-of-a-bitch. And thank the children: they make the decisions in Paris now. *(He and Coco lead Guy and the Nun away.)*

FRANÇOIS *(to the Children):* Let's get on with our work. *(They start working again. Mme. Cabet tries to lead Geneviève away, but she shakes her head and sits down; starts sewing her bags.)* There are some evil men among us. In some battalions, they're even letting criminals fight.

MME. CABET: Yes. Well, let them be among us! It's the only good they'll ever do in their lives.

FRANÇOIS: Even on top, there are those who fill their own pockets.

MME. CABET: You get what you get.

FRANÇOIS: I'm going to have to chop down that apple tree.

MME. CABET: Must you? Really? *(Enter Jean and Babette.)* Jean, Babette, François wants to chop down the apple tree!

BABETTE: No! Don't let him!

JEAN: It won't be a conventional barricade with a tree smack in the middle of it. But it won't hurt. Leave it. *(Pats the cannon.)* Ammunition or not, it's good to have you, whatever the generals say. Including our own. *(He and Babette unfold a sign reading YOU ARE A WORKER TOO. Pointing to it:)* That's my slogan, François. *(They hang it above the barricade, facing in the direction from which the enemy will be coming.)* They'll have to see that.

MME. CABET: Jean, I don't know if they've been in the army before, if they're straight from the provinces. Those peasants, working sixteen hours a day, and those sons of penniless shopkeepers—yes, even the shoemakers—have always thought of themselves as better than plain workers.

JEAN: Maybe they'll think again when they see my slogan, Mama—especially when it's accompanied by rifle fire.

SCENE THIRTEEN

Place Pigalle, Bloody Week, May, 1871. Geneviève Géricault, Jean Cabet, François Faure, and Two Civilians are on the barricades with rifles. The German Prisoner and Papa are dragging a case of ammunition into a corner. A Woman, badly wounded, is lying in another corner. Heavy artillery fire. Drums signaling the attacking of neighboring streets. The apple tree is in full bloom.

FRANÇOIS *(calling out loudly):* Langevin and Coco should have been here a long time ago if they were still alive. It's been three days.

PAPA: O, I'm sure Coco's still alive. And if Paris is too by the end of this week, the whole Versailles bunch'll be finished forever.

FRANÇOIS: They're pretty well armed— with grapeshot. You know, the New Time first gives its newest weapons to the Zouaves of the Old Time.

PAPA: On the 18th of March we could've cleaned out their nests in two hours.

FRANÇOIS: What do *you* think about that, Jean?

JEAN: I told you: we just don't know.

GENEVIÈVE: Well, we're learning, Jean.

JEAN: By dying? That's not gonna help very much.

GENEVIÈVE: It will one day, Jean. Here they come again.

JEAN: Not yet. What good is it for me and you to know, if we're dead, Geneviève?

GENEVIÈVE: I'm not talking about you and me. I said "We." That's more than you and me.

JEAN: I only hope we have enough "We" on our side, and behind us. *(The noise of the cannon dies down a bit.)*

WOMAN *(suddenly):* Hey . . . You . . . I live at 15 Rue des Cygnes. Write on the wall next to the door what's happened to me. . . . For my husband. . . . The name is Jardain.

FRANÇOIS: 15 Rue des Cygnes. O.K.

WOMAN: We wanted to keep fighting the Prussians 'cause they wouldn't send back the soldiers they'd taken prisoner, didn't we? I had two there. Now they're coming back *(pointing to the barricade:)* I wonder what they told them about us! Oh! I think I . . . oh! *(She sinks down in a fever, moaning.)*

FRANÇOIS: They're all worked up just because *they* had to do it.

JEAN: Somebody ought to carry her into the house.

FRANÇOIS: Not if she doesn't want us to. . . . She's afraid it'll burn.

JEAN: But she's in our way here.

FRANÇOIS: Not very much, Jean. And she did fight, didn't she?

JEAN: Yeah, she knows how to use a gun. *(Drums, nearer.)* That's from the Rue du Bac.

LANGEVIN *(entering, followed by a child whom he tries to send away):* Go away! That's an order! You're only in the way here. *(The child starts to go, stops, and waits for him.)* They need more help in the Rue de Bac.

JEAN *(shrugging his shoulders):* Where's Coco?

LANGEVIN *(shaking his head; to Papa):* Can you spare M. Kraus here?

PAPA: Salut, Coco! No, he only understands my language. What's going on at the Hôtel de Ville?

LANGEVIN: There's no one there any more. They're all at the barricades. Delescluze fell at the Place du Château d'Eau. Vermorel's been wounded. Varlin's fighting in the Rue Lafayette. The fighting at the Gare du Nord is so severe that women run into the streets, smack an officer in the face, and then on their own stand up against the wall. *(Exit, followed by the child.)*

JEAN: Things must be pretty bad—he didn't even ask about Mother.

MME. CABET *(entering with Babette, bringing soup):* Children, you've got to eat, even if there isn't any garlic! And why do you have to keep your caps on? They'll only show them who you are. You ought to eat with a soup spoon, my. . . .

JEAN *(taking the soup spoon; suddenly, as she collapses):* Mama!

FRANÇOIS: From the rooftops!

PAPA *(screaming):* Get inside! It's only her arm. *(He rushes forward and drags Mme. Cabet into the house. Babette, stupefied, gathers her eating utensils together. Halfway to the house she falls too.)*

GENEVIÈVE *(holding Jean back):* Jean, you can't go over there!

JEAN: But she's not badly wounded.

GENEVIÈVE: Yes she is.

JEAN: No she isn't!

FRANÇOIS: There they are! Fire! *(He shoots.)*

JEAN *(returning to the barricade, also*

231

begins firing): You sons of bitches! You bastards!

(One of the Civilians runs away. Papa comes back out of the house. In the alley, to the left, Soldiers enter, kneel and fire. François falls. The shots have knocked down the sign. Jean points to it as he falls. Geneviève takes the red flag to the barricade, then turns back to the corner where Papa and the German are firing. The German falls. Geneviève is hit.)

GENEVIÈVE *(falling):* Long live the . . . *(Madame Cabet drags herself out from the house and sees all the fallen, dead. Papa and the Civilian continue firing. From all the alleys emerge Soldiers who now move toward the barricades with drawn bayonets.)*

SCENE FOURTEEN

The Walls of Versailles. The bourgeoisie is watching the demise of the Commune, through lorgnettes and opera glasses.

BOURGEOIS WOMAN: My only regret is that they'll escape to Saint-Ouen.

A GENTLEMAN: Not a chance, Madame. We have already signed a traité with the Crown Prince of Saxony, to insure that the Germans will let none of them escape. Where is your pique-nique basket, Émilie?

ANOTHER GENTLEMAN: Quel spectacle merveilleux! The fires, the mathématique mouvement of the troops! Now we can recognize the génius of Haussman, to supply Paris with boulevards. One can say that they improve the looks of the capital, and of course they do. But they help its pacification even more! *(Big explosion. All applaud.)*

VOICE: That was the Mairie at Montmartre, a particularly dangerous nest.

ARISTOCRATIC WOMAN: Les lorgnettes, Philine. *(Looks through the opera glasses:)* Magnifique!

WOMAN NEXT TO HER: If only the poor Archbishop had lived long enough to see this. Not to have exchanged him for Blanqui, that was a little hard.

ARISTOCRATIC WOMAN: Nonsense, my dear. He said it so well himself: "Blanqui, ce fanatique de la violence," was worth a whole army corps for that mob. And the execution of the Archbishop, may he rest in peace, was worth *two* army corps for us! Oh look! Look who's coming.

(Enter Thiers, flanked by his adjutant, Guy Suitry. He is greeted by applause, and smiles and bows to all.)

ARISTOCRATIC WOMAN *(softly):* Monsieur Thiers, this means immortality for you. You have returned Paris to her true mistress, France.

THIERS: Ah! Messieurs, mesdames, la France, c'est vous.

FIN

LOUIS ADOLPHE THIERS *Painting by* Leon Bonnat

EUGENE VARLIN *Anon. Engraving*

CHARLES DELESCLUZE *Bust by* Michel-Léonard Béguine

EXECUTION *Sketch by* Georges Tiret-Bognet

EDMUND de GONCOURT *Anon. Painting*

ERNEST RENAN *Photograph*

BURNING OF PARIS

LA PAIX *Lithograph by* Honoré Daumier

THIERS: "WHOSE TURN IS NEXT" *Caricature by* Paul Klenck

"PARIS IN ITS OWN JUICE." THIERS AND THE PRUSSIANS

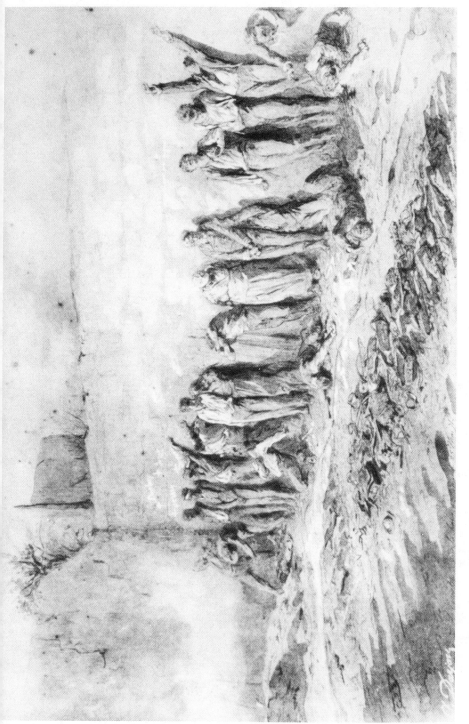

EXECUTIONS AT THE WALL IN PERE LACHAISE CEMETERY
Painting by Henri Alfred Darjou

SELECTED BIBLIOGRAPHY

Ronald Tobin

The purpose of this bibliography is twofold. First, the intention is to give the general reader a reference list for further investigation of the topic. But there has been no intent to make an exhaustive list for the use of the specialist. For more titles and sources one should consult the bibliographies cited below. General works with helpful bibliographical notes are also pointed out.

The secondary aim of this compilation seems, at least partially, to contradict the first. For this does provide a relatively full catalog of publications issued during the centenary season of 1969 through 1972. Proportionately greater space is allotted to works of this period. Included in the latter category are reprints of older works whose revival will contribute to the modern reader's appreciation of the cultural and political circumstances of the Commune.

Bibliographies

Bo, Giuseppe del. *La Commune de Parigi: saggio bibliographico.* Milan: Feltrinelli, 1957.
Rougerie, J., and Haupt, G. "Bibliographie de la Commune de 1871: travaux parus de 1940 à 1961." *Le Mouvement social,* no. 37, October–December 1961, pp. 70–92; no. 38, January–March 1962, pp. 51–82.
The First International and the Paris Commune. In Russian. Moscow, 1964. A. comprehensive list of all printed works held in institutes and libraries of the Soviet Union.
Weerdt, D. de, and Oukhow, C. *La Commune de Paris 1871 dans le livre et l'image.* Brussels: Bibliothèque royale Albert Ier, 1971.

Accounts by Contemporaries and Participants

Arnould, Arthur. *Histoire populaire et parlementaire de la Commune de Paris.* 1878. Reprint. New York: AMS Press, 1971.

Claris, Aristide. *La Proscription française en Suisse 1871–1872.* 1872. Reprint. Paris: Editions d'histoire sociale, 1968.

Clère, Jules. *Hommes de la Commune: biographie complète de tous ses membres.* 1871. Reprint. New York: AMS Press, 1971.

Commune de Paris. *Les proces-verbaux de la Commune de 1871.* Critical edition of minutes. 2 vols. Paris, 1924 & 1945.

Commune de Paris. *Les 31 Séances officielles de la Commune de Paris.* Revue de France, 1871. Reprint. Paris: F. Maspero, 1970.

Coulonges, George. *La Commune en chantant.* Paris: Les Editeurs français réunis, 1970.

Darcel, Albert. "Les Musées, les arts et les artistes pendant la Commune," *Gazette des beaux arts* 30 (1872).

Descaves, Lucien. *Les Émmures.* Paris, 1899.

———— *Philemon, vieux de la vieille.* Paris, 1913.

Dupuy, A. 1870–1871, *La Guerre, la Commune et la presse.* Paris, 1959.

Du Camp, Maxime. *Paris after the Prussians.* Translated by Philip A. Wilkins. London and Melbourne: Hutchinson and Co., 1940.

Goncourt, E. *Paris under Siege, 1870–1871. From the Goncourt Journal.* Edited and translated by George J. Becker. Ithaca and London: Cornell University Press, 1969.

Jeanneret, Georges. *Paris pendant la Commune révolutionnaire de '71.* 1871. Reprint. Paris: Editions d'histoire sociale, 1968.

Malon, Benoît. *La Troisième Défaite du prolétariat français.* 1871. Reprint. Paris: Editions d'histoire sociale, 1968.

Martine, Paul. *Souvenirs d'un insurgé: la Commune, 1871.* Edited by Jacques Suffel. Paris: Librairie académique Perrin, 1971.

Massenet, Léon, et al. *Hommes et choses du temps de la Commune.* 1871. Reprint. Paris: Editions d'histoire sociale, 1968.

Mendes, Catulle. *Les 73 Jours de la Commune.* Paris: Lachaud, 1871.

Michel, Louise. *La Commune: histoire et souvenirs.* 2 vols. 1898. Reprint. Paris: F. Maspero, 1970.

Thiers, Adolphe. *Notes et souvenirs de M. Thiers 1870–1873.* Paris: Calmann-Lévy, 1901.

Varloot, Jean. *Les Poetes de la Commune.* Paris: Les Editeurs français réunis, 1951.

The Paris Commune of 1871: Inventory of the Collection of the University of Sussex Library. Sussex, England, 1973. An important collection of materials which includes contemporary accounts, extensive newspaper files, documents, graphic materials, and a wide range of works on the Commune published up to World War II.

The Paris newspapers of the time are available in a collection at the

Bibliothèque nationale in Paris as well as at the University of Sussex Library, England.

Wall posters. See *Murailles politiques françaises.* 2 vols. Paris: 1873–1874.

General Works on the Commune

Adamov, Arthur. *Anthologie de la Commune.* Paris: Editions sociales, 1959.

Anthony, Jonquil. *The Siege of Paris and the Commune.* New York: Grossman Publishers, 1971.

Bernstein, Samuel. *The Beginnings of Marxian Socialism in France.* Rev. ed. New York: Russell and Russell, 1965.

Bourgin, G. *La Guerre de 1870–1871 et la Commune.* Paris, 1938. Extensively and handsomely illustrated.

Bruhat, J.; Dautry, J.; and Tersen, E. *La Commune de 1871.* Rev. ed. Paris: Editions sociales, 1970.

Choury, Maurice. *Le Paris communard.* Paris: Librairie académique Perrin, 1970.

Dautry, J., and Scheler, L. *Le Comité Central des vingt arrondissements de Paris: septembre 1870–mai 1871.* Paris: Editions sociales, 1960. One of the first important works using scholarly techniques with previously unedited documents.

Delesalle, Paul. *Paris sous la Commune.* Paris: Bureau d'editions, n.d.

Decloufle, A. *La Commune de Paris, 1871.* Paris, 1969.

Dominique, Pierre. *La Commune de Paris.* Paris: Grasset, 1970.

Edwards, Stewart. *The Paris Commune, 1871.* London: 1971; New York: Quadrangle Books, 1973.

Elton, Sir Godfrey E. *The Revolutionary Idea in France, 1789–1871.* New York: H. Fertig, 1969.

Faucher, Jean-Antoine. *La véritable histoire de la commune.* 3 vols. Paris: 1960. Reprint (2 vols.). Paris: Editions du Gerfaut, 1969.

Gallo, Max. *Tombeau pour la Commune.* Paris: Editions Robert Laffont, 1971.

Guillemin, Henri. *Cette curieuse guerre de 1870.* Paris: Gallimard, 1956.

———— *L'Héroïque Défense de Paris.* Paris: Gallimard, 1959.

———— *La Capitulation.* Paris: Gallimard, 1960.

———— *L'Avènement de M. Thiers et réflexions sur la Commune.* Paris: Gallimard, 1971.

Horne, Alistair. *The Terrible Year: The Paris Commune 1871.* New York: Viking Press, 1971.

Jellinek, Frank. *The Paris Commune of 1871.* 1937. Reprint. New York: Grosset and Dunlap, 1965.

Joughin, Jean T. *The Paris Commune in French Politics, 1871–1880: The History of the Amnesty of 1880.* Baltimore: Johns Hopkins Press, 1955.

Kamenka, Eugene. *Paradigm for Revolution: The Paris Commune 1871–1971.* Melbourne: Australian National University Press, 1972.

Lambert, Susan. *The Franco-Prussian War and the Commune in Caricature.* London: 1971.

Lefebvre, Henri. *La Proclamation de la Commune.* Paris, 1965.

Lenin, V. I. *On the Paris Commune.* Moscow: Progress Publisher, 1970.

Lhospice, Michel. *La Guerre de '70 et la Commune en 1,000 images.* Paris: Cercle européen du livre, 1965.

Lissagaray, Prosper O. *Histoire de la Commune de 1871.* 3 vols. 1896. Reprint. Paris: F. Maspero, 1967. The classic history which is still worth reading.

———— *The History of the Commune of 1871.* Translated by Eleanor Marx Aveling. New York: Monthly Review Press, 1967.

Marx, Karl. *The Civil War in France.* New York: International Publishers, 1968.

Marx, Karl, and Engels, Friedrich. *Writings on the Paris Commune.* Edited by Hal Draper. New York: Monthly Review Press, 1972.

Mason, E. *The Paris Commune.* 1930. Reprint. 1967.

Molok, A. *Les Ouvriers de Paris pendant la Commune.* Translated from Russian. *Cahiers du Communisme,* no. 5 (1951).

Noel, Bernard. *Dictionnaire de la Commune.* Paris: F. Hazan, 1971.

Rihs, C. *La Commune de Paris: ses structures et ses doctrines.* Geneva: Droz, 1955.

Rougerie, Jacques. *Paris libre 1871.* Paris: Editions du Seuil, 1971. This excellent little volume has a very helpful bibliographical section.

————, ed. *Procès des communards.* Paris: Julliard, 1964.

Schulkind, E. W., ed. *The Paris Commune of 1871: The View from the Left.* London: Jonathan Cape, 1972. Includes a useful bibliographical section.

————. *The Paris Commune of 1871.* London: The Historical Association, 1971. Pamphlet G. 78. An excellent overview, illustrated, with short but helpful bibliographical notes.

————. *University of Sussex Colloquium: The Paris Commune of 1871.* Forthcoming. A wide variety of essays on different aspects of the Commune presented at the University of Sussex, England, April 1971.

Selected Bibliography

Soria, Georges. *Grande histoire de la Commune.* 5 vols. Paris: Livre club Didérot, 1969–1971.

Trotsky, Leon. *Leon Trotsky on the Paris Commune.* New York: Pathfinder Press, 1971.

Villain, Jean. *Die grosen 72 Tage: ein Report über die Pariser Kommunarden.* Berlin: Verlag Volk und Welt, 1971.

Voici l'aube: l'immortelle Commune de Paris. Colloque de l'institut Maurice Thorez du 6 au 9 mai 1971. Paris: Editions sociales, 1972.

Williams, Roger L. *The French Revolution of 1870–1871.* New York: Norton, 1969.

Williams, S. L. *Commune of Paris, 1871.* New York: John Wiley and Sons, 1971.

Wolfe, Robert. "The Parisian Club de la Revolution, 1870–1871," *Past and Present*, no. 39 (April 1968).

Special Topics

BIOGRAPHY

Cerf, Marcel. *Edouard Moreau: l'âme du comité central de la Commune.* Paris: Les Lettres nouvelles, 1971.

Feld, Charles. *Pilotell, dessinateur et communard.* Paris: Livre club Didérot, 1969.

WOMEN

Thomas, Edith. *The Women Incendiaries.* Translated by J. and S. Atkinson. New York: George Braziller, 1966.

———. *Louise Michel: ou la Velléda de l'anarchie.* Paris: Gallimard, 1971.

SECTIONS OF THE CITY

Choury, M. *La Commune au quartier Latin.* Paris: Club des amis du livre progressiste, 1961.

Rémy, Tristan. *La Commune à Montmartre: 23 mai 1871.* Paris: Editions sociales, 1970.

THE PROVINCES

Gaillard, Jeanne. *Communes de province, Commune de Paris, 1870–1871.* Paris: Flammarion, 1971.

Girault, Jacques. *La Commune et Bordeaux, 1870–1871.* Paris: Editions sociales, 1971.

Greenberg, Louis M. *Sisters of Liberty: Marseille, Lyon, Paris and the Reaction to a Centralized State, 1868–1871.* Cambridge: Harvard University Press, 1971.

LITERATURE

Adamov, A. *Le Printemps '71.* Paris: Gallimard, 1961.
Brecht, B. *Die Tage der Commune.* Berlin: Suhrkamp Verlag, 1957.
Choury, M., ed. *Les Poètes de la Commune.* Paris: Seghers, 1970.
Lidsky, Paul. *Les Ecrivains contre la Commune.* Paris: F. Maspero, 1970. Contains comparisons between the Commune and the events in Paris of May 1968.
Vallès, Jules. *La Commune de Paris: pièce inédite en 5 actes et 11 tableaux.* Edited by M. C. Bancquart and L. Scheler. Paris: Les éditeurs français réunis, 1970.
———. *L'Insurgé.* Paris: Les éditeurs français réunis, 1967.
———. *The Insurrectionist.* Translated by Sandy Petrey. Englewood Cliffs, N.J.: Prentice Hall, 1971.

SPECIAL ISSUES OF PERIODICALS

Europe, revue mensuelle 48, nos. 499–500. *La Commune de Paris.* Paris: Les éditeurs français réunis, 1970.
——— 49, nos. 504–5. In *Documents sur la Commune.* Paris: Les éditeurs français réunis, 1971.
International Review of Social History 17 (1972), pts. 1, 2. Special issue. *1871: Jalons pour une histoire de la Commune de Paris.*
The Massachusetts Review 12, no. 3 *Revolution and Reaction: The Paris Commune of 1871.* Amherst, Mass., 1971.
La Nouvelle critique, special number. *Expériences et langage de la Commune de Paris.* Paris, 1971.

ADDENDA

Horne, Alistair. *The Fall of Paris: The Siege and the Commune 1870–71.* London: Macmillan and Co., 1965.
Kranzberg, Melvin. *The Siege of Paris, 1870–1871: A Political and Social History.* Ithaca: Cornell University Press, 1950.